State Compensation for Criminal Injuries

For John and Anne

State Compensation for Criminal Injuries

David Miers, LLM, D.Jur

Professor of Law, Cardiff Law School

BLACKSTONE PRESS LIMITED

First published in Great Britain 1997 by Blackstone Press Limited,
9-15 Aldine Street, London W12 8AW. Telephone: 0181-740 2277

© D. Miers, 1997

ISBN: 1 85431 505 6

British Library Cataloguing in Publication Data
A CIP catalogue record for this book is available from the British Library

Typeset by Montage Studios Limited, Tonbridge, Kent
Printed by Bell and Bain Ltd, Glasgow

Contents

Preface   ix

Table of Statutes   xiii

Table of Cases   xvii

Annual Reports of the Criminal Injuries Compensation Board   xxiii

Abbreviations   xxv

1   Creating the Criminal Injuries Compensation Scheme   1

1.1 Introduction   1.2 Justifications   1.2.1 General justifications for State compensation for victims of crime   1.2.2 Specific justifications for the Criminal Injuries Compensation Scheme   1.3 The old Scheme 1.3.1 Legal status of the old Scheme   1.3.2 Amending the old Scheme   1.4 The new Scheme   1.4.1 The White Paper: funding, clarity and delivery   1.4.2 Criminal Injuries Compensation Authority 1.4.3 Implementation and transitional arrangements   1.4.4 Standard of proof   1.5 Accountability   1.5.1 Parliamentary   1.5.2 Judicial 1.5.3 Internal   1.6 Interpreting the Scheme

2   Applications and awards   30

2.1 Application rates   2.1.1 Number of crimes of violence   2.1.2 Claims consciousness   2.1.3 The decision to apply   2.2 Applying for compensation   2.2.1 Making the application   2.2.2 Verifying the application   2.2.3 False, fraudulent and abandoned applications   2.2.4 Initial determination of the application   2.3 The award   2.3.1 Notification of the outcome of the application   2.3.2 Entitlement to the award 2.3.3 Interim awards   2.3.4 Reopening awards   2.3.5 Reconsideration of decisions   2.3.6 Payment and the administration of awards   2.4 Costs

3   *Hearings, reviews and appeals*   52

3.1 The old Scheme: hearings 3.1.1 Hearing requests and
client satisfaction 3.1.2 Grounds for a hearing 3.2 The new
Scheme 3.2.1 Introduction 3.2.2 Review of decisions (paras
58–60) 3.2.3 Appeals (paras 61–71) 3.2.4 Oral hearings

4   *Criminal injuries: victimising events*   76

4.1 Introduction 4.2 Jurisdiction 4.3 Victimising events: crimes of
violence 4.3.1 Defining a crime of violence 4.3.2 Constituent elements
of a crime of violence 4.4 Victimising events: trespass on a railway 4.5
Victimising events: law enforcement 4.5.1 Introduction 4.5.2 Interpretation of para. 8(c) 4.5.3 The exceptional risk qualification: para.
12 4.6 Traffic accidents

5   *Defining and proving a personal injury*   104

5.1 Definition of personal injury 5.1.1 Physical injury 5.1.2 Disease
5.1.3 Mental injury 5.2 Establishing the criminal injury 5.2.1 Proof
of a victimising event 5.2.2 Causation

6   *Eligible persons*   128

6.1 Introduction 6.2 Compensable persons: personal injuries
6.2.1 Adult victims 6.2.2 Child victims 6.3 Compensable persons:
fatal injuries 6.3.1 Fatal injuries sustained in the womb
6.3.2 Non-survival of compensation 6.3.3 Qualifying claimants
6.4 Potentially uncompensable persons: domestic violence

7   *Eligibility*   140

7.1 Introduction 7.2 Limitation of actions 7.2.1 Time limit
7.2.2 Implementation 7.3 The financial minimum 7.3.1 The policy 7.3.2
The provision 7.3.3 Implementation 7.3.4 Impact of increases in the
threshold 7.4 Cooperation with the authorities 7.4.1 Reporting the
circumstances of the injury 7.4.2 Cooperating in bringing the offender to
justice 7.4.3 Assistance in connection with the application
7.5 Undeserving applicants 7.5.1 The policy 7.5.2 The provision
7.5.3 Implementation

8   *Assessment of compensation*   186

8.1 Background: the common law basis of assessment 8.2 Size of
awards 8.3 The tariff Scheme 8.4 Personal injuries 8.4.1 General
damages 8.4.2 Special damages 8.5 Fatal injuries 8.5.1 Cause of
death 8.5.2 General damages: the standard amount of compensation
8.5.3 Special damages 8.5.4 Loss of parental services

9 Deductions 226

9.1 Introduction 9.2 Basic operation of the two schemes 9.2.1 Deductible benefits and payments 9.2.2 Non-deductible payments 9.2.3 Impact of the deduction on the award 9.2.4 Payments received, present and future entitlements 9.3 Social security benefits 9.3.1 Scope of the old and new schemes 9.3.2 Incidence of income tax 9.3.3 Prospects of remarriage 9.3.4 Impact of the provisions 9.4 Insurance and pensions 9.4.1 Personal and non-employer insurance 9.4.2 Occupational pension and insurance arrangements 9.5 Offender and other State compensation 9.5.1 Recovery of damages or of compensation from the offender 9.5.2 Other criminal injury compensation payments

Appendix 1   *The old Scheme* 242

Appendix 2   *Criminal Injuries Compensation Act 1995* 251

Appendix 3   *The new Scheme* 261

Appendix 4   *The new Scheme's Guide to Applicants for Loss of Earnings and Special Expenses* 293

Appendix 5   *The new Scheme's Guide to Applicants for Compensation in Fatal Cases* 301

Index 309

Preface

In 1964 the government introduced innovative arrangements providing State-funded compensation for victims of crimes of violence within Great Britain. At that time the Criminal Injuries Compensation Scheme was frankly experimental; thereafter it became a primary aspect of the Home Office's response to personal victimisation. In its first full year of operation (1965–66), the Criminal Injuries Compensation Board, the body charged with the responsibility for the administration of the Scheme, received 2,452 applications and paid £407,912 in compensation; in 1993–94 (its last year before the introduction of the first, unlawful, tariff Scheme), there were 73,473 applications and £165,110,651 was paid in compensation.

During its first 30 years the Scheme underwent a number of revisions. But its defining characteristics remained substantially unaffected: anyone who sustained personal injury as the result of the commission of a crime of violence or an act of law enforcement would, assuming his or her eligibility, receive compensation based on the common law principles governing a personal injury action. Where the victim died as a result of the crime, his or her dependants would receive compensation akin to that available in an action under the Fatal Accidents Act 1976. There were also some significant differences between the common law's and the Scheme's treatment of delinquent victims and of the impact of collateral benefits upon the award of compensation, though the latter are less marked now.

Another of the original Scheme's defining characteristics was that it had no authority in law, being introduced by written parliamentary answer. This extraordinary arrangement, justified by reference to the need to be able quickly to amend the Scheme, persisted until 1988. In that year a revised version of the Scheme was enacted as ss. 108–117 of and sch. 6 and 7 to the Criminal Justice Act 1988. However, no commencement order was ever made to bring these provisions into force. The primary reason was that the Board was, because of an upsurge in the number of applications in the late 1980s, virtually at breaking point; it was thought that the introduction of the statutory Scheme would merely exacerbate an already very difficult state of affairs.

These concerns were themselves overtaken by the government's growing recognition during the early 1990s that, being essentially demand led, and imposing few costs on anyone wishing to make an application, the Scheme's operation offered little scope for control over its increasing rate of expenditure. Accordingly, the Home Office proposed and introduced on 1 April 1994, again by written parliamentary answer, a new Scheme. Divorced from any common law principles governing the assessment of compensation, this Scheme provided a tariff of fixed amounts of compensation for nominated injuries. There was no scope for individual assessment, nor any compensation for loss of earnings or earning capacity or for long-term care; nor, in fatal cases, was there any provision for loss of dependency. This new Scheme was compatible with neither the extant version of the original Scheme, nor its statutory counterpart; indeed, the Home Secretary added that he intended to repeal the provisions in the Criminal Justice Act 1988 when the opportunity arose.

This new Scheme provoked bitter opposition from the whole range of organisations offering support to victims of crime, as well as from the legal profession. Indeed, five current or former Lords of Appeal, together with a member of the Court of Session, joined in a highly critical Lords debate in March 1994. It was initiated by Lord Ackner, who concluded his speech: 'I find it difficult to imagine a more arrogant refusal by a Minister to carry out his statutory duty. I await with interest the first of the set of proceedings for judicial review to test the legality of the Government's action.' Lord Ackner did not have to wait long. In April 1995 the House in its judicial capacity delivered its judgment in *R* v *Secretary of State for the Home Department, ex parte Fire Brigades Union* [1995] 2 AC 513 that the Home Secretary had indeed acted unlawfully.

This decision meant first that all of the applications to the Board which had been submitted during 1994–95 under the terms of the new Scheme were now to be reconsidered under the terms of the old, and second that if the government did wish to pursue its intentions, it would have to enact legislation. This was done in the Criminal Injuries Compensation Act 1995, s. 1 of which requires the Secretary of State to 'make arrangements for the payment of compensation to, or in respect of, persons who have sustained one or more criminal injuries'. The Scheme so required was approved by both Houses of Parliament on 12 December 1995 and came into force on 1 April 1996. This is also a tariff Scheme, but unlike its unlawful predecessor, does provide for compensation for pecuniary loss for victims or their dependants. All applications made after that date to the Criminal Injuries Compensation Authority, which succeeds the Board, are to be dealt with under the terms of the new Scheme, but all earlier applications will continue to be dealt with under the terms of the common law version. Both the old and the new Schemes will therefore coexist for some time.

This book describes the interpretation and implementation of the Criminal Injuries Compensation Scheme, in both its old and new versions. The first chapter explains some more of the background to the introduction of the two Schemes; the second and third deal with the procedures governing the making of an application, and those relating to the Schemes' systems of internal review and appeal. The following six chapters deal with the Schemes' substantive provisions: the scope of the victimising events that may give rise to compensable injuries; the definition of a criminal injury; the range of eligible applicants; eligibility criteria; the assessment of awards and the deduction of collateral benefits.

The book is primarily addressed to those who work with or wish to make use of the Scheme. But it should also be recognised that the continuation (even in attenuated form) of arrangements under which the taxpayer provides compensation for those who, *prima facie*, have a civil action against their offenders (assuming their identification) raises broader issues concerning the range of alternative compensation systems for accident victims. Where appropriate, the scope of the old and new Schemes is compared with the approach taken by the law of tort to the recovery of damages for personal injuries; this in turn raises the more general initial question so trenchantly analysed by Atiyah, whether this unique provision for victims of personal crime is justifiable.

I should like to thank my colleague Richard Lewis, who kindly commented on drafts of the later chapters. I owe a particular debt of gratitude to Anne Johnstone, the Head of Legal Services at the Criminal Injuries Compensation Authority, and to her colleagues, who read and commented on the whole of the draft text. In addition to the usual disclaimer, I should stress that none of what is said in what follows should be read as having the Authority's approval.

David Miers
January 1996

Table of Statutes

Administration of Justice Act 1982
134, 193
s. 1(1)(a)   133
s. 5   213

Channel Tunnel Act 1987   78, 283
Children and Young Persons Act 1933
s. 53   178
Civil Aviation Act 1982
s. 92   77, 283
Civil Evidence Act 1995   210
Continental Shelf Act 1964
s. 1(7)   77, 243, 283
Criminal Damage Act 1971
s. 1(1)   80, 85, 86
s. 1(2)   80, 84, 85, 86, 92
Criminal Injuries Compensation Act
1995   2, 9, 13, 20, 60, 76, 197, 198,
203, 227, 241, 251–60, 265
s. 1   x, 251, 261
s. 1(1)–(2)   2, 252
s. 1(3)   252
s. 1(4)   20, 252
s. 2   251, 261
s. 2(1)   252
s. 2(2)   25, 252
s. 2(3)   252–3
s. 2(3)(A)   197
s. 2(4)   197, 253
s. 2(5)   198, 253
s. 2(6)   199, 253
s. 2(7)   253
s. 3   251, 261
s. 3(1)   253
s. 3(1)(a)   140

Criminal Injuries Compensation Act
1995 — continued
s. 3(1)(b)   50
s. 3(1)(c)   241
s. 3(1)(d)   50
s. 3(1)(e)   142
s. 3(2)   23, 38, 63, 64, 67, 253
s. 3(3)   241, 253
s. 3(4)   20, 39, 253
s. 3(5)   254
s. 3(5)(b)   24
s. 3(6)   24, 254
s. 3(7)   254
s. 4   60, 251, 261
s. 4(1)   254
s. 4(2)   62, 254
s. 5   60, 251, 261
s. 5(1)–(2)   20, 254
s. 5(3)   254
s. 5(3)(a)   61
s. 5(3)(c)   61
s. 5(3)(d)(i)   61, 69
s. 5(4)   254
s. 5(5)–(8)   255
s. 5(9)   71, 255
s. 6   251, 261
s. 6(1)   255
s. 6(1)(b)(ii)   25
s. 6(2)–(4)   255
s. 6(5)   255–6
s. 6(6)   256
s. 7   24, 251
s. 7(1)–(2)   256
s. 8   50, 251, 256–7
s. 8(3)(b)   51

Criminal Injuries Compensation Act
   1995 — *continued*
  s. 9   251
  s. 9(1)–(7)   257
  s. 10   251
  s. 10(1)   257–8
  s. 10(2)–(3)   258
  s. 11   2, 25, 251
  s. 11(1)–(2)   20, 258
  s. 11(3)   25, 258
  s. 11(4)   25, 61, 259
  s. 11(5)   259
  s. 11(6)–(7)   25, 259
  s. 11(8)   259
  s. 12   251, 261
  s. 12(1)–(6)   259
  s. 12(7)   259, 260
  s. 13   251
  s. 13(1)–(2)   260
  Sch.   260
Criminal Injuries to Persons
   (Compensation) Act (Northern Ireland)
   1968 77
Criminal Justice Act 1987 16
Criminal Justice Act 1988   x, 14, 82, 106,
   251
  s. 108   ix, 1, 16, 54, 259, 260
  s. 109   ix, 1, 16, 54, 80, 259, 260
  s. 109(1)(a)(ii) 82
  s. 109(3)(a) 87
  ss. 110–117   ix, 1, 16, 54,
   259, 260
  s. 171(1)   1, 2
  s. 171(2)–(4)   260
  s. 172(2)   260
  s. 172(4)   260
  Sch. 6   ix, 259, 260
  Sch. 7   ix, 259, 260
   para. 9   213
Criminal Justice Act 1991   190
  s. 2(2)(a)   190, 191
  s. 2(2)(b)   111, 190
  s. 2(2)(c)   190
  s. 2(2)(d)   191
  s. 2(3)(b)   203
  s. 2(7)(a)   191
  s. 31(1)   111
Criminal Justice and Public Order
   Act 1994
  s. 142 86
Crown Proceedings Act 1947
  s. 2(1) 4

Damages (Scotland) Act 1976
   133, 217, 224
  Sch. 1   134, 246
   para. 1(aa)   250
Damages (Scotland) Act 1993   217, 219

Explosive Substances Act 1883
  s. 2   80, 84

Fatal Accidents Act 1976   ix, 133, 134,
   135, 161, 186, 217, 224, 227, 303
  s. 1(3)   134, 135, 246
  s. 1(3)(b)   250
  s. 1A   133
  s. 1A(2)   135, 217, 219
  s. 3(2)   219
  s. 3(3)–(4)   222
  s. 4   221
Finance Act 1996
  s. 150 50
Firearms Act 1968
  s. 16A   110

Health and Safety at Work etc. Act 1974
  s. 7(a)   120
Hovercraft Act 1968   77, 283

Income and Corporation Taxes Act 1988
   50
  s. 329B   256
  s. 329C(1)–(2)   256
  s. 329C(3)   256–7
Infant Life (Preservation) Act 1929   132

Law Reform (Contributory Negligence)
   Act 1945
  s. 1(1)   162
Law Reform (Miscellaneous Provisions)
   Act 1934   219
  s. 1   133, 217
Law Reform (Miscellaneous Provisions)
   Act 1971
  s. 4   234
Law Reform (Personal Injuries) Act 1948
  s. 2   232
  s. 2(1)   229
  s. 2(4)   213, 215
Limitation Act 1980
  s. 2   141
  s. 11(1)   141
  s. 14(1)   141
  s. 28   141

Mental Health Act 1959   95
Mental Health Act 1983   128

Occupiers' Liability Act 1984
   s. 1   183
Offences against the Person Act 1861
      83, 91
   s. 16   110, 111
   s. 18   32, 86, 88, 103, 112, 171, 180
   s. 20   32, 80, 86, 88, 171
   s. 23   80, 84, 129
   s. 24   129
   s. 34   33, 81, 91, 121
   s. 35   102
   s. 38   93
   ss. 44–45   89
   s. 47   32, 83, 88, 89, 110, 112,
         121, 125
   s. 58   132

Parliamentary Commissioner Act 1967
   s. 11A   257
   s. 11B(1)–(2)   257
   s. 11B(3)   257–8
   s. 11B(4)   258
   Sch. 3
      para. 6B   258
      para. 6C   258
Police and Criminal Evidence Act 1984
   s. 24(4)(b)   90
   s. 24(5)   94
   s. 24(5)(b)   90
Powers of Criminal Courts Act 1973
   s. 37   240
   s. 38   240
Prevention of Terrorism (Temporary
      Provisions) Act 1989   184
Public Order Act 1986
   ss. 1–3   109
   s. 5   169

Rehabilitation of Offenders Act 1974
      173, 175, 176, 177, 178, 180, 268
Road Traffic Act 1972
   s. 25   94
Road Traffic Act 1988
   ss. 1–3   102
   s. 224   103

Sexual Offences Act 1956
   s. 1   86
   s. 1(3)   87, 119

Sexual Offences Act 1956 — *continued*
   s. 2   105
   s. 3   87, 119
   ss. 5–6   86, 119
   ss. 10–12   86, 119
   s. 14   119
   s. 14(2)   86
   s. 15   119
   s. 15(2)   86
   s. 16   119
Sexual Offences (Scotland) Act 1976
   s. 2(b)   87
Social Security Act 1989   188, 232
   s. 22   226
Social Security Administration Act 1992
      227, 229, 233
   s. 81   226
   s. 81(1)   227
   s. 81(3)   227
   s. 81(3)(c)   227
   s. 81(7)   226, 229
   s. 82   226
   s. 82(1)   226
   s. 88(1)(f)   227
Social Security (Incapacity for Work)
      Act 1994   205, 232
Supreme Court Act 1981
   s. 32A   46, 189
   s. 35A   189

Theft Act 1968
   s. 12A   102
   s. 15   39
Tribunals and Inquiries Act 1992
   Sch. 1   255
   Sch. 2
      para. 1   260

Vagrancy Act 1824
   s. 4   112

International legislation

Channel Tunnel Treaty   241
   Protocol   78
      art. 1(d)   283
EC Treaty
   art. 7   79
European Convention on the Compensation
      of Victims of Violent Crimes
      78, 241
   art. 4   19

European Convention on Human Rights
  art. 14   142

French Code of Criminal Procedure
  art/s. 706–15   78

Table of Cases

Alcock v Chief Constable of South Yorkshire Police
  [1992] 1 AC 310 — 106, 114, 115, 116
Alcock v Chief Constable of South Yorkshire Police — 116
Alexandrou v Oxford [1993] 4 All ER 328 — 5, 6
Ancell v McDermott [1993] 4 All ER 355 — 6
AP (Female), Re [1991] CLY 1363 — 196
Ashton v Turner [1981] QB 137 — 158
Associated Provincial Picture Houses Ltd v Wednesbury Corporation
  [1948] 1 KB 223 — 27, 184
Attia v British Gas plc [1987] 3 All ER 455 — 106
Attorney-General's Reference (No. 6 of 1980) [1981] QB 715 — 167
Attorney-General's Reference (No. 3 of 1994) [1996] 2 WLR 412 — 132

Beckford v The Queen [1988] AC 130 — 89
Bolton Metropolitan District Council v Secretary of State
  for the Environment [1995] 1 WLR 1176 — 26
Bradburn v Great Western Railway Co. (1874) LR 10 Ex 1 — 228, 236
Burns v Edman [1970] 2 QB 541 — 162, 184, 222
Burton v Islington Health Authority [1993] QB 204 — 129

C, Re [1991] CLY 1367 — 196
C (A Minor) v Director of Public Prosecutions [1996] AC 1 — 79, 122
Chadwick v British Railways Board [1967] 1 WLR 912 — 119
Chan Wing-Siu v The Queen [1985] AC 168 — 168
Colledge v Bass Mitchells and Butlers Ltd [1988] 1 All ER 536 — 232
Cookson v Knowles [1979] AC 556 — 210
Council of Civil Service Unions v Minister for the Civil Service [1985] AC 374 — 59
Cowan v Trésor Public (case 186/87) [1989] ECR 195 — 78
Cresswell v Eaton [1991] 1 WLR 1113 — 225
Cunningham v Harrison [1973] QB 942 — 213, 239

Davies v Director of Public Posecutions [1954] AC 378 — 168
Davies v Powell Duffryn Associated Collieries Ltd [1942] AC 601 — 220
Denman v Essex Area Health Authority [1984] QB 735 — 232
Dews v National Coal Board [1988] AC 1 — 208
Dingwall v Walter Alexander and Sons (Midland) Ltd 1980 SC 64 — 224
Director of Public Prosecutions v K (A Minor) [1990] 1 WLR 1067 — 83

Director of Public Prosecutions v Morgan [1976] AC 182   90, 121
Donnelly v Joyce [1974] QB 454   215

E, J, K and D (Minors), Re [1990] CLY 1596   196
Ellis v Home Office [1953] 2 QB 135   5

Fairclough v Whipp [1951] 2 All ER 834   86

G (A Minor) (Ward: Criminal Injuries Compenstion), Re [1990] 1 WLR 1120   130
Gammell v Wilson [1982] AC 27   205
Gardner v Moore [1984] AC 548   103
Gaskill v Preston [1981] 3 All ER 427   232
Graham v Dodds [1983] 1 WLR 808   220, 222
Gray v Barr [1971] 2 QB 554   125, 184
Gray v Criminal Injuries Compensation Board 1993 SLT 28   87

H, Re [1988] CLY 1104   196
Harris v Empress Motors Ltd [1984] 1 WLR 212   205
Hayden v Hayden [1992] 1 WLR 986   221, 225
Hegarty v Shine (1878) 14 Cox CC 145   158
Hewson v Downs [1970] 1 QB 73   232
Hicks v Chief Constable of the South Yorkshire Police [1992] 2 All ER 65   133, 217
Hill v Chief Constable of West Yorkshire [1989] AC 53   5, 6
Hodgson v Trapp [1989] AC 807   210, 232
Home Office v Dorset Yacht Co. Ltd [1970] AC 1004   5
Housecroft v Burnett [1986] 1 All ER 332   201, 215
Hughes v National Union of Mineworkers [1991] 4 All ER 278   6
Hunt v Severs [1994] 2 AC 350   215
Hussain v New Taplow Paper Mills Ltd [1988] AC 514   228, 236, 239

Jobling v Associated Dairies Ltd [1982] AC 794   200, 207
John Munroe (Acrylics) Ltd v London Fire and Civil Defence Authority
   [1996] 4 All ER 319   6

L v Director of Public Prosecutions (1996) The Times, 31 May 1996   124
Lancaster's Application, Re [1977] CLY 496   44
Lane v Holloway [1968] 1 QB 379   163, 166
Lim Poh Choo v Camden and Islington Area Health Authority [1980] AC 174   192

Mallett v McMonagle [1970] AC 166   210
Marcel v Commissioner for the Metropolis [1992] Ch 225   72
McCamley v Cammell Laird Shipbuilders Ltd [1990] 1 WLR 963   239
McLoughlin v O'Brian [1983] 1 AC 410   106, 109, 117
Meah v McCreamer [1985] 1 All ER 367   195
Mehmet v Perry [1977] 2 All ER 529   221
Metropolitan Police Commissioner v Caldwell [1982] AC 341   85, 88
Mulcahy v Ministry of Defence [1996] 2 WLR 474   6
Murphy v Culhane [1977] QB 94   166

Nabi v British Leyland (UK) Ltd [1980] 1 WLR 529   232

O'Dowd v Secretary of State [1982] NI 210   117

Ogwo v Taylor [1988] AC 431 — 164
Osman v Ferguson [1993] 4 All ER 344 — 5

Page v Smith [1996] AC 155; [1995] 2 All ER 736 — 106, 109
Palfrey v Greater London Council [1985] ICR 437 — 232
Parry v Cleaver [1970] AC 1 — 236
Payne-Collins v Taylor Woodrow Construction Ltd [1975] QB 300 — 137
Pepper v Hart [1993] AC 593 — 29
Pickett v British Rail Engineering Ltd [1980] AC 136 — 205
Pidduck v Eastern Scottish Omnibuses Ltd [1990] 1 WLR 993 — 222
Pitts v Hunt [1991] 1 QB 24 — 158, 163, 182
Plummer v P.W. Wilkins and Son Ltd [1981] WLR 831 — 232
Povey v Governors of Rydal School [1970] 1 All ER 841 — 214

R v Anderson [1966] 2 QB 110 — 168
R v Blaue [1975] 1 WLR 1411 — 162
R v Brown [1994] 1 AC 212 — 84, 87
R v Burstow [1996] Crim LR 331 — 111, 112
R v Chan-Fook [1994] 1 WLR 689 — 110, 111
R v Chief Constable of Cheshire, ex parte Berry (CICB, 1986, para. 42) — 72
R v Cogan [1976] QB 217 — 90, 125
R v Criminal Injuries Compensation Board, ex parte A (1992) LEXIS,
  20 February 1992 — 145
R v Criminal Injuries Compensation Board, ex parte Aston (1994) LEXIS,
  9 May 1994 — 152
R v Criminal Injuries Compensation Board, ex parte Barrett
  [1994] 1 FLR 587 — 223, 228
R v Criminal Injuries Compensation Board, ex parte Brady, The Times,
  11 March 1987 — 72
R v Criminal Injuries Compensation Board, ex parte Brindle (unreported,
  4 February 1982, DC) — 44, 48
R v Criminal Injuries Compensation Board, ex parte Brown
  (unreported, 12 December 1987, DC) — 46, 47
R v Criminal Injuries Compensation Board, ex parte Carr [1981] RTR 122 — 94
R v Criminal Injuries Compensation Board, ex parte Clowes
  [1986] QB 184; [1977] 1 WLR 1353 — 80, 84, 87
R v Criminal Injuries Compensation Board, ex parte Cobb (1994) LEXIS,
  26 July 1994 — 153
R v Criminal Injuries Compensation Board, ex parte Comerford
  (CICB, 1981, para. 20(a)) — 166
R v Criminal Injuries Compensation Board, ex parte Cook
  [1996] 1 WLR 1037 — 26, 58, 152, 171, 172, 179
R v Criminal Injuries Compensation Board, ex parte Cragg (unreported,
  23 April 1982) — 170
R v Criminal Injuries Compensation Board, ex parte Crangle (1981)
  LEXIS DC/369/81 — 67
R v Criminal Injuries Compensation Board, ex parte Cummins (1992)
  LEXIS, 17 January 1992 — 188
R v Criminal Injuries Compensation Board, ex parte Dickson (1995)
  The Times, 20 December 1995 — 57
R v Criminal Injuries Compensation Board, ex parte Earls
  (LEXIS DC/456/80, 21 December 1982) — 44

R v Criminal Injuries Compensation Board, ex parte Emmett
(CICB, 1989, para. 26.3)   100, 101

R v Criminal Injuries Compensation Board, ex parte Evans (1995)
LEXIS, 17 May 1995   171, 172

R v Criminal Injuries Compensation Board, ex parte Fox (unreported,
8 February 1972)   137

R v Criminal Injuries Compensation Board, ex parte Gambles
[1994] PIQR 314   27, 28

R v Criminal Injuries Compensation Board, ex parte Gould (unreported,
6 February 1989, DC)   72, 73

R v Criminal Injuries Compensation Board, ex parte Hobson LEXIS,
7 July 1995   27

R v Criminal Injuries Compensation Board, ex parte Ince [1973]
1 WLR 1334   95, 96, 97, 125, 163

R v Criminal Injuries Compensation Board, ex parte Jobson
LEXIS, 4 May 1995   27, 28, 152, 153

R v Criminal Injuries Compensation Board, ex parte Johnson (1994)
21 BMLR 48   115, 117, 127

R v Criminal Injuries Compensation Board, ex parte Lain [1967]
2 QB 864   13, 26

R v Criminal Injuries Compensation Board, ex parte Lawton [1972]
1 WLR 1589   95

R v Criminal Injuries Compensation Board, ex parte Lazzari (1993)
LEXIS, 14 May 1993   232

R v Criminal Injuries Compensation Board, ex parte Letts (CICB, 1989,
para. 26.2)   102

R v Criminal Injuries Compensation Board, ex parte Lloyd (unreported,
4 July 1980, DC)   69

R v Criminal Injuries Compensation Board, ex parte Maxted (1994)
LEXIS 8 July 1994   171, 172

R v Criminal Injuries Compensation Board, ex parte McGuffie [1978]
Crim LR 160   224

R v Criminal Injuries Compensation Board, ex parte P [1994]
1 All ER 80   14, 23, 130, 137

R v Criminal Injuries Compensation Board, ex parte Parsons (1981)
The Times, 22 May 1981 (DC); (1982) The Times, 25 November
1982 (CA)   25, 81, 127

R v Criminal Injuries Compensation Board, ex parte Parsons (unreported,
17 January 1990, DC)   70, 73

R v Criminal Injuries Compensation Board, ex parte Pearce (1993)
LEXIS, 5 December 1993   153

R v Criminal Injuries Compensation Board, ex parte Penny [1982]
Crim LR 298   83

R v Criminal Injuries Compensation Board, ex parte Powell (1993)
LEXIS, 16 July 1993   153

R v Criminal Injuries Compensation Board, ex parte Richardson [1974]
Crim LR 99   211

R v Criminal Injuries Compensation Board, ex parte RJC (An Infant)
[1978] Crim LR 220   179

R v Criminal Injuries Compensation Board, ex parte S (1995) LEXIS,
24 March 1995   154

R v Criminal Injuries Compensation Board, ex parte Schofield [1971]

1 WLR 926   29, 96, 100, 101, 125
R v Criminal Injuries Compensation Board, ex parte Staten
[1972] 1 WLR 569   137
R v Criminal Injuries Compensation Board, ex parte Thomas (1994)
LEXIS 18 October 1994   172
R v Criminal Injuries Compensation Board, ex parte Thompstone
[1984] 1 WLR 1234   159, 171, 172, 185
R v Criminal Injuries Compensation Board, ex parte Tong [1976]
1 WLR 1237   28, 43, 44
R v Criminal Injuries Compensation Board, ex parte Webb [1986] QB 184   79, 81
R v Criminal Injuries Compensation Board, ex parte Webb [1987]
QB 74   29, 81, 87, 88, 90, 121, 122
R v Criminal Injuries Compensation Board, ex parte Whitelock (CICB,
1987, para. 53)   73
R v Criminal Injuries Compensation Board, ex parte Williams (1993)
LEXIS 7 April 1993   168
R v Criminal Injuries Compensation Board, ex parte Wilson (1991)
LEXIS, 5 February 1991   144
R v Cunningham [1957] 2 QB 396   88
R v Dawson (1985) 81 Cr App R 150   105
R v Gelder (1994) The Times, 16 December 1994   111, 112
R v Hodgson [1973] QB 565   86
R v Ireland (1996) The Times, 22 May 1996   112
R v Linekar [1995] QB 250   87, 119
R v Mahmood [1994] Crim LR 368   101, 102
R v Martin (1881) 8 QBD 54   81, 103
R v Miller [1983] 2 AC 161   83
R v Ragg [1995] 4 All ER 155   111
R v Richart (1995) The Times, 14 April 1995   111
R v Savage [1992] 1 AC 699   83, 88
R v Secretary of State for the Home Department, ex parte Fire Brigades
Union [1995] 2 AC 513   2
R v Self [1992] 1 WLR 657   90, 94
R v Seymour [1983] 2 AC 493   102
R v Shannon (1980) 71 Cr App R 192   110
R v Steer [1988] AC 111   85
R v Warburton-Pitt (1990) 92 Cr App R 136   123
R v Watson [1989] 1 WLR 684   105
R v Webster [1995] 2 All ER 168   92
R v Williams [1987] 3 All ER 411   89
Ravenscroft v Rederiaktiebolaget Transatlantic [1992] 2 All ER 470   115
Redpath v Belfast and County Down Railway [1947] NI 167   228
Revill v Newbery [1996] QB 567   158, 159, 163, 182, 183
Roberts v Johnstone [1989] QB 878   215
Robertson v Lestrange [1985] 1 All ER 950   223
Rookes v Barnard [1964] AC 1129   193

S v Meah [1986] CLY 1049   195
Smith v Chief Superintendent, Woking Police Station (1983)
76 Cr App R 234   112
Smoker v London Fire and Civil Defence Authority [1991] AC 502   238
Spittle v Bunny [1988] 1 WLR 847   221, 224

Stanley v Saddique [1992] QB 1   224
Stubbings v United Kingdom The Times, 24 October 1996   142
Stubbings v Webb [1993] AC 498   141

Taylor v O'Connor [1971] AC 115   220
The Mediana [1900] AC 113   194
Treadaway v Chief Constable of West Midlands (1994) The Times,
    25 October 1994   159

Vernon v Bosley The Times, 4 April 1996   106

W v Meah, D v Meah [1986] 1 All ER 935   195
West, H., and Son Ltd v Shephard [1964] AC 326   193
Wise v Kay [1962] 1 QB 638   193
Wright v British Railways Board [1983] 2 AC 773   210

Annual Reports of the Criminal Injuries Compensation Board

Paragraph 3 of the old Scheme requires the Board to submit annually to the Home Secretary and the Secretary of State for Scotland a full report on the operation of the Scheme together with accounts. A list of Reports cited in this book is set out below.

In the text, the Annual Reports will be referred to simply as, for example: CICB, 1995, para. 1.

CICB 1965: 1st Report, Accounts for the year ended 31 March 1965, Cmnd 2782, London: HMSO, December 1965.

CICB 1966: 2nd Report, Accounts for the year ended 31 March 1966, Cmnd 3117, London: HMSO, December 1966.

CICB 1967: 3rd Report, Accounts for the year ended 31 March 1967, Cmnd 3427, London: HMSO, December 1967.

CICB 1968: 4th Report, Accounts for the year ended 31 March 1968, Cmnd 3814, London: HMSO, December 1968.

CICB 1969: 5th Report, Accounts for the year ended 31 March 1969, Cmnd 4179, London: HMSO, December 1969.

CICB 1970: 6th Report, Accounts for the year ended 31 March 1970, Cmnd 4494, London: HMSO, December 1970.

CICB 1971: 7th Report, Accounts for the year ended 31 March 1971, Cmnd 4812, London: HMSO, December 1971.

CICB 1972: 8th Report, Accounts for the year ended 31 March 1972, Cmnd 5127, London: HMSO, December 1972.

CICB 1973: 9th Report, Accounts for the year ended 31 March 1973, Cmnd 5468, London: HMSO, December 1973.

CICB 1974: 10th Report, Accounts for the year ended 31 March 1974, Cmnd 5791, London: HMSO, December 1974.

CICB 1975: 11th Report, Accounts for the year ended 31 March 1975, Cmnd 6291, London: HMSO, December 1975.

CICB 1976: 12th Report, Accounts for the year ended 31 March 1976, Cmnd 6656, London: HMSO, December 1976.

CICB 1977: 13th Report, Accounts for the year ended 31 March 1977, Cmnd 7022, London: HMSO, December 1977.
CICB 1978: 14th Report, Accounts for the year ended 31 March 1978, Cmnd 7396, London: HMSO, December 1978.
CICB 1979: 15th Report, Accounts for the year ended 31 March 1979, Cmnd 7752, London: HMSO, December 1979.
CICB 1980: 16th Report, Accounts for the year ended 31 March 1980, Cmnd 8081, London: HMSO, December 1980.
CICB 1981: 17th Report, Accounts for the year ended 31 March 1981, Cmnd 8401, London: HMSO, December 1981.
CICB 1982: 18th Report, Accounts for the year ended 31 March 1982, Cmnd 8752, London: HMSO, December 1982.
CICB 1983: 19th Report, Accounts for the year ended 31 March 1983, Cmnd 9093, London: HMSO, December 1983.
CICB 1984: 20th Report, Accounts for the year ended 31 March 1984, Cmnd 9399, London: HMSO, December 1984.
CICB 1985: 21st Report, Accounts for the year ended 31 March 1985, Cmnd 9684, London: HMSO, December 1985.
CICB 1986: 22nd Report, Accounts for the year ended 31 March 1986, Cm 42, London: HMSO, December 1986.
CICB 1987: 23rd Report, Accounts for the year ended 31 March 1987, Cm 265, London: HMSO, December 1987.
CICB 1988: 24th Report, Accounts for the year ended 31 March 1988, Cm 536, London: HMSO, December 1988.
CICB 1989: 25th Report, Accounts for the year ended 31 March 1989, Cm 900, London: HMSO, December 1989
CICB 1990: 26th Report, Accounts for the year ended 31 March 1990, Cm 1365, London: HMSO, December 1990.
CICB 1991: 27th Report, Accounts for the year ended 31 March 1991, Cm 1782, London: HMSO, December 1991.
CICB 1992: 28th Report, Accounts for the year ended 31 March 1992, Cm 2122, London: HMSO, December 1992.
CICB 1993: 29th Report, Accounts for the year ended 31 March 1993, Cm 2421, London: HMSO, March 1993 (*sic*; in fact published March 1994).
CICB 1994: 30th Report, Accounts for the year ended 31 March 1994, Cm 2849, London: HMSO, May 1995.
CICB 1995: 31st Report, Accounts for the year ended 31 March 1995, Cm 3169, London: HMSO, March 1996.

Abbreviations

Act (without further qualification)	Criminal Injuries Compensation Act 1995
Authority	Criminal Injuries Compensation Authority
BCS	British Crime Survey
Board	Criminal Injuries Compensation Board
CICB (followed by date)	Annual Report of the Board
DSS	Department of Social Security
Guide	the Guide in CICB, 1995 (old Scheme); *Guide to the Criminal Injuries Compensation Scheme*, issue number one 4/96 (Glasgow: Criminal Injuries Compensation Authority, 1996) (new Scheme)
Guide to Earnings and Expenses	*Guide to Applicants for Loss of Earnings and Special Expenses*, issue number one 4/96 (Glasgow: Criminal Injuries Compensation Authority, 1996)
Guide to Fatal Cases	*Guide to Applicants for Compensation in Fatal Cases*, issue number one 4/96 (Glasgow: Criminal Injuries Compensation Authority, 1996)
new Scheme	the Criminal Injuries Compensation Scheme made by the Secretary of State on 12 December 1995
old Scheme	the non-statutory Criminal Injuries Compensation Scheme which came into operation on 1 February 1990 and earlier versions
Panel	Criminal Injuries Compensation Appeals Panel
Scheme	Criminal Injuries Compensaton Scheme

1 Creating the Criminal Injuries Compensation Scheme

1.1 INTRODUCTION

The Criminal Injuries Compensation Scheme (the 'Scheme'), by which the State makes unique financial provision for the victims of crimes against the person, was first established in 1964 by written parliamentary answer (HC Debs, vol. 697, cols. 89–94, 24 June 1964). In its non-statutory form, this Scheme, with some changes, continued in force for over 30 years, administered by the Criminal Injuries Compensation Board (the 'Board').

On 1 April 1994 the government introduced a variation which replaced the common law basis for the assessment of compensation under the Scheme with a tariff of 186 named injuries valued at between £1,000 and £250,000. The tariff Scheme was set out in a White Paper published in December 1993 (Home Office, *Compensating Victims of Violent Crime: Changes to the Criminal Injuries Compensation Scheme*, Cm 2434, London: HMSO, 1993). It was introduced against the background of the Criminal Justice Act 1988, ss. 108–117, which, though not in force, had, for the first time, placed the original Scheme on a statutory footing. In addition to the departure from the common law assessment of general damages, the tariff made no provision for loss of dependency or for loss of earnings and earning capacity, both of which had been features of the Scheme since its inception. The government's intention was that claims lodged with the Board before 1 April 1994 would continue to be dealt with under the original Scheme, but that the tariff would in due course become the sole measure of compensation. In the meantime, ss. 108–117 would be repealed.

Contemplating a wholly different measure of compensation from that envisaged by the statutory version, the introduction of the tariff Scheme necessarily made it impossible for the Secretary of State to exercise his discretion under s. 171(1) to bring ss. 108–117 into force. This explicit contradiction between the future intentions of the executive and the declared intentions of Parliament prompted a judicial review of the legality of the tariff Scheme. In *R* v *Secretary of State for the Home Department, ex parte Fire Brigades Union* [1995] 2 AC 513, the House of Lords held by a 3 : 2 majority that by bringing the tariff into effect the Home Secretary had acted unlawfully. Lord Browne-Wilkinson, with whom Lords Lloyd of Berwick and Nicholls of Birkenhead agreed, said (at p. 554):

> By introducing the tariff Scheme he debars himself from exercising the statutory power for the purposes and on the basis which Parliament intended. For these reasons, in my judgment the decision to introduce the tariff Scheme at a time when the statutory provisions and his power under s. 171(1) were on the statute book was unlawful and an abuse of the prerogative power.

Committed to the introduction of a tariff, the government's response was the publication, within a month of the Lords' decision, of the Criminal Injuries Compensation Bill. This received the Royal Assent on 8 November 1995. By s. 1(1) of this framework legislation (which is reproduced as Appendix 2), the Secretary of State 'shall make arrangements for the payment of compensation to, or in respect of, persons who have sustained one or more criminal injuries', which shall include the making of a scheme (s. 1(2)). The Criminal Injuries Compensation Act 1995 (hereafter, 'the Act') further provides by s. 11 that a draft Scheme shall be laid before Parliament and that its making shall be subject to affirmative resolution procedure. The draft was laid before Parliament on 16 November 1995 and the Scheme was made by the Secretary of State on 12 December 1995. Its details are part of the subject matter of this book. We turn first to review briefly the justifications for the introduction and maintenance of a criminal injuries compensation scheme.

1.2   JUSTIFICATIONS

Commending the Bill to Parliament, the Minister of State said (HL Debs, vol. 566, col. 292, 19 July 1995):

> Its aim is to provide statutory backing for the payment of compensation to blameless victims of violent crime. The Bill will provide the framework for an enhanced tariff scheme. That new scheme will concentrate on a simple tariff approach for the majority of victims, while ensuring that generous compensation is paid to those most seriously affected by their injuries. In this way we believe that the enhanced tariff scheme provides the right balance between the needs of victims while protecting the interests of taxpayers.

But for some, such sentiments alone continue to be insufficient to justify the preferment that victims of personal crime enjoy by comparison with other accident victims. Over 25 years ago Atiyah commented that 'what has to be justified is giving compensation to this particular type of case rather than in others, in giving more than is given by welfare state benefits, in giving where the welfare state gives none, and in giving by methods wholly rejected by the welfare state' (Atiyah, P., *Accidents, Compensation and the Law*, London: Weidenfeld and Nicolson, 1970, p. 324). Similar questions were raised by the government spokesman in a Lords debate in 1978. Looked at rationally, he remarked, the distress suffered by victims of crime 'is very little different from the shock and suffering caused by being casualties on the roads, by industrial accidents and the tragic births of children with severe physical and mental handicaps.... We have to ask ourselves whether we can say that victims of crime are intrinsically different from other disabled people in the community' (HL Debs, vol. 395, col. 306, 18 July 1978). These questions were not answered then, nor, in Lord Simon of Glaisdale's view, during the two debates on the first and second tariff Schemes in 1994 and 1995. If the new arrangements continue, as the government asserts, to amount to the most generous criminal injuries compensation scheme in the world, then it also needs to say why taxpayers are being asked to make these exceptional payments. Lord Simon observed (HL Debs, vol. 566, col. 1616, 6 November 1995; to like effect, HL Debs, vol. 552, col. 1089, 2 March 1994):

A whole number of anomalies exist, both external and internal....

There is the anomalous fact that we are compensating victims of violence, not victims of crime generally. Crimes against property are not within the scheme any more than they were within the common law Scheme or the original tariff Scheme. The only justification that I can see for compensating victims of violence is that society owes a duty to protect its citizens from criminal activity. But if that is so, then crimes against property should equally be the subject of compensation. That would make it even more expensive than the original Scheme. That was quite exorbitant (far more than we could possibly afford) and was rightly withdrawn.

When introduced, the Scheme was only the second to be established in a common law jurisdiction. Against the background of the rhetoric of the victims' movement of the late 1960s and early 1970s, recurring efforts were made by their promoters to justify the introduction of victim compensation schemes funded by general taxation. Apart from the constant repetition of the apparent injustice implicit in the discrepant treatment by 'the system' of victims and offenders, reliance was placed on the commonly observable fact that, for most victims of violent crime, the civil remedy that is in theory available to them is in reality hollow, given that most offenders go unapprehended or, if apprehended, typically have insufficient means to make compensation other than in cases involving minor injury. Clearly the victim of violent crime is at a disadvantage in these respects, but so too is the victim of property offences and of fraud. The difficulty with the argument that the State should stand behind the offender is that it argues too much; when the Scheme was introduced in 1964 the government was, as Lord Simon remarked, at pains to deny that any equivalent 'liability' existed for victims of property offences.

The further suggestion, that a compensation scheme is justifiable on the ground that the welfare state does nothing for the victim of crime 'as such', can be resisted on the ground that it has as yet done nothing for the victims of cancer or multiple sclerosis 'as such'; but, as Atiyah commented at the time, both points of view miss the target. No welfare state disburses money to the disadvantaged 'as such'; what it does is to attempt to alleviate the *consequences* of such misfortunes — loss of earnings and earning capacity, the costs of coping with permanent or temporary disability. (See generally, Cane, P., *Atiyah's Accidents, Compensation and the Law*, 5th ed., London: Weidenfeld and Nicolson, 1993, p. 253.)

1.2.1   General Justifications for State Compensation for Victims of Crime

Some of the justifications for State compensation for victims of crime that appeared in the 1960s and 1970s emphasised a doctrinal analogy with common law concepts and remedies; others appealed to notions of social justice or to the optimality of loss spreading. More recently, as the political argument that victims should be given a more prominent role within the criminal justice system has gained momentum, other justifications have been advanced. These depend on notions of equity within criminal justice, rather than on principles external to that system.

Traditional justifications have been based upon notions of a contract between the State and the citizen or upon the law of negligence. Neither is especially convincing. The contractarian argument relies on the premise that in consideration for the acceptance of laws regulating the private use of force in the pursuit of grievances and of the State's effective monopoly over the prosecution, trial and disposition of offenders, the State promises to compensate citizens if they suffer criminal injuries. But no common law system entails a proposition to the effect that its enforcement agencies promise to protect all people at all times. Moreover, the argument would presumably extend to theft and criminal damage, a liability which, as has been noted, the Home Office denied when the *ex gratia* scheme was introduced in 1964. A second pragmatic objection is that citizens gain far more than they lose as a result of the State's intervention in the policing and prosecution of offences (Ashworth, A., 'Punishment and Compensation: Victims, Offenders and the State', *Oxford Journal of Legal Studies*, 1986, vol. 6, p. 86 at pp. 102–4). The contractarian argument also overstates the force of recognising citizens' rights. Allowing that the State does have an obligation to protect its citizens says no more than that it has an obligation to provide health care or education. These obligations give citizens a right to a fair share of what might reasonably be allocated to these and other public goods; moreover, the right may be dependent on the citizen satisfying some criteria of eligibility. In the case of criminal injuries, the obligation to protect does not imply the satisfaction of an equivalent to the right to damages as measured in the law of contract, but only to the allocation of an equitable share in public resources (Haldane, J. and Harvey, A., 'The Philosophy of State Compensation', *Journal of Applied Philosophy*, 1995, vol. 12, p. 273 at p. 279).

Reliance on the law of negligence, in which the State is regarded as a tortfeasor because of its failure to prevent criminal activity, is also unconvincing. One obvious point is that the police are not Crown servants for the purposes of s. 2(1) of the Crown Proceedings Act 1947. The question whether a duty of care could inhere in a government department, for example, concerning the supervision of a borstal institution (*Home Office* v *Dorset Yacht Co. Ltd* [1970] AC 1004), a prison (*Ellis* v *Home Office* [1953] 2 QB 135), or a psychiatric hospital (Miers, D., 'Liability for Injuries Caused by Violent Patients', *Journal of Personal Injury Litigation*, 1996, p. 314) is complex and on the present law is likely to be answered in the negative. Even if it could be demonstrated, for example, that an assault on an elderly person in an enclosed area on a council estate was foreseeable because (a) insufficient police officers had been assigned to a high crime rate district, or (b) the local authority had made inadequate provision for lighting the pathways and vestibules or had allowed the estate to become run down and further vandalised, or (c) because the architect's designs, as approved by the relevant planning authorities, can now be shown to facilitate rather than to deter crime, this would not, as Lord Keith of Kinkel emphasised in *Hill* v *Chief Constable of West Yorkshire* [1989] AC 53, be a sufficient test of liability. Some further ingredient would be needed to establish that proximity of relationship between the victim/plaintiff and the police/defendant which the law would recognise as creating a duty of care. As *Hill* v *Chief Constable of West Yorkshire* clearly establishes, such a duty does not exist between the police and members of the public at large. Moreover, even if there were such a relationship, their Lordships held that the police ought, for reasons of public policy, to be immune from actions for negligence in the performance of their routine policing function. The police may make mistakes; but it would be wrong to open their operational decisions to the possibility of actions for negligence, the result of which, in Lord Keith's words, would be 'the significant diversion of police manpower and attention from their most important function, that of the suppression of crime' (p. 64).

The further ingredient was also not present in *Alexandrou* v *Oxford* [1993] 4 All ER 328. There the Court of Appeal held that if an intruder alarm installed in the plaintiff's premises which, when triggered, sent a 999 call to the local police station, created a special relationship between them, then the police would have the same relationship with any other member of the public who used the 999 service. Glidewell L.J. held that this was not what was envisaged by Lord Diplock in *Home Office* v *Dorset Yacht Co. Ltd* as a special relationship. By contrast, in *Osman* v *Ferguson* [1993] 4 All ER 344, P, a schoolteacher, formed an unhealthy attachment to Ahmed Osman, a 15-year-old pupil at the school at which he taught, an attachment to which Osman and his family objected. A sequence of actual and threatened violent episodes against the Osman family and their property over the succeeding 18 months, all of which were reported by the Osmans to the police, culminated in P injuring Ahmed Osman and killing his father with a shotgun. Mrs Osman and her son brought an action against the Metropolitan Police Commissioner for negligence. The gist of the action was that, by virtue of their knowledge of P's actions, the police were in a special relationship with the Osmans and owed them a duty of care. Because the police had failed to apprehend P or to bring appropriately serious charges sooner, they were in breach of that duty. Giving the main judgment McCowan L.J. concluded ([1993] 4 All ER 344 at p. 350):

... it seems to me that it can well be said on behalf of the plaintiffs that the second plaintiff [Ahmed Osman] and his family were exposed to a risk from [P] over and above that of the public at large [that is, unlike the 999 call in *Alexandrou* v *Oxford*]. In my judgment the plaintiffs have an arguable case that as between the second plaintiff and his family on the one hand, and the investigating officers, on the other, there existed a very close degree of proximity amounting to a special relationship.

Ahmed Osman was a known victim of a known offender, unlike Jacqueline Hill, who was 'one of a vast number of the female general public who might be at risk' from Peter Sutcliffe's activities (per Lord Keith, [1989] AC 53 at p. 62), or Alexandrou, whose burgled shop was linked to a police station by an intruder alarm triggered by unknown offenders, or the owner of premises to whose emergency call the fire brigade had responded (*John Munroe (Acrylics) Ltd* v *London Fire and Civil Defence Authority* [1996] 4 All ER 319). But applying Lord Keith's dicta, and echoing Glidewell L.J. in the *Alexandrou* case, that 'it is not fair or reasonable that the police should be under any such common law duty as is here proposed' ([1994] 4 All ER 328 at p. 340), McCowan L.J. held that the public policy objection was fatal to the Osmans' case.

Lord Keith's unequivocal rejection of liability on the ground of public policy is illustrated also in *Ancell* v *McDermott* [1993] 4 All ER 355. The plaintiff's wife sustained fatal injuries when the car she was driving skidded on some oil on the road surface and collided into an oncoming lorry. Beldam L.J. held that the police had no duty to warn road users of hazards created by other drivers (see also *Hughes* v *National Union of Mineworkers* [1991] 4 All ER 278, which also concerns the police, and *Mulcahy* v *Ministry of Defence* [1996] 2 WLR 474, where the Court of Appeal applied Lord Keith's dictum in holding that one serviceman owed no duty to another in battle conditions).

If *Hill* v *Chief Constable of West Yorkshire* confirms that the argument that the State should compensate victims where it has failed to comply with its duty to protect them from harm is untenable because its major premise is unsupportable as a matter of law, the Court of Appeal's decision in that case also contains an interesting reversal of the argument under review, namely, that, were it not for the existence of the Scheme, it might be argued that a duty should exist (Markesinis, B. and Deakin, S., *Tort Law*, Oxford: Oxford University Press, 1994, p. 45). Fox L.J. said [1988] QB 60 at p. 73:

Historically, English law has left the consequences of the tortious acts of criminals to be borne by the members of the public who suffered them. What we are concerned with in this case is whether it is just and reasonable that, or, if it be preferred, whether as a matter of policy, a cause of action should lie against the police in the alleged circumstances of the present case.... If the State made no provision at all for criminal injuries that might be a reason for imposing a legal duty of care upon the police in the conduct of their investigations, though, for the reasons which I have indicated, I think that would produce unfair results between the victims of crime. . . .

[The Scheme has made] quite wide provision for compensation for such persons as are likely to suffer financial loss as a result of a crime of violence. It would not be desirable that inequalities should be produced by providing additional remedies for negligence. Either such remedies will merely duplicate the scheme, or they will give rise to inequalities [between victims of crime and victims of other actionable injuries] which may be offensive to the families of other victims of crimes of violence in cases where no negligence by the police was involved.

More persuasive is the argument based on social welfare. This suggests that as the State is prepared to allocate funds from general taxation towards the relief of financial hardship occasioned by chronic unemployment, physical or mental disability or illness, so it should intervene where such consequences are occasioned by criminal violence. But the Scheme in Great Britain does not seem to be based on social welfare considerations. A system of social welfare is characterised by the payment of benefits designed to alleviate poverty or serious hardship, these payments typically being conditional upon proof of need. While there continues to be a financial threshold in the Scheme, its express purpose is not to filter out the unneedy, but to enable transfers of expenditure to other parts of the Scheme and to reduce administrative costs. Apart from this, and a further financial limit on the total payable for loss of earnings, the original Scheme provided, to all intents and purposes, the measure of compensation that would be payable in a civil action against the offender. Thus conceived, it went far beyond the occasions for, and the amount of, the financial help available as Department of Social Security (DSS) payments. Once a government envisages compensating for such losses as pain and suffering and loss of amenities, the expenses incurred by a victim employing domestic help or private nursing care, or not taking into account money received from other non-taxpayer sources, it has moved beyond benefiting a person in need and as such its decision cannot be based on welfare philosophy alone. Nor can the tariff Scheme be justified by such philosophy. It is true that the measure of compensation has been curtailed, but it remains significantly more extensive than welfare provision.

Some supporters of compensation schemes have sought justification in the argument that it is economically more sensible to distribute losses occasioned by criminal activity at large, rather than let them fall on the individual concerned. This argument has traditionally been based on an analogy with no-fault automobile accident schemes (Cane, P., *Atiyah's Accidents, Compensation and the Law*, 1993, pp. 415–420; Markesinis and Deakin, *Tort Law*, 1994, ch. 4). These are justified in part on the reasoning that as most accidents on the roads are referable to risks inherent in the activity, those who benefit from it should bear its concomitant costs. Likewise, as criminal behaviour is seen, by many, as being endemic in our social-structural and economic arrangements, so those who ultimately benefit from those arrangements — taxpayers — should also bear the costs. But because both the original and the tariff Schemes recognise elements of general damages as being compensable, the argument in favour of the optimality of loss spreading is less persuasive since such items as pain and suffering are referable to other notions of social equity, in particular to restitution and the notion of full compensation implicit in personal injury actions. Moreover, where the victim of crime continues to be afforded from the taxpayer compensation assessed on principles and to a level inapplicable to the victims of other risks which might also be considered endemic to our economic arrangements — industrial injuries are an obvious case — the argument will not support what is claimed for it. It is implicit in the loss distribution argument that we regard the loss sustained, and not the manner of its occurrence, as the relevant ground on which to compensate. So long as we continue to have a separate criminal injuries scheme that gives victims of crime greater compensation than is available to other accident victims, or gives it in circumstances where it is denied to others, there will be difficulty in justifying it on this argument.

> One reason for according special treatment for crime victims would be the presumption of a distinctive harm suffered by those who have been wronged. But equally a reason for not singling out this group might be the thought that what constitutes crime is a highly relative matter, and to attach special significance to this gives inappropriate emphasis to these misfortunes and stigmatises their victims. Furthermore, to treat crime victims differently is, in effect, to compensate them for a loss additional to those shared with victims of accident or disease. (Haldane, J. and Harvey, A., 'The Philosophy of State Compensation', *Journal of Applied Philosophy*, 1995, vol. 12, p. 273 at p. 277).

More recent writing seeks to justify State compensation of victims for personal crime by reference to values associated with the maintenance of the criminal justice and penal systems (see further Miers, D., 'The Responsibilities and the Rights of Victims of Crime', *Modern Law Review*, 1992, vol. 56, p. 482). It is a matter of mundane note that the interests of victims of crime have traditionally been subordinated to powerful and persisting objectives of the criminal justice system. The response of the police to a victim's reported crime determines its status and the nature of any subsequent dealings with it. This response is informed by consider-ations which may have little to do with the victim's interests: clear-up criteria, offence priorities, the usefulness of the offender as a Crown witness, sentencing factors and so on. Bureaucratic and operational imperatives likewise inform the trial and sentencing processes. A major impetus for change in the way in which victims of crime are perceived and their injuries dealt with has come about as the result of the efforts of Victim Support. Reviewing its work Maguire concluded (Maguire, M., 'Victim's Needs and Victim Services: Indications from Research', *Victimology*, 1985, vol. 10, p. 539 at p. 554) that the evidence:

> ... has already supplied ample ammunition for the victim movement to support its case for a major reappraisal of society's response to victimisation. It has demonstrated beyond much doubt that the majority of victims of all kinds of crime

experience problems of some kind, however major or minor, and however short-lived or long-lasting these may be. It has shown that even minor crime can have a severe emotional impact on victims. It has revealed a widespread need for information, about the progress of police investigations, about crime prevention and about compensation. It has demonstrated a need for special service agencies, from which victims of all types of crime can obtain information, practical help and emotional support. It has also uncovered an inexcusable phenomenon.... that of 'secondary victimisation', the creation of extra distress for victims through insensitive behaviour by policemen, court officials or other agents of the criminal justice system.

The British Crime Survey has confirmed that it is victims who are the gatekeepers to the mobilisation of the personnel of the criminal justice system (Hough, M., and Mayhew, P., *Taking Account of Crime*, Home Office Research Study 85, London: HMSO, 1985). Victims who feel unsympathetic to the system's goals and values will be less likely to supply or validate information sought by the police. Research unequivocally confirms the importance victims attach to being kept informed (Skogan, W., *Contacts between Police and Public*, Home Office, Research Study 134, London: HMSO, 1995), and in line with recommendation R(87) 21.1 of the Council of Europe (Council of Europe, *Recommendation of the Committee of Ministers on Assistance to Victims and the Prevention of Victimisation*, 1987), a number of propositions concerning good practice with regard to victims were included in the *Victim's Charter* as a set of 'Standards for the Criminal Justice Services'. These standards, which are repeated in the revised version of the *Charter* published in 1996, address among others the police, the CPS and the courts, and concern such matters as giving information to victims, recording their losses and injuries for the purpose of compensation orders, providing facilities in court buildings for victims and their families, and being solicitous for victims who have to give evidence. The original *Victim's Charter* was published on 1 February 1990 (European Victims Day), which unhappily coincided with an increase in the minimum loss provision of the Criminal Injuries Compensation Scheme then in force to £750. Despite the changes brought about by the Act, the Scheme remains one of the major aspects of the government's commitment to the amelioration of the victim's contact with the criminal justice system (Dignan, J. and Cavadino, M., 'Towards a Framework for Conceptualising and Evaluating Models of Criminal Justice from a Victim's Perspective', *International Review of Victimology*, 1996, vol. 4, p. 153; Newburn, T., *Crime and Criminal Justice Policy*, Longman, 1995, ch. 7).

1.2.2 Specific Justifications for the Criminal Injuries Compensation Scheme

The original Scheme was based on the recommendations which took shape in the deliberations of a Home Office Working Party. This reported in 1961 (Home Office, *Compensation for Victims of Crimes of Violence*, Cmnd 1406, London: HMSO, 1961) and addressed two options. One was based on the industrial injury scheme.

The second, which was ultimately accepted in the 1964 White Paper, was modelled on common law damages (Home Office, *Compensation for Victims of Crimes of Violence*, Cmnd 2323, London: HMSO, 1964); but neither really came to terms with what was being contemplated by the introduction of the Scheme; namely, the creation of a system of State-funded compensation for the victims of intentional torts to the person.

These reports were themselves the product of a distinct shift in governmental concern about the place of the victim in the criminal justice system. In his account of the rise of the 'victim movement' and in particular of the government's eventual recognition of the National Association of Victim Support Schemes (as Victim Support was then known) as its official mouthpiece, Rock notes that general shifts in social values are generally not attributable to single events (Rock, P., *A View from the Shadows*, Oxford: Oxford University Press, 1984). Nevertheless, one of the most notable features of the introduction of criminal injury compensation schemes in common law jurisdictions has been that they have often been immediately preceded by the commission of a particularly serious crime of violence against a vulnerable or altruistic victim, which in turn occasioned a public campaign in favour of 'doing something' for victims of crime. For example, the first full debate in the Lords for 17 years was prompted by the murder of an MP's daughter (HL Debs, vol. 395, col. 255, 18 July 1978). It is typical also for such crimes to prompt an anti-offender rhetoric in which calls for more condign punishment figure prominently. What took place in Great Britain in the 1960s was a politicisation of the experience of personal victimisation; that is, the explicit use of that experience in connection with the integrity and credibility of penal and criminal justice policy. The critical response to the more liberal ideology which informed penal policy during the 1960s focused on the apparent discrepancies between the State's treatment of offenders, cared for at the taxpayer's expense, while the victim, whose needs were ignored, was sidelined until needed as a Crown witness and then discarded as being of no further use. This juxtaposition continues to have a powerful rhetorical pull, especially when played upon by right-wing governments, and has been instrumental in justifying for them a return to more retributive penal values (Henderson, L., 'The Wrongs of Victims' Rights', *Stanford Law Review*, 1985–86, vol. 37, p. 937).

If critics of the system were quick to rely upon apparent discrepancies between the State's treatment of offenders and victims, neither were those responsible for formulating penal and criminal justice policy slow to recognise the political capital which could be made from such comparisons. In its White Paper, *Penal Practice in a Changing Society*, in which many of the penal reforms of the 1960s were canvassed, the Home Office observed (Cmnd 645, London: HMSO, 1959, p. 7):

> The assumption that the claims of the victim are sufficiently satisfied if the offender is punished by society becomes less persuasive as society in its dealing with offenders increasingly emphasises the reformative aspects of punishment. Indeed in the public mind the interests of the offender not infrequently seem to be placed before those of the victim. This is certainly not the correct emphasis.

This observation was cited approvingly in the 1964 White Paper which included the specific proposals which became the Criminal Injuries Compensation Scheme.

Elsewhere the 1959 White Paper extolled the virtues of offenders making direct financial reparation to their victims, which now assume the form of compensation orders (see Miers, D., *Compensation for Criminal Injuries*, London: Butterworths, 1990, chs 8–11), but it also recognised the inescapable fact that many offenders are never caught, or if caught, are not convicted of any offence. In these cases, it suggested, society owes an obligation to the victim whom it has failed to protect and whom it alone can effectively compensate. While accepting the desirability of making provision for the victims of crimes of personal violence, a provision which had been independently argued by the Quaker reformer, Margery Fry (Rock, *Helping Victims of Crime*, 1986, pp. 50–59), the Home Office Working Party nevertheless made it quite clear when it addressed this issue directly that there was no question of the government acknowledging a right to compensation. Such a contention was both fallacious and dangerous (Home Office, Cmnd 1406, 1961, para. 17):

Fallacious because we do not believe that the State has an absolute duty to protect every citizen all the time against other citizens: there is a distinction between compensation for the consequences of civil riot, which the forces of law and order may be expected to prevent, and compensation for injury by individual acts of personal violence, which can never be entirely prevented. Dangerous, because acceptance of public liability for offences against the person could be the basis for a demand for acceptance of liability for all offences against property.

This categoric rejection of liability, reiterated 20 years later by the 1986 Working Party established to pave the way for the introduction of a statutory scheme (Home Office, *Criminal Injuries Compensation: A Statutory Scheme*, London: HMSO, 1986, para. 4.2) and in 1993 by the White Paper announcing the tariff Scheme (Home Office, Cm 2434, 1993, para. 4), was, from the outset, consistently undermined by government spokesmen referring to the desirability of the State accepting a 'responsibility' for the victims of violent crime. Elsewhere, the Home Office urged that compensation was justifiable on 'practical' grounds. Since these grounds were not regarded as being a sufficiently sound base on which to enact legislation, it is unclear precisely what they did comprise, apart from well-meaning expressions of sympathy. Being sufficient, however, to warrant the expenditure of public money, the denial of any liability upon which equivalent treatment for the victims of property crime could be based amounts to little more than the pragmatic objection that the cost would be too great.

Forced to the point, the Home Office Working Party could find 'no constitutional or social principle on which State compensation could be justified' (Home Office, Cmnd 1406, 1961, para. 18). Given the background, it is hardly surprising that those who supported the introduction of special arrangements for victims of personal crime should find it difficult to identify a justificatory base beyond appeals to humanitarianism or the political need to redress the balance between the victim and the offender as part of a broader law and order package. Equally, the intended beneficiaries of the Scheme made (and continue to make) it virtually impossible for any critical evaluation of its content or justification to take place. As Edelhertz and Geis observed in their review of the genesis in the 1960s of schemes in the United States, it is 'not the best kind of politics for an elected official to be seen as antagonistic to the interests of innocent victims of violent crime' (Edelhertz, H., and Geis, G., *Public Compensation of Victims of Crime*, New York: Praeger, 1974, p. 1). The legislative confusion which accompanied the introduction of the Scheme was, for others, 'compelling evidence that compensation is not and never was conceived as anything more than a symbolic palliative for victims of crime' (Chappell, D. and Sutton, L., 'Evaluating the Effectiveness of Programs to Compensate the Victims of Crime', in Drapkin, I., and Viano, E., eds., *Victimology: a New Focus*, Lexington, Mass: Lexington Books, 1974, p. 207 at p. 212). Viewed simply as an expression of populist values about crime, the question whether the Scheme serves any instrumental values thus assumes a secondary importance to its symbolic value.

However it is viewed, there is little doubt but that the failure to identify sound reasons for its introduction led directly to many of the problems which the Scheme encountered in its early years, and indeed which have continued to beset its implementation. Nor have its more recent supporters shown any greater sophistication. The Royal Commission on *Civil Liability and Compensation for Personal Injury* devoted a short chapter to the Scheme, concluding lamely that 'compensation for criminal injury is morally justified as in some measure salving the nation's conscience at its inability to preserve law and order' and that it was right that victims of crimes of violence should receive appropriate compensation (Cmnd 7054, London: HMSO, 1978, paras 1588, 1591). What amounted to appropriate compensation was substantially equated with common law damages, but whether this equation was appropriate to a criminal injuries compensation scheme has always been arguable and was not questioned by the Royal Commission. By contrast, the 1961 Working Party had canvasssed the alternatives of loss and need as the basis for the assessment of compensation, and set out an option modelled on the industrial injury scheme which emphasised its characteristic features: awards payable by pension and not as a lump sum, thus allowing variation for deterioration in the victim's condition, adjustment for inflation and protection against dissipation; flexibility and easy dovetailing with social security benefits and payments by the offender; and administrative convenience (Home Office, Cmnd 1406, 1961, paras 12–13). But with some modifications, the common law model was preferred.

The 1986 Working Party continued in this largely unreflective tradition. Criminal injury compensation could be justified because it gives effect to 'the strong public sympathy for those innocent victims of crime, who are unlikely to obtain redress against the offender'. Having accepted the desirability of such financial provision, the Working Party considered the common law model to be 'the best available basis for the compensation of victims by the State', but offered no reasons why this should be so (Home Office, *Criminal Injuries Compensation: A Statutory Scheme*, 1986, paras 4.2 and 12.4). This preference was not seriously questioned until the Home

Office published its White Paper (Cm 2434) in 1993 on which the tariff scheme is based. But even while rejecting the common law model on the grounds of delay and lack of transparency in the assessment of general damages, the 1993 White Paper made no attempt to answer the question why victims of crime should be singled out, even for the reduced compensation contemplated by the tariff. It is simply 'right for this feeling [of responsibility for and sympathy with the innocent victim] to be given practical expression by the provision of a monetary award on behalf of the community' (para. 4). So also said the Secretary of State when introducing the Criminal Injuries Compensation Bill at its Second Reading (HC Debs, vol. 260, col. 734, 23 May 1995).

1.3   THE OLD SCHEME

We turn now to consider the formal standing of the original non-statutory Scheme before detailing the introduction of the tariff Scheme under the Criminal Injuries Compensation Act 1995 ('the new Scheme'). There are two good reasons why it is necessary to continue to pay attention to the original Scheme (which, following para. 84 of the new Scheme, will be called 'the old Scheme'). The first is that the substantive terms of the new Scheme are, with the exception of the tariff, essentially the same as those of its predecessor. Accordingly, the interpretation that has been placed upon them both by the Board and, in consequence of applications for judicial review, by the courts, will continue to be persuasive. The second is that the old Scheme will continue to apply to claims lodged before 1 April 1996. Experience suggests that it may take some years before such claims are finalised. In the text which follows, references to individual paragraphs of the old and new Schemes will be noted as, for example: old Scheme, para. 6 or new Scheme, para. 23.

1.3.1   Legal Status of the Old Scheme

Although established as a purely ex gratia arrangement which the executive could cancel at will, and thus having no basis in law, the administration of the old Scheme was nevertheless recognised by the courts as being amenable to judicial review. The *locus classicus* is the judgment of Diplock L.J. in *R* v *Criminal Injuries Compensation Board, ex parte Lain* [1967] 2 QB 864 at pp. 883–4:

> The Criminal Injuries Compensation Board is not constituted by statute or statutory instrument but by act of the Crown, that is the executive government, alone. It administers on behalf of the executive government moneys granted by Parliament to Crown for distribution by way of compensation to persons who have suffered personal injury directly attributable to criminal offences, the prevention of crime, or the apprehension of offenders. So far there is nothing novel about this. If the matter rested there no person would have any right to obtain any payment out of those moneys which would be enforceable in courts of law by action or controllable by prerogative writ.

But the matter does not rest there. The executive government announced in Parliament and published to intending applicants a document called 'The Scheme'. It took the form of a statement expressed in the future tense of how the distribution of compensation to applicants would be carried out. It stated that the Board would entertain applications for payment of compensation where specified conditions were fulfilled, and laid down the procedure for the determination by the Board of such applications. The procedure at any rate bears all the characteristics of a judicial or quasi-judicial procedure; and the Board when determining applications in accordance with that procedure is clearly performing de facto quasi-judicial functions, that is, acting as an inferior tribunal. Its authority to do so is not derived from any agreement between Crown and applicants but from instructions by the executive government, that is, by prerogative act of the Crown. The appointment of the Board and the conferring on it of jurisdiction to entertain and determine applications, and of authority to make payments in accordance with such determinations, are acts of government, done without statutory authority but nonetheless lawful for that.

A decision of the Criminal Injuries Compensation Board made under its non-statutory authority could not, his Lordship added, 'give the applicant any right to sue either the Board or the Crown for that sum' (p. 888). Or in the more recent words of Leggatt L.J. commenting on amendments to the old Scheme:

> ... the reality is that the circumstances have been amended in which public money may be paid out to applicants, none of whom has any entitlement to it. It is a manifestation of the bounty of the Crown. (*R v Criminal Injuries Compensation Board, ex parte P* [1994] 1 All ER 80 (DC))

But the Board's decisions were not without legal effect; they made lawful a payment from the government that would otherwise have been unlawful. So far as applicants were concerned, though in theory the Secretary of State could have disallowed or reduced payment even where they fell within the terms of the Scheme, in practice the Board had no such discretion: 'the Board has always regarded itself as obliged to award compensation to anyone who satisfied the conditions for payment of compensation' (Home Office, *Criminal Injuries Compensation: A Statutory Scheme*, 1986, para. 2.2). The denial of a right to sue for payment was therefore of little moment.

Two reasons were commonly advanced at the time for the creation of this 'constitutional anomaly' (Lord Bridge, HL Debs, vol. 446, col. 297, 14 December 1983). The first was that to place the Scheme on a statutory basis would be to create rights in law which the government had consistently denied during the period of consultation prior to its introduction. The second was that in any event the Scheme was intended to be an experiment. Some years before it achieved statutory status in the Criminal Justice Act 1988, the Scheme had, it may be argued, long since moved from the experimental stage. Writing in 1980 the Board observed: '... we think that it can be said with confidence that the Scheme is now part of the nation's legal and social system' (CICB, 1980, para. 1). Even allowing for the fact that this was a partial judgment, few would question the significance of the old Scheme for the many thousands — over 500,000 — of victims of crimes against the person compensated under its terms in the 30 years since 1 August 1964.

1.3.2   Amending the Old Scheme

One consequence of the old Scheme's mode of creation was that it was readily susceptible to amendment, as indeed was intended by the 1964 White Paper: 'there being virtually no previous experience anywhere in the world to draw upon', for example, as to the numbers of applicants or amount of compensation which would be payable to them, 'the Government . . . do not claim that the arrangements proposed . . . are incapable of further improvement in the light of experience' (Home Office, Cmnd 2323, 1964, para. 29). Apart from regular changes to the financial minimum, major changes to the Scheme (all effected by written parliamentary answer) took place in 1969 and 10 years later.

The most important of the 1969 changes reformulated the definition of offences attracting compensation, and extended the scope of the provision entitling the Board to reject undeserving applicants. The 1979–80 changes were more extensive, implementing recommendations published in 1978 (Home Office, *Review of the Criminal Injuries Compensation Scheme: Report of an Interdepartmental Working Party*, London: HMSO, 1978). The most significant were the introduction of:

(a)   powers to compensate the victims of domestic violence and to reopen cases where there had been a marked deterioration in the victim's medical condition following the making of an award,

(b)   time limits for the submission of claims and of requests for hearings, and

(c)   an increase in the Board's powers to administer awards where that would be in the victim's interest.

A further review was initiated in 1984 following the announcement in 1983 that the government intended to place the Scheme on a statutory basis (HL Debs, vol. 446, col. 283, 14 December 1983). This review reported in 1986 (Home Office, *Criminal Injuries Compensation: A Statutory Scheme*, London: HMSO, 1986), the year after a Commons Home Affairs Committee report recommended a number of changes to the way in which the Home Office met the needs of victims of crimes of personal violence (House of Commons, Home Affairs Committee. *Compensation and Support for Victims of Crime*, House of Commons Paper, Session 1984–85, London: HMSO, 1984). Such of the 1986 working party's recommendations as were accepted by the Home Office were introduced in the 1990 revision of the old Scheme. They are dealt with in their appropriate places in the following chapters.

Until the announcement in 1983, the government had resisted attempts to place the old Scheme on a statutory basis. The demand for legislation was prompted by a number of factors: a desire to see victims 'properly' treated (that is, by law) and to hold the government to its promise to introduce legislation; a feeling that there was insufficient parliamentary scrutiny of cost; and the continuing unease that, while it had never happened, it remained theoretically possible for the Crown to deny the payment of an award notwithstanding an applicant's eligibility within the Scheme. As a government minister once put it, 'In theory, a Secretary of State could wake up one morning and say, "That's enough of criminal injuries compensation"', and that would be it' (HC Debs, Standing Committee F, col. 738, 24 February 1987). The government's reluctance to legislate stemmed from a variety of factors. Not the least of these was the wish to avoid political controversy, which would arise because, although legislation for victim compensation is bound to attract wide support, many will think it does not go far enough.

The promised statutory version of the old Scheme was first introduced in the Bill which was enacted as the Criminal Justice Act 1987. The relevant clauses were, however, omitted before that Bill received the Royal Assent because the government, which had announced a general election to be held in May 1987, jettisoned them so as to ensure that the provisions dealing with serious fraud were enacted before Parliament was prorogued. A very similar set of clauses was finally enacted in ss. 108–117 of the Criminal Justice Act 1988. However, it became clear during 1989 that their introduction would only exacerbate the serious difficulties which the Board was then experiencing in the timely resolution of applications (CICB, 1990, para. 1.5). Accordingly, no commencement order was made (House of Commons, Home Affairs Committee, *Compensating Victims Quickly: the Administration of the Criminal Injuries Compensation Board*, House of Commons Paper 92, Session 1989–90, London: HMSO, 1990, para. 16). Nevertheless, substantial procedural changes were introduced by way of revisions to the old Scheme. These came into force on 1 April 1990 (HC Debs, vol. 163, written answers, cols. 411–417, 8 December 1989). It is this version of the old Scheme which will continue to apply to applications lodged before 1 April 1996. It is set out in Appendix 1.

1.4   THE NEW SCHEME

1.4.1   The White Paper: Funding, Clarity and Delivery

From the outset, the old Scheme was funded out of the votes of the Home Office and of the Scottish Home and Health Department. In 1993–94 the grant was £181,359,000 (CICB, 1995, p. 24). In addition the Board has had a small income from operating receipts (principally money recovered by victims from their offenders), which in 1993–94 amounted to £286,429. From this fund has been paid the awards made to successful applicants, the wages and salaries of the Board members and its staff, and the Board's various operating costs. In its first full year of operation, the Board received 2,452 applications and made 1,164 awards totalling about £4m at 1993 prices. By 1992–93, those figures had risen, in round numbers, to 66,000 new applications and 37,000 awards totalling £152m (Home Office, Cm 2434, 1993, para. 7).

During the late 1980s and the early 1990s the number of applications lodged with the Board increased very substantially by comparison with earlier years. Apart from 1990-91, which showed a decrease over the previous year, there was a 26% increase between 1988–89 and 1989–90, a 20% increase between 1990-91 and 1991–92, and an 11% increase between 1992–93 and 1993–94. In 1979–80, the Board received 22,801 new applications. It took 10 years for that figure to double to 43,385 new applications; but within five years of 1988–89 that figure had nearly doubled again, to 73,473. These increases were in turn matched by the government's growing concern about its relative lack of financial control over the Scheme and the burgeoning cost of compensation (HC Debs, vol. 260, col. 735, 23 May 1995). Traditionally, the Board has sought to forecast from year to year the expected increase in the number of new applications, and hence its likely expenditure, but three major factors affecting the old Scheme meant that these forecasts were always likely to be inexact. In chapter 2 we return to a fourth major factor, the crime rate.

Two of the three factors are linked: expenditure is demand led and claims are risk-free (Home Office, Cm 2434, 1993, para. 11; CICB, 1994, para. 2.1). While legal aid eligibility is limited to the Green Form Scheme and the costs of legal advice or representation are not reimbursed, the expense of making an application for criminal injuries compensation is low, typically amounting to little more than completing a form and supplying medical and employment evidence. Since legal aid is not generally available, no judgment is made on an application's likely success; about 35% are rejected. In recent years Victim Support, the national organisation giving advice and support to victims of crime, has become very experienced in assisting victims to make applications. When coupled with the publicity that the Home Office has given to its *Victim's Charter*, which includes reference to the old Scheme, the inexorable increase in new applications is not a matter of surprise.

But the primary reason why the old Scheme would inevitably continue to be expensive is that compensation was based on common law damages. With some qualifications victims would receive the award which they could expect in a civil action against their attackers. Where the injuries are severe, involving paraplegia, blindness or other disablement, the general damages award in particular could be substantial. The old Scheme was unusual in this respect. Almost all other criminal injury compensation schemes impose not only a minimum, but a maximum amount that will be compensated. In the 1993 White Paper, the government argued that as there is objectively no 'right' figure for pain and suffering, and that in many cases the determination of an appropriate sum can be both complex and time-consuming, reliance on the common law as the measure of compensation worked to the disadvantage of most applicants. This disadvantage was threefold: only a minority of applications were being resolved within six months; the basis on which they were resolved was unclear; and there were evident disparities between victims presenting similar injuries (Home Office, Cm 2434, 1993, paras 2, 10–12).

By contrast, a tariff Scheme, in which injuries of comparable severity would be grouped together in bands for which a single fixed payment would be made, would permit applications to be resolved more quickly and clearly. Because no discretion could be exercised once an applicant's injury had been placed in the appropriate band, it also followed that decisions could be taken by relatively junior officials, rather than by the more experienced, and more expensive, members of the Board. A significant advantage to the government would be that, no longer tied to increases in common law damages, it could control exactly the sums payable for each level of injury; holding any increases at or below the level of inflation. But this was not all that was proposed in the White Paper. First, no award, whether single or multiple, would exceed £250,000, and second, no compensation would be payable for loss of earnings or earning capacity, or for future medical care. Because the tariff Scheme would break the link with common law damages, substituting for the subjective element of assessment a more objective test which would be easier to apply, '. . . a separate or additional payment for loss of earnings or future medical care is no longer appropriate. Such expenses will therefore no longer be paid separately' (Home Office, Cm 2434, 1993, para. 21). And, thirdly, '. . . since loss of earnings is no longer to be paid as a separate head of damage under the tariff scheme, it would be inappropriate and inconsistent to continue paying dependency/loss of support in fatal cases' (ibid., para. 25). Accordingly, in fatal cases there would be a single payment of £10,000. The government estimated that altogether these changes would reduce expenditure on the old Scheme by about £85m a year. Over the forthcoming five years, the Scheme would cost £175m in 1996–97, rising by £15m for two years and then by £20m to £260m in the fifth year (HC Debs, Standing Committee A, col. 58, 13 June 1995).

Promised for the summer of 1993, the publication of the White Paper in December of that year prompted immediate and widespread hostility. This was due in part to the delay, which meant that there were now only some four months before the date on which the proposed Scheme was scheduled for implementation, but was more substantially due to the content of its proposals and the manner in which the Secretary of State intended to deal with the existing Scheme. In a powerful speech in the Lords debate in March 1994, Lord Ackner (one of five current or former Lords of Appeal in Ordinary who, together with a member of the Court of Session who had also been a member of the Board, spoke against the White Paper) condemned the government's proposals as hypocritical, unfair and an abuse of power. Lord Ackner did not have to wait long for, nor would he have been surprised by, the eventual outcome of the 'first of the set of proceedings for judicial review to test the legality of the Government's action' (HL Debs, vol. 552, col. 1075, 2 March 1994).

Not the least of those who expressed disquiet about its proposals was the Board's Chairman, Lord Carlisle of Bucklow who, incredible as it seems, was not consulted by the government prior to the announcement on 23 November 1992 (HC Debs, vol. 214, col. 457) that it intended to replace it with the tariff Scheme (CICB, 1993, para. 31.1; HL Debs, vol. 552, col. 1081, 2 March 1994). Indeed, one member who had been with the Board for many years resigned in protest at the government's proposals. The White Paper's critics' objections centred, in the Board's words, 'on the inherent unfairness of a system of compensation which made no specific allowance for victims' financial losses or more general differences in impact on different people of the same injury' (CICB, 1995, para. 1.1; see also HL Debs, vol. 552, col. 1081, 2 March 1994). Prime among those who would be disadvantaged by the proposals were dependants, who would no longer be eligible for compensation for loss of dependency; those very seriously injured victims who required continuing medical and domestic care; victims whose injuries resulted in a significant loss of earnings or of earning capacity; and victims for whom an objectively less serious injury could, because of their own circumstances, have a significant subjective value. In Lord Ackner's words (HL Deb., vol. 552, col. 1074, 2 March 1994):

As the government have conceded, the new scheme is not intended to provide compensation to reflect a particular victim's losses. The effects on the particular individual of his injuries are irrelevant. All victims would be lumped together and would receive a payment based solely on the category of injury without regard to the age or sex of the victim. Victims will either receive too much or too little, and those who lose out most are the most vulnerable, that is to say, those whose injuries and loss are the greatest. They fall into the following three categories: first, those who have suffered the most severe injuries; secondly, those whose injuries have resulted in significant impairment of earning capacity and loss of employment; and thirdly, families of victims of murder and manslaughter.

It was also observed that the government's proposals ran directly counter to the principles enunciated in art. 4 of the European Convention on the Compensation of Victims of Violent Crimes which it had enthusiastically ratified in 1990: 'Compensation shall cover, according to the case under consideration, at least the following items: loss of earnings, medical and hospitalisation expenses and funeral expenses, and as regards dependants, loss of maintenance' (HL Debs, vol. 552, col. 1074, 2 March 1994). The government's retrenchment was, for the official opposition, evidence of a hollow commitment to the welfare of crime victims, and to its claim that the new Scheme would continue to be the most generous in the world, it was observed that there were no unambiguous criteria by which this could properly be judged (HC Debs, vol. 260, cols. 741, 789, 23 May 1995).

The government's basic response to Victim Support, the Association of Personal Injury Lawyers and its other critics, was that 'the majority of claimants will be no worse off under the new arrangements than they would be under the present ones' (Home Office, Cm 2434, 1993, para. 21). This was so, it argued, because in determining the amount for each tariff band, it had taken the median award for each injury based on a 20,000 sample from 1991–92, which thus reflected 'more closely the value of the pain and suffering element of the award', undistorted by special factors such as loss of earnings and payment for medical or other expenses (ibid., para. 15). But because the Board does not keep figures which separate the general damages awards for particular injuries from the special damages payable in any case, it was inevitable that when determining what the median award for any injury would be, the resultant figure, based as it was on the global sums payable to applicants presenting such injury, would include any special damages payable to those applicants (ibid., para. 14). Accordingly, the government urged, since the bands as published in the White Paper contained an element of compensation going beyond pain and suffering, each tariff amount was (to an unspecified degree) greater than would have been the case if the median award could have been based solely on the Board's general damages awards. Moreover, since the median awards were subsequently reflated by 19% to bring them to 1994 prices, there was in effect a nominal element of loss of earnings (HC Debs, Standing Committee A, cols. 135–8, 15 June 1995). The government also argued that the number of applicants who would have received greater compensation under the old than under the new arrangements would be small; in fatal cases, 25 out of 252 applicants in 1991–92 (Home Office, Cm 2434, 1993, para. 25).

Undeterred by its critics, the government introduced the tariff Scheme with effect from 1 April 1994. A year later the House of Lords held that the Home Secretary had acted unlawfully (*R v Secretary of State for the Home Department, ex parte Fire Brigades Union* [1995] 2 AC 513). One consequence of that decision was that the Board was required to reopen some 16,000 applications determined under the tariff Scheme and reconsider another 55,000 registered under it, in order to assess them on the basis of the old Scheme. This will inevitably have an impact on the speed with which new applications will dealt with (CICB, 1995, paras 1.5–1.6). The second consequence was the enactment of the Criminal Injuries Compensation Act 1995. Since the White Paper proposals have, from their critics' standpoint, been substantially improved under the new Scheme, it is now impossible to determine the accuracy of the government's 1993 predictions about their impact. The amendments to the White Paper proposals which the government introduced in the new Scheme will be considered in chapter 8.

1.4.2   Criminal Injuries Compensation Authority

The new Scheme will be administered by the Criminal Injuries Compensation Authority (the 'Authority'). This non-departmental public body is not explicitly provided for in the Act but is established by virtue of the Scheme laid before Parliament on 16 November and made on 12 December 1995 in compliance with s. 11(1) and (2), which is reproduced as Appendix 3. The Authority employs 'claims officers', who will determine applications for compensation, and 'adjudicators', who will hear appeals against those determinations. They are appointed by the Secretary of State under ss. 3(4) and 5(1) of the Act respectively. Adjudicators are appointed as members of the Criminal Injuries Compensation Appeals Panel (the 'Panel'), one of whom is its Chairman (new Scheme, para. 2). Their appellate work is described in chapter 3. The Secretary of State may also appoint a 'Scheme manager' to have overall responsibility for managing the provisions of the Scheme, with the exception of those dealing with appeals to the adjudicators (Act, ss. 1(4) and 5(2)).

Some concern was expressed in the Lords concerning the absence in the Act of any reference to the Authority. The Minister's response was that (HL Debs, vol. 566, col. 1354, 31 October 1995):

... it is not necessary for parliamentary, public accountability or other purposes for the Bill to create a statutory body through which the Secretary of State's arrangements can be carried out. In law, unless and until a scheme manager is appointed, claims officers will carry out the functions conferred on them by the Bill with respect to the determination of claims and the award of compensation. In practice, all claims officers will be part of the CICA, even though it has no distinct legal personality. The authority will be a recognisable entity to which the public can look in matters concerned with the day-to-day running of the scheme.

As a non-departmental public body, the Authority has the same status as the Board. The White Paper canvassed a variety of options, including the creation of an executive agency and bringing its activities within central government. The latter was rejected as being contrary to the current policy to devolve functions; the former, while not objectionable for that reason, would nevertheless have brought the Authority closer to government (Home Office, Cm 2434, 1993, para. 30). Privatisation was rejected as unacceptable in principle. The White Paper also suggested that the Scheme's administration might be market tested once established, but in debate the government indicated that it had at that time no intention to do so (HC Debs, Standing Committee A, cols. 63–89, 13 June 1995; HL Debs, vol. 566, col. 295, 19 July 1995). Even if its administration were to be market tested, its systems for review and appeals would not.

The adjudicators replace the members of the Criminal Injuries Compensation Board who hitherto, in addition to determining applications, have had responsibility for deciding internal appeals by dissatisfied applicants. The 1978 Working Party described them as being responsible 'individually or in small panels at hearings, for considering and deciding upon all applications for compensation' and collectively, as having responsibility 'for internal policy and practice relating to the day-to-day operation of the Scheme' (Home Office, *Review of the Criminal Injuries Compensation Scheme: Report of an Interdepartmental Working Party*, 1978, para. 1.2). Board members are barristers or solicitors appointed by the Home Secretary or, in Scotland, solicitors or advocates appointed by the Secretary of State for Scotland. Despite their jurisdictional origins, Board members may determine applications from either side of the border. Appointments have been part-time and have been for an initial period of five years. In 1995 there were 43 members, including the Chairman, Lord Carlisle. The Chairman has also been a member of the Board but has had additional responsibilities to discharge, for example, concerning the acceptance of applications made after the three-year time limit (chapter 7.2.2) or the reopening of awards to take account of deterioration in the applicant's condition (chapter 2.3.4). These and other instances of the Chairman's discretion are discussed in later chapters.

It is likely that a number of the former Board members will be reappointed as members of the 50-strong Panel, which 'will be drawn from a broad constituency including the legal and medical professions, the business and commercial world and other professional or responsible groups' (Home Office, Cm 2434, 1993, para. 35). In addition to their adjudicatory work, Panel members will 'advise the Secretary of

State on matters on which he seeks its advice, as well as on such other matters and at such times as it considers appropriate' (new Scheme, para. 5). This advice will be referred to in the Authority's annual reports. The opposition was keen that a separate advisory body including appointments from outwith the Panel should be established for this purpose, but this was resisted by the government (HC Debs, Standing Committee A, cols. 39–49, 224–6, 13 and 22 June 1995).

Throughout its life the Board has been supported by clerical and administrative staff whose complement was substantially increased in 1992 following the critical comments made by the Home Affairs Committee (House of Commons Paper 92, Session 1989–90, para. 19). In recent years there have been other major changes in its operation, not the least of which was the establishment in 1987 of a second office in Glasgow, which now employs more staff than its London headquarters. In addition to these, members conduct hearings in a number of cities in Great Britain, at which they also undertake inspections of applicants' injuries as a preliminary to the assessment of compensation.

1.4.3   Implementation and Transitional Arrangements

Revisions to the old Scheme have applied only to applications relating to injuries incurred after the date on which the revisions commenced. Conversely, applications received before the date on which revisions were to commence have been dealt with under the unrevised Scheme, and in some cases, on the basis of a yet earlier version than that. Thus the 1990 version of the old Scheme provides that applications received by the Board before 1 February 1990 would, subject to the procedural changes introduced in 1990, continue to be determined in accordance either with the 1969 or with the 1979 version, depending on the date on which the injury was incurred (old Scheme, para. 29).

In the case of applications received after the date of commencement but relating to injuries incurred before it, the arrangement under the old Scheme was that the unrevised Scheme should apply. Thus, under the 1990 version of the old Scheme, applications received on or after 1 February 1990 in respect of injuries incurred before that date were dealt with on the basis of the 1979 Scheme (old Scheme, para. 28). This has meant, for example, that an injury directly attributable to an offence of trespass on a railway that was sustained on 31 January 1990 would not have come within the terms of the old Scheme, but would if it had been sustained a day later. This is so because that particular criminal injury was only introduced in the 1990 version.

Because there has been a three-year limitation period for applications, this arrangement has meant that the Board would, for some years after the introduction of any revisions, have been determining applications on the basis of the earlier version of the Scheme. Moreover, because the Board has been prepared to accept applications in respect of injuries incurred when the applicant was a child, but which only come to light some 10 or even 20 years later, those applications are covered by that version of the old Scheme in force at the date of the injury. In the particular case of child abuse committed before 1 October 1979 by a member of the child's family, this has meant that where the child and the offender were living together at the time as members of the same family, the applicant would be ineligible for compensation. This is so because para. 7 of the 1969 Scheme, which was revised with effect from 1 October 1979, provided that the Board could not award compensation in such cases (old Scheme, para. 28(b)). The Board continues to emphasise these limitations on its discretion to award compensation in such cases (CICB, 1995, para. 5.7).

The rationality of the maintenance of this rule in the light of the change which, subject to some qualifications, permitted compensation in such cases, was tested in *R* v *Criminal Injuries Compensation Board, ex parte P* [1994] 1 All ER 80. The Divisional Court held that in excluding this class of victim at the outset, the Scheme was not irrational, nor was it rendered so in the light of the subsequent amendments (per Leggatt L.J.):

> The making of a claim is a not a right but a privilege. It follows that the only legitimate expectation that a claimant can have is of recovering an award in accordance with the scheme in force for the time being ... the fact that some claimants are or continue to be excluded from the scheme by force of amendments made to it neither demonstrates that it is perverse nor renders it so.

By contrast, the new Scheme provides that any application received on or after 1 April 1996 will be dealt with on the basis of that Scheme, irrespective of the date on which the injury was incurred (new Scheme, para. 83). Applications received before 1 April 1996 will continue to be dealt with under the 1990 version of the old Scheme, subject to the applicability of any earlier version to the injury in question (new Scheme, para. 84), as will any applications to reopen a case under para. 13 of the old Scheme (new Scheme, para. 87).

The new Scheme gives power to the Secretary of State to fix a 'transfer date' on which the Board will cease to exist, and any outstanding para. 84 applications will be dealt with by the Authority (new Scheme, para. 86). Paragraph 86(a) of the new Scheme further provides for the decisions of the Authority's legally qualified Panel members to have the same authority for the purposes of the new Scheme as had the Board's Members for the purposes of the old Scheme.

1.4.4 Standard of Proof

Section 3(2) of the 1995 Act provides: 'Where, in accordance with any provision of the Scheme, it falls to one person to satisfy another as to any matter, the standard of proof required shall be that applicable in civil proceedings'. This was always the case under the old Scheme, and it most obviously means that wherever the burden falls on the applicant, he must, as to any matter requiring proof, satisfy the Authority (a claims officer) or the Panel (an adjudicator) on the balance of probabilities. But the section is not limited to the applicant's burden. It applies to any person who is required to satisfy another as to any matter. This will include, for example, the

Authority, where the Panel is hearing an appeal against a review decision (see also new Scheme, para. 64).

1.5   ACCOUNTABILITY

1.5.1   Parliamentary

Paragraph 3 of the old Scheme provided that the Board's decisions would not be subject to Ministerial review. This followed from the views of the 1961 Working Party to the effect that compensation decisions should not be made by a government department acting administratively, nor by any body which was not independent of such a department (Home Office, Cmnd 1406, 1961, para. 66). The Working Party envisaged that these decisions, being judicial in character, would be taken by the courts (as was then the case in Northern Ireland) or a specially created tribunal. The latter suggestion was proposed in the 1964 White Paper (Cmnd 2323) and given effect in para. 3 of the original old Scheme:

> The Board will be entirely responsible for deciding what compensation should be paid in individual cases and their decisions will not be subject to appeal or to Ministerial review.

Parliamentary accountability was thought to be sufficiently met by keeping the general working of the Scheme under review, and by the imposition on the Board of a requirement to submit annually to the Home Secretary and the Secretary of State for Scotland a full report on the operation of the Scheme. But with the exception of the Lords debate in December 1983 (HL Debs, vol. 446, cols. 283–309, 14 December 1983), the Annual Reports have excited little interest, typically prompting parliamentary questions about delay in resolving cases, or about the minimum threshold. By contrast, two reports of the Home Affairs Committee in the mid to late 1980s did bring about a number of beneficial changes to the Home Office's support for the Board's administrative arrangements (House of Commons Papers, Papers 43, Session 1984–85; 92, Session 1989–90).

Neither was the Board made subject to supervision by the Council on Tribunals, which omission the 1986 working party recommended should be rectified (Home Office, *Criminal Injuries Compensation: A Statutory Scheme*, 1986, para. 3.5). As the Board was not a Crown body, it did not fall within the jurisdiction of the Parliamentary Commissioner for Administration, but as he is an *ex officio* member of the Council, he has been able to direct to it complaints to him of maladministration.

The Act provides that the individual decisions of claims officers (s. 3(5)(b) and (6)) and of the Scheme manager (s. 7) shall not be regarded as decisions taken by the Secretary of State. This provision caused considerable concern during debate, the question being whether, and to what extent, it reduced the Secretary of State's accountability for the new Scheme. In reply, the government gave an assurance that its intention was no more than to reproduce exactly the position obtaining under para. 3 of the old Scheme, which provided that the general working of the Scheme will be kept under review by the Secretary of State (new Scheme, para. 4, repeating with minor amendment para. 3 of the old Scheme), who will be answerable to Parliament on matters of policy and funding (HC Debs, Standing Committee A, cols. 201–7, 22 June 1995), while operational decisions are taken by the Scheme's claims officers and adjudicators. Section 6 of the Act requires the Secretary of State to nominate an appropriate person to make an annual report to him, and to lay the report before Parliament. In addition to the usual statement of accounts, the report must (s. 6(1)(b)(ii)) 'cover the operation of, and the discharge of functions conferred by, the Scheme during the year to which it relates'.

There was also considerable disquiet that, as framework legislation, the Act says virtually nothing about how the new Scheme will operate. Two major issues emerged. The first was that in giving power to the Secretary of State to introduce and amend the Scheme as he saw appropriate, there was a significant attenuation of parliamentary control (see, for example, Lords Ackner, Windlesham and Simon of Glaisdale, HL Debs, vol. 566, cols. 307, 584 and 595, 19 July and 16 October 1995). When first published the Bill provided essentially that only the tariff element of the Scheme would need to be approved by Parliament; such matters as the definition of a criminal injury, eligibility and the range of qualifying persons were to be dealt with administratively. As the result of sustained pressure in the Lords, a number of important changes were made by the government. Prime among these were the amendments that were enacted as s. 11. The Secretary of State is required to seek parliamentary approval for the introduction of the entire Scheme, and any change, however minor, to the Scheme's 'key' elements will also require parliamentary approval by the affirmative resolution procedure. These key elements include (s. 11(3)): changes to the 'additional amounts' of compensation specified in s. 2(2) (that is, loss of earnings, special expenses and compensation in fatal cases), the calculation of compensation in respect of multiple injuries and children conceived as a result of rape; limits on compensation; and the circumstances in which compensation may be withheld or reduced. The affirmative resolution procedure also applies where any change is proposed to rights of appeal or the circumstances in which an appeal is to be dealt with by a hearing (s. 11(4)). Changes to any other aspect of the Scheme will be subject to approval by the negative resolution procedure (ss. 11(6) and (7)) (HL Debs, vol. 566, col. 1610, 6 November 1995).

A second major change was to bring the decisions of the Scheme's administrative officers within the jurisdiction of the Parliamentary Commissioner for Administration (PCA). The opposition's first attempt to amend the Bill to this effect was resisted by the government on the ground that it was likely that many of the new applicants rejected each year (some 35%) would apply to the PCA, clogging the system with bogus claims (HC Debs, vol. 262, cols. 1093–1104, 29 June 1995). However, it gave an undertaking to review the matter, and introduced an amendment during the Lords stages (HC Debs, vol. 265, col. 741, 7 November 1995).

1.5.2   Judicial

At its establishment, the old Scheme explicitly excluded the possibility of an appeal on the merits of a decision of the Board. However, it was shortly established in *R* v *Criminal Injuries Compensation Board, ex parte Lain* [1967] 2 QB 864 that the Board's decisions were subject to judicial review, the court rejecting its argument that as the Scheme was no more than an administrative arrangement, certiorari could not go since the Board had no legal authority and could not determine questions affecting the rights of subjects. Considering the total number of applications (779,400 taking account of those abandoned; CICB, 1995, App. A), the number of applications for judicial review that are heard is small. A LEXIS search showed 42 cases between May 1981 and May 1995. Many of those cases concern the application of the Board's discretion in para. 6 of the old Scheme to refuse or reduce an award where the applicant has failed to cooperate with the police (para. 6(a); chapter 7.4.1), or where his character (para. 6.(c); chapter 7.5.3.2) makes it inappropriate that he should receive an award from public funds. The question which was considered at length in *R* v *Criminal Injuries Compensation Board, ex parte Cook* [1996] 1 WLR 1037 (CA) was the degree of detail which the Board should give when advising applicants of its decision to refuse or reduce an award having exercised its discretion under this or other paragraphs of the old Scheme.

The facts of *ex parte Cook* were that the applicant made a claim arising from the murder of her husband, who was the victim of a contract killing. At the time of his murder he was on day release from prison where he was completing a 16-year sentence for armed robbery. Mrs Cook was wholly unassociated with any of her husband's criminal activities. Her application was rejected under para. 6(c) because of her husband's character as shown by his criminal convictions, a matter which para. 15 permits the Board to take into account when dealing with applications arising from fatal injuries (chapter 7.5.2.1). Her application for judicial review was refused by Potts J., and before the Court of Appeal she argued that the Board had failed to take account of her own good character or that if it had, it had failed to give any indication in its reasons that it had done so, and, secondly, that the Board had wrongly refused her application for an oral hearing. This second point is dealt with in chapter 3.1.2.2.

Giving the leading judgment, Aldous L.J. held that the Board had no duty to consider the applicant's good character (see further 7.5.2.1), and that being the case, it was not necessary to refer to her character in the reasons it gave for refusing the application. The reasons given were, in his view, adequate. Adapting the decision of the House of Lords in *Bolton Metropolitan District Council* v *Secretary of State for the Environment* [1995] 1 WLR 1176 concerning the adequacy of reasons given by the Secretary of State in a planning matter, his Lordship said ([1996] 1 WLR 1037 at p. 1043):

... it is clear that the board's reasons should contain sufficient detail to enable the reader to know what conclusion has been reached on the principal important issue or issues, but it is not a requirement that they should deal with every material consideration to which they have had regard. If the reasons given are sufficient, they cannot be reviewed in judicial review proceedings unless the board misconstrued their mandate or the decison is *Wednesbury* unreasonable.

The matter did not, however, end there. Before the Court of Appeal the appellant argued that the 'more exacting approach' (Hobhouse L.J., p. 1049) to be found in Sedley J.'s judgment in *R* v *Criminal Injuries Compensation Board, ex parte Gambles* [1994] PIQR 314 (DC) should be adopted. What Sedley J. had sought in that case was the introduction of a three-stage test in which the Board, when faced with such applications, should ask itself first, whether the applicant's conduct made a full award inappropriate; second, if so, to what extent the applicant's conduct impacted on the award; and third, what award if any should the applicant consequently receive? Sedley J. held that in its rejection of an application arising from injuries sustained in a fight in which the applicant was a willing participant, the Board had moved from the first to the third question, omitting the second entirely. It had thus failed to 'establish a rational and proportionate nexus between the conduct of applicant' and the rejection of the application.

Aldous L.J. was emphatically of the view that Sedley J. was wrong. A decision that no award was appropriate was equivalent to deciding that the award should be nil; only if the Board should decide that some award was appropriate did the third question become relevant. So far as the nexus to which Sedley J. referred was concerned, Aldous L.J. said (at p. 152):

> ... I am clear that the board do not have to establish anything. Their duty is to consider the material circumstances and to arrive at a decision as to whether there should be an award out of public funds and, if so, what. That requires judgment not a complicated step-by-step approach.

Hobhouse L.J. (whose judgment is largely confined to a consideration of Sedley J.'s decision) went further. Reviewing other decisions of the Divisional Court in which *ex parte Gambles* had been discussed, his Lordship noted that none had adopted Sedley J.'s approach (save in *R* v *Criminal Injuries Compensation Board, ex parte Jobson* (LEXIS, 4 May 1995, in which Dyson J. adapted but did not base any finding of invalidity in the Board's decision on it; chapter 7.5.2.1), and that in two cases it had been distinguished. One of these was *R* v *Criminal Injuries Compensation Board, ex parte Hobson* LEXIS, 7 July 1995, in which Buxton J. decided not to follow *ex parte Gambles* — a decision which was specifically approved by Aldous L.J. Concluding his review, Hobhouse L.J. said (pp. 1050–1):

> In my judgment, *ex parte Gambles* seeks improperly to extend the scope of judicial review from an assessment of the propriety of the decision to an evaluation of its merits.

... the decision of the Board in *ex parte Gambles* was not on its face irrational nor did it seek to found upon some consideration which should have been excluded.... What Sedley J. was doing was, in truth, not identifying any defect in the decision but criticising the clarity and the completeness of the thought processes as set out in the reasons....

Such considerations may be relevant to an appeal but do not suffice for setting aside by way of judicial review a decision which is not prima facie irrational or improper.

In holding, with Aldous L.J., that *ex parte Gambles* should be overruled, Hobhouse L.J. nevertheless indicated that he would have preferred a fuller statement of reasons by the single member of the Board. Stressing that the reasons given were adequate for the purpose of informing the applicant why she had been unsuccessful, his Lordship said that 'it is usually a better practice to make explicit what is otherwise only implicit' (p. 1053). This *dictum* may be seen as coincident with Dyson J.'s remarks in *ex parte Jobson* that while there is no need to make detailed findings of fact or give exhaustive reasons and justifications for the exercise of its discretion, the short reasons which the Board gives 'must be sufficient to enable the applicant to see the factual basis on which the relevant conclusion has been arrived at, what considerations have been taken into account, and whether the decision on the issue is lawful'.

The new Scheme derives its authority from statute and as a public body the Authority's decisions are inevitably subject to judicial review. It will be seen that throughout the Scheme, there is an obligation on the Authority, or where the applicant appeals, the Panel, to give written reasons for its decision.

1.5.3   Internal

Both the Board and the Authority have a complaints procedure (old Scheme, Guide; new Scheme, Guide, Part 11). Part 10 of the Guide to the new Scheme specifies a set of return dates for acknowledging and dealing with applications, reviews and appeals, and for making payments. A senior member of staff will investigate complaints about the way in which an application has been dealt with, but not the correctness of the decision, which may be the subject of a hearing or, in the case of the new Scheme, a review. The Guide also draws attention to the role of the Parliamentary Commissioner for Administration.

1.6   INTERPRETING THE SCHEME

In its original and all its revised versions, the language of the old Scheme has been both prescriptive and descriptive, informing the reader of the limits of the Board's discretion and giving examples of its exercise. General propositions about the Board's interpretation of the old Scheme were until 1990 annexed to its Reports as the 'Statement', thereafter known as the 'Guide'. Issued for the benefit of applicants and their advisers, this was, the Board emphasised, written for guidance only (CICB, 1995, Guide). It will, for some years to come, continue to be an important indication of the scope of the Scheme as it applies to applications lodged before 1 April 1996.

In compliance with para. 21 of the new Scheme, the Authority has published a Guide to its operation, which contains the tariff of awards. It is very similar in style to the Guide to the old Scheme. It is a useful summary of the Scheme, but is not a substitute for it. Readers are warned that it cannot cover every situation or set of circumstances. In this book, a reference to the 'Guide' in relation to the old Scheme refers to the Guide appearing in the Board's 1995 Report, unless otherwise indicated. In the case of the new Scheme, the 'Guide' means Issue Number One (4/96) of the Authority's *Guide to the Criminal Injuries Compensation Scheme*. This is a lengthy document which has not been reproduced in this book. Its main provisions are, however, quoted *verbatim* and dealt with at the appropriate section of the narrative. The Authority has also published two further Guides to specific aspects of the Scheme; these are reproduced in Appendices 4 and 5.

When interpreting the old Scheme the courts repeatedly said that it should not be approached as though it were a statute, but that '... members of the Board ought to be free to deal with these eventualities when they arise in a flexible manner having regard to the whole object of the scheme' (per Wien J., *R v Criminal Injuries Compensation Board, ex parte Tong* [1976] 1 WLR 47 at p. 51). Likewise, courts were enjoined to interpret the Scheme so as to give effect to its underlying policy, adopting the interpretation of a reasonable and literate man (Bridge J., *R v Criminal Injuries Compensation Board, ex parte Schofield* [1971] 1 WLR 926 at p. 931) (and to the same effect, Lawton L.J. in *R v Criminal Injuries Compensation Board, ex parte Webb* [1987] QB 74 at p. 77). Whether, in practice, the courts always reached interpretations of the Scheme's provisions that were consonant with their policy is open to question: in *ex parte Tong* the award did survive for the benefit of the victim's estate, which was clearly out of line with the Scheme's intentions; in *ex parte Schofield* the Court of Appeal permitted a bystander to an act of law enforcement to recover compensation for an accidental injury when she herself was making no effort to engage in any such act which, again, was inconsistent with the Scheme's intentions. Though authorised by statute, the new Scheme is in many key respects similar in its wording to the old. It may therefore be expected that the courts will approach its interpretation in a similar fashion.

This book makes frequent reference to the debates on the Criminal Injuries Compensation Bill. The reason is that because it was a framework Bill, the government was unable to detail the workings of the new Scheme. Instead, it gave a number of assurances about how the Scheme would operate once in force. Following *Pepper v Hart* [1993] AC 593, these assurances are of importance to the interpretation of the new Scheme. References to the government's replies are references to the Secretary or Minister of State as appropriate; speakers' names are given only where they were not speaking for the government.

2 *Applications and Awards*

This chapter deals with the volume of work that the Authority may expect, the procedures for making and determining an application, the status of an award of compensation, the circumstances in which an award may not be final, and the payment of the costs associated with making an application.

2.1 APPLICATION RATES

In its 15th Report the Board commented (CICB, 1979, para. 3):

> The predominant factors in the volume of our work must relate to the number of crimes of violence, awareness of the Scheme and the decision of a victim to apply for compensation.

In the following year it added to this list the revisions to the Scheme made in 1969 and 1979 (CICB, 1980, para. 4). The picture is, however, more complex than this: while the numbers of new applications have, with only a few exceptions, increased every year, it is difficult to relate changes in the number of applications to changes in the Scheme. This is so first, because, as a matter of definition, volume of work cannot be equated simply with the annual total of new applications: it involves a qualitative as well as a quantitative dimension, as the Board's observations on the difficulties that attend the consideration, for example, of late applications and applications concerning child abuse attest (see CICB, 1986, para. 7; and 1991, para. 1.8). Secondly, it is in practice very difficult to identify either the relationship between different subsets of figures that may be attributable to these revisions, or the impact that they may have had on the total of new applications. The issue is made more difficult because these revisions have both widened and narrowed the scope of the Scheme. For example, in 1979–80, it was widened to include victims of intra-family violence and to empower the Board to reopen cases where there had been a serious deterioration in the applicant's medical condition. On the other hand, another change in 1979–80 narrowed the ground on which compensation would be available to those accidentally injured while engaged in law enforcement. Neither is it clear what impact increases in the financial minimum have upon the application rate (CICB, 1988, para. 2.2).

One of the primary reasons given by the government for the introduction of the tariff Scheme is that it will, in time, permit applications to be dealt with more quickly than has been the case in the past. That may be so; in the meantime, it is likely that the number of applications will continue to rise with the annual increase in the crime rate.

2.1.1 Number of Crimes of Violence

The first and most obvious factor affecting the volume of work to be dealt with by the Authority is the number of recorded crimes of violence. In 1994–95 there were 61,355 new applications in England and Wales (CICB, 1995, para. 3.1). This represents 19.7% of the 311,700 notifiable offences of violence against the person, sexual offences and robbery recorded by the police in 1994 (Home Office, *Criminal Statistics England and Wales 1994*, Cm 3010, London: HMSO, 1995, table 2.1). While this proportion is in line with the previous 10 years' figures, the actual number represents a decrease of 2.5% on the previous year. This was, however, expected, as there had been a similar increase in 1993–94 as applicants sought to bring their claims within the more generous terms of the old Scheme (CICB, 1995, para. 3.1).

Table 2.1   Number of Applications and Number of Crimes 1985–94

Applications in fiscal year	*Notifiable offences in calendar year (thousands)*	*Column 1 as percentage of column 2*
1985–86: 33,420	1985: 170.7	19.6
1986–87: 35,967	1986: 178.2	20.2
1987–88: 35,940	1987: 198.8	18.1
1988–89: 36,285	1988: 216.1	16.8
1989–90: 36,285	1989: 239.9	15.1
1990–91: 45,700	1990: 249.9	18.3
1991–92: 52,100	1991: 265.1	19.7
1992–93: 55,993	1992: 284.2	19.7
1993–94: 62,511	1993: 294.2	21.2
1994–95: 61,355	1994: 311.7	19.7

Table 2.1 lists the number of applications to the Board and the number of recorded crimes of violence between 1985 and 1994. Care must be taken when drawing inferences from these figures. There is, first, no direct chronological correspondence

between the number of recorded crimes of violence and the number of new applications. Secondly, there is no direct correlation between the number of applications the Board receives in any year and the number which are successful, as the Board's Reports do not distinguish, in the tables showing how live applications have in any one year been resolved, the year in which the application was made. Neither does the number of recorded crimes say anything about the size of the eligible population within the terms of the Scheme; and the figures offer no firm basis for determining how successful the Scheme has been in reaching that population. Nor, as the Home Office emphasised in its evidence to the Home Affairs Committee in 1989, is there a stable relationship between the number of crimes of violence and applications for compensation; it is instead a matter both of complexity and of some uncertainty (House of Commons Home Affairs Committee, *Compensating Victims Quickly: the Administration of the Criminal Injuries Compensation Board*, House of Commons Paper 92, Session 1989–90, London: HMSO, 1990). Two issues arise. First: how many more incidents than the 311,700 recorded in 1994 might have given rise to compensable injuries had they been reported? Second: given that the number of applications received by the Board was 19.7% of the offences that were recorded, how many more of them might have sustained a successful application?

The British Crime Survey (BCS) estimates that there are four times as many offences of wounding than the recorded figure. It also estimates eight times as many for robbery and theft from the person, but whereas robbery could lead to an award under the Scheme, theft from the person generally could not; this grouping is therefore omitted from the analysis which follows. I have also omitted consideration of the dark figure of sexual offences, primarily because they appear to give rise to a very small number of applications, which are dominated by offences under ss. 18, 20 and 47 of the Offences against the Person Act 1861. Let us suppose, therefore, that in 1994 there were 876,800 offences of wounding, rather than the 219,200 that were notified to the police. While the quantity of offences is clearly an important factor in determining the likely rate of applications for compensation and, by extension, the likely administrative and compensation costs, numbers alone will be poor aids to prediction. What is critical is the *severity* of the injuries sustained, since applications to the Authority will not succeed unless the total value of the awardable compensation exceeds the minimum threshold, currently £1,000. Thus while the true rate of offences of wounding may be higher than the recorded figure, the dark figure 'does not indicate that there is four to five times as much crime of the *same severity* as is now recorded in *Criminal Statistics*' (Hough, M. and Mayhew, P., *The British Crime Survey*, Home Office Research Study 76, London: HMSO, 1983, p. 13). One criterion which has been used by the BCS to refine severity is whether the victim required medical help. On this basis, the BCS concluded that 'most assaults and crimes of violence did not result in any serious physical injury; in only 12% of cases did the victim need any sort of professional medical attention, and in less than 1% of cases the victim was admitted to hospital' (Hough, M. and Mayhew, P., *Taking Account of Crime*, Home Office Research Study 85, London: HMSO, 1985, p. 9). This suggests that in 1994 some 105,216 victims of offences of wounding required medical or hospital attention. This figure is comfortably within the 219,200 such offences recorded in that year, most of which would almost certainly have been reported to the police, but many more than the 61,355 applications received by the Board in 1994–95. Before considering how many of that estimate might have given rise to compensable injuries, some other complicating factors should be mentioned.

Since, as a general proposition, one precondition to obtaining compensation is that the incident be reported to the police, the very fact that an injury does result from an unreported crime will almost always be fatal to an application in respect of it. That proposition is subject to the Board's exercise of its discretion to accept an application arising from an unreported offence, for example, in the case of assaults on staff committed by patients in mental hospitals. But in this formal sense the number of recorded offences does indeed represent the outer limit of the potentially eligible population of victims of personal crime, but not, of course, the outer limit of those injuries that are sufficiently severe to warrant compensation. Secondly, the BCS classification 'crime of violence' (of which wounding is one instance) is not coterminous with notifiable offences for the purposes of *Criminal Statistics* and neither of these is coterminous with what constitutes a criminal injury for the purposes of the Scheme, which includes injuries arising from arson and acts of law enforcement. To predict how many of all the offences which can constitute criminal injuries for the purposes of the Scheme could give rise to compensable injuries, it would be necessary to know their proportion of the total of applications. As the Board's Reports give no guidance on this issue, it is a matter of conjecture how many of the BCS estimate for medically attended victims of wounding offences in 1994 did apply, and how many victims of other offences made applications. Thus as it is not possible to say how many more victims of wounding offences might be eligible, neither is it possible to say how many more victims of, for example, offences under s. 34 of the Offences against the Person Act 1861 (trespass on a railway, a criminal injury included in 1990) fall within the eligible population.

When discussing the BCS estimate of severity above, it was estimated that 105,216 victims of wounding offences would have required medical or hospital attention in 1994. What remains a matter of speculation is how many of these incidents might have given rise to injuries sufficiently severe to meet the Scheme's lower limit. McClintock's 1963 study indicated that a large proportion of victims suffer no serious injury; 75% were back at work within a week, about 12% were off work for 10 days and less than 2% suffered permanent disability (McClintock, D., *Crimes of Violence*, London: Macmillan, 1963, p. 54). A similar picture emerges from a compensation survey conducted by the Centre for Socio-Legal Studies in the 1970s (Harris, D., et al., *Compensation and Support for Illness and Injury*, Oxford: Oxford University Press, 1984). A sample of 5,036 people who had sustained personal injury (from any source) resulting in two weeks' interruption in normal activities was derived from an initial sample of 35,085 individuals. Of these 5,036, only 21 were victims of crime, and only seven made successful claims to the Board. Failure to obtain an award may be explained by factors other than a relatively unserious injury; nevertheless this Survey underlines two points that have been stressed by the BCS: first, the relative infrequency of crimes against the person, and secondly, the relatively non-serious consequences of personal victimisation (Hough, M. and Mayhew, P., *The British Crime Survey*, 1983).

Two other surveys, specifically of crime victims, point to a greater degree of harm, and suggest that the population of eligible victims (that is, victims who could expect an award) is certainly larger than the number who actually apply. Shapland's study of 218 victims of criminal violence in the Midlands showed that 45 of the 54 who applied to the Board received either full or reduced awards (Shapland, J. et al., *Victims in the Criminal Justice System*, London: Gower, 1985). The application rate here was 25%, compared with the figure of 19% given earlier; the success rate 83% by comparison with the success rate of 63% over the life of the Board (the cumulative total to 1995 of all applications received throughout Great Britain (and not abandoned) was 848,544; the number of applicants who received either full or reduced awards was 533,098: CICB, 1995, para. 2.1 and App. A). The second, more recent study is Maguire and Corbett's account of their interviews with victims previously sampled by the BCS. Over a third of their sample who had suffered personal victimisation reported themselves as being 'very much affected' by the offence (Maguire, M. and Corbett, C., *The Effects of Crime and the Work of Victim Support Schemes*, London: Gower, 1987, ch. 3). Allowing for the small sample in Shapland's study and the fact that Maguire and Corbett were reporting victims' own perceptions of injury, these studies suggest that the eligible population of victims who have suffered injury as a result of a crime of personal violence in England and Wales could be between 25% and 30% of the total of such reported crime, which, in 1995, would be between 77,925 and 93,510 individuals.

The fact that the proportion of new applications has remained relatively constant over many years' increases in the rate of recorded crimes of violence while at the same time the Scheme must have become very much better known to potential applicants and their advisers, suggests that there is no substantial number of eligible victims hidden within that rate. These estimates must of course remain tentative so long as there are so little reliable data on the relationship between the number of recorded offences, the measurable impact of the offence, and the relative proportions of the various criminal injuries that comprise the global figure of applications to the Board. As noted in chapter 1.4.1, forecasting the annual increase in crimes of violence against the person and the proportion of that figure who might be expected to apply to the Board assumed increasing budgetary importance during the late 1980s. The lack of financial control implicit in the Board's inability to be exact about its future commitments was one of the reasons why the new Scheme was introduced. A tariff cannot control the rate of recorded crimes of violence or of applications to the Authority, but it can bring greater rectitude to forecasts based on a range of injury levels implicit in different rates of application.

2.1.2   Claims Consciousness

What is clear is that, with very few exceptions, the number of new applications received each year has consistently exceeded both the Board's annual predictions and the annual percentage increases in the number of notifiable offences. Thus there may be some support for the view expressed by the Board some 20 years ago that the growth in the number of new applications is indicative of a greater willingness on the part of victims to seek compensation (CICB, 1977, para. 1), though exactly what the determinants of such willingness are is a complex and largely untested issue. Equally unclear is the extent to which this 'steady upward trend' reflects the uncovering of the dark figure of eligible victims on the one hand, or an absolute increase in that population on the other (CICB, 1988, para. 2.2).

No doubt pure ignorance accounts in many cases for failure even to consider making a claim (Cane, P., *Atiyah's Accidents, Compensation and the Law*, 5th ed., London: Weidenfeld and Nicolson, 1993, pp. 173–177). It is trite to observe that knowledge of the existence of the Scheme is a precondition to making an application, but despite the Board's constant efforts to publicise its terms, there has in the past been an apparently widespread ignorance about it. In the early 1980s Shapland found that while 39% of her sample knew of the existence of the Scheme, 51% knew of no method by which they could be compensated (Shapland, J. et al., *Victims in the Criminal Justice System*, 1985, p. 124), a level of ignorance underlined in Newburn's survey of the use of compensation orders, in which he tested awareness of compensation possibilities (Newburn, T., *The Use and Enforcement of Compensation Orders in Magistrates' Courts*, Home Office Research Study 102, London: HMSO, 1988, pp. 36–7). The issue of publicity will be of importance both to victims and to the Authority. For the Authority, decisions as to when, how and to whom to target information will have implications for the efficacy of its publicity effort, and for the allocation of its financial and staffing resources should that effort produce an increase in applications. There is also the consideration that a better informed applicant can submit a more complete application, anticipating matters which the Authority would otherwise have to follow up itself (CICB, 1989, para. 17).

Shapland's research suggests that the quality of information which victims are given by the police or other groups, such as Victim Support, is the most significant factor predicting whether victims will seek compensation. Since the source of information will almost always be the police, their contribution is crucial. In 1988 the Home Office published a circular encouraging the police to give advice and assistance to victims about the possibility of compensation (including compensation orders), and giving information about the Board (Home Office Circular No. 20/1988), advice that is repeated in abbreviated form in the *Victim's Charter*. Given that the incidence of personal victimisation among the general population which is sufficiently severe to be compensable under the Scheme is low, the Board's own efforts have tended to avoid unfocused publicity (CICB, 1995, para. 7.2). Such publicity can be dysfunctional, creating misconceptions and false expectations in some applicants. The fact that awards under the old Scheme were *ex gratia* apparently encouraged the view among some of those who made unsuccessful applications, that the Board was free to compensate those for whom it felt sympathy, but who did not fall within its provisions (CICB, 1979, para. 15). Its efforts have therefore been directed to particular groups likely to be responsible for making applications, or to the victims of major criminal incidents. Thus, in response to the marked increase during the late 1980s in the number of applications arising from child abuse, the Board sent a new circular on this matter to local authorities and other interested organisations (CICB, 1989, paras 1.7, 21.4, 21.5; CICB, 1995, App. H). And 'once the cause of the Lockerbie disaster had been established the Board confirmed that the circumstances would be regarded as a ''crime of violence'' for the purposes of the Scheme ... [and] members of the staff visited Lockerbie to explain the Board's position to those responsible for coordinating assistance to the victims there' (CICB, 1989, para. 7.1). Despite these intensive and focused efforts, which in some previous instances have included sending application forms directly to known victims, three years later the Board noted 'that many of those affected [by the Lockerbie disaster] remain in ignorance of the Scheme' (CICB, 1992, para. 7.2).

2.1.3   The Decision to Apply

As might be expected, the primary reason why victims choose not to make an application is because they regard their injuries as being too trivial. This was the main reason (385 of respondents) given in Shapland's sample when asked why they had not applied to the Board. In a healthy and robust person a sprained wrist sustained, for example, while attempting to prevent the offender from snatching a camera or handbag may indeed raise no issue about the 'triviality' of the injury (although this need say nothing of the victim's sense of anger or loss), but in marginal cases the exact components of this judgment become critical. Since we can hardly expect victims untutored in CICB Reports to be able to determine whether their injuries were ones for which, by para. 5 of the old Scheme, 'the total amount of compensation payable after deduction of social security benefits, but before any other deductions under the Scheme, would be not less than the minimum amount of compensation', the judgments of others, such as the police, victim support groups or the victims' friends, family and workmates are likely to be influential; but there is little hard evidence on this matter.

One factor which clearly emerged from Shapland's research as being significant is the possibility of the victim being able to quantify the loss or injury. The reasons given by the applicants in her sample were dominated by the wish to recover for lost earnings, medical and dental expenses, lost or ruined clothing and for property loss or damage (in particular, to spectacles). It is perhaps not surprising that victims are more likely to make an application where their injuries can be translated into real and tangible losses, but this possibility does not assist victims whose special damages are not significant by comparison with the effects of the injury to their health.

Yet, as the Board's comments on the outcome of its efforts following the Lockerbie disaster indicate, there continues to be a significant proportion of victims who, though fully aware of the Scheme, and whose injuries would surely have warranted an award, do not apply. In 1973 the Board sent application forms to all 223 victims of the terrorist bomb explosion at the Old Bailey in March that year. Of the Board's estimate that 186 of them were eligible for compensation (the others suffering only minor injuries), only 103 (55%) made an application. As to the possible reasons for the shortfall, the Board commented that this was probably attributable to their 'desire to forget their painful experience as quickly as possible', which factor was 'of paramount importance to them' (CICB, 1974, paras 1 and 10). The shortfall between eligibility and take-up is an experience that is by no means unique to the CICB; it is a perennial feature of schemes in other common law jurisdictions, and is a common phenomenon in other areas of public benefit allocation. A number of factors may explain this discrepancy: divergent perceptions of loss, of need and of the utility of the benefit to meet those losses or needs; differences in beliefs and feelings about the application procedure, including in the case of the Scheme, an unwillingness on the part of victims of crime to have their conduct or character investigated; inability to cope with official forms and enquiries; and a desire simply to forget a distressing experience. These are no doubt all factors which singly or in combination may discourage victims from applying; their precise role remains, however, a matter of speculation.

2.2 APPLYING FOR COMPENSATION

2.2.1 Making the Application

'An application for compensation under this Scheme in respect of a criminal injury ... must be made in writing on a form obtainable from the Authority (new Scheme, para. 17). There are two application forms: one for personal and one for fatal injuries. The application may relate to any criminal injury sustained after 1 August 1964. The applicant may be the person who directly sustained the injury (new Scheme, para. 6(a)), or, where the victim has since died, an applicant who is a 'qualifying claimant' for the purposes of the payment of compensation in fatal cases (new Scheme, para. 6(b); see chapter 6.3.3). Applications received by the Authority before 1 April 1996 will continue to be dealt with under the terms of the old Scheme; applications received after that date will be dealt with under the new Scheme, irrespective of the date on which the criminal injury was sustained (see chapter 1.4.3). Paragraph 7(a) of the new Scheme precludes the possibility of an applicant who has already made an application before 1 April 1996 benefiting twice by making a further application after that date. For the purposes of the new Scheme, 'applicant' means 'any person for whose benefit an application for compensation is made, even where it is made on his behalf by another person' (new Scheme, para. 6). For the special provisions concerning applications on behalf of children, see chapter 6.2.2).

2.2.2 Verifying the Application

The personal injury application form requires applicants to give details of the incident and of the injuries to which it gave rise. It asks for details of the offence, whether and how the circumstances were reported to the police; the extent of the injuries and the treatment received; loss of earnings and special expenses; and particulars of any previous applications. The applicant is also required to sign a section of the form authorising the provision of information to the Authority by the police, medical authorities, employers, relevant central and local government authorities or 'any other person, body or organisation with information relevant to [the] application'. In relation to any matter concerning the application upon which the claims officer must be satisfied, the applicant (or any other person seeking to prove the matter) must be able to satisfy the claims officer on the balance of probabilities (Act, s. 3(2); chapter 1.4.4).

Once received, each application will be given a reference number personal to the applicant, acknowledged and dealt with by a claims officer. The main initial task, to be completed within two weeks (the Board gave priority to applications arising from fatal injuries and from injuries to children), will be the verification with the police or the medical authorities named in the application of the information given by the applicant, and with any other relevant person or agency. The police will be asked to confirm that the injury was reported to them, and whether, in their view, it was attributable to a crime of violence (or other criminal injury) or resulted to any extent from the applicant's own conduct. They will also be asked whether the applicant is known to them, and the outcome of criminal proceedings. Where these are pending, it has been the Board's practice to defer determination of the application, but only if it considers that the proceedings are likely to have a bearing on the outcome of the application. This supersedes its earlier approach, which was to delay the determination of an application on the ground that its decision might prejudice the fair trial of the defendant. As a result of criticism, this approach was modified to the practice set out in para. 52 of the Guide to the old Scheme. It may be assumed that the Authority will continue this practice.

This process of verification can take some time. In dealing with applications, a claims officer can 'make such directions and arrangements for the conduct of an application, including the imposition of conditions, as he considers appropriate in all the circumstances' (new Scheme, para. 19). Should discrepancies appear or sufficient information has been given or is unavailable (for example, as to the victim's medical condition or prognosis), the claims officer will seek further information from the applicant, or await the outcome of treatment. In this connection, the new Scheme provides (para. 20) that 'Where a claims officer considers that an examination of the injury is required before a decision can be reached, the Authority will make arrangements for such an examination by a duly qualified medical practitioner'. The Authority will reimburse the applicant's reasonable expenses in such cases.

2.2.3 False, Fraudulent and Abandoned Applications

Occasionally, applications are revealed as being false or fraudulent. In some instances applicants may simply invent an injury for the purpose of applying for compensation or to draw attention to themselves (CICB, 1991, para. 13.3; CICB, 1994, para. 8.1), or imagine that they were the victim of an offence (CICB, 1995, para. 8.1). More common are cases in which injuries are presented as being inflicted during an assault that were in fact self-inflicted or sustained when the applicant fell over while drunk (CICB, 1987, para. 56; 1991, para. 13.2). There are also cases in which applicants falsify receipts or records of their income for the purpose of increasing the award (CICB, 1989, para. 13.2; 1994, para. 8.1).

It has been the Board's practice to ask the police to investigate applications such as these, and, where appropriate, to instigate proceedings. These typically rely on a completed or attempted offence under s. 15 of the Theft Act 1968 (CICB, 1994, para. 8.1); on occasion, wasting police time (CICB, 1990, para. 13.3). The recommendation made by the 1986 Working Party (Home Office, *Criminal Injuries Compensation: A Statutory Scheme*, London: HMSO, 1986, para. 22.4) that there should be a specific statutory offence, akin to those common in social security legislation, of knowingly or recklessly, and without reasonable excuse, making a statement to the Board which is false in a material particular, has not been acted upon, perhaps because, as the Board's Reports indicate, the number of such cases is very small by comparison with the total number of applications received.

Of applications that are genuine, about 2.5% are abandoned each year. The Board's Annual Reports do not indicate the reasons why these applications are not pursued.

2.2.4 Initial Determination of the Application

Section 3(4) of the Act provides for the appointment of claims officers for the purpose of determining claims and making awards and payments of compensation. It is they who 'will be responsible for deciding, in accordance with [the] Scheme, what awards (if any) should be made in individual cases' (new Scheme, para. 3). Claims officers are therefore pivotal to the implementation of the new Scheme. Under the old Scheme, individual applications were, prior to the 1990 revision, determined by a single member of the Board on the basis of the documentary evidence submitted by the applicant and generated in response to the case-working officer's inquiries. The single member could make either a full or a reduced award, reject the application altogether, or, where he considered that he could not make a just and proper decision himself, refer it to a hearing by at least two members. It may be noted that this last option is not possible under the new Scheme. This is so because the new Scheme establishes a procedure whereby initial decisions may be reviewed by more senior claims officers before the applicant may invoke the appeals procedure at which her claim may be heard by the equivalent of a member of the Board. The government thus opposed Lord Carlisle of Bucklow's amendment which would have given claims officers the opportunity to refer an application to a member of the appeals Panel: 'If the authority were able to refer cases directly to the appeals panel for first decision there would then be no further body to which the claimant could appeal if he were dissatisfied with the panel's decision' (HL Debs, vol. 566, col. 1382, 31 October 1995).

Because it was concerned that Board members' talents were often being expensively employed on matters that its administrative staff were, by virtue of their experience with the Scheme, wholly competent to decide, the 1986 Working Party recommended that in a limited range of cases, the initial determination of an application should be devolved to the Board's staff (Home Office, *Criminal Injuries Compensation: A Statutory Scheme*, 1986, para. 22.4). The concomitant potential for a speedier resolution of applications became much more urgent towards the end of that decade as the proportion of applicants who could expect their application to be resolved within six months fell from 23% in 1986–87 to 7.9% in 1989–90; conversely, whereas in 1986–87 50% of applications took over 12 months to resolve, by 1989–90, that figure had risen to 73%. As the Home Affairs Committee put it in their enquiry that year: 'in simple terms, most victims can now expect to wait at least a year until their claim is met. Fifteen years ago, around 1 in 20 had to do so' (House of Commons Paper 92, Session 1989–90, para. 5). These delays inevitably contributed to an 'appalling backlog' (CICB, 1986, para. 1), which, by 1989–90, amounted to two years' work for the Board, without any new applications. As the Board observed at the time: '. . . the backlog itself now contributes substantially to the overall delay if only on account of the time spent on essentially non-productive work dealing with queries and representations about partially completed cases' (CICB, 1989, para. 1.4).

There are, essentially, three main causes of delay. The first, investigative delay, is 'inevitable in every case because of the enquiries we have to make and our dependence on third parties for the necessary information' (CICB, 1989, para. 1.4; see also Lord Carlisle, HL Debs, vol. 565, col. 306, 19 July 1995). The second is that in serious cases, it may simply not be possible for the applicant's medical advisers to agree quickly a prognosis sufficiently exact to provide the basis for an assessment of compensation (though interim awards can be made in such cases; see chapter 2.3.3). The third, which in the opinion of the Home Affairs Committee seriously compounded the problem, is bureaucratic inefficiency. The Committee encountered 'a world of filing cabinets and heaps of paper, not of VDUs and instant data retrieval' (House of Commons Paper 92, Session 1989–90, para. 26). It made a number of recommendations designed both to increase the Board's efficiency and to prompt the Home Office to inject additional resources. The introduction of IT facilities and training, along with new staff (the number of staff appointed over the years had fallen in proportion to the annual increase in the number of new applications) and restructured internal procedures based on a management review, all accompanied the completion of the Board's relocation from London to Glasgow in the early 1990s (CICB, 1990, paras 1.1–1.11; 1993, paras 1.1, 1.8; 1994, paras 1.5, 1.7).

In addition to these, a number of changes were made to the Scheme's procedures. Those concerning its internal appeal provisions (hearings) are dealt with in chapter 3.1.2. They also gave effect to the 1986 Working Party's recommendation to delegate some decisions to the administrative staff. Paragraph 22 of the 1990 version of the old Scheme provided that the 'initial decision on an application will be taken by a single member of the Board, or by any member of the Board's staff to whom the Board has given authority to determine applications on the Board's behalf'. As a precautionary measure, para. 22 also provided that the 'designated member of the

Board's staff' could exercise the option which has always existed for the benefit of the single member, of referring an application to a hearing 'where he considers that he cannot make a just and proper decision himself'.

In response to concern that the delegation of substantive issues to administrative staff might lead to an increase in applications for judicial review, the new power was at first used only to devolve decisions to the Board's legal staff and only in respect of the questions whether the applicant had complied with the requirements of para. 6(a) (reporting to and co-operating with the police) and whether the injury was a criminal injury (para. 4(a)) which had occurred within Great Britain (para. 4(b)). But within a short time, the Board's staff, including those without legal qualifications, were routinely making initial decisions on applications on these matters, and also on whether the applicant had co-operated with the medical authorities (old Scheme, para. 6(b)) and whether the injury met the financial minimum (CICB, 1992, para. 15; 1993, para. 15). Between 1991 and 1994, the proportion of applications resolved by initial decisions taken by the Board's staff rose from 6% to 19% (CICB, 1991, para. 1.7; 1994, para. 2.3).

The opportunity to delegate decisions, together with the technological and resourcing improvements to the administration of the Board, have proved to be an undoubted success, contributing significantly to a marked increase in the number of cases resolved each year. Thus, in 1990 the Board received an increase of 24% in new applications (53,655) over the previous year and resolved 38,620 (CICB, 1990, para. 1.1); in 1994 it received 73,473 new applications (an increase of 11% over the previous year) and resolved 65,293 (CICB, 1994, para. 1.1). This improvement in the number of case resolutions (from 72% to 89%), which reflects an increase in the number of applications resolved at a hearing as well as by delegated decision, has been accompanied by a substantial improvement in the time taken to resolve them. By comparison with the figures given to the Home Affairs Committee, in 1994 42.7% of applications were resolved within six months, and the proportion of applicants waiting more than 12 months had fallen to just under 30% (CICB, 1994, para. 3.12). These improvements were not maintained into 1995, largely as a consequence of the additional burdens created by the introduction of the unlawful tariff Scheme in April 1994 (CICB, 1995, paras 1 and 2). Leaving aside the particular circumstances accompanying the tariff Scheme, the Board found itself, perhaps for the first time for many years, in a position to be proactive in the handling of applications, rather than merely reacting to their inexorable accumulation with the backlog from the late 1980s (CICB, 1993, para. 1.1).

There can be no doubt that this delegation has been a considerable help in increasing the throughput of cases and in speeding up the process. By deciding these straightforward cases at an early stage we have not only relieved the pressure on Board members but staff have been able to concentrate their efforts on those cases that are likely to attract awards. This, coupled with changes in our procedures, has meant that cases can be more *actively managed* from a much earlier stage. (CICB, 1992, para. 1.7)

A less welcome consequence was that as the Board became more efficient, so it found that its progress with applications was being held up as it waited for other agencies, notably the police and health authorities, to respond to its enquiries. The Board has sought to introduce, with these agencies, procedures that will generate quicker responses, but investigative delay will always be a critical factor in the speedy resolution of applications (CICB, 1991, para. 1.5).

This is, in essence, the model for the new Scheme. All initial decisions will be taken by claims officers: 'An application for compensation under this Scheme will be determined by a claims officer' (new Scheme, para. 50). That decision will comprise two principal steps. The first is whether the applicant is eligible for compensation; in particular, whether the injury was a criminal injury, whether the applicant complied with the rules governing the reporting of the injury, and whether the applicant's conduct or character make an award inappropriate (new Scheme, Guide, para. 4.5). The burden of proof here lies, as it does in all matters, on the applicant: 'The standard of proof to be applied by a claims officer in all matters before him will be the balance of probabilities' (new Scheme, para. 19). The second step, assuming eligibility, is the determination of the appropriate tariff level.

Following notification of the claims officer's decision, an applicant under the old Scheme had three months within which to ask for a hearing, if dissatisfied with the decision (old Scheme, para. 22). In the case of the new Scheme, a dissatisfied applicant may first seek to have the decision reviewed, provided that the Authority receives the application for review within 90 days of the date of the decision (new Scheme, para. 59). Hearings, reviews and appeals are dealt with in chapter 3.

2.3 THE AWARD

2.3.1 Notification of the Outcome of the Application

Under both the old and new Schemes, the Board or the Authority notifies applicants or their representatives in writing of the outcome of the application (old Scheme, Guide, para. 62; new Scheme, para. 50). Awards will either be for the full amount claimed, or, in the exercise of the discretion conferred under the Scheme, for a reduced amount (in which case the applicant is told why, new Scheme, Guide, para. 61). The number of reduced awards is typically small (see App. A in any CICB Annual Report).

The proportion of successful applications is 62–3% (CICB, 1995, para. 2.1). In 1994–95 there were 19,594 rejected applications. Of the nil awards, 13% were rejected because of the victim's conduct, character or way of life, 14% were not crimes of violence, 27% did not meet the lower limit and 25% were not reported to the police in time (CICB, 1995, App. A). Though not defined, 'a full award' has meant an assessed award which comprises compensation for all verified and allowable items of special damage, together with an appropriate sum (based on common law damages) for general damages, less any sums deductible under the terms of the Scheme. In 1994–95, of 55,807 applications resolved and decisions made (after those that had been abandoned), 27,644 full awards were made at an initial determination, with a further 3,842 made at hearings. Under the new Scheme, a 'full' award will mean compensation based on the tariff, together with any special expenses (see chapter 8.4.2.2) and any compensation for loss of earnings or dependency (see chapters 8.4.2.1 and 8.5.3.1).

2.3.2 Entitlement to the Award

Under both the old and new Schemes, applicants are entitled to payment only after the Board or the Authority has received notification in writing that they have accepted the award (old Scheme, para. 22; new Scheme, para. 50). This proposition, which will apply in all straightforward cases, may be subject to variation by the claims officer, in particular where the award is in the form of a structured settlement (see chapter 2.3.6) or the decision is reconsidered before final payment of the award (see chapter 2.3.5).

This continues the position that has obtained since the 1979 revisions to the old Scheme. One of these specifically addressed the Court of Appeal's decision in *R v Criminal Injuries Compensation Board, ex parte Tong* [1976] 1 WLR 1237. The victim, a rent collector, had been injured in a robbery. He was made an interim award, and some time later a final assessment was made by a single member of the Board. Before he was notified of this award, the victim died from other causes. The Scheme then provided (old Scheme, para. 15), as it does now (new Scheme, para. 37), that 'where the victim has died in consequence of the injury, no compensation other than funeral expenses will be payable for the benefit of the estate': *actio personalis moritur cum persona*. After a special hearing, the Board decided that if the victim died before he had accepted the award offered, the offer lapsed. While the dependants specified in the Scheme were free to apply for compensation, they would only be eligible for an award based on a fatal accident action, thus excluding any compensation for general damages. The Scheme also provided (old Scheme, para. 16), as, subject to its new limitations, it does now (new Scheme, para. 44), that where the victim dies otherwise than in consequence of the injury, an award can be made to a dependant in respect of a reduction in earnings sustained by the victim between the injury and the date of death, and any expenses incurred by him as a result of the injury (see chapter 8.5.1.1). This did not, however, avail the victim's dependants in *ex parte Tong*, as his loss of earnings had been wholly met by his employer; the Board's final assessment was for general damages, which would not survive for the benefit of the widow, or be available under the Fatal Accidents Act 1976. They applied for judicial review of the Board's decision not to pay them the award offered to him.

Reversing the Divisional Court, the Court of Appeal held that compensation vested as soon as the award was decided, irrespective of whether the applicant had been notified of it. The Court was especially concerned that the Board's view would mean that an applicant's entitlement could well depend on the speed with which offers of compensation were dispatched. If, in *ex parte Tong*, notification of the award had been sent the day after it was made (25 February 1971), the applicant would, since he died on 6 March 1971, have become 'entitled' to it ('entitled' because, the old Scheme, having no basis in law, conferred no enforceable rights on applicants; see chapter 1.3.1), and his widow likewise. Lord Denning MR thus preferred the common law analogy, that once the verdict is given, the entitlement to compensation inheres in the applicant.

This created some difficulty for the Board, which held some awards as provisional pending the outcome of the Home Office review then being conducted. This agreed with the Board's view that an applicant should have no title to an award offered until the Board had received notification in writing that it had been accepted (Home Office, *Review of the Criminal Injuries Compensation Scheme: Report of an Interdepartmental Working Party*, London: HMSO, 1978, para. 21.7).

It follows therefore that the applicant who responds to the notification of an award by requesting a hearing (old Scheme) or a review of the initial decision (new Scheme), has yet to become entitled to it and runs the risk that at the hearing or the review, the original award may be reduced or even denied altogether. The Guide to the old Scheme is explicit: 'If you are made an award with which you are dissatisfied and are granted an oral hearing no part of the award will become payable, if at all, until your case has been considered at the hearing' (old Scheme, Guide, para. 63). Both the old and the new Schemes provide that a hearing or a review should be treated as applications *de novo*; the new Scheme states (para. 60; see also para. 50): 'The officer conducting the review will reach his decision in accordance with the provisions of this Scheme applying to the original application, and he will not be bound by any earlier decision either as to the eligibility of the applicant for an award or as to the amount of an award'.

Moreover, for so long as the applicant delayed accepting the offered award, she ran the risk that the Board might vary it if fresh information should come to light raising a question, for example, about her eligibility. This occurred in *R v Criminal Injuries Compensation Board, ex parte Brindle* (unreported, 4 February 1982, DC). Following a hearing, the Board agreed that an award should be made, but deferred the decision as to the exact amount as it wished to obtain some further information. While awaiting this, the applicant was arrested on suspicion of having committed very serious offences. The Board now deferred its decision until the outcome of the ensuing criminal proceedings, which Woolf J. held it was entitled to do. As noted below (chapter 2.3.5), under the new Scheme a claims officer may reconsider an award at any time prior to its actual payment.

The award is personal to the applicant, so where a personal representative (or executor or administrator) requests a hearing or a review in respect of an award which was communicated to an applicant who died without accepting it, the personal representative has no right to receive the original award. This applies whether, as in *R v Criminal Injuries Compensation Board, ex parte Earls* (LEXIS DC/456/80, 21 December 1982), the victim dies from the injuries he received, or as in *Re Lancaster's Application* [1977] CLY 496, the victim dies from other causes. By s. 7

of the Act, an award cannot be assigned or be made subject to a charge; nor does an award pass to the benefit of the applicant's creditors should he become bankrupt.

2.3.3 Interim Awards

With three important exceptions, a decision by a claims officer (or, in the case of adjourned appeals, the Panel, see chapter 3.2.4.5) to make an award will be final. The first of these concerns interim awards, one or more of which 'may be made where a claims officer considers this appropriate' (new Scheme, para. 51) in advance of the final decision on the application. Interim awards have been available under the Scheme since its inception and are typically used in medically complex cases where it is clear that the applicant is eligible for an award, that it is likely to be substantial, and that there has already been, or is likely to be, a substantial delay before a final award can be made. In such cases the Board may feel that it is desirable to make a part payment (old Scheme, Guide, para. 52). Between 1991–92 and 1994–95, the Board made between 4,885 and 6,492 such awards a year; some 12–16% of resolved applications (CICB, 1995, para. 3.9).

The making of an interim award does not, however, mean that a final award will inevitably follow. Paragraph 53 of the new Scheme provides: '... the fact that an interim payment has been made does not preclude a claims officer from reconsidering issues of eligibility for an award' (see chapter 2.3.5). This follows para. 12 of the old Scheme, which provided that in a case where an interim award had been made, the Board may thereafter 'decide to make a reduced award, increase any reduction already made or refuse to make any further payment at any stage before receiving notification of acceptance of a final award'. It has not been the Board's practice to require the repayment of an interim award should it subsequently decide that the applicant is ineligible for an award.

2.3.4 Reopening Awards

A distinguishing feature of the Scheme was introduced in the 1979 revisions: the power to reopen final awards in narrowly defined circumstances. In its 1978 Report the Board had indicated that it would welcome such a power, though it noted that it could achieve a similar effect by the use of 'permanent interim awards' (CICB, 1978, para. 55). These could be made where there was a known risk of future medical deterioration, such as epilepsy or sympathetic ophthalmia, but they afforded no discretion where unexpected complications arose. The change was recommended by the 1978 Working Party (Home Office, *Review of the Criminal Injuries Compensation Scheme*, 1978, para. 4.6) and took effect as para. 13 of the old Scheme:

Although the Board's decisions in a case will normally be final, they will have discretion to reconsider a case after a final award of compensation has been accepted where there has been such a serious change in the applicant's medical condition that injustice would occur if the original assessment of compensation were allowed to stand, or where the victim has since died as a result of his injuries. A case will not be reopened more than three years after the date of the final award unless the Board are satisfied, on the basis of evidence presented with the application for reopening the case, that the renewed application can be considered without a need for extensive enquiries. A decision by the Chairman that a case may not be reopened will be final.

The availability of this power also meant that the Board did not have to rely on the Rules of the Supreme Court made under s. 32A of the Supreme Court Act 1981 permitting the award of provisional damages for personal injuries. By para. 87 of the new Scheme, applications made after 1 April 1996 to reopen a final award accepted before that date will be dealt with by the Authority under the terms of para. 13 of the old Scheme (or any corresponding earlier provision).

With minor amendments, the power to reopen final awards is continued in the new Scheme. Decisions made by a claims officer (or, in the case of adjourned appeals, the Panel, see chapter 3.2.4.5), and which have been accepted by an applicant may subsequently be reopened by a claims officer 'where there has been such a material change in the victim's medical condition that injustice would occur if the original assessment of compensation were allowed to stand, or where he has since died in consequence of the injury' (new Scheme, para. 56).

Since this power was first introduced, there has been a small but regular number of applications to reopen final decisions; around 150 a year during the 1990s, of which some 60%-70% are successful. As para. 13 of the old Scheme makes clear, the desire to do justice was tempered by strong bureaucratic considerations. The possibility that a case might be reopened (or reopened more than once) requires that files be held back which would otherwise be destroyed (though this is less of a problem once all files are stored on computer). Sometimes the medical prognosis will contemplate a foreseeable risk of deterioration; in other cases a judgment as to the future must be made.

The 1986 Working Party considered the administrative problems posed by the exercise of this discretion, which, like any other, must be exercised reasonably (*R v Criminal Injuries Compensation Board, ex parte Brown* (unreported, 12 December 1987, DC); CICB, 1989, paras 50.1–50.2). Its recommendation that no application to reopen a case should be contemplated more than three years after the original award was not acted upon in the 1990 revision to the old Scheme (Home Office, *Criminal Injuries Compensation: A Statutory Scheme*, 1986, para. 13.3), but the substance finds expression in para. 57 of the new Scheme. This imposes a two-year limit on reopening final awards, unless the claims officer is satisfied (this reproduces the test in para. 13 of the old Scheme, see CICB, 1994, para. 6.17), 'that the renewed application can be considered without a need for further extensive enquiries'. This limit also reflects the reduction from three to two years of the period within which the original application must be made (see chapter 7.2.1). The applicant can request that the decision not to reopen the case be reviewed (new Scheme, para. 58(b); chapter 3.2.2).

The Board's Reports observe that, while limited in number, these applications involve a substantial amount of staff time. They almost invariably concern complex medical conditions and pose considerable difficulty in establishing the link between the incident and the subsequent deterioration (CICB, 1982, para. 11; 1990, para. 23.5). In some cases there is no causal connection (CICB, 1989, para. 22.2; 1991, para. 27.3), but applicants may come to believe that ill-health experienced subsequent to the criminal injury is necessarily connected to it. This in turn may be productive of ill will on their part when their applications are refused (CICB, 1982, para. 11). Even where a connection is shown, the change in the applicant's medical condition must be 'serious' (CICB, 1992, paras 24.2–24.9; 1994, para. 6.17), or, as specified in para. 56 of the new Scheme, 'material'. Paragraph 4.25 of the Guide to the new Scheme gives three examples of circumstances justifying the reopening of a case: 'where the injuries are now serious enough to justify an award; where the applicant would now qualify for an award from a higher injury band; and where the applicant's medical condition has deteriorated to such an extent that he or she is no longer able to pursue his or her occupation'. Assuming that the application to reopen is supported by the medical evidence, the substantive test under the new Scheme remains the same as under the old; namely, that the change in the victim's medical condition is such 'that injustice would occur if the original assessment of compensation were allowed to stand'.

An initial award should not be reopened where the award made took specific account of the possibility of deterioration in the applicant's medical condition (CICB, 1991, para. 27.2), as was the case in *R v Criminal Injuries Compensation Board, ex parte Brown*. Here the award included a reference to the small possibility that the site of a bullet wound in the applicant's leg might become reinfected. This indeed occurred, and the Divisional Court supported the Chairman's refusal to reopen the award precisely because the original compensation contemplated what had transpired. Nor should an original decision to refuse an award be reopened, even though the consequences of the injury are now much worse (CICB, 1991, para. 27.4; 1994, para. 6.17). In this connection, it may be noted that the Board would have been able to refuse further compensation, even where all the conditions of para. 13 were met, if, subsequent to the original award, the Board took the view that in the light of the applicant's subsequent conduct, it was inappropriate that a full award or any award at all be granted. This possibility will apply also in the case of the new Scheme.

2.3.5 Reconsideration of Decisions

Whereas the two established exceptions from finality of awards — interim awards nd reopened awards — are intended to benefit applicants, the third is primarily intended to permit the claims officer to reduce, or even disallow, an award, notwithstanding that it may have been accepted by the applicant. Although this has no exact predecessor, the old Scheme did provide that where an applicant was asked to attend a regional hearing so that Board members could inspect the applicant's injuries for the purpose of a proper assessment, the Board could, before making a final determination, 'take account of any fresh information (e.g., about criminal convictions) between the date of calling for the inspection and the date of the Board's determination which would affect the applicant's eligibility under the Scheme' (old Scheme, Guide, para. 54).

Subject to para. 77, para. 53 of the new Scheme provides that 'A decision made by a claims officer ... may be reconsidered at any time before the actual payment of a final award where there is new evidence or a change in circumstances'. This reconsideration may take place either before the applicant is notified of the award (normal administrative practices may imply the lapse of a few days between the claims officer's decision and the dispatch of a letter to the applicant) or afterwards. In the latter case, the applicant must be sent a written notice that the decision is to be reconsidered and, in due course, written notification of the outcome of the reconsideration, either confirming the original decision or specifying the revised decision (new Scheme, para. 54). Paragraph 4.23 of the Guide alerts the reader to the existence of the discretion in para. 53 of the new Scheme, but the Authority has no obligation to inform the applicant that the decision has been reconsidered if the reconsideration took place before the applicant was notified of the initial decision.

The Scheme does not indicate what this new evidence or change in circumstances might comprise. The language of para. 53 would permit an award to be increased if the change of circumstance were, for example, a sudden and serious deterioration in the victim's medical condition which had come to the Authority's attention independently of the applicant. It is also conceivable that in reaching a decision on the application, a claims officer could overlook a vital piece of medical evidence suggesting a worse prognosis, with the result that the award could at once be corrected to a higher tariff band before notification is sent to the applicant. However, the procedural arrangements relating to the reconsideration of decisions suggest that any variation in the award will be downwards.

First, the initiative to reconsider is envisaged as coming from the claims officer rather than the applicant. There is nothing in paras 53 and 54 giving applicants the right to request a reconsideration on the basis of new evidence or a change of circumstances known to them and which they wish to bring to the claims officer's attention. (Equally, there is nothing to stop applicants or their legal representatives proffering such information to a claims officer at any time.) On the contrary, the applicant's role in any reconsideration is limited to the making of representations in the case where written notification of the award has already been sent; in such cases '... any representations which he sends to the Authority within 30 days of the date of such notice will be taken into account in reconsidering the decision' (new Scheme, para. 54). These procedures alone suggest that the new evidence or change in circumstances (for example, further reports from the police concerning the incident or the applicant's history or contribution to it, or, as in *R* v *Criminal Injuries Compensation Board, ex parte Brindle* (unreported, 4 February 1982, DC), concerning his involvement in a new offence) is such that it raises the question for the claims officer whether the award is too high, or even whether the applicant is eligible for an award. Thus para. 53 provides that the payment to date of interim awards does not preclude the claims officer 'from reconsidering issues of eligibility for an award'.

Secondly, whether the reconsideration took place before or after the applicant was notified of the initial decision, that decision may be reviewed at the applicant's request. It is clear from the provisions governing the review of claims officers' decisions that paras 53 and 54 contemplate that the reconsideration of a decison may result either in the reduction of an award (new Scheme, para. 58(d)) or its complete refusal (new Scheme, para. 58(c)).

Thirdly, reconsideration may also take place following the adjudicators' determination of an appeal. That determination may involve the adjudicators in giving directions to a claims officer as to how the application should be decided (new Scheme, para. 77). If, before an award made in compliance with these directions has been paid, the claims officer considers that there is new evidence or a change in circumstances 'which justifies reconsidering whether the award should be withheld or the amount of compensation reduced', the case will be referred to the Panel of adjudicators for a rehearing under para. 82 (new Scheme, para. 55; chapter 3.2.4.5).

2.3.6 Payment and the Administration of Awards

Assuming no reconsideration under paras 53 and 54, once determined and accepted, an award of compensation will normally be paid to the applicant by cheque as a single lump sum (new Scheme, para. 51). The Board was never enamoured of periodic payments, which it regarded as a disincentive to a prompt return to work. It also had more sympathy with the Law Commission's identification of the practical difficulties which would accompany a power to permit damages for loss of future earnings to be paid periodically — and which would impinge upon the Board (Law Commission, *Report on Personal Injury Litigation — Assessment of Damages*, Law Com. No. 56, 1973) than by the benefits which the Pearson Commission claimed for it (Royal Commission on Civil Liability and Compensation for Personal Injury, *Report*, Cmnd 7054, 1978, ch. 14).

Both the Board and the Authority may make other arrangements for the payment of the award, including its administration on the applicant's behalf. Paragraph 9 of the old Scheme provides:

If in the opinion of the Board it is in the interests of the applicant (whether or not a minor or a person under an incapacity) so to do, the Board may pay the amount of any award to any trustee or trustees to hold on such trusts for the benefit of all or any of the following persons, namely the applicant and any spouse, widow or widower, relatives and dependants of the applicant and with such provisions for their respective maintenance, education and benefit and with such powers and provisions for the investment and management of the fund and for the remuneration of the trustee or trustees as the Board shall think fit. Subject to this the Board will have a general discretion in any case in which they have awarded compensation to make special arrangements for its administration, In this paragraph 'relatives' means all persons claiming descent from the applicant's grandparents and 'dependants' means all persons who in the opinion of the Board are dependent on him wholly or partially for the provision of the ordinary necessities of life.

Section 3(1)(b) of the 1995 Act provides that the Scheme may make provision 'for an award to be made subject to conditions'. In its turn, para. 50 of the new Scheme provides that the claims officer 'may make such directions and arrangements, including the imposition of conditions, in connection with the acceptance, settlement, payment, repayment and/or administration of an award as he considers appropriate in all the circumstances'.

The terms of both Schemes thus permit the claims officer to make arrangements for the management of awards not only where applicants are incapable of managing their own affairs, but if the officer considers it to be in their best interests. In the past this has included withholding full payment from applicants whose personal history suggests that they might dissipate the award if paid in full (CICB, 1983, para. 32). These powers will, however, be more commonly used in cases where the applicant is incapable by reason of mental disorder as defined by the Mental Health Act 1983 of managing his or her own affairs, and in the case of awards to minors. The Board's guide on child abuse (old Scheme, App. H) indicates that awards up to £1,000 may be released to those having parental responsibility and that higher awards will usually be invested and managed by the Board through the Bank of Scotland. Where a child is in care, the award will usually be managed by the local authority. Awards for minors will be held on trust where the offender — typically a parent — might otherwise benefit (CICB, 1993, para. 1.13). For the same reason, the Board has on occasion postponed making a final award where the child's life is at risk and there is a danger that it might die intestate. In such cases the Board might make interim awards for specific needs, subject to stringent control (CICB, 1995, App. H, para. 9). These arrangements may be expected to continue under the new Scheme.

An important addition to the new Scheme provides for the making of structured settlements (s. 3(1)(d) of the 1995 Act). In its non-statutory form, there was some doubt about whether the Board had the power to make such a settlement. Because the applicant had no right to the award, there was no antecedent debt for annuity payments to be treated as payments of capital and not subject to tax (Law Commission, *Structured Settlements and Interim and Provisional Damages*, Consultation Paper 125, 1992, London: HMSO, para. 3.34; Final Report, Law Com. 224, Cm 2636, London HMSO, 1994, paras 3.101–3.105). This doubt is cured by s. 8 of the Act, which amends the Income and Corporation Taxes Act 1988 to provide that an award of compensation under which payments from annuities purchased in accordance with the provisions of the Scheme are made to the applicant (or another person on his behalf), or held in a trust of which the applicant is the sole beneficiary, is a 'qualifying award', and that the income from such an award shall not be regarded for the purposes of income tax as the applicant's income (Finance Act 1996, s. 150).

Paragraph 52 of the new Scheme provides for an agreement to be made between the Authority and the applicant that the award is to consist of annuities, and that the applicant may direct the Authority as to which annuities should be purchased.

In debate, the government agreed to introduce arrangements whereby awards made under the old Scheme could also be made as structured settlements (HC Debs, Standing Committee A, cols. 234–7, 27 June 1995; HL Debs, vol. 566, cols. 594, 596 and 722, 16 and 17 October 1995). These take effect as s. 8(3)(b) of the Act.

2.4 COSTS

The cost of making an application for compensation falls upon the applicant. An applicant who seeks legal advice may be eligible for advice under the Green Form scheme, but in common with other tribunals, legal aid is not available if he wishes to be represented at a hearing or an appeal. The Authority will not meet the costs of legal representation for the purposes of an appeal (new Scheme, para. 61); neither it nor the Board will meet the cost of representation at an oral hearing (old Scheme, para. 25; new Scheme, para. 74). However, both of these paragraphs give a discretion to reimburse the applicant's expenses in attending the hearing, together with those of any witnesses called by her, the Board or the adjudicators.

The Authority will reimburse the applicant's expenses (and those of a carer) where a claims officer, considering that an examination of the injury is required before a decision can be reached, requests that the applicant be examined by a duly qualified medical practitioner (new Scheme, para. 20). In the same vein, para. 65 permits the Panel to reimburse expenses where it has requested inspection of the appellant's injuries. This was also the practice under the old Scheme.

The cost of photographs showing the extent of injury is usually reimbursed at a standard rate. In its 22nd Report, the Board indicated that it was then prepared to reimburse the cost of advice for a straightforward claim obtained by a parent or guardian in connection with an application made on his or her child's behalf (CICB, 1986, para. 47). This is no longer the case.

3 Hearings, Reviews and Appeals

Both the old and the new Schemes make provision for a dissatisfied applicant to seek a fresh determination of an initial decision. This chapter is concerned with the applicant who believes that an initial decision reached by a member of staff, a Board member, or a claims officer employed by the Authority, was substantively wrong. Applicants who are dissatisfied with the way in which their applications were dealt with should invoke the complaints procedure (chapter 1.5.3); thereafter judicial review. The provisions in both the old and new Schemes are complex. Chapter 3.1.2 deals with the grounds for a hearing under the old Scheme, a procedure that is likely to be invoked for some time yet. Chapter 3.2 deals with the two-tiered system of review and appeal introduced by the new Scheme. Appeals in the new Scheme will involve an oral hearing very similar to that already provided for under the old Scheme. Chapter 3.2.4 deals with the conduct of oral hearings and appeals in both Schemes.

3.1 THE OLD SCHEME: HEARINGS

3.1.1 Hearing Requests and Client Satisfaction

As noted in chapter 2.3.1, most applications to the Board have resulted in a full award, and most single-member decisions (to whatever effect) have been accepted. The Board's Reports do not permit a comparison to be made simply between the number of applications resolved and the number of hearing requests made in any one year, since the latter may well refer to applications resolved in the previous year; at the time of the Home Affairs Committee's enquiry in 1989, when the delay in resolving applications was at its worst, this would have been true of most hearing requests. However, making this comparison over a number of years suggests that until the late 1980s, about 90% of single-member decisions were accepted; the level of requests between 1984 and 1988 was around 5,000 a year. Thereafter, it rose by about 1,000 a year, an increase which the Board attributed to a higher number of case resolutions (CICB, 1989, para. 10.2; 1993, para. 10.11 and App. D) brought about in part by the delegation to its staff of some initial decisions: 'There has been little change in the rate of applications for hearings but the increased output at the first decision stage has led to a consequential increase in the number of hearings applications' (CICB, 1991, para. 1.6). By 1993–94, the number of hearing requests had risen to 15,192 (CICB, 1994, para. 4.11), more than twice the number (7,203) recorded in 1989–90, the year before the 1990 revisions to the old Scheme, which included the power to delegate decisions, came into effect. These figures should be set against the substantial increases over the same period in the number of new applications (53,655 in 1989–90, 73,473 in 1993–94 (+37%) and of applications resolved (38,620 in 1989–90, 65,293 in 1993–94 (+69%)). The number of hearing requests fell in 1994–95 to 11,152, a decrease the Board attributed to the absence, in consequence of the introduction of the tariff, of new applications under the old Scheme which could be quickly processed to an initial decision (CICB, 1995, para. 4.11).

In the absence of any research, it is not easy to tell whether the number of hearing requests by applicants is indeed representative of the overall level of satisfaction. There is no way of knowing how many were dissatisfied but were discouraged from pursuing matters to a hearing by the unavailability of legal aid, the advice of those they consulted, the further delay in a final resolution of their application, or by their perception of the risk that the hearing might find against them. Other considerations which Shapland noted in her sample were an inability to understand how the award was made up, with a consequent inability to identify the appealable issue, while others felt that given the *ex gratia* nature of the award, it would be wrong to complain about what they perceived to be a gift (Shapland, J. et al., *Victims in the Criminal Justice System*, London: Gower, 1985). The first of these two findings is underlined by Newburn's small study of 23 hearing requests at the Board during the mid 1980s (Newburn, T., *The Settlement of Claims at the Criminal Injuries Compensation Board*, Home Office Research Study 112, London: HMSO, 1989). Noting the substantial discrepancies between initial assessments and the outcome of the hearings, Newburn asked (pp. 22–3):

> ... what proportion of those applicants whose injuries are underestimated, actually request a hearing? It is difficult to see how members of the public would be in a position to judge whether the sum of money they have been offered by the Board is a realistic one or not, and unless they have specialist legal advice it seems likely that the majority of applicants who request hearings will be those who contest the rejection of the application rather than the size of the award.

The Home Office expects that applicants' mystification about how the award is made in their case will, to a substantial extent, be dispelled by the tariff Scheme (Home Office, *Compensating Victims of Violent Crime*, Cm 2434, London: HMSO, 1993, para. 9). Nevertheless, it is likely that applicants will continue to challenge the chosen level; indeed, precisely because they will be able to see clearly from the published tariff how the level in their case compares with similar injuries, they will be better informed and perhaps more ready to request a review. The other main occasion for requesting a hearing before the Board, the refusal or reduction of an award, will be unaffected by the clarity of the tariff.

Paragraph 22 of the old Scheme permitted single members or members of the Board's staff to refer to a hearing an application about which they considered they could not make a just and proper decision by themselves. Such referrals have been relatively infrequent, comprising 1–2% of applications — 960 in 1994–95 — but they have typically dealt with difficult issues concerning the applicant's eligibility for an award, in particular where there is a dispute about the evidence, and the assessment of compensation in complex cases (HL Debs, vol. 566, cols. 1380-1, 31 October 1995; CICB, 1991, paras 30.2 and 30.3; 1992, paras 26.2–26.4; 1993, para. 28.2; 1994, para. 7.1; 1995, para. 7.1).

3.1.2   Grounds for a Hearing

By para. 22 of the old Scheme, an application for a hearing by a dissatisfied applicant has to be made in writing 'within three months of notification of the initial decision', although the Chairman, whose decision on the matter is final, can waive this limit where an extension is requested within the three-month period, or where it is otherwise 'in the interest of justice to do so'. In general terms, this means that there is an arguable case and that a hearing is justified, or that it is arguable that the Board erred in its original decision and that a reconsideration is justified (Greer, D., *Criminal Injuries Compensation*, London: Sweet & Maxwell, 1991, p. 217). The application must set out the reasons why the hearing is sought, and include any additional evidence that the applicant wishes to draw to the Board's attention and which may assist it to decide whether a hearing should be granted.

Until 1990 all applicants had an automatic right to an oral hearing, but important changes were introduced in the 1990 revised Scheme which imposed restrictions on this right. In essence, the revised Scheme draws a distinction between hearing requests which can be dealt with on documentary evidence alone (reconsideration) and those which might involve an oral inquiry. As we shall see, that distinction has been further developed in the new Scheme, so that every dissatisfied applicant must first request a review of a decision before invoking the appeals procedure, which carries with it the opportunity of an oral hearing in some cases.

The reason for the change was that during the 1980s the Board became increasingly concerned about the demands placed upon its resources by applicants' unqualified right to a hearing before three members of the Board, excluding the member who made the initial decision. In formulating the recommendations that were introduced in 1990, the 1986 Working Party's principal concern was to balance the desirability of reducing the Board's workload by eliminating some hearing requests with that of retaining for applicants a right to have the initial decision upon their applications reviewed in any case where there were grounds upon which the Board could reach a different decision. Once it became clear that ss. 108–117 of the

Criminal Justice Act 1988 were unlikely to be brought into force, the Board sought to have these controls introduced into the existing Scheme, as:

> a way of sifting out obviously unmeritorious as well as frivolous hearing applications so that the time can be more profitably spent on those cases which plainly require the Board's attention. By the same token we consider that the Scheme ought to provide for certain cases to be reconsidered on paper rather than invariably by oral hearing. (CICB, 1989, para. 1.8)

These controls were contained in paras 23 and 24 of the 1990 revision. They give effect to these objectives in two ways.

3.1.2.1　Reconsideration (para. 23)

'Reconsideration' in this context should not be confused with the procedures specified in paras 53–55 of the new Scheme discussed in chapter 2.3.5.

As an initial step, para. 23 seeks to eliminate from the hearing procedure applications which simply raise questions about the accuracy of the primary facts. Where the reasons given in support of an application for a hearing suggest that 'the initial decision was based on information obtained by or submitted to the Board which was incomplete or erroneous' the application will be remitted for reconsideration by the single member who made the initial decision or, where this is not practicable or the initial decision was made by a member of the Board's staff, by any other Board member. For example, an applicant whose application was disallowed on the ground that she had failed to report the incident to the police or co-operate with them may have her application reconsidered if it becomes apparent that she did inform them or that the reason for not making a complaint was because the assailant had been killed in a separate incident (CICB, 1994, para. 7.2). The paragraph would also allow the reconsideration of an award if further medical information suggests that the original assessment was wrong (CICB, 1991, para. 10.4; 1993, para. 28.4; 1995, para. 7.2). Another example drawn from the Board's reports shows its use in connection with the question whether the applicant's injuries were caused by a crime of violence (CICB, 1992, para. 26.6).

This paper reconsideration does not preclude the possibility of a subsequent hearing, which is expressly preserved by para. 23. If an applicant is dissatisfied following a reconsideration and applies for a hearing, the three-month time limit applies not from the date of notification of the initial decision but from the date of notification of the reconsidered decision.

3.1.2.2　Review (para. 24)

The changes introduced by para. 24 are substantively more important. Although it is clear that they were designed to prevent an application going to a hearing unless it satisfies one of the criteria specified in para. 24(a)–(c), its wording, when taken with the Board's own commentary upon it, is not perspicuous. The paragraph begins with a statement of the three criteria. It continues: 'An application for a hearing which appears likely to fail the foregoing criteria *may* [emphasis added] be reviewed by not less than two members of the Board, other than any member who made the initial or reconsidered decision'. This suggests that the review succeeds rather than precedes a decision on whether the application meets any of the three criteria, and that the review is discretionary. It thus raises the questions: who decides whether an application 'appears likely to fail', and under what circumstances is the discretion to review not exercised? The Board's Reports indicate that the answer to both is that all applications for a hearing are reviewed by Board members who decide whether or not the criteria are met in any case. Paragraph 4.4 of the 1994–95 Report (which substantially repeats the equivalent paragraph in previous Reports) says:

> Paragraph 24 of the Scheme allows the Board to review an application for a hearing on the papers. This review *must* [emphasis added] be carried out by at least two members of the Board who [depending on their findings] may reject the application for a hearing or allow the application to proceed to an oral hearing.

In practice the Board has always allocated three members to para. 24 reviews. Paragraph 7.1 of the same Report (which likewise repeats earlier Reports) adds: 'All applicants retain a right to have their case reviewed on the papers by at least two members of the Board but an oral hearing will be held only if the case warrants it'. This in turn can be read as implying that even if the applicant is refused a hearing, the application will be reviewed on the papers, with the possibility of variation in the initial decision. But it is clear that there is no halfway house between the refusal and the grant of an application for a hearing. If the application does not satisfy one of the tests set out in para. 24(a)–(c), there will be no hearing in respect of it, and no further review of the initial decision. A decision to refuse an application for a hearing is final.

A dissatisfied applicant will therefore be granted a hearing (which will be an oral hearing) only if:

> (a)   no award was made on the ground that any award would be less than the sum specified in para. 5 of the Scheme and it appears that applying the principles set out in para. 26 below, the Board might make an award; or
> (b)   an award was made and it appears that, applying the principles set out in para. 26 below, the Board might make a larger award; or
> (c)   no award or a reduced award was made and there is a dispute as to the material facts or conclusions upon which the initial or reconsidered decision was based or it appears that the decision may have been wrong in law or principle.

Paragraph 26 provides that at a hearing:

> ... the amount of compensation assessed by a single member of the Board or a designated member of the Board's staff will not be altered except upon the same

principles as the Court of Appeal in England or the Court of Session in Scotland would alter an assessment of damages by a trial judge.

The first two grounds are quite specific: para. 24(a) is concerned only with the minimum loss provision (CICB, 1993, para. 28.7; 1994, para. 7.3; 1995, para. 7.3), and para. 24(b) only with cases in which the applicant is seeking an increase in the award. By contrast, para. 24(c) is considerably wider in scope: it contemplates all those cases in which the Board has discretion to withhold or reduce compensation. Hearing requests invoking para. 24(c) will typically involve applications rejected because: the injury did not constitute a criminal injury as defined by the Scheme (CICB, 1992, para. 26.10) or was sustained outwith the jurisdiction (CICB, 1994, para. 7.3); was made out of time, or resulted in an award being withheld or reduced in value because: the applicant had failed to notify the police of the incident (CICB, 1991, para. 31.3; 1992, para. 26.9), had not co-operated with them (CICB, 1991, para. 31.4; 1992, para. 26.8), had provoked the incident in which he was injured or had a series of convictions for offences of violence (CICB, 1993, para. 28.6; 1994, para. 7.3; 1995, para. 7.3). In *R v Criminal Injuries Compensation Board, ex parte Dickson* (1995) *The Times*, 20 December 1995, Carnwarth J. held that 'conclusion' in para. 24(c) means any conclusion drawn from the facts, including a conclusion as to the extent to which the award should be affected by the information available to the Board. The language of this paragraph was not confined to raw facts, but extended to any conclusions which were to be drawn from them, inferences, 'and also value judgments as to significance and weight, in reaching a final evaluation'. It therefore applied to a dispute about the applicant's character and its relevance to his application. This decision was under appeal at the time of writing.

Accordingly, neither an applicant whose application was initially rejected by a Board member or by a designated member of staff or was rejected by a Board member upon a reconsideration under para. 23 because his injuries were valued at less than the sum specified in para. 5 (para. 24(a)), nor one who seeks to challenge the award made (para. 24(b)), will be entitled to a hearing unless the initial decision was wrong in principle or the amount awarded was so very small as to make it (in the judgment of the Court of Appeal) an entirely erroneous estimate of the damage to which the applicant is entitled (adapted from Greer L.J. in *Flint v Lovell* [1935] 1 KB 354).

Given that it applies to cases in which there is a dispute about the material facts or, perhaps, the inferences drawn from them, or in which it appears that the initial or reconsidered decision may have been wrong in law or principle, para. 24(c) would be of much wider scope were it not for a further qualification. Should the Board members who are reviewing the application consider that:

... if any facts or conclusions which are disputed were resolved in the applicant's favour it would have made no difference to the initial or reconsidered decision, or that for any other reason an oral hearing would serve no useful purpose, the application for a hearing will be refused.

A question which arose in *R* v *Criminal Injuries Compensation Board, ex parte Cook* [1996] 1 WLR 1037 (chapter 1.5.2) was whether this proviso merely imposed a 'low threshold' as a condition of the applicant being granted an oral hearing. Such threshold would be satisfied where the applicant could show that her application raised a point of principle, and that it was far from self-evident that the Board's decision was right. The Court of Appeal was firmly of the view that para. 24 imported no such condition. Aldous L.J. held (p. 1046):

> ... there can be no doubt as to the meaning of para. 24 of the scheme. The Board have a discretion whether to appoint an oral hearing. Paragraph 24 makes it clear that the applicant will only be entitled to a hearing if no award was made or there is a reduced award and there is a dispute as to the facts or conclusions upon which the initial or reconsidered decision was based, or if it appears that decision may have been wrong in law or principle. There was no dispute in this case as to the material facts or the conclusion upon which the decision was based. The application for an oral hearing raised nothing new. Thus it was quite open to members of the Board to conclude that the decision was right in law and in principle. I therefore conclude that their decision that an oral hearing would serve no useful purpose, because it would make no difference to the single member's decison which was not wrong in law or principle, was right.

The proviso applies to all three of the criteria specified in para. 24(a)–(c), and contains two conditions upon which a hearing may be refused. First, suppose that while struggling to arrest the offender, the applicant had been deliberately pushed by him against a wall, thereby sustaining slight bruising on the upper arm. An application for compensation would surely be refused on the ground that these injuries would not exceed the minimum loss provision. An application for a hearing would likewise be refused on the basis of para. 24(a), and it would also be refused following the two-member review even were they to give the applicant the benefit of a doubt, for example, about whether the bruising would take three rather than two weeks to heal. It might be otherwise where, drawing on the facts recounted in the Board's 25th Report (CICB, 1989, para. 18.1), the offender also bit the applicant. In this instance the Board would almost certainly be told of the applicant's concern that he might have contracted hepatitis B or become HIV positive, in which case a hearing would be granted.

Similarly, where there is a dispute about the facts upon which the award for general damages was based, then on the assumption that there would have been no alteration to the assessment had the Court of Appeal been considering the facts as found by the Board, the application would fail under para. 24(b), and would also fail under this additional qualification where, even giving the applicant the benefit of a doubt, for example, about his medical prognosis, there would have been no other outcome but that reached at the initial decision or reconsideration. Such a decision might, however, be reopened some years later if there is medical evidence showing a serious deterioration (chapter 2.3.4). Finally, suppose that the applicant had been assaulted as he stepped off a British cross-Channel ferry at Calais, and that he had a conviction a few years earlier for armed robbery. The Board could dismiss the application on the ground that, the injury being sustained in France, it had no jurisdiction (see chapter 4.2). But it would also almost certainly refuse a hearing on the basis of the qualification as it applies to para. 24(c) because, even allowing him the benefit of any evidence that the assault took place on the ferry, the Board would very rarely compensate applicants having recent convictions for serious offences, and thus the conclusion reached at the initial or reconsidered decision would have been no different.

It is also possible for the two-member review to refuse a hearing in any one of these three instances if for 'any other reason' they consider that a hearing 'would serve no useful purpose' (CICB, 1991, para. 31.2). This is intended to allow the Board to refuse hearing requests on the ground that they are vexatious, frivolous or otherwise unmeritorious, as for example if the Board were to receive an application in which it is alleged that the applicant's injuries have been caused by the use of invisible rays projected by ill-disposed beings from foreign planets (HL Debs, vol. 489, col. 749, 23 November 1987). While this second condition gives the Board a wide power to refuse a hearing application, such refusal will be unlawful if it is 'so outrageous in its defiance of accepted logic or of accepted moral standards that no sensible person who had applied his mind to the question to be decided could have arrived at it' (Lord Diplock, *Council of Civil Service Unions* v *Minister for the Civil Service* [1985] AC 374 at p. 410).

While, as the Home Affairs Committee observed, these new provisions held out the possibility of a significant increase in applications for judicial review (House of Commons Home Affairs Committee, *Compensating Victims Quickly: the Administration of the Criminal Injuries Compensation Board*, House of Commons Paper 92, Session 1989–90, London: HMSO, 1990, para. 12), the Board sought to preserve the judicial model in the hearing procedures. This can be seen in the requirements first that reconsiderations under para. 23 must be conducted by a Board member where the initial decision was taken by a designated member of staff; secondly that in paras 24(a)–(c) an oral hearing will, subject to the further qualification in para. 24, be granted where a court would interfere with a trial judge's decision or where there is a dispute about the facts or it appears that the Board erred in law; and thirdly in the need for two members to decide upon hearing requests that are subject to review.

3.1.2.3   Reconsideration and Review: Summary
In summary, the procedures established by paras 23, 24 and 26 of the old Scheme provide:

   (a)   where the application for a hearing suggests that the initial decision was based on erroneous or incomplete information, it will be remitted for reconsideration, without prejudice to the applicant's right, if then dissatisfied, to apply for a hearing (para. 23);

   (b)   all other applications (including those made subsequent to a reconsideration) for a hearing will be reviewed by two Board members against the criteria set out in paras 24(a)–(c): if the application relates to the assessment of compensation or to whether the injuries met the lower limit, a hearing will be granted if it appears to be wrong in principle or the amount awarded was so very small as to make it an entirely erroneous estimate of the damage to which the applicant is entitled; if no award or a reduced award was made, a hearing will be granted if there is a dispute about the evidence or it appears that the decision was wrong in law or principle; but

(c)   should the members decide, having given the applicant the benefit of any factual or inferential doubts, that the initial or reconsidered decision would have been no different or for any other reason a hearing would serve no useful purpose, the application will be rejected. That decision is final, though open to judicial review; and

(d)   if granted, the hearing will be oral (chapter 3.2.4).

As was intended, these procedures have had the effect of reducing the number of oral hearings held each year, and thus of increasing the number of cases resolved. Between 1991–92 and 1994–95, the number of hearing applications resolved rose from 8,090 to 11,279 (CICB, 1992, para. 10.12; 1995, para. 4.12). In 1993–94, of the total of 10,948, 1,455 applications were resolved under para. 23 and 1,384 under para. 24 (CICB, 1994, para. 4.12). Until 1994–95, it had also had the effect of shortening the interval between the request for a hearing and its resolution. In the year before the introduction of the new procedures, 72% of hearing applications took more than 12 months to resolve; only 4% were resolved within six months (CICB, 1990, para. 10.5). By 1993–94, these proportions were 39% and 23% respectively (CICB, 1994, para. 4.14.). The final year of the old Scheme saw a deterioration in these figures, a reflection 'of the drop in relatively straightforward decisions taken at the first decision stage. As a result of this a higher proportion than usual of cases at hearings were those which had been waiting for some time, often by reason of the need to obtain further medical assessments and schedules of financial loss' (CICB, 1995, para. 4.15). Despite the improvement in the Board's productivity, there were, at 31 March 1995 some 18,808 hearing applications awaiting resolution. This represents well over a year's work on the current rate of approximately 11,000 hearing resolutions a year (CICB, 1994, para. 4.15).

3.2   THE NEW SCHEME

3.2.1   Introduction

By s. 4 of the Act, the Scheme 'shall include provision for the review, in such circumstances as may be specified, of any decison taken in respect of a claim for compensation' and, by s. 5, provision 'for rights of appeal against decisions taken on reviews under provisions of the Scheme made by virtue of s. 4'. The procedures governing reviews and appeals are therefore to be found in the Scheme rather than the Act, a matter about which there was considerable dissatisfaction in the Lords. Amendments were moved which would have placed the appeals procedures in the

Act, but these were defeated (HL Debs, vol. 566, cols. 1358–66, 31 October 1995). A major criticism was met when the government brought forward the amendment which was enacted as s. 11(4). This provides that no change can be made to the rights of appeal or the circumstances in which an appeal is to be dealt with by an oral hearing unless it is approved by Parliament by affirmative resolution.

The distinction between reviews and appeals builds upon, but takes considerably further, the distinction introduced in the 1990 revision to the old Scheme whereby applications for oral hearings are reviewed to determine whether they merit a hearing:

> ... an applicant will be able to request an administrative review by the authority of its original decision on his or her claim. This new feature was introduced in the earlier tariff scheme with a view to delivering decisions quickly, cutting out unnecessary appeals, and relieving some of the pressure on the appeals process. Reviews will also help towards quality control. Applicants will have to have been through the review process before formally appealing (HL Debs, vol. 566, col. 711, 17 October 1995).

Under the new Scheme, virtually every decision taken by a claims officer is open to review (except decisions taken on review under para. 60 and decisions taken by a claims officer following a direction by the adjudicators under para. 77) and every review decision is open to appeal. Some of those appeals will be dealt with by an oral hearing.

Reviews will be heard by other, more senior, claims officers. Appeals will be heard by adjudicators, all of whom are members of the Criminal Injuries Compensation Appeals Panel. They are appointed by the Secretary of State under s. 5(3)(a) of the Act and are wholly independent of the Authority. The appeals system will be administered by its own staff, the 'hearings secretariat', appointed by the Secretary of State for that purpose (s. 5(3)(c)). While they decide appeals, no member of the Panel will have any involvement in the determination of applications. Where they allow an applicant's appeal, they direct the Authority to act accordingly. Conversely, with the exception of some 'specified functions' (s. 5(3)(d)(i)), no claims officers will have any involvement in the hearing or deciding of appeals.

3.2.2 Review of Decisions (Paras 58–60)

The first step for a dissatisfied applicant is to seek a review of the decision reached by the claims officer. This application must be made in writing on the form obtainable from the Authority and be supported by reasons together with any additional information. With the *Application for Review*, the applicant will be sent a copy of the Authority's Guide, *Applying for a Review of Our Decision* (this is a single page document all of whose points are covered in the text; it is not therefore reproduced as an Appendix). The application for review must be received by the Authority within 90 days of the decision to be reviewed. In exceptional circumstances a claims officer more senior than the one who took the original decision may grant an extension of time requested by the applicant within the 90 days if that request is based on good reasons, or may otherwise waive the time limit if it would be in the interests of justice to do so (new Scheme, para. 59). These reproduce in substance the two grounds to waive the three-month time limit for hearing applications under para. 22 of the old Scheme (chapter 3.1.2). However, unlike the old Scheme, where the Chairman's decision on this matter was final, the new Scheme provides for the applicant to seek a review of the senior claims officer's decision not to waive the limit (new Scheme, para. 58(a)).

There are five grounds on which an applicant may seek a review of a claims officer's decision. These are set out in para. 58:

(a)   a decision not to waive the two-year time limit for the submission of the original application for compensation (para. 17; see chapter 7.2.1) or, as just noted, to waive the time limit for the application for review under para. 59;

(b)   a decison not to reopen a case under paras 56–57 (chapter 2.3.4);

(c)   a decision to withhold an award, including such a decision made on the reconsideration of an award under paras 53–54;

(d)   a decision to make an award, including a decision to make a reduced award whether or not as a result of the reconsideration of an award under paras 53–54); and

(e)   a decision to seek repayment of an award under para. 49 (repayment where the successful applicant subsequently receives damages in a civil action, compensation under a compensation order, or payment under any other criminal injuries compensation scheme: chapter 9.5).

Paragraph 58 of the new Scheme provides for two categories of decision made by claims officers which cannot be the subject of review. The first is the review decision itself, in which case the dissatisfied applicant's course of action is to appeal. The second is a decision made by a claims officer in compliance with directions made by the adjudicators having determined an appeal (new Scheme, para. 77). There can be no further appeal against this decision since it was itself the outcome of the applicant's application for an appeal.

The procedure for review involves a claims officer more senior than any other who has dealt with the application to date determining the decision afresh on the basis of the original application together with the reasons for requesting the review and any additional information provided by the applicant. The Act requires that the review of a decision 'must be conducted by a person other than the person who made the decision under review' (s. 4(2)). The additional specification in the Scheme that the review officer be more senior was initially contained in an amendment which was withdrawn when the Minister gave a firm undertaking that the government would bring forward its own amendment (HC Debs, Standing Committee A, cols. 208–9, 22 June 1995; HL Debs, vol. 566, cols. 711–12, 17 October 1995). This claims officer is not bound by any earlier decision about the eligibility of the applicant for or the amount of an award (new Scheme, para. 60). Accordingly, an applicant who has, for example, been made an award reduced by 50%, because of his conduct at the time of the incident, runs the risk that the more senior claims officer will take a more serious view of his conduct. The applicant could of course appeal this decision, but the burden of proof will be on him to satisfy the adjudicators that an award should not be reduced or withheld (new Scheme, para. 64(b)).

To be successful, the supporting reasons and any other information supplied by the applicant must satisfy the claims officer on the balance of probabilities that the initial decision should be reviewed (Act, s. 3(2)). The Authority is required to give the applicant written notification of and reasons for the review decision. If the applicant does not appeal, the Authority will ensure that 'a determination of the original application is made in accordance with the review decison' (new Scheme, para. 60).

3.2.3 Appeals (Paras 61–71)

The procedure for making an appeal against a review decision is very similar to that for requesting the review. The applicant must complete the *Application for Appeal* (which the Authority will have sent, together with the *Guide to Appeal Procedures*, with the notification of the review decision), so that the Criminal Injuries Compensation Appeals Panel (the 'Panel') receives it within 30 days of the date of the review decision. The applicant must set out the reasons for making the appeal, supported by any relevant additional material (new Scheme, para. 61).

In exceptional circumstances a member of the Panel's staff may grant an extension of time requested by the applicant. The discretion is exercised on the same basis as in the case of applications for the review of a decision; that is, if the request is made within the 30 days and is based on good reasons, or it would be in the interests of justice to do so (new Scheme, para. 62). It is for the applicant to satisfy the member of staff on the balance of probabilities that the case for a waiver of the time limit is made out (new Scheme, para. 64(a)). Unlike the position with reviews, where the decision by a claims officer not to waive the time limit is itself amenable to review, if the member of staff is minded not to waive the time limit in the case of an appeal, the request must be referred to the Chairman of the Panel (or such adjudicator as has been nominated by the Chairman to deal with such requests for waiver). A decision by the adjudicator not to waive the time limit is then final and is not open to review. The Panel is required to notify the applicant of the outcome of the request for an extension of time, and, if the request is refused, the reasons why it was refused. As with the original notice of appeal, this notification must be copied to the Authority.

The new Scheme distinguishes two categories of appeal. The significance of the distinction is that the first category will only be decided on documentary evidence whereas the second can, in specified circumstances, lead to an oral hearing. The following two sections describe these categories; we then consider the conduct of oral hearings. It should be noted that in both cases, should the Authority submit any evidence or material for the Panel's attention, the applicant must be given the opportunity to make representations on it before the appeal is determined (new

Scheme, para. 64(b)). If those representations are made at a hearing which the applicant, without reasonable excuse, fails to attend, this opportunity is lost.

3.2.3.1   Appeals Concerning Time Limits and Reopening of Cases (Paras 66–68)

The first category of appeal concerns the first two of the five grounds on which an applicant may request a review. These are:

(a)   cases in which the applicant is appealing against the review decision made by a claims officer not to waive the two-year time limit on the original application (new Scheme, para. 17) or by a more senior claims officer not to waive the 90-day time limit on a request for a review (new Scheme, para. 59) (new Scheme, para. 66(a)); and

(b)   cases in which the applicant is appealing against the review decision made by a claims officer not to reopen a case under paras 56–57 (new Scheme, para. 66(b)).

Both of these appeals will be dealt with by the Chairman of the Panel or another adjudicator appointed by him (new Scheme, para. 66) on documentary evidence alone; that is, the initial or reviewed decision together with the applicant's reasons for making the appeal and the evidence tendered in support. If the Authority submitted to the Panel any material in support of its decision, the documentary evidence must also include the applicant's representations on that material (new Scheme, para. 64(b)).

As in all other matters, the burden of proof lies on the applicant to satisfy the adjudicator on the balance of probabilities that his case is made out (Act, s. 3(2); new Scheme, para. 64). The adjudicator will allow the appeal 'where he considers it appropriate to do so' (new Scheme, para. 67). Where the appeal concerns a decision not to reopen a case, and the application was made more than two years after the date of the final decision, the adjudicator must (like a claims officer exercising the discretion under para. 57; see chapter 2.3.4) be satisfied that the renewed application can be considered without a need for further extensive enquiries by the Authority. If this appeal is allowed, the adjudicator will direct the Authority to reopen the case (para. 68(c)). Where the adjudicator allows an appeal that concerns the time limits, she will, in the case of a decision not to waive the limit imposed by para. 17, direct the Authority to deal with the application as if the time limit had been waived (new Scheme, para. 68(a)), and in the case of a decision not to waive the time limit imposed by para. 59, direct it to conduct a review in accordance with para. 60 (new Scheme, para. 68(b)).

In cases where the adjudicator considers that it would be inappropriate to allow the appeal (this discretion is clearly subject to judicial review), the applicant (and the Authority) will be given in writing the reasons why the appeal was dismissed. Apart from any judicial review, the adjudicator's decision is final (new Scheme, para. 67).

3.2.3.2 Appeals Concerning Awards (Paras 69–71)

The second category of appeal concerns the last three of the five grounds on which an applicant may request a review. These are:

(a)   cases in which the applicant is appealing against the review decision made by a claims officer to withhold an award, including the withholding of an award following its reconsideration under paras 53–54 (new Scheme, para. 69(a));

(b)   cases in which the applicant is appealing against the review decision made by a claims officer to make a full or a reduced award, including the making or reduction of an award following its reconsideration under paras 53–54 (new Scheme, para. 69(b)); and

(c)   cases in which the applicant is appealing against the review decision made by a claims officer in which the applicant is required to repay an award under para. 49 (new Scheme, para. 69(c)).

If the applicant's appeal falls within any of these three grounds, the Authority may also make a request for the appeal to be referred to an oral hearing (new Scheme, para. 69).

The government successfully opposed amendments which would have required all such appeals to lead automatically to an oral hearing. Giving the example of an applicant who had made an unqualified admission in his application and on review that he had started the fight in which he was injured, the Lord Advocate observed that if the appeal was to the effect that it was improper for a reduction to be made at all (as distinct from the amount of the reduction), then it would be bound to fail, since nothing said at a hearing could justify the proposition that the adjudicator would not be entitled to make a reduction. Thus, 'to require that if the appellant says that he desires a hearing there should be a hearing would be to expend a great deal of time and energy on a matter which could not succeed' (HL Debs, vol. 566, col. 716, 17 October 1995). Similarly, if the application would be bound to fail because the injury was not sustained in Great Britain. The government's position was supported by the Board's chairman, Lord Carlisle of Bucklow, who observed that in 1994–95 (by comparison with the 11,152 requests made that year), 644 hearing applications had been refused under the provisions in para. 24 of the old Scheme (HL Debs, vol. 566, col. 1398, 31 October 1995).

Accordingly, the first step is for a member of the Panel's staff to decide whether to refer the appeal for an oral hearing. If the staff member decides not to refer it, then she must submit it to an adjudicator for further consideration. The adjudicator is required to refer the appeal to an oral hearing if either one of two conditions is met (new Scheme, para. 70). They are:

(a)   in a case where the review decision was to withhold an award on the ground that the injury was not sufficiently serious to qualify for an award equal to at least the minimum amount payable under the Scheme, that an award in accordance with the Scheme could have been made; or

(b) in any other case, that there is a dispute about the material facts or conclusions upon which the review decision was based and that a different decision in accordance with the Scheme could have been made.

The first condition is specific; it applies only to appeals concerning the question whether the applicant's injuries meet the lowest tariff level (£1,000). In this respect, it is similar to the first of the three criteria set out in para. 24(a) of the old Scheme by which an application for an oral hearing is to be determined (chapter 3.1.2.2). The second covers all other appeals. These will typically include appeals concerning the applicant's compliance with the requirements of para. 13(a) and (b) (reporting to and co-operating with the police), para. 13(c) (co-operating with the Authority); whether the injury was a criminal injury (paras 8–12); the reduction or refusal of an award because of the applicant's conduct or character (para. 13(d) and (e)); issues concerning loss of earnings and special expenses (paras 31–6); and the appropriate tariff level for the applicant's injuries (paras 25–9). This second condition therefore deals with the cases contemplated by para. 24(b) and (c) of the old Scheme, and does so, like the first condition, on a much simpler basis, namely, could the decision have been decided differently? It is for the adjudicators at the hearing to decide whether it would. It is the government's expectation that 'in the vast majority of cases an oral hearing would be heard by the panel' (HL Debs, vol. 566, col. 716, 17 October 1995).

If the adjudicator considers that the decision being appealed could not have been decided differently, then he will dismiss the appeal and the review decision will stand. The dismissal is final. As in all other cases, the applicant and the Authority are to be sent written notification of the dismissal, together with the reasons for it.

Apart from the test specified by para. 70, the adjudicator also has a discretion to refer an appeal for an oral hearing 'where he considers that the appeal cannot be determined on the basis of the material before him or that for any other reason an oral hearing would be desirable' (new Scheme, para. 70).

3.2.4   Oral Hearings

3.2.4.1   A Fresh Determination
Oral hearings have been a feature of the Scheme since its inception and will continue to be so under the appeals procedures of the new Scheme. Despite the heading in the new Scheme, 'Oral hearing of appeals', a hearing never has been and should not be regarded as an appeal in the sense that that term is normally understood. So much is clear from the fact that under the old Scheme a single member or designated member of staff could refer an application to a hearing without first deciding any issues of law or fact. And under the new Scheme, the adjudicator to whom the Panel's member of staff refers an appeal may choose to refer it for an oral hearing if for any reason she considers that desirable.

At the hearing applicants are reminded, under the old Scheme, that the Board 'looks at the application afresh and may take into account matters not mentioned', while para. 6.1 of the Guide to the new Scheme tells them that the Panel has 'wide powers within the Scheme to consider afresh your original application'. Accordingly the outcome of the appeal may entail the reversal of any findings or inferences of fact or any conclusions drawn from them concerning eligibility or quantum, though it would be unusual to come to a radically different decision in the absence of new information. Under both the 1990 revision to the old Scheme, and para. 70 of the new Scheme, no case will come to a hearing which does not *prima facie* raise the question whether, if the Board members or the Panel were acting as an appeal court, they would not reverse the initial or reconsidered decision on a matter of fact, or does not *prima facie* raise the question whether the initial or reconsidered decision was wrong in law or principle, in which case it would have to be reversed.

3.2.4.2 Burden of Proof

The Scheme has always placed a substantive burden of proof on the applicant at a hearing. Both para. 25 of the old Scheme and that aspect of the Guide to the old Scheme which comments upon it make it clear that the burden lies on the applicant not only to prove on a balance of probabilities that his injuries were directly attributable to the victimising event, but 'also the negative ingredient that the violence was not inflicted upon him by someone acting in self-defence' (per Hodgson J. in *R v Criminal Injuries Compensation Board, ex parte Crangle* (1981) LEXIS DC/369/81), that is, that it was not the victim who initiated the aggression towards him. In addition the applicant is required to satisfy the hearing that compensation ought not to be reduced or withheld for any other reason under para. 6 or, in the case of domestic violence, under para. 8 of the old Scheme. Likewise, the applicant has to satisfy the Board members of the nature and consequences of the injuries sustained and of the loss of earnings, dependency and expenses claimed. Paragraph 14 of the old Scheme provides that the applicant may (which effectively means, 'usually will') be required to produce evidence of such loss.

The position under the new Scheme remains unaltered, though more shortly stated. By s. 3(2) of the 1995 Act and para. 64 of the new Scheme, it is for the applicant to make out his case on the balance of probabilities, and in particular, to satisfy 'the adjudicator or adjudicators responsible for determining his appeal that an award should not be reconsidered, withheld or reduced under any provision of this Scheme'.

3.2.4.3 Procedure

The new Scheme provides that written notice of the date of the hearing will be sent to the applicant and the Authority at least 21 days in advance (new Scheme, para. 73). This notice may be accompanied by a copy of the documents submitted by the applicant and the Authority for the adjudicators' attention. Any other documents will be made available at the hearing itself, in particular, witness statements (see chapter 3.2.4.4). Under the old Scheme, one of the Board's advocates for the hearing would prepare a 'schedule of documents before the Board' to be sent to the applicant a few weeks before the day on which it was listed. This schedule would contain a copy of the applicant's request and a 'hearing summary', comprising a resumé of the incident, a note of the outcome of any criminal proceedings, a statement of the issues to be decided, the reminder about the nature of the hearing and a statement of the applicant's injuries and financial loss. This summary would be followed by copies of the original application for compensation, any statements made by the applicant, the initial decision (which might be annotated by the single member to show that a particular fact was taken into account), the hearing request and finally police and medical reports.

For his part, the applicant was expected to inform the Board of the names and addresses of any witnesses he proposed to call, and where he disputed the Board's medical reports or assessment, to provide his own account. Likewise, where there was a dispute about pecuniary loss, the applicant was expected to provide further evidence supporting his case. In both instances the hearing would be unlikely to take place until the Board had received from the applicant what it considered to be sufficient evidence upon which to make a decision.

A hearing under the new Scheme will take place before at least two adjudicators (new Scheme, para. 72). It used to be the case under the old Scheme that all hearings took place before three Board members, but following the views expressed by the 1986 Working Party, the 1990 revisions provided that two members would be sufficient (old Scheme, para. 24). This change was prompted, like the others relating to its procedures, by a wish to make more effective use of the Board's members. In its 1991 Report, the Board noted that while it continues to allocate three members to more complex cases, many are decided by two. 'This has assisted us greatly in achieving the excellent results during the year [that is, a 49% increase in the resolution of hearing applications in 1990–91] whilst at the same time helping us to ensure that we have not made unreasonable demands on members' time' (CICB, 1991, para. 10.5). In providing for the hearing procedures under the new Scheme, the government was keen to maintain this improved productivity (HC Debs, Standing Committee A, col. 217, 22 June 1995). Neither of the two members can include the member who made the initial or reconsidered decision; similarly, neither of the two adjudicators before whom the hearing takes place under the new Scheme may include the adjudicator who, under para. 70, referred the appeal for the hearing.

The procedure to be followed for any particular appeal will be a matter for the adjudicators hearing the appeal (new Scheme, para. 72), and is to be as informal as is consistent with the proper determination of appeals (old Scheme, para. 27; new Scheme, para. 75). Under the old Scheme, the hearing was essentially inquisitorial and many were determined quickly, often in no more than 30 minutes. One reason for this is that the members of the hearing would have become familiar with the paperwork before the hearing began. The chairman might recount briefly the essential elements of the application and the Board's decision to date and then invite the applicant to put his or her account (CICB, 1991, para. 10.7). The chairman's resumé could often amount to a verbatim repetition of the grounds given by the applicant in the hearing request. Following these preliminaries the hearing would proceed to the point(s) in issue. Where the issue concerned quantum, Board members might take the initiative by asking the applicant what additional factors, for example, concerning scarring or continued pain or discomfort, she thinks they ought to take into account.

In some instances the point(s) in issue would be rehearsed by the Board's advocate. While its advocates normally would take an active part only in applications raising questions of eligibility, such applications have constituted the majority of hearing requests. The advocate's primary function under the old Scheme has been to bring out the truth of the circumstances relating to the incident giving rise to the injury, and to any other matters relevant to application, whether these advance or detract from the applicant's case. Sometimes this will require the advocate to adopt an adversarial stance, cross-examining the applicant on her statement and cross-examining her witnesses, whether or not the applicant is herself represented. Applicants may bring a friend or legal adviser to assist in putting their case (but not just for moral support); where they are unrepresented, the Board members themselves have often examined its own witnesses on the applicant's behalf.

The new Scheme likewise makes provision for an appeal to be presented by someone other than the adjudicators (new Scheme, para. 75), but unlike the old Scheme, it is clear that the claims officer acts on behalf of the Authority. This is an instance of the 'specified function' in relation to an appeal which can be conferred on a claims officer under s. 5(3)(d)(i) of the Act. The Lord Advocate put the matter thus:

> As under the 1990 Scheme, and the 1994 tariff scheme, we envisage that cases will be presented to the appeals panel by presenting officers. Their job — I stress this — will be to present the facts of the case and to facilitate the appeals process (HL Debs, vol. 566, col. 719, 17 October 1995).

This function assumes greater significance by virtue of the fact that, unlike the old Scheme, not all the adjudicators will be legally qualified (chapter 1.4.2), though each hearing will contain one who is (HC Debs, Standing Committee A, cols. 220–6, 22 June 1995).

The new Scheme follows its predecessor in giving all the parties to the hearing the right to call, examine and cross-examine witnesses. In this connection, it should be noted that neither the Board nor the Panel are bound by any rules of evidence which may prevent a court from determining any document or other matter or statement in evidence (old Scheme, para. 25; new Scheme, para. 75). The hearing may therefore take into account any hearsay or opinion evidence, whether or not its author is present. In *R* v *Criminal Injuries Compensation Board, ex parte Lloyd* (unreported, 4 July 1980, DC), the statements of two men acquitted of assault arising from the incident in which the applicant claimed to have sustained his injury were preferred to the applicant's own oral testimony given at the hearing, and even to that given by a police officer (whose evidence is generally respected). The Divisional Court held that the evidence had probative value whose weight was for the Board to judge. A corollary of its informal status is that neither the Board nor the Panel has the power to subpoena witnesses; it may only invite them to attend. It is for applicants to arrange for their own witnesses to attend.

Under para. 25 of the old Scheme, the Board members' determination must be made 'solely in the light of evidence brought out at the hearing'. This means, first, that the hearing is not bound by the summary prepared by the Board's advocate. The members may base their decision on any matter raised at the hearing, even though it is raised for the first time, provided that it is relevant to the application. Conversely, where relevant evidence is not brought out, the Board's decision may be open to judicial review. In *R* v *Criminal Injuries Compensation Board, ex parte Parsons* (unreported, 17 January 1990, DC) the applicant alleged that she had been raped. The Board rejected her application because some of the evidence before the hearing refuted the allegation. It was later discovered that the investigating officer had failed to make available to the Board the notes of an interview he had held with the defendant. Rejecting the application for judicial review the Divisional Court held that in the context of the evidence that was before the Board, there was no realistic possibility that it would have reached a different conclusion.

The decision taken under para. 25 is final, save that:

> ... where the only issue remaining is the assessment of compensation [the Board] may remit the application to a single member of the Board for determination in the absence of the applicant but subject to the applicant's right to apply under para. 22 above for a further hearing if he is not satisfied with the final assessment of compensation.

In other words, there may be two hearings rather than one where the difference between the applicant and the Board is resolved to one concerning only the assessment of compensation. Where the application was referred under para. 22 by a single member or a designated member of staff the decision taken at the hearing is both the first and final decision.

The following are examples of the kinds of decision made at hearings (they are all drawn from the Board's reports, and relate to paragraphs within the old Scheme):

(a)   Paragraph 4: the injury was not a criminal injury, but self-inflicted (CICB, 1992, para. 26.14), was caused accidentally (CICB, 1993, para. 28.16), or, though the fire causing the injury was deliberately lit, was not arson (CICB, 1993, para. 28.17); or injuries caused by an animal known to its owner to be dangerous and normally kept secure could amount to a criminal injury (CICB, 1993, para. 28.10), as could a cut caused to a police officer searching a suspect in whose pocket there was an unprotected syringe (CICB, 1994, para. 7.4).

(b)   Paragraph 5: the trauma subsequent to an assault may, where additional evidence is submitted, bring the injury within the lower limit (CICB, 1992, para. 26.23).

(c)   Paragraph 6(a): the applicant did not timeously report the incident to the police (CICB, 1992, paras 26.15–26.17); or the failure to report could be explained by the fact that the applicant could not identify her assailant in a crowd, but upon release from hospital did return to assist the police (CICB, 1992, para. 26.22), by the fact that as the police attended the scene and conveyed him to hospital the applicant assumed that they would deal with it without his making a complaint (CICB, 1992, para. 26.24), or by the fact of the trauma induced by the attack (CICB, 1993, para. 28.11).

(d) Paragraph 6(b): the applicant's failure to correspond with the Board did not warrant the application being disallowed where he had been in contact with his solicitors whom he expected would be writing on his behalf (CICB, 1992, para. 26.21); or because the applicant had failed to admit to having a conviction, his award could be reduced by 10% (CICB, 1993, para. 28.18).

(e) Paragraph 6(c): the applicant had sufficient responsibility for the incident giving rise to the injury to deny an award altogether (CICB, 1992, para. 26.19) or reduce its amount (CICB, 1993, para. 28.13; 1994, para. 7.4); conversely, that there was a good reason for the applicant not taking precautions which would have prevented an injury (CICB, 1995, para. 7.4); or the applicant's convictions made it inappropriate that he should be made an award at all (CICB, 1992, para. 26.20;).

(f) Paragraph 8: although living in the same house as the assailant (her father), the applicant was not living there as a member of his fanily, and thus could be made an award (CICB, 1993, para. 28.15).

(g) Paragraph 12: the applicant's injuries were so severe as to require an increase in quantum (CICB, 1993, para. 28.9), had hastened his move into a nursing home thus requiring special damages to meet its fees (CICB, 1993, para. 28.16), had significantly affected the applicant's earning capacity (CICB, 1994, para. 7.4) or had prejudiced his chance (because of medical retirement) of purchasing a service house at a discount (CICB, 1994, para. 7.4).

Under the new Scheme the adjudicators may, on determining the appeal, make such direction as they think fit (provided of course that they conform to the Scheme's provisions) as to the decision to be made by a claims officer on the application for compensation (new Scheme, para. 77). In this respect, the procedure resembles the remission to magistrates of a decision taken on appeal by way of case stated. Whatever the determination reached by the adjudicators, the parties will normally be informed, with reasons, at the end of the hearing. In other cases, they will be sent written notification.

The adjudicators also have the power to reduce the amount of an award where they consider that the appeal was frivolous or vexatious (Act, s. 5(9); new Scheme, para. 77). In cases where such a conclusion is apt, it is likely that the request for the hearing will have been turned down by the adjudicator to whom it is referred by the member of the Panel's staff. However, that the appeal is vexatious 'might only appear during the hearing, for example, where the claim had been based on the idea that a person had no previous conviction, whereas the claim had been determined on the basis that he had' (HL Debs, vol. 566, col. 722, 17 October 1995). The government opposed a Lords amendment which would have required the applicant to be warned that his appeal might be judged vexatious, but accepted that it would be appropriate to give advice about this matter in the Guide to Appeals.

3.2.4.4 Privacy and Confidentiality

Under both Schemes, hearings are to be held in private (old Scheme, para. 27; new Scheme, para. 76). With the applicant's consent, they both permit observers to attend provided that they undertake in writing not to disclose the identity of any of the participants in any subsequent reporting or any material from which their identity could be discovered. The 1986 Working Party's recommendation that the presumption should be in favour of public hearings, has not been accepted.

The Board has in the past published information about its decisions, normally in the form of press releases; but it has never referred to applicants by name. When the Board's Reports recorded the details of the applications leading to the highest awards in any year, it was, in widely publicised cases, possible to identify the recipient. In 1990 the Board changed its practice, so that it now records only the sums awarded (CICB, 1990, para. 9.1).

Confidentiality has extended also to the police reports supplied to the Board in connection with its inquiries concerning the victim or the event giving rise to the alleged criminal injury (*Marcel* v *Commissioner for the Metropolis* [1992] Ch 225). The reports themselves are not disclosed either to the applicant or to the members participating in the hearing. They are instead retained by the Board's advocate, who will seek to elicit from the police at the hearing, the substance of what appears in the report. This may in turn be used as the basis for cross-examination about matters of fact or opinion so expressed.

Witness statements are, on the other hand, made available to the applicant, but only on the day of the hearing, and will be recovered from him at its conclusion. This practice was called in question in *R* v *Chief Constable of Cheshire, ex parte Berry* (CICB, 1986, para. 42) (DC). This application for judicial review arose from the refusal of the Chief Constable to make available to Berry, whose application for compensation had been rejected under para. 6(c) of the old Scheme and who had subsequently requested a hearing, a list of the previous convictions (if any) of the witnesses to be called by the Board. The case principally turned upon the applicant's rights as against the Chief Constable, but it was also argued that the Board's practice amounted to a denial of natural justice, inasmuch as the applicant would have access to these reports only upon the day of the hearing, and would thus be quite unprepared to meet or to challenge them. Nolan J. rejected this argument, accepting the Chairman's evidence that the Board's procedures do not prejudice those with valid points to make, and observing that applicants are, when presented with such reports, always entitled to an adjournment, as was the case in *R* v *Criminal Injuries Compensation Board, ex parte Gould* (unreported, 6 February 1989, DC).

The point was further considered by Nolan J. in *R* v *Criminal Injuries Compensation Board, ex parte Brady, The Times*, 11 March 1987 (DC), where his Lordship held that the Board was entitled to take the view that the agreement by chief constables to make available witness statements for the purpose of proceedings before the Board (as recorded in a memorandum to chief constables from the Home Secretary in May 1969), was an agreement to supply them to the Board alone. The Board's failure to supply copies until the day of the hearing did not amount to a denial of natural justice. Paragraph 73 of the new Scheme indicates that this practice, which is summarised in the Board's reports for the old Scheme (CICB, 1995, para. 4.6), will continue; documents which are not sent to the applicant prior to the hearing will be made available at the time.

Neither was the Board acting unlawfully when, in *R* v *Criminal Injuries Compensation Board, ex parte Whitelock* (CICB, 1987, para. 53) (DC), it did not formally produce such witness statements at the hearing. The statements were before the Board and had been supplied to the applicant; McCowan J. held that the phrase 'brought out at the hearing', contained in para. 25 of the old Scheme, while not especially clear, meant 'no more than what is before the Board at the hearing'. The duty of the Board's staff is to take reasonable steps to obtain such material and to place it before the Board (*R* v *Criminal Injuries Compensation Board, ex parte Parsons* (CICB, 1990, para. 27.2) (DC)).

3.2.4.5 Adjournments and Rehearings

Paragraph 25 of the old Scheme permits the Board to adjourn a hearing once commenced 'for any reason'. This may be of its own motion, perhaps because the evidence it requires to make a decision is not available, or at the applicant's request. Where the applicant is refused such a request judicial review will not lie if the basis upon which the applicant made the request could not in any way have affected the members' decision (*R* v *Criminal Injuries Compensation Board, ex parte Gould* (CICB, 1989, para. 26.4) (DC). Paragraph 77 of the new Scheme gives the adjudicators power to adjourn the hearing; in doing so they may make an interim award (chapter 2.3.3).

As a further concession to the desire to reduce the workload of Board members, an application considered at an adjourned hearing may be remitted for determination by a single member in the absence of the applicant if the only issue remaining is the assessment of compensation. However, in such a case the applicant has a right to apply for a further hearing if he is not satisfied with the final assessment. This hearing application is subject to the provisions in paras 22–4 of the old Scheme.

Cases set down for hearing, whether as the result of referral or at the applicant's request, have been shared between teams of Board members sitting at various centres in England, Scotland and Wales. The substantial increase in the number of hearing requests over the past few years has placed a very considerable burden upon Board members, a burden which is exacerbated by requests that are abandoned or by applicants (or their representatives) who are not fully prepared for the hearing. In its 1987 Report the Board commented (CICB, 1987, para. 12):

The number of cases prepared for hearings was substantially higher than the number actually resolved. There are still far too many applicants who simply fail to attend or who give insufficient notice of their unpreparedness thus creating last-minute gaps in the Board's hearing lists. Other cases may have to be adjourned for further medical evidence or for the purposes of resolving some dispute as to the applicant's financial loss. A common example is the case in which the applicant's solicitors have failed to supply the Board before the hearing with a properly quantified and substantiated documentary account of their client's loss of earnings.

Observing that such poor preparation would, in litigation, be reflected in the order for costs, the Board amended its forms so as to underline to applicants their obligations prior to the hearing. This did not, however, resolve a problem for which, for many years, the Board could find no effective sanction (CICB, 1993, para. 10.10). From 1994, however, the Board has taken the view that where a hearing has to be adjourned unnecessarily because the applicant (or his adviser) has failed to deliver to the Board medical or special damage evidence that has been in his possession for some time, it may disallow the application under para. 6(b) of the old Scheme, that is, the failure to give all reasonable assistance to the Board in connection with the application (CICB, 1995, para. 4.10). Where the applicant is dilatory, he only has himself to blame if his application is disallowed; but if it is his solicitor, a negligence action against the firm might succeed.

Nor, until the 1990 revision, was there any sanction for simple absenteeism. Paragraph 25 of the old Scheme now provides that the Board may dismiss an application if the applicant fails to attend the hearing and has offered no reasonable excuse. The Board's Reports give examples of the use of this power in cases involving dispute as to whether the injury met the lower limit (CICB, 1991, para. 32.2), the applicant's share of responsibility for the injury (CICB, 1991, para. 32.3; 1992, para. 26.12), and quantum (CICB, 1991, paras 32.4–5). The Chairman may relist the hearing upon a request in writing, but his discretion is final.

These procedures are maintained in the new Scheme, but with some elaboration of the possibility of a rehearing of an appeal determined in the applicant's absence. The new Scheme provides, first, that the adjudicators may determine an appeal where the applicant fails, without reasonable excuse, to attend the hearing (new Scheme, para. 78). If the applicant wishes to seek a rehearing, he must apply to the Panel in writing so that it receives his application within 30 days of the date of his notification of the outcome of the hearing (new Scheme, para. 79). As in the case of the applications for the review of a decision or giving notice of appeal, this time limit may be waived; unlike those instances, there is only one ground for waiver: that it is in the interests of justice. A favourable decision may be taken by a member of the Panel's staff; in other cases she must refer the application to the Panel's Chairman or the adjudicator who has been appointed to hear requests to waive the time limits affecting appeals (new Scheme, para. 80). The decision concerning waiver is final and written notification of it, with reasons in a case where it is refused, must be sent to the applicant and to the Authority.

The application for the rehearing must be supported with reasons for the applicant's non-attendance. If a member of the Panel's staff considers that there are 'good reasons' for the appeal to be reheard, she will refer it for a rehearing. If not, she will refer it to the Chairman or another adjudicator nominated by the Chairman for the purpose, who will decide whether to refer it. That decision is final and written notification of it, with reasons in a case where it is refused, must be sent to the applicant and to the Authority (new Scheme, para. 81).

It should also be noted that the applicant who fails, without reasonable excuse, to attend the initial hearing, and whose application for it to be relisted is refused, will have lost the opportunity to make representations before the adjudicators on any evidence or other material submitted by the Authority for their consideration at the hearing (new Scheme, para. 64(b)).

Where an appeal is reheard, none of the adjudicators who heard the original appeal may take part. Otherwise, all the provisions of the new Scheme governing the hearing procedure (paras 72–8) and the burden of proof on the applicant (para. 64) apply.

4   Criminal Injuries: Victimising Events

4.1   INTRODUCTION

Applications for compensation under both Schemes are made in respect of 'criminal injuries'. These are defined in essentially the same terms in para. 4 of the old Scheme and para. 8 of the new. Broadly speaking, criminal injuries are personal injuries (that is, physical or mental injuries) sustained in Great Britain and directly attributable to:

(a)   a crime of violence (including arson or an act of poisoning) (old Scheme, para. 4(a); new Scheme, para. 8(a)); or

(b)   an offence of trespass on a railway (old Scheme, para. 4(c); new Scheme, para. 8(b)); or

(c)   the apprehension or attempted apprehension of an offender or a suspected offender, the prevention or attempted prevention of an offence, or the giving of help to any constable who is engaged in any such activity (old Scheme, para. 4(b); new Scheme, para. 8(c)).

Although there are some minor differences between them, it was the government's intention 'from the outset that those issues that qualified under the old scheme will be carried forward and built into the new scheme' (HC Debs, Standing Committee A, col. 247, 27 June 1995). Consistent with its wish to publish the Scheme's details as a separate document, the government resisted efforts in the Lords to place the definition of a criminal injury in the Act (HL Debs, vol. 566, cols. 594–60, 16 October 1995). Not all criminal injuries qualify for compensation: injuries arising from road traffic offences are generally excluded (old Scheme, para. 11; new Scheme, para. 11); and where a person is accidentally injured while engaged in law enforcement activity, both Schemes require that he should at the time have been taking an exceptional risk which was justified in the circumstances (old Scheme, para. 6(d); new Scheme, para. 12). This chapter considers the jurisdictional requirements of the two Schemes, the defining characteristics of the three victimising events, and the exclusion of injuries caused by road traffic offences. Chapter 5 deals with the definition of a personal injury and the question of proof of the injury.

4.2 JURISDICTION

An injury caused by one of the events specified in para. 4 of the old Scheme or para. 8 of the new is a criminal injury only if it is sustained in Great Britain, that is, England, Wales and Scotland. Besides the specific extensions of jurisdiction mentioned below, this includes British territorial waters. For the purposes of both Schemes, an injury is sustained in Great Britain if it is sustained (old Scheme, para. 4; new Scheme, para. 8, note 1):

(a) on a British vessel, aircraft or hovercraft (the new Scheme substitutes 'ship' for 'vessel'); or

(b) on, under or above an installation in a designated area within the meaning of s. 1(7) of the Continental Shelf Act 1964 or any waters within 500 metres of such an installation; or

(c) in a lighthouse off the coast of the United Kingdom.

The new Scheme specifies the terms 'British aircraft' and 'British hovercraft' as being a British controlled aircraft or hovercraft within the meaning of s. 92 of the Civil Aviation Act 1982 and as it applies to hovercraft under the Hovercraft Act 1968, or one of Her Majesty's aircraft or hovercraft. It also specifies 'British ship' as meaning any vessel used in navigation wholly owned by British citizens or bodies corporate (CICB, 1990, para. 26.3: the successful applicant was assaulted on board a ship owned by a British company, registered in Bermuda, and at the time in Spanish waters), Scottish partnerships, or one of Her Majesty's ships (new Scheme, para. 8, note 2).

The Scheme thus extends first to the land borders of England, Wales and Scotland. In Northern Ireland criminal injury compensation was governed prior to the introduction of direct rule by the Criminal Injuries to Persons (Compensation) Act (Northern Ireland) 1968 and is now governed by Order in Council (Criminal Injuries to Persons (Compensation) (Northern Ireland) Order 1977 as amended in 1988; see Greer, D., *Compensation for Criminal Injuries to Persons in Northern Ireland*, 2nd ed., Belfast: SLS Publications, 1990). Whereas the land border between Northern Ireland and the Republic may generate some jurisdictional difficulties arising from the territorial extent of the criminal law, even if the injury were potentially compensable under both sets of arrangements, there can be no double recovery of compensation since each set contains a provision requiring deduction of other moneys received from the State in respect of the injury (chapter 9.5.2).

Though the Scheme is not explicit, a criminal injury sustained within the limits of the territorial waters adjacent to the United Kingdom will also qualify, as will injuries sustained by or to officers of the United Kingdom when exercising their duties in that part of the Channel Tunnel designated part of Great Britain by the

Channel Tunnel Act 1987, or in its control zone. This amendment to the 1990 version of the old Scheme was introduced as para. 4A in 1993 (CICB, 1993, App. E), and is contained in note 1(b) to para. 8 of the new Scheme. The amendment affects both Schemes identically. It provides that anyone injured by a UK 'officer' (as defined in the Protocol made under the Channel Tunnel Treaty of 25 November 1991) in the exercise of his duties may be regarded as having sustained a criminal injury for the purposes of the Scheme, where the injury occurs within that part of the Tunnel designated as British. Injuries inflicted on British citizens by non-UK officers are not criminal injuries; neither are injuries inflicted by British citizens (or by a citizen of any other country) on non-UK officers. The UK officer who sustains an injury at the hands of a British or other citizen, or at the hands of a non-UK officer, sustains a criminal injury within the Scheme.

Apart from these special arrangements affecting the Channel Tunnel, the Scheme's extent is defined by reference to the place where the injury is sustained, not by reference to British nationality or citizenship. Injuries sustained by a British national as a result of a fight in a Spanish discotheque (CICB, 1992, para. 18.1) or on an American naval base in Japan (CICB, 1991, para. 18.2) are not criminal injuries for the purposes of the Scheme. Neither did the British passengers taken prisoner by the Iraqi army after their plane landed in Kuwait in August 1990 and then used as part of the army's 'human shield' at the beginning of the Gulf War sustain a criminal injury within para. 4 of the old Scheme: their injuries were sustained in Kuwait, not on the aircraft (CICB, 1994, para. 6.5). Similarly, a British passenger on a Danish North Sea ferry who is criminally injured by another passenger will not qualify (CICB, 1984, paras 19–20; 1988, paras 19.1–19.2). An injury would, however, qualify if it were sustained on a British cross-Channel ferry (or other British-owned vessel: CICB, 1990, para. 26.3), on a British aircraft, hovercraft or oil rig, or if the foreign-owned ferry were in British territorial waters (CICB, 1993, para. 17.4). Since the geographical extent of the Scheme is defined by reference to the place where the criminal injury was sustained, foreign nationals visiting Great Britain have always qualified.

The terms of the European Convention on the Compensation of Victims of Violent Crimes, Cm 1427, London: HMSO, 1988, which the United Kingdom ratified on 1 February 1990 and which came into force on 1 June 1990, provides that British citizens are eligible for compensation under the arrangements established in any other State which is a party to the Convention and within whose jurisdiction a criminal injury was sustained. It also appears that British citizens will be able to benefit under any such arrangement made by a member State of the European Union. In *Cowan* v *Trésor Public* (case 186/87) [1989] ECR 195, a British citizen was seriously injured in a robbery on the Paris Metro. His application to the *Commission d'indemnisation des victimes d'infraction* was turned down on the basis that Article 706–15 of the French Code of Criminal Procedure provides that compensation shall be payable to foreign nationals only if there is a reciprocal agreement with the other State, or the foreign national has a residence permit. Neither applied in his case. The applicant then referred to the Court of Justice of the European Communities for a preliminary ruling on the question whether the conditions attached to the eligibility for compensation of foreign nationals constituted a breach of art. 7 of the EC Treaty, which prohibits discrimination on the grounds of nationality. The Court ruled that, as it had previously held that tourists are recipients of services and are free to move from one member State to another to receive those services, so the protection afforded to each person as a corollary of that freedom of movement could not be qualified by reference to nationality. Thus compensatory arrangements for acts of criminal violence could not be made dependent on such conditions as reciprocity with another member State, or the possession of a residence permit.

Within Great Britain the old Scheme applies for the most part uniformly. To the extent that it is based upon the common law or upon statutory provisions peculiar to England and Wales on the one hand, and to Scotland on the other, there will continue to be differences in its detailed application. An area of obvious difference is the age of criminal responsibility, which is 10 years in England and Wales and eight in Scotland. In *C (A Minor)* v *Director of Public Prosecutions* [1996] AC 1 the House of Lords emphatically reversed the Court of Appeal's efforts to alter the law of England and Wales concerning the presumption of *doli incapax*. At the same time the House was highly critical of an area of law which Lord Lowry considered had been inconsistently applied over the years. Until Parliament accepts their Lordships' invitation to investigate, deliberate and legislate upon the matter, this difference will remain. However, it has no practical significance for the Scheme which has always provided that the fact that the 'offender' cannot be convicted by reason of his age is no bar to a finding that the injury was attributable to the commission of an offence (chapter 5.2.1).

By contrast, there is one area where differences between the two jurisdictions which did affect the application of the old Scheme have been eliminated. Shorn of any reference to the law governing the assessment of damages in personal and fatal accident actions, such substantive differences as did exist on this matter no longer obtain. A good example concerns compensation to a child for the death of its parent. If such a criminal injury occurred in Scotland, the award to the relatives for loss of society would, under the old Scheme, include an award for the benefit of any person regarded by the deceased as a child of his or her family. In England and Wales, however, no bereavement award could be made to the deceased's children. Under the new Scheme, any child accepted by the deceased (or dependent on the victim) is a qualifying claimant, and may be eligible for the standard amount of compensation at level 10 of the tariff (new Scheme, para. 39). Moreover, where the child was under 18 at the time of the victim's death, additional compensation may be paid for the loss of the parent's services (new Scheme, para. 42).

4.3   VICTIMISING EVENTS: CRIMES OF VIOLENCE

4.3.1   Defining a Crime of Violence

Neither the old nor the new Scheme defines what constitutes a crime of violence. This may seem odd, or, in the stronger opinion of the Divisional Court in *R* v

Criminal Injuries Compensation Board, ex parte Webb [1986] QB 184 at p. 198, 'highly unsatisfactory', but given that the vast majority of applicants under this heading could be predicted to have sustained their injuries as the result of the commission of indisputable instances of such an offence, there may have seemed little point in endeavouring to do what many, including the Scheme's sponsors and subsequent Home Office working parties, have found to be a difficult exercise (see generally Duff, P., 'Criminal Injuries and "Violent" Crime', *Criminal Law Review*, 1987, p. 219). Nevertheless, the absence of a definition did create difficulties in the interpretation of para. 4(a) of the old Scheme. The judicial attention that it received was in large measure responsible for the inclusion in the 1990 revision of injuries attributable 'to an offence of trespass on a railway', but this revision did not go by any means as far as the changes made in s. 109 of the Criminal Justice Act 1988. If that statutory Scheme had been brought into force, the Scheme would, for the first time, have defined this phrase and have done so, unusually for a criminal injury compensation scheme, both generically and by reference to specific offences. Because the new Scheme is identical to the old in its statement of this victimising event, it is important to be aware both of the judicial background and of earlier decisions taken by the Board.

The question, what is a crime of violence for the purposes of para. 4(a), was directly confronted in *R* v *Criminal Injuries Compensation Board, ex parte Clowes* [1977] 1 WLR 1353. There a policeman was injured in an explosion caused by the build-up of gas escaping from a main which had been broken open by a suicide who had gassed himself. The Board rejected his application on two grounds: that the deceased had not committed a crime of violence, and that the applicant's injuries were not in any event directly attributable to any crime that the deceased had committed. As to the first point, the Board decided that if there were a crime of violence, it was a crime against property (s. 2 of the Explosive Substances Act 1883: maliciously causing an explosion likely to endanger life or property) and, being such an offence, it did not fall within para 4: 'to come within the terms of the Scheme, the crime must be one which concerned violence to the person rather than violence to property' (CICB, 1976, para. 5(2)). Second, even if the facts of the applicant's injury could be regarded as being within the scope of an offence against the person, for example, ss. 20 or 23 of the Offences against the Person Act 1861, the Board concluded that the deceased had not formed, prior to his death, the requisite fault element of either of them.

Clearly, the suicide had committed the basic offence under the Criminal Damage Act 1971, s. 1(1), but, by a majority, the Divisional Court took the view that the Board should also have considered s. 1(2), which provides that it is an offence, without lawful excuse, to damage or destroy property being reckless as to whether the life of another would thereby be endangered. The Court agreed with the Board's view that the expression 'a crime of violence' connoted violence to a person; but this, it held, was not confined to offences against the person. Where an offence against property involved violence in the sense that its consequences, as opposed to its definition, involved a violent injury being caused to another, then it would fall within the Scheme, provided that the offender had, or could be inferred to have had, the requisite fault element. Lord Widgery C.J., dissenting, preferred the Board's approach. This he thought more closely gave effect to the purpose of the Scheme, which he took to compensate for acts of criminal violence directed against the person. He expressly refused any attempt to define the phrase 'crime of violence' beyond commenting that the Board's submission, that it 'should mean a crime of which violence is an essential ingredient', was 'a very neat and tidy package in which to put this problem' (at p. 1364).

The meaning of the phrase was later reconsidered in judicial review applications arising from claims for compensation made by train drivers in respect of the mental injuries they had sustained when witnessing suicides on railway lines. The two decisions are *R* v *Criminal Injuries Compensation Board, ex parte Parsons* (1981) *The Times*, 22 May 1981 (DC); (1982) *The Times*, 25 November 1982 (CA), and the test case, *R* v *Criminal Injuries Compensation Board, ex parte Webb* [1987] QB 74 (CA). In *ex parte Parsons* the Board had conceded that when he had trespassed on the railway track (CICB, 1981, para. 21), the suicide had committed a crime of violence, contrary to s. 34 of the Offences against the Person Act 1861. This provides that a person commits an offence who, by any unlawful act, or by any wilful omission or neglect, endangers or causes to be endangered the safety of any person conveyed or being in or upon a railway. A violent injury would be caused to the passengers if, for example, the driver had to brake suddenly to avoid running over a body on the line, so causing the passengers to fall against each other or against the compartment's fittings. The concession made, the only question in *ex parte Parsons* was whether the applicant's injuries were directly attributable to the commission of the offence. The concession was, however, questioned in the Divisional Court, and Cumming-Bruce L.J.'s repetition in the Court of Appeal of Glidewell J.'s misgivings about *ex parte Clowes* encouraged the Board that its revised position, namely, that a s. 34 offence did not constitute a crime of violence, was correct. Accordingly, it refused the applications made in *ex parte Webb* (CICB, 1983, para. 17).

After reviewing the history of the Scheme, the Divisional Court in *R* v *Criminal Injuries Compensation Board, ex parte Webb* [1986] QB 184 rejected the applicants' argument that 'in deciding whether a crime is a crime of violence what matters is the impact on the victim, not the intent of the offender', preferring the Board's submission that a crime of violence is 'one where the definition of the crime itself involves either direct infliction of force on the victim, or at least a hostile act directed towards the victim or class of victims' ([1986] QB 184 at p. 195). This too was the conclusion reached by the Court of Appeal, which added that while this interpretation was wider than that suggested by Lord Widgery C.J. in his dissenting judgment in *ex parte Clowes*, the second clause in particular was 'necessary to bring within the Scheme conduct amounting to causing grievous bodily harm even though no violence is used by the offender' ([1987] QB 74 at p. 79). This would include such behaviour as that in *R* v *Martin* (1881) 8 QBD 54, where the accused, by his unlawful conduct, caused panic among a crowd of people as the result of which a number were injured.

Commenting unfavourably on the absence of any definition of the phrase 'crime of violence', the Divisional Court offered: 'any crime in respect of which the prosecution must prove as one of its ingredients that the defendant unlawfully and intentionally, or recklessly, inflicted or threatened to inflict personal injury upon another' ([1986] QB 184 at p. 198). But while it accepted the underlying distinction, that it is for the Board to decide 'whether unlawful conduct because of its nature, not its consequence, amounts to a crime of violence', the Court of Appeal did not think it prudent to attempt a definition, preferring Lord Widgery's view, that the question is essentially one of fact for the Board ([1987] QB 74 at pp. 79–80).

The 1986 Home Office Working Party preferred the Divisional Court's approach, accepting 'the need for a clear definition of a crime of violence' as a way of indicating that the Scheme 'should not be regarded as underwriting any injury loosely connected with a breach of the criminal law' (Home Office, *Criminal Injuries Compensation: A Statutory Scheme*, London: HMSO, 1986, paras 4.4–4.6). However, like its predecessors, the Working Party quickly found that the task was easier said than done. A list, to or from which offences could be added or removed by statutory instrument, would suffer from the problem both of exclusivity (eliminating meritorious and otherwise eligible claimants) and of inclusivity (arousing false expectations by specifying offences that were 'too wide' for the Scheme's purpose). The debates on the statutory definitions in the Criminal Justice Act 1988 are ample evidence of these difficulties (HL Debs, vol. 489, cols. 784–93, 2 November 1987). The Working Party took the view that 'a crime of violence' should include an offence which was intended to cause death or personal injury, and one which caused the death or injury of any person, the offender being reckless as to whether death or injury was caused. But such a formulation would have excluded the mental injuries sustained by train drivers in the railway suicide cases, and in response to effective lobbying by ASLEF, the 1990 revision specifically identified trespass on a railway as a victimising event (chapter 4.4).

4.3.2   Constituent Elements of a Crime of Violence

The following two sections seek to exemplify how the Board has interpreted para. 4(a) of the old Scheme. Though it was not brought into force, the definition given in the Criminal Justice Act 1988, s. 109(1)(a)(ii), can be taken as capturing the essence of its approach: a personal injury is a criminal injury when it is directly attributable to conduct constituting an offence which requires proof of intent to cause death or personal injury or recklessness as to whether death or personal injury is caused. An attempt to commit a crime of violence is also a 'crime of violence' for the purposes of the Scheme.

4.3.2.1   External Elements of a Crime of Violence
Personal injuries are not criminal injuries even though they are caused by a breach of rules under which the 'offender' may be punished, if that breach cannot be construed as constituting the external elements of a crime of violence. If a prison

officer strains his back trying to carry a heavy and unco-operative prisoner, there is no act or omission on the part of the prisoner which can render this a criminal injury, no matter how much he may desire the officer to hurt himself in the process, and irrespective of the fact that his refusal to comply with the officer's instruction to move was itself a breach of the Prison Rules (*R v Criminal Injuries Compensation Board, ex parte Penny* [1982] Crim LR 298). Similarly, a nurse who was injured while trying to extinguish the flames lit by a psychiatric patient who set herself on fire, did not sustain a criminal injury. Whatever else she may have done, the patient's behaviour did not constitute the external elements of a crime of violence (CICB, 1990, para. 17.3).

The external elements of the offence will typically comprise acts rather than omissions, but omissions and states of affairs created by the offender may cause injuries which will be criminal injuries for the purpose of the Scheme. In 1990, an electrician was convicted of manslaughter when the person in whose house he had installed some electrical equipment was electrocuted some months later as a direct result of his reckless wiring (*The Times*, 31 January 1990). The householder's death was a criminal injury. Similarly, should an offender hide in his clothing a razor blade, an open knife or a hypodermic needle, being reckless as to whether a police officer, when conducting a 'pat down' search might cut his hand on it, there may be an assault on the reasoning in *R v Miller* [1983] 2 AC 161 and *Director of Public Prosecutions v K (A Minor)* [1990] 1 WLR 1067 that, having created a dangerous situation, the offender had failed to neutralise it. Since no foresight or foreseeability of actual bodily harm is required, an offence under s. 47 of the Offences against the Person Act 1861 would readily be made out (*R v Savage* [1992] 1 AC 699).

These external elements must also by definition be attributable to human action or inaction. The Board has regularly received applications arising from injuries caused as the result of an attack by a dog (CICB, 1989, paras 16.5–6; 1992, para. 17.5; 1993, paras 17.6–7). These, like injuries inflicted by other animals, may constitute a crime of violence under the 1861 Act if the person in charge of the dog deliberately set it on the applicant or if the attack was a result of the owner's failure to control an animal known to be vicious, and the lack of control was reckless (new Scheme, Guide, para. 7.20). Thus where, because his farm had been set alight in an arson attack, a farmer let out a ram he knew to be violent (he had written 'Dangerous' in red paint on its fleece and normally masked it whenever he let it out) and it attacked a firefighter, the Board concluded that the applicant had been the victim of a crime of violence (CICB, 1993, para. 28.10). The injury was, presumably, considered to be too remote a consequence of the arson, and the fact that the farmer was seeking to save the ram's life did not render his conduct otherwise lawful. A more difficult application arose from the death of a driver whose car hit a horse which had been deliberately chased from a field on to a public road (CICB, 1992, para. 25.7). At the inquest, the coroner reached a verdict of unlawful killing; it would be open to the Board to find that the offender was at least reckless as to whether a road user would suffer serious bodily harm as a result of the intentional driving of the horse on to the road.

An act or omission may *prima facie* constitute the external elements of a crime of violence, but be rendered lawful by the applicant's consent. One instance was that of a professional escapologist who sustained injury when he was unable to free himself from the rope with which two volunteers from the audience, one a climber and the other himself an escapologist, had bound him (CICB, 1989, paras 16.7–9). Another example, though rather more bizarre, is recorded in the Board's 1988 Report. The victim allowed the offender, who was completely unqualified as a doctor, to perform 'surgical' operations upon his penis, including the removal of part of the foreskin. The victim consented, it appears, because of the offender's plausible manner and his collection of surgical instruments. On a later occasion he consented to being placed under a general anaesthetic. The offender was ultimately convicted of an offence under s. 23 of the 1861 Act, but the victim's application was disallowed because 'what was done was done with his consent' (CICB, 1988, paras 18.1–4). Comment is speculative in the absence of a full statement of the circumstances, but even on the assumption that it was freely given, a victim's consent to serious bodily harm does not in general relieve the person inflicting it of criminal liability (*R* v *Brown* [1994] 1 AC 212). Irrespective of the criminal liability of the person causing the harm, however, it would always be open to a claims officer to deny or reduce compensation by the application of para. 13(d) (the equivalent of para. 6(c) of the old Scheme), for example if the injury were sustained as the result of sadomasochistic practices. Where consent can be given to an act which would otherwise constitute an offence, for example, medical treatment, the consent must be freely given and be informed. An applicant who permits a person who falsely states that he is a dentist to engage in acts of dental treatment does not consent to the injuries which he receives (CICB, 1992, para. 26.6).

Personal injuries directly attributable to the commission of a 'crime of violence' do not obviously include those attributable to crimes against property. A person who suffers a mental injury when he discovers upon returning home after an absence that his property and clothing have been criminally damaged or that his possessions have been stolen does not sustain a criminal injury (CICB, 1992, paras 16.10 and 17.3). Nor does an applicant who sustains a physical injury by tripping over a cable which had been criminally damaged (CICB, 1990, para. 17.4). Likewise, no compensation could be awarded on the following facts. Upon her arrival at work, the applicant found the alarm bells ringing. The policeman who arrived in answer to her call asked her to accompany him on to the premises. In one room they found a man, later convicted of burglary, hiding in the roof space, behind some ceiling tiles. As the first tile was removed, his leg fell limply down, causing the applicant to believe that there was a dead body there. Subsequently she developed alopecia, a condition often diagnosed as being induced by shock (CICB, 1985, para. 21).

However, some crimes against property, such as s. 2 of the Explosive Substances Act 1883 and s. 1(2) of the Criminal Damage Act 1971, also contemplate violent injury to the person; their commission, if personal injury is caused, can constitute crimes of violence for the purpose of the Scheme. If the conduct of the suicide in *R* v *Criminal Injuries Compenstion Board, ex parte Clowes* [1986] QB 184 could, when he broke open the gas main in order to gas himself, be construed on the objective test in *Metropolitan Police Commissioner* v *Caldwell* [1982] AC 341 as recklessness as to whether the life of another would be endangered, the injured policeman would have sustained a criminal injury. It would be otherwise if the offence committed were under s. 1(1) of the 1971 Act, as this is confined to the destruction of or damage to property. Where criminal damage under s. 1(1) is caused by fire, it will be charged as arson, which is specifically included in the two Schemes. Thus, to destroy a person's property by fire may constitute a criminal injury if that causes personal injury, but where the destruction is by other means, though it has the same effect, it will not be. Suppose a defendant, angered by some aspect of the victim's behaviour, drives a JCB into his front garden, knocking down the front wall and destroying his garden. This is witnessed by the victim standing at his front door; so long as the defendant makes no attempt to assault the victim (for example, by driving the JCB at him), there is no crime of violence which could support an application should the victim suffer a mental injury. It would be otherwise if the defendant damaged or destroyed the victim's house, being reckless as to whether the victim's life was endangered (*The Times*, 13 April 1991).

It is important in such cases to be clear about what aspect of the offender's conduct may suggest an intention to cause death or personal injury, or recklessness as to either of these. In *R* v *Steer* [1988] AC 111, the offender shot at the victim through the windows of his house, breaking them. The victim was physically unhurt. The House of Lords dismissed the appeal from the Court of Appeal, which had allowed an appeal against a conviction under s. 1(2) of the Criminal Damage Act 1971. The issue was whether the defendant intended to endanger the victim's life (or was reckless as to such endangerment) as a consequence of the bullets being discharged from his gun, or of the damage to property caused by the bullets. The House held that on the true construction of s. 1(2), '... the prosecution are required to prove that the danger to life resulted from the destruction of or damage to the property; it is not sufficient for the prosecution to prove that it resulted from the act of the defendant which caused the destruction or damage' (Lord Bridge, [1988] AC 111 at p. 119). Thus if the victim in this case had suffered a mental injury as a consequence of the shock of being shot at, he would have sustained a criminal injury not because the offender had intended to endanger his life or had been reckless as to whether or not it was endangered in the terms of s. 1(2) of the Criminal Damage Act 1971, but because he had committed some other crime of violence, such as an attempt to inflict grievous bodily harm. The 'dismal distinction' drawn in *R* v *Steer* was applied by Lord Taylor of Gosforth CJ in *R* v *Webster* [1995] 2 All ER 168 at p. 173. In one of the appeals the defendants had dropped masonry from a bridge on to a train passing below. The masonry broke through its roof, the passengers within being injured both by the masonry and parts of the broken roof falling on to them. The Court of Appeal allowed the appeal against the trial judge's misdirection, confirming that where it is alleged that the defendant intended to commit the offence in s. 1(2), the Crown must prove not that he intended that the masonry itself would endanger life, but that life would be endangered as a result of the damage that it caused. Nevertheless, the passengers would have sustained criminal injuries, either because of the alternative verdict of reckless endangerment under the section, or because a claims officer would be able to conclude that an offence under s. 18 or 20 of the 1861 Act had occurred.

The absence of any definition of 'crime of violence' from the Scheme has necessitated the specific inclusion of arson and poisoning as criminal injuries. Although their fault elements contemplate death or personal injury being caused to another, both offences can be committed without violence being directed against an individual (CICB, 1990, para. 17.6; 1991, para. 17.4 (poisoning); 1992, para. 25.3 (arson)). An offence under s. 1(1) of the Criminal Damage Act 1971 will be charged as arson where the damage or destruction is caused by fire. In cases where the fire is set on waste ground and involves the burning of foliage and the like, the claims officer will need to be satisfied both that a fire so located would be classified as arson by the police, and second, that what was being burnt was 'property' within the meaning of s. 10 of the Act (CICB, 1993, para. 28.17).

An important new qualification concerning those injured as a result of arson is that contained in para. 12(b) of the new Scheme. This provides that a person who is accidentally injured while engaged in activity 'directed at containing, limiting or remedying the consequences of a crime' does not sustain a criminal injury unless he was at the time taking an exceptional risk which was justified in the circumstances. This qualification includes only those whose activity is so 'directed', which will include firefighters but exclude persons not in the emergency services. Where the fire is set not merely to damage or destroy property (Criminal Damage Act 1971, s. 1(1)) but to endanger life (s. 1(2)), and thus an injury sustained by a firefighter is not 'accidental' but intended or recklessly caused by the offender, it may be argued that the qualification does not apply (see chapter 4.5.3).

The absence of definition has also had the potential for creating some difficulty in connection with the commission of sexual offences. Although most sexual offences do not require the Crown to prove that the offender used or threatened violence in their commission, they will almost always be capable of constituting crimes of violence where the victim was under 16. This is so because in cases of rape (s. 1 of the Sexual Offences Act 1956 as amended by s. 142 of the Criminal Justice and Public Order Act 1994 to include the rape of a man), unlawful sexual intercourse (ss. 5 or 6), buggery (s. 12), or incest (ss. 10 and 11), the claims officer will be able to conclude that there must also have been an indecent assault. This is an alternative verdict for all of these offences, and since by ss. 14(2) and 15(2), a person under 16 'cannot in law give any consent which would prevent an act being an assault', once the indecency is shown, the offence is made out (*R* v *Hodgson* [1973] QB 565). Thus the Authority's *Guide on Child Abuse and the Criminal Injuries Compensation Scheme* is able to say that rape, incest and buggery are clear examples of crimes of violence for the purpose of applications on behalf of sexually abused children (CICB, 1989, para. 25.8). Difficulty may arise where the claims officer cannot be sure that the alleged offender (in such cases, typically the victim's brother, uncle or father) did not simply invite the child to commit an indecent act, in which case there would be no assault (*Fairclough* v *Whipp* [1951] 2 All ER 834).

Where the victim is over 16 years of age, consent to an act which would otherwise constitute a necessary external element of a sexual offence will be relevant (CICB, 1992, para. 17.2), subject to the limits set out in *R* v *Brown* [1994] 1 AC 212 (even though offences were committed in this case, there were no victims who would have been successful in a claim for compensation; chapters 7.5.3.2.2 (old Scheme) and 7.5.3.2.3 (new Scheme)).

Although the point never appears to have arisen, there must be some doubt as to whether rape is a crime of violence where the rapist obtains a woman's consent by deception and no violence is used. In *R* v *Linekar* [1995] QB 250, the Court of Appeal confirmed that the deception must go to the nature of the act or the defendant's identity (a consent obtained by pretending to be the woman's husband is invalid: Sexual Offences Act 1956, s. 1(3)) rather than some characteristic of the accused, even though the woman would not have consented to intercourse had she known the truth. Where the deception is of the former kind, the consent so obtained is, apart from the rape offence, invalid for the purpose of an offence of indecent assault. For this reason, a claims officer could therefore conclude that the woman had been the victim of a crime of violence. In the latter case, however, the consent is good, and there is no rape. There may instead be an offence under s. 3 of the 1956 Act (procuring a woman, by false pretences, to have sexual intercourse), but dicta in *Gray* v *Criminal Injuries Compensation Board* 1993 SLT 28 suggest that this does not amount to a criminal injury. There the offender, a bigamist, procured sexual intercourse by purporting to marry the applicant. Lord Weir, sitting in the Outer House of the Court of Session, held that she was not the victim of a crime of violence. The applicant's case before the Outer House was founded on s. 2(b) of the Sexual Offences (Scotland) Act 1976, which creates the same offence as that in s. 3 of the Sexual Offences Act 1956. The court held that this offence was not one attended with violence. Moreover, the question whether she had been the victim of a crime of violence (possibly an indecent assault) was, as Lord Widgery put it in *R* v *Criminal Injuries Compensation Board, ex parte Clowes* [1986] QB 184 (and confirmed by Lawton L.J. in *R* v *Criminal Injuries Compensation Board, ex parte Webb* [1987] QB 74), very much a jury point. In general, Lord Weir held, the proper approach was to look not at the effect of the offender's behaviour, but at the nature of the crime and ask, were the acts of sexual intercourse crimes of violence?

It is of interest in this connection to note that para. 10 of the old Scheme specifically provided that 'The Board will consider applications for compensation arising out of acts of rape and other sexual offences' and that s. 109(3)(a) of the Criminal Justice Act 1988 also specified rape as a victimising event. The Act included two other offences whose commission need not involve violence, kidnapping and false imprisonment; this suggests that the drafter thought it necessary to include these three offences precisely because they are not obviously crimes of violence. The inclusion of rape and sexual offences as victimising events in the old Scheme has naturally pre-empted the need to look for an underlying offence of indecent assault. Thus an applicant who, under hypnosis, had been raped and buggered by the offender, sustained a criminal injury within the scope of para. 10 of the old Scheme, without more (CICB, 1992, para. 27.5). By contrast, the new Scheme makes no direct reference to sexual offences in its specification of victimising events or of what constitutes a 'personal injury' (new Scheme, para. 9). They come within the Scheme, however, by virtue of their inclusion in the tariff of injuries under the headings 'sexual abuse of children' and 'sexual assault'.

4.3.2.2 Fault Elements of a Crime of Violence

As the Court of Appeal made clear in *R v Criminal Injuries Compensation Board, ex parte Webb* [1987] QB 74, where it is not obvious that the offence constituted 'a crime of violence', it is necessary to look to the nature of the crime rather than its consequences (old Scheme, Guide, para. 2). It is not possible to state exhaustively what offences are included in this category; this remains a matter for the Authority to determine, but indisputably included are all offences of homicide and offences under ss. 18, 20 and 47 of the Offences against the Person Act 1861. These constitute the bulk of criminal injuries that have been dealt with by the Board. As suggested earlier, a crime of violence is typified by an offence whose fault elements include any one of an intention to cause death or personal injury or recklessness as to whether death or personal injury is caused. Recklessness will have to be determined in its subjective or objective sense, depending on the offence which the claims officer considers is made out in the victim's application. Where an offence against the person involves an assault or proof of malice, it will be necessary for the claims officer to be satisfied that the offender himself appreciated the risk he was running (*R v Cunningham* [1957] 2 QB 396; *R v Savage* [1992] 1 AC 699), but in the case of an offence under s. 1(2) of the Criminal Damage Act 1971, objective recklessness will suffice (*Metropolitan Police Commissioner v Caldwell* [1982] AC 341).

Whether subjectively or objectively determined, recklessness is the minimum level of fault acceptable for the purposes of the Scheme. Though an injury is clearly consistent with conduct constituting the external elements of an offence such as ss. 20 or 47 of the Offences against the Person Act 1861, for example, being struck by a javelin thrown during a school sports day (CICB, 1985, para. 20), being knocked over by another skater and breaking one's leg on the ice (CICB, 1986, para. 16), or having one's fingers crushed by a hinged drainage gate dropped by another person (CICB, 1989, paras 16.3–4), it will not constitute a criminal injury if it was only negligently inflicted. What has made the Board's task more difficult is that it often has to deal with applications in which no conviction for an offence requiring proof of the fault elements identified above has been reached. In such cases a claims officer will have to determine whether recklessness can be inferred from the factual circumstances disclosed in the application and in the police report of the incident. We return to this point in the discussion on proof in chapter 5.2.1, but one example may be given here as an illustration of this difficulty. An application was brought on behalf of an eight-year-old girl who had developed foetal alcohol syndrome and cerebral palsy as the result of her mother's alcohol abuse during pregnancy. Such conduct could amount to a crime of violence, for example, if it were the mother's intention to harm the child while in the womb; but the single member concluded that no fault element consistent with such an offence could be inferred from the facts (CICB, 1988, 16.1–16.4).

An 'offender's' belief that he is entitled to use reasonable force in self-defence or to effect an arrest may negative the fault elements. A person who is injured while being lawfully arrested does not sustain a criminal injury; but the matter is less easy where the person effecting the arrest was operating under a mistake. Suppose a wholly innocent applicant is mistaken by a store detective for a person whom he has reasonable grounds to suspect is committing theft, and in the struggle between them, as the applicant seeks to break free from what, from his point of view, is an unlawful arrest, he is struck and injured by the detective. In *R* v *Williams* [1987] 3 All ER 411 the Court of Appeal held that if a defendant were labouring under a mistaken view of the facts, for example, that his victim was consenting to the use of force, that it was necessary to defend himself, or that a crime was being committed, then he is entitled to be judged on the facts as he believed them to be (see also *Beckford* v *The Queen* [1988] AC 130 (PC)). Accordingly the store detective would, assuming that he had reasonable grounds for his suspicion and that his use of force was reasonable, be entitled to be acquitted on a charge arising from the injuries caused to the applicant. Thus there would be no offence upon which to sustain an application. This may seem harsh from the innocent applicant's perspective, but his position is no different from that which obtains in civil law, since an action against the store detective would (leaving aside ss. 44 and 45 of the Offences against the Person Act 1861) fail for the same reason.

However, he may think himself unfairly treated by comparison with what happened in *R* v *Williams*. There the victim saw a youth attempt to rob a woman. He gave chase, knocked the youth to the ground and attempted to immobilise him. The defendant, who had not witnessed the attempted robbery, came upon the scene. The victim told him that he was a police officer, which was untrue, and that he was arresting the youth. When he failed to produce a warrant card the defendant punched him in the face. The defendant's conviction under s. 47 of the 1861 Act was quashed for the reasons given above. If a crime of violence were the only class of victimising event, then the victim would be unable to sustain an application for compensation on these facts, there being no crime of violence. However, assuming that the claims officer would not regard his pretending to be a policeman as disentitling him under para. 13(d), it seems clear that the victim's injury was caused by his apprehension or attempted apprehension of an offender or suspected offender (the youth), which would come within para. 8(c) of the Scheme. There is nothing in this paragraph which requires that the injury be caused by conduct constituting an offence, or indeed, even by a human agency (chapter 4.5.2). If it is fair that these facts should give rise to a successful application for compensation, whereas the innocent victim injured by the mistaken store detective will fail, then the distinction must lie in the pro-social behaviour of the victim who seeks to enforce the law.

One further variant may be considered. Whereas a store detective acts lawfully in arresting someone whom she has reasonable grounds for suspecting is committing an arrestable offence, even though no such offence was being committed (Police and

Criminal Evidence Act 1984, s. 24(4)(b)), she acts unlawfully where she arrests someone who she has reasonable grounds for suspecting has committed an arrestable offence, if no such offence was actually committed (Police and Criminal Evidence Act 1984, s. 24(5)(b); *R* v *Self* [1992] 1 WLR 657). In the latter case, therefore, the victim of the wrongful arrest, if injured in a struggle with the detective, may have a successful claim under the Scheme (as well as a civil action for wrongful arrest and false imprisonment against the detective — in which event any damages will have to be repaid to the Authority: chapter 9.5.1). But the victim mistakenly arrested under the power in s. 24(4) who is injured in the struggle will, as we have seen, have no remedy, assuming the detective's use of force was reasonable.

An offender may mistakenly believe the victim to be consenting when he is not. Suppose, for example, a victim such as the wife in *R* v *Cogan* [1976] QB 217 were to make an application under the Scheme. There it was held that as the offender need only honestly believe that the woman was consenting to sexual intercourse, he would not commit rape despite the fact that he had no reasonable grounds for so believing (*Director of Public Prosecutions* v *Morgan* [1976] AC 182). On the assumption that rape can entail the commission of a crime of violence, an application under the Scheme would surely succeed, for the Authority, like the Court of Appeal's robust confirmation of the husband's conviction for aiding and abetting, would never deny that the victim was indeed raped, whatever the 'rapist's' state of mind. Indeed, under the terms of the new Scheme, a claims officer could simply conclude that she had suffered a sexual assault.

The difference between an application arising on the facts in *R* v *Cogan* and one arising from the mistaken actions of the store detective is that the rapist's beliefs merely served to excuse him from liability for what remained throughout an unlawful act; the store detective's beliefs, however, constituted a justification for his actions. A case in point was decided by the Board in 1987. The victim and the offender had smoked some cannabis together in the house occupied by the victim. Later she was accosted by the offender outside the toilet, but, following her protestations, he was ejected by the householder. The offender was later readmitted and allowed to sleep in the house in a room separate from the victim's. Two days later she reported to the police that she had been raped, but at his first trial, where the defence was that she consented, the jury could not agree and was dismissed. At the second trial, with the same defence, the offender was acquitted. The victim made a claim which was initially denied because the single member was not satisfied that she had not consented. At the hearing, however, the Board held that the outcome of the two trials was irrelevant, and on the basis of her evidence and that of the householder, made a full award (*Legal Action*, June 1987, p. 16).

4.4   VICTIMISING EVENTS: TRESPASS ON A RAILWAY

Introduced in the 1990 revision, para. 4(c) of the old Scheme was the government's concession to the train drivers over the matter of railway suicides, which the Court of Appeal had held in *R* v *Criminal Injuries Compensation Board, ex parte Webb*

[1987] QB 74 not to be attributable to the commission of a crime of violence (chapter 4.3.1). Under para. 8(b) of the new Scheme, which is in identical terms to para. 4(c) of the old Scheme, a train driver (or any other railway worker) who suffers mental injury as a result of coming across the body of a person who had committed suicide on a railway track, or as a result of his unsuccessful attempts to stop the train before it hit a person standing between (CICB, 1991, para. 19.2) or lying on the railway lines (CICB, 1991, para. 19.3; 1992, para. 19.4), sustains a criminal injury within the Scheme (HC Debs, Standing Committee A, col. 246, 27 June 1995). It can also cover a case where the person killed was not seeking to commit suicide, but was instead simply playing or otherwise walking on the tracks or the railway embankment (CICB, 1992, para. 19.3; 1994, para. 6.7).

Neither the old nor new Schemes make reference to s. 34 of the Offences against the Person Act 1861, by which a person commits an offence who, by any unlawful act or by wilful omission or neglect, endangers the safety of any person conveyed or being in or upon a railway. This is so, first because the 1861 Act does not extend to Scotland, and second, because the offence would extend the scope of the Scheme to negligently inflicted injuries, caused, for example, by a passenger insecurely placing a heavy suitcase on an overhead luggage rack from which it falls on to the passenger sitting below (HL Debs, vol. 489, col. 788, 2 November 1987).

Mental injury alone is, by para. 9 of the new Scheme, compensable only under limited conditions. In the case of a person employed in the business of a railway, compensation is payable where that person 'witnessed and was present on the occasion when another person sustained physical (including fatal) injury directly attributable to an offence of trespass on a railway, or was closely involved in its immediate aftermath' (chapter 5.1.3.3.4). This clearly covers train drivers. Paragraph 12(b) of the new Scheme does not apply to train drivers seeking to invoke para. 9(d). Paragraph 12(b) is a new provision which seeks to limit compensation when members of the emergency services are accidentally injured while they are engaged in activity directed to 'containing, limiting or remedying the consequences of a crime'; they will be compensated for accidental injury only if, at the time of the injury, they were taking an exceptional risk. A driver who, seeing a body on the line ahead, stops his train without having to brake hard, phones the next signal box, and, having secured his train, walks along the track to the body, is engaged in activity remedying the consequences of a crime, but might not be considered to be taking an exceptional risk. Without the final sentence of para. 9(d) (which excludes the application of para. 12(b)), the driver would not be compensable for the mental injury he later suffers.

This one item well illustrates the underlying problems of justifying criminal injury compensation schemes. For the drivers' union, ASLEF, it was argued that it would be a grave injustice that those who had been completely blameless should receive no compensation for the mental and physical pain that could haunt them for the rest of their lives. As special pleading, this applies equally, of course, to any child born with a physical or mental handicap or to anyone who sustained such an injury as a result of the overcrowding at the Sheffield Wednesday football ground in 1988, and so on.

Since there has never been any basis for criminal injury provision other than, as the Home Office Working Party put it, 'a narrow and rather specific one: to reflect the strong public sympathy for the innocent victims of violent crime, who are unlikely to be able to obtain redress against the offender' (Home Office, *Criminal Injuries Compensation: A Statutory Scheme*, 1986, para. 4.1; chapter 1.2.2), it is difficult either to draw anything but an arbitrary borderline between one victim and another, or to resist (upon what grounds?) yet another group of victims being included in the Scheme's ambit. As Duff puts it in 'Criminal Injuries and ''Violent'' Crime', *Criminal Law Review*, 1987, at p. 229:

> The difficulty is that public sympathy is a crucial element in justifying the Scheme but non-eligible victims may also attract it and there is no other cogent reason which can be given to explain compensating only the victims of 'violence'.

Railway suicides are not, of course, the only kind of conduct constituting a trespass on a railway which can cause personal injury. Other examples are cases where the offender leaves planks of wood across the track to derail the train, abandons a car on a level crossing in order to cause a crash (CICB, 1993, para. 19.3), or stands on a trackside embankment throwing stones or other objects at or through the train's windows (CICB, 1994, para. 6.7). However, injuries caused to train drivers or passengers by a person standing on a bridge over the railway and dropping objects on to the train are criminal injuries under para. 8(a), not para. 8(c), because they can simply be construed as crimes of violence under s. 1(2) of the Criminal Damage Act 1971, as in *R* v *Webster* [1995] 2 All ER 168 (chapter 4.3.2.1).

4.5   VICTIMISING EVENTS: LAW ENFORCEMENT

4.5.1   Introduction

Compensation for injuries sustained by a person engaged in an act of law enforcement (whether or not it concerned a crime of violence) has been a feature of the Scheme from the beginning. This feature is maintained in the new Scheme, para. 8(c) of which is in substantively identical terms to para. 4(b) of the old. This provides that personal injury directly attributable to the apprehension or attempted apprehension of an offender or suspected offender, to the prevention or attempted prevention of an offence or to the giving of help to any constable who is engaged in any such activity is a criminal injury. The provision is intended to apply in particular to injuries sustained by private citizens engaged in one of these activities, but in respect of which it might be difficult to say that the injuries were caused by a crime of violence. If, during the struggle, the offender intentionally or recklessly caused injury to the applicant, there would clearly be a victimising event under para. 8(a), but where an injury is 'accidental', in the sense that the circumstances cannot support the conclusion that the offender had the fault element of a crime of violence at the time that he caused the injury, the applicant would, but for para. 8(c), be uncompensable. Similarly, if the applicant, such as a store detective or security guard, were to sustain an injury while chasing an offender who had just committed a theft, the injury would, but for this provision, be uncompensable as it would not be directly attributable to a crime of violence. In practice, it is police officers who are the more likely to benefit from this provision. However, because the Board's figures do not indicate which of the three victimising events in para. 4 (now para. 8) was the cause of the criminal injury, it is impossible to say how many of the applications made in any one year fall within this category, or were made by police officers.

However, not all accidentally sustained injuries which are directly attributable to an act of law enforcement come within the terms of the Scheme. Both Schemes further provide that such injuries will qualify for compensation only where the claims officer (or the Board) is satisfied that when the injury was sustained, the applicant was taking an exceptional risk which was justified in all the circumstances (old Scheme, para. 6(d); new Scheme, para. 12). As the definitions of what constitutes a criminal injury are alternatives, it is quite possible that a victim who sustains a personal injury while engaged in an act of law enforcement will be able to support an application for compensation under either para. 8(a) or para. 8(c). This is of importance, as it is only in respect of criminal injuries caused by law enforcement activity that the exceptional risk qualification applies. Thus, if in the struggle to apprehend an offender the applicant is injured by him or by his accomplice, perhaps by a missile thrown by one of the group whose unlawful conduct he is going to investigate, his personal injury can be said to have been caused by a crime of violence (CICB, 1990, paras 26.6–26.7), and there is no further requirement associated with the law enforcement activity to make it a qualifying injury. If, however, the injury is 'accidental', for example, where the applicant trips and falls while trying to restrain or to pursue the offender (CICB, 1991, paras 20.2–20.3), or the offender did not have the fault element of a crime of violence (such as s. 38 of the Offences against the Person Act 1861: assault with intent to resist arrest), it will only be a criminal injury if the applicant meets the exceptional risk condition. The following section considers the interpretation of para. 8(c); the exceptional risk qualification is discussed in chapter 4.4.3.

4.5.2   The Interpretation of Para. 8(c)

The significance of the words 'apprehension' and 'offender', and the phrase 'the prevention of an offence' each posed some difficulty in the early years of the old Scheme. As all three figure in the new Scheme, the decisions, discussed in the following sections, continue to be of importance. Like its predecessor, para. 8(c) is generally intended to treat as criminal injuries personal injuries accidentally sustained by police or citizens while engaged in law enforcement activity. The offence to which the apprehension, prevention or assistance is related can be any criminal offence, including any offence against property, and offences triable only summarily; in addition, the injury may be sustained at the hands not only of the suspected offender, but also where the applicant coming to assist in the law enforcement activity is struck and injured by the constable or another citizen who has come to assist. Moreover, it may include an injury sustained otherwise than at some other person's hands, as where the applicant slips and falls while assisting police officers.

The decisions discussed below show that injuries attributable to law enforcement activity may be criminal injuries notwithstanding that the victim has no power of arrest or that he was mistaken about the existence of an offence, or that the offender was escaping a custody which was not exclusively justified by reference to his suspected or proven offending. These decisions stand in contrast to the liability that a citizen bears should he arrest or attempt to arrest someone he has reasonable grounds for suspecting has committed an arrestable offence, no such offence having been committed. If the citizen should be injured in such circumstances he will sustain a criminal injury (providing, if it were accidentally caused, that he was taking an exceptional risk); but, not complying with s. 24(5) of the Police and Criminal Evidence Act 1984, the arrest is unlawful, and the citizen will be liable in an action for false imprisonment brought by the person he arrested (*R* v *Self* [1992] 1 WLR 657).

4.5.2.1   The *Apprehension* or *Attempted Apprehension* of an Offender

Prior to the 1979–80 changes to the Scheme, this aspect of law enforcement was described as the 'arrest or attempted arrest' of an offender or suspected offender. The change was made in response to the decision in *R* v *Criminal Injuries Compensation Board, ex parte Carr* [1981] RTR 122 (DC), where the applicant witnessed a motorcycle collision and was injured while trying to prevent one of the motorcyclists from leaving the scene of the accident. The Board held that there could be no attempted arrest, since the applicant had no power of arrest in the circumstances, and that there was no attempt to prevent the commission of a crime (namely, failure to stop after an accident contrary to s. 25 of the Road Traffic Act 1972) since the offence had been committed when the motorcyclist sought to leave the scene and before the applicant unsuccessfully chased after him (CICB, 1977, paras 12–13). The Divisional Court held that albeit the motorcyclist had intended to leave the scene of the accident and had started to do so, he had not completed that process when the applicant began his pursuit, and thus the motorcyclist had not completed the offence under s. 25 at the time when the applicant was injured. When reconsidered by the Board, an award was made, presumably on the basis that the applicant was injured while attempting to prevent the commission of a crime (CICB, 1981, para. 20(1)), but the Scheme was also amended so as to make it clear that even if the Divisional Court had upheld the Board's view of when the offence of failure to stop was completed, the applicant would still have sustained his injuries while attempting to apprehend an offender.

'Apprehension', then, has no specifically legal connotation: an applicant may, for the purposes of the Scheme, apprehend or attempt to apprehend an offender or suspected offender although he has no power to arrest or detain that person.

4.5.2.2   An *Offender* or Suspected *Offender*

In *R* v *Criminal Injuries Compensation Board, ex parte Lawton* [1972] 1 WLR 1589 (DC), the question arose whether an application could be sustained where the offender, at the time when the applicant was injured trying to apprehend him, had in fact ceased to be detained as having committed an offence, but was instead being detained under different statutory powers. In this case the Board refused an application by a policeman who had accidentally injured his back when he jumped through a police station window to prevent the escape of a man being detained under the emergency provisions of the Mental Health Act 1959. The detainee had initially been brought in on suspicion of theft, but had subsequently been identified as a former in-patient at a mental hospital, and was consequently detained with a view to his being seen by a doctor and readmitted to hospital. The Board took the view that as at the material time the detainee was being held under non-criminal regulations, he committed no offence by attempting to escape custody and was thus not an offender or suspected offender. However, the Divisional Court decided that the initiation by the police of procedures under the Mental Health Act 1959 did not terminate the original ground for the man's detention, and thus (Lord Widgery C.J. at p. 1592):

> ... where as here the police officer had authority ... to act in one of two capacities, it seems to me to be wholly unreal and quite unnecessary to pause and consider whether at the moment when he jumped through the window, he had in mind one or the other. If it were necessary to make fine distinctions of that kind we should be introducing an unduly legalistic note into this essentially informal procedure. It is quite impossible to suppose that any officer in his situation would ever apply his mind to the situation as to which of his hats he was wearing or which authority he was exercising.

The court accepted the Board's argument that an injury would not be compensable where the only hat the policeman was wearing meant that the person he was attempting to place into custody was not in law an offender or suspected offender. However, where there is a multiplicity of hats, one of which includes the possibility that there was an offender or suspected offender, then the injuries he sustains will constitute criminal injuries.

4.5.2.3   The *Prevention of an Offence*

A third matter was considered in *R* v *Criminal Injuries Compensation Board, ex parte Ince* [1973] 1 WLR 1334 (CA). This was whether an application could succeed under the heading, 'prevention of crime', if at the time when the applicant was injured in trying to prevent it, there was actually no crime being, or about to be, committed. In this case the applicant's husband, who was on duty in a police car, was killed when, answering a general alarm, he shot a set of traffic lights and was killed in a collision with another police car crossing with the lights. Subsequently it was discovered that this was a false alarm. The Board held that the deceased was not at the material time actually engaged in the prevention of a crime. Both the Divisional Court and the Court of Appeal held that this decision was in error.

The Court of Appeal held that it was unduly restrictive to interpret the relevant words of the Scheme as implying that a precondition of compensation was that an offence must have been committed. Neither, the court held, would it matter if the offence never could be committed because the circumstances in reality did not disclose an offence, provided that the policeman believed that they could. If, as was the case in *ex parte Ince*, the policeman was acting in response to a false alarm, his injury would be a criminal injury provided that he was actually engaged in preventing an offence, albeit one about whose existence he was mistaken.

4.5.3   The Exceptional Risk Qualification: Para. 12

The treatment of accidental injuries sustained while a citizen or policeman was attempting to apprehend an offender or prevent a crime caused some problems in the interpretation of the old Scheme. One of the obvious difficulties is the systematic ambiguity of the phrase 'accidental injuries'. It could mean first, injuries which are remote to the law enforcement activity, such as a police officer cutting his hand on the glass door of the police station as he leaves in answer to an emergency call (CICB, 1968, para. 6). However, since both Schemes require that the injury caused by the law enforcement activity be 'directly attributable' to it, 'accidental' is not employed as a causal concept. Secondly, it could refer to injuries directly attributable to the activities of the offender whom the applicant is trying to arrest or restrain, but who does not have the fault element of a crime of violence whose external elements entail the injury the applicant has sustained. In this sense, an 'accidental' injury may be contrasted with one intentionally or recklessly caused (and thus also includes negligently inflicted injuries). But this does not take account of the cases in which the applicant sustains her injury otherwise than at the hands of anyone at the scene of the law enforcement activity; for example, falling over while running to assist a police officer to restrain the offender. Thus, by 'accidental', the Schemes mean to include injuries which are directly attributable to acts of law enforcement, but which are not necessarily caused by anyone; they are, simply, injuries attributable to events which occur while the applicant is engaged in law enforcement activity. However, there remains some doubt about what kinds of 'accidental' injuries are within the new Scheme.

Although the 1964 Scheme contained no limitation (other than the causal connection) on the scope of these events, the Board sought to draw the line at compensating those who were accidentally injured while an arrest was taking place but who themselves were not in any way engaged in assisting to effect the arrest (CICB, 1971, para. 8). However, in *R v Criminal Injuries Compensation Board, ex parte Schofield* [1971] 1 WLR 926, the Court of Appeal held that since there was indeed nothing in the Scheme to limit an award of compensation to those who were actually engaged in the law enforcement activity, the Board acted improperly where it refused an application on behalf of a bystander who had been accidentally injured while someone else was effecting an arrest.

A further substantial extension followed the Court of Appeal's decision in *R* v *Criminal Injuries Compensation Board, ex parte Ince* [1973] 1 WLR 1334. Combining Megaw L.J.'s interpretation of the phrase 'attempted prevention of an offence' as including an instance where a police officer 'goes towards the place or supposed place of the supposed offence' (p. 815) with the court's interpretation of the phrase 'directly attributable' as meaning not solely attributable, but attributable in whole or in part to the offence or supposed offence, this decision meant that (Home Office, *Criminal Injuries Compensation: A Statutory Scheme*, 1986, para. 6.9):

> Compensation was likely to be payable not only to a police officer injured at the scene of a crime while taking active steps to prevent its commission, but also to any officer who believed that an offence was about to take place and took some action to prevent it; in the case of an attempted arrest, any injury accidentally sustained from the time that a police officer received instructions and responded to them was likely to be within the scope of the Scheme.

In response to the Board's unease, the 1978 Working Party proposed that such injuries should only be compensable, in the words of para. 6(d) of the old Scheme, 'if the applicant was at the time taking an exceptional risk which was justified in all the circumstances' (Home Office, *Review of the Criminal Injuries Compensation Scheme: Report of an Interdepartmental Working Party*, London: HMSO, 1978, para. 5.23). By this means:

> ... the scheme properly excluded cases where, for example, a police officer tripped over a kerb while following an offender in broad daylight. Such injuries were to be regarded as a normal hazard of the job and not an exceptional risk (HC Debs, Standing Committee A, col. 253, 27 June 1995).

Although directed specifically at accidental injuries sustained by those engaged in law enforcement activity, it was, it seems, assumed that this qualification would also have the effect of excluding bystanders. At all events, following its introduction in 1980, the Board's Reports suggest that the qualification had met its primary objective, and that the only issue was what was meant by an exceptional risk. Injured bystanders simply do not figure in the Board's Reports during the 1980s. The qualification was maintained in the 1990 revision and is reproduced and extended in para. 12 of the new Scheme. This provides that:

> Where an injury is sustained accidentally by a person who is engaged in:
> (a)   any of the law-enforcement activities described in para. 8(c), or
> (b)   any other activity directed to containing, limiting or remedying the consequences of a crime,
> compensation will not be payable unless the person injured was, at the time he sustained the injury, taking an exceptional risk which was justified in all the circumstances.

The exceptional risk qualification is couched in exactly the same terms as para. 6(d) of the old Scheme. The interpretation which the Board put upon it will therefore be relevant to its interpretation by the Authority. It will also be seen that the new Scheme extends the qualification to those who are injured while engaged in activity directed towards 'containing, limiting or remedying the consequences of a crime'. This was included so as to place firefighters and other members of the emergency services on the same footing as police officers *vis-à-vis* the normal hazards of their job. Under the old Scheme, 'a firefighter accidentally injured in the normal course of attending a fire call which was subsequently ascribed to arson — a crime of violence under the Scheme — is eligible for an award even though no activity beyond that normally expected of a firefighter as a matter of routine has been undertaken' (HC Debs, Standing Committee A, col. 253, 27 June 1995). The government's intention was that if a police officer is properly ineligible under the Scheme if he should trip over a kerbstone while walking up to an offender (CICB, 1990, para. 18.5), then so also should be a firefighter who trips over a hose when the fire he was called to put out is later discovered to be the result of an arson attack. It could also extend to accidental injuries sustained by ambulance teams, paramedics and others who give first aid to a person injured in a fight (HL Debs, vol. 566, col. 704, 17 October 1995). Notwithstanding its extension to firefighters, the government considered that '... injuries sustained in actually rescuing people from the consequences of an arson attack, although perhaps seen as a traditional part of a firefighter's job, are likely to involve a degree of risk well beyond the norm, and would thus qualify under the "exceptional risk" provisions of the scheme' (HC Debs, Standing Committee A, col. 253, 27 June 1995).

In one respect, para. 12(b) may extend the range of compensable injuries. The 1991 Report refers to an application by a police officer who, having arrested a burglar in the loft of a house, was injured when, on his way down its ladder, the loft door fell shut on to his hand (CICB, 1991, para. 20.4). Assuming that the burglar did not slam the door, there was no crime of violence, and hence the officer had to rely on para. 4(b). The Board found that as the arrest had been effected, the officer was no longer engaged in the apprehension etc. of an offender or suspected offender. The Board also found that the officer had not, in any event, been taking a risk. Allowing that the taking of an exceptional risk following the effecting of an arrest is quite possible (for example, an officer has to climb across a roof to assist the offender to the ground, or has to rescue the offender's victim from a dangerous place), if those actions can be regarded as activity 'directed to ... remedying the consequences of a crime', then the officer's application might be successful.

'In assessing whether or not [the applicant] was taking an exceptional risk, we will look at all the facts to decide whether the risk [the applicant] took was exceptional and justified in all the circumstances' (new Scheme, Guide, para. 7.16). This assessment thus contains two components: that the risk was exceptional and, secondly, that the applicant was justified in taking it.

The question whether the risk which the applicant took was exceptional itself comprises two elements. The first is subjective, relating to the applicant: was the risk out of the ordinary for this particular applicant? Like the Board, the Authority is able to employ different standards as between different law enforcers; what is exceptional for a citizen, for example, tackling a man armed with a knife, may not be so for a policeman (CICB, 1987, para. 22). 'Police officers, or, for example, firefighters because of their training and experience should be in a better position to assess the consequences of their actions and we believe that it would be unjust to apply the same tests to "civilians"' (new Scheme, Guide, para. 7.17). In this way the Authority could go some way to reflect the reservations which the 1986 Working Party expressed about the extension of the Scheme to those who are paid to enforce the law and who have been, if injured in the course of their employment, eligible for industrial injury benefit (Home Office, 1986, para. 6.13). A good example of how these variable standards may apply is provided by an application reported in 1995. The female applicant was woken at night by noises coming from her kitchen. Going downstairs to investigate, she was confronted in the kitchen by two men, one outside the window, the other moving backwards through it. She suffered no physical violence nor was threatened with any, but sustained mental injury. Her application was initially refused on the ground that it disclosed no crime of violence; at a hearing the Board concluded that she was engaged in the prevention or attempted prevention of an offence (burglary), and that as 'an unarmed female civilian' she took a justified exceptional risk in confronting 'an unknown number of suspected burglars who might or might not have been armed and willing to resort to violence' (CICB, 1995, para. 6.9).

The second element relates to the incident in which the applicant was injured. This entails an objective assessment of the balance between the gravity of the situation, the immediacy of the threat posed to the public, and the danger posed by the steps needed to neutralise that threat. The Guide proceeds to give some general instances of what may or may not amount to such a risk. These can be traced to earlier decisions taken by the Board, most of which concern the last of these three factors. Thus injuries sustained while walking or running towards an incident or going to apprehend an offender in broad daylight (CICB, 1989, para. 17,2; 1990, para. 18.3; 1992, para. 20.1), or escorting a non-violent prisoner, are not within the Scheme (CICB, 1982, paras 31, 36 and 37; 1988, paras 28.1–28.5; new Scheme, Guide, para. 7.16); neither are those sustained when climbing, or jumping over walls, fences, parapets or other obstructions, unless the applicant cannot see what is on the other side, or the incident occurs at night (CICB, 1982, para. 38; 1988, paras 29.1–29.3; 1989, paras 17.2–17.3; new Scheme, Guide, para. 7.16). Falling from a height or down an embankment, or through a roof or a skylight should normally be regarded as taking an exceptional risk (CICB, 1982, paras 39–41; 1983, para. 30; 1990, paras 18.2–18.4), as may falling when pursuing an offender in icy conditions (CICB, 1994, para. 6.10). Answering a 999 call concerning intruders in an unoccupied building has not normally been within the Scheme, although the Board would consider the nature of the premises in question.

The Guide to the new Scheme also indicates that the Authority will not normally consider police officers eligible for compensation where they are injured in traffic accidents as a result of chasing or trying to intercept a car which has refused to stop, 'unless there was some exceptionally risky additional factor, such as severe adverse weather conditions' (new Scheme, Guide, para. 7.17). This follows from the decision of the Divisional Court in *R* v *Criminal Injuries Compensation Board, ex parte Emmett* (CICB, 1989, para. 26.3). Prior to this case, the Board had allowed some applications in such circumstances (CICB, 1986, paras 24 and 18). Here the police officer's car was struck by a third car entering a road junction when she had come to a standstill behind the offender's car which had halted in the middle of the junction. The court held that the Board's decision, that on the facts the officer was not taking an exceptional risk, was neither unreasonable nor perverse.

Like its predecessor, the new Scheme also provides that the risk must be justified. There are no claims noted in the Board's reports illustrating the application of this criterion. It is intended to exclude applicants injured while neutralising a trivial threat or one which, though real enough, their actions would be unlikely to affect.

The purpose behind the introduction in 1980 of the exceptional risk condition was, as we have seen, to limit the scope of the Scheme where injuries are 'accidentally' sustained by those about to engage in law enforcement activity. It was also intended to exclude bystanders such as the applicant in *R* v *Criminal Injuries Compensation Board, ex parte Schofield* [1971] 1 WLR 926, since even if the person engaged in the law enforcement activity was taking an exceptional risk, the bystander who sustained the accidental injury was not. However, para. 7.14 of the Guide to the new Scheme states:

> You may also be entitled to an award if you were injured during the course of such an action [law enforcement] even though you were not yourself taking part in it. If you were, for example, an innocent bystander and were knocked over and injured by the offender or the pursuer, you could be entitled to an award.

It is difficult to see how this can follow from the terms of the Scheme, or if it does, what sense it makes. If the innocent bystander is knocked over and the claims officer is satisfied that at the time the offender (or the pursuer) had the fault elements of a crime of violence, then the bystander would clearly fall within para. 8(a). But if not, then the bystander can only be brought within the terms of the Scheme if a distinction is drawn between two kinds of victim of law enforcement activity: the participating and the non-participating bystander. In the former case, a bystander who, seeing someone trying to break into her neighbour's car and, having shouted at him chases after him, will not sustain a criminal injury when she slips and breaks her ankle because she is not taking an exceptional risk (CICB, 1990, para. 18.3). (Neither does the victim of theft who slips and falls when chasing the man who stole his wallet (CICB, 1991, para. 20.3)). But, in the latter, if, in a struggle between a police officer and the offender in a confined space, the offender's arm were to swing out and strike a bystander who is trapped in a corner of the room, this accidental injury would, according to para. 7.14 of the Guide, come within the terms of the Scheme. In short, and assuming that in both cases the accidental injury is directly attributable to the law enforcement activity, the 'good citizen' qualifies for compensation only if he meets the exceptional risk condition, while the non-participating bystander apparently qualifies without more.

Yet the purpose of the introduction in the old Scheme of the exceptional risk qualification was to exclude bystanders as well as those who, though engaged in an act of law enforcement, had 'no more than a slender connection with the crime or suspected crime' (HC Debs, Standing Committee A, col. 253, 27 June 1995). Nowhere in the debates on the new Scheme did the government indicate that it wished to revert, in the case of bystanders, to the position which obtained in *ex parte Schofield*. As Lord Archer of Sandwell observed: '. . . there is no obvious reason why a person who is present at the scene of a fight, simply from idle curiosity, and who is injured, should be compensated while someone who is public spiritedly trying to restore order or protect someone should be denied compensation' if he were not taking an exceptional risk (HL Debs, vol. 566, col. 700, 17 October 1995).

4.6 TRAFFIC ACCIDENTS

Both Schemes provide that a personal injury sustained as the result of a road traffic offence is not a criminal injury. Neither a pedestrian struck by a stolen car whose driver had lost control of it (CICB, 1991, para. 26.3) or by a car which skidded in wet conditions (CICB, 1993, para. 25.3) or reversed into him and drove off (CICB, 1995, para. 6.13), nor a pedestrian who had been knocked over by a cyclist who had ignored a red traffic signal (CICB, 1991, para. 26.5), nor a cyclist who had been knocked off his bike by a pedestrian stepping into the road without looking (CICB, 1991, para. 26.4), were compensable under the old Scheme. Nor will they be under the new.

But the old Scheme also provided that a personal injury would be a criminal injury where it was due to a deliberate attempt to run the victim down (old Scheme, para. 11). In *R v Criminal Injuries Compensation Board, ex parte Emmett* (CICB, 1989, para. 26.3) (DC) the Board appeared to construe this fairly broadly. The facts of this case were noted earlier (chapter 4.5.3). Although no award was made, the Board was prepared to accept that the action of a driver committing a road traffic offence causing the applicant, driving another car, to be stranded in the road where she was likely to be struck by other cars, could amount to a deliberate attempt to run her down. But there have been few such applications reported by the Board (CICB, 1984, para. 33; 1988, para. 41.1; 1994, para. 6.16; see Spencer, J., 'Motor Vehicles as Weapons of Offence', *Criminal Law Review*, 1985, p. 29). In some of the successful cases it seems that the driver was in effect committing a crime of violence and using the vehicle to cause the victim harm, though without seeking to run him down. For example, an award was made where the applicant was grabbed by a passenger in a car and dragged along the road (CICB, 1991, para. 33.1). The Board also accepted an application where the driver of a stolen car abandoned it while it was still moving, leaving it to collide with and kill a baby being wheeled along the pavement in its pram (CICB, 1992, para. 25.2). The facts are superficially very close to those in *R v Mahmood* [1994] *Crim LR* 368, where the defendants were guilty of aggravated vehicle taking under s. 12A of the Theft Act 1968. It is not clear from the Board's Report whether the driver was engaged in a deliberate attempt to run the victim down, though he was clearly reckless; the inference must be that he could be convicted of manslaughter.

The new Scheme also contains this qualification, though it is differently worded; an injury attributable to the use of a vehicle is not a criminal injury 'except where the vehicle was used so as deliberately to inflict, or attempt to inflict, injury on any person' (new Scheme, para. 11). This more nearly covers the applications mentioned above; that is, cases in which the car is intentionally used as the injury-causing agent, even though the driver does not intend to run the victim down. But the use of the word 'deliberately' must exclude recklessness as exhibited in the application resembling the facts of *R* v *Mahmood*; in cases such as these, the claims officer will need to be satisfied that a crime of violence which can be committed recklessly was committed. If not, the application must be refused.

There is another difference in substance between the formulations in the two Schemes. The new Scheme makes it clear that the applicant may be someone other than the person targeted by the driver. A person who has a close relationship with the person so targeted and who suffers mental injury directly attributable to the driver's attempt to injure that person sustains a compensable criminal injury (chapter 5.1.3.3.2).

The justification for the exclusion of road traffic offences, even where they constitute crimes of violence, as in the case of causing death by dangerous driving or causing bodily harm by wanton or furious driving, does not arise 'from the nature of the offences, but from the purely practical consideration of avoiding the need for the Board to embark upon detailed consideration of cases which are eligible for compensation under motor insurance arrangements, including the agreements between the Motor Insurers' Bureau and the Secretary of State for Transport' (Home Office, *Criminal Injuries Compensation: A Statutory Scheme*, 1986, para. 11.1). In *R* v *Seymour* [1983] 2 AC 493, the House of Lords held that causing death by reckless driving may be equivalent to manslaughter, but if the death is caused by what constitutes an offence under s. 1 of the Road Traffic Act 1988, it will be excluded from the Scheme if it is covered by the MIB agreements.

Conversely, where an injury is directly attributable to the commission of an offence under ss. 1 or 2 of the 1988 Act or under s. 35 of the Offences against the Person Act 1861, compensation will be payable under the Scheme if the circumstances of the injury fall outside the terms of the MIB agreements, for example, if the injury occurred on private land, or in the case of the untraced drivers agreement, the vehicle was being deliberately used as a weapon. Whereas offences under ss. 1 and 2 of the Road Traffic Act 1988 can constitute crimes of violence, in *R* v *Criminal Injuries Compensation Board, ex parte Letts* (CICB, 1989, para. 26.2), the Court of Appeal doubted whether an offence of careless driving (s. 3) could ever satisfy para. 4(a), though it was not prepared to rule out the possibility altogether.

Clause 1(e) of the untraced drivers agreement eliminates liability where the vehicle was being deliberately used as a weapon; in such cases the MIB and the

Scheme are mutually exclusive. This is not so, however, under the uninsured drivers agreement, which deals with injuries caused by identified but uninsured drivers. Here the MIB and the Scheme overlap, and the relationship between them was considered by the House of Lords in *Gardner* v *Moore* [1984] AC 548. The driver was convicted under s. 18 of the Offences against the Person Act 1861 for deliberately driving his car at the plaintiff, causing him serious injury. The plaintiff brought an action against the driver and, as second defendants, the MIB, seeking a declaration that, under the uninsured drivers agreement, they were liable to indemnify him for any unsatisfied judgment against the driver. The issue to be determined by the House of Lords was whether the driver could, notwithstanding his deliberate use of the car as weapon, rely upon this agreement. The MIB argued that the well-established principle of insurance law that a person was not entitled to profit from his own wrong should be applied in this case. The House of Lords rejected this, holding that since the satisfaction of the driver's liability to the plaintiff was incidental to the main purpose of the MIB agreement, which was the protection of innocent victims, the principle was not compromised by such a declaration. In argument, the MIB suggested that as the facts showed a deliberate hit and run, the proper source of compensation was not the MIB, but the Board. Lord Hailsham of St Marylebone LC rejected this: 'the two remedies are not necessarily mutually exclusive alternatives and were not designed to be so' (p. 562).

The Board has received a number of applications arising from injuries sustained on the road, but where the victim was, for example, pushed or forced into the path of an oncoming vehicle whose driver is entirely blameless for the ensuing injury (CICB, 1983, para. 25), or simply pushed or forced off his bike (CICB, 1982, para. 29; 1988, paras 43.1–43.2). These are not excluded under para. 11 of either Scheme; indeed such injuries are materially indistinguishable from a case where the offender pushes the victim into a canal or river, or over a cliff or other natural or artificial embankment intending to cause death or personal injury, or being reckless as to whether these are caused. These would also include cases where an offender ties rope or tape across a path causing a cyclist to fall off her bike when hitting it at speed, possibly into the path of a following vehicle (CICB, 1986, para. 26; 1992, para. 23.4). The applicants' claims in these cases succeeded, but the side notes in the Report are misleading in their reference to 'traffic offences'; these are surely straightforward examples of a crime of violence, such as the old authority, *R* v *Martin* (1881) 8 QBD 54 (Chapter 4.3.1). Another example of a criminal injury caused by a crime of violence, though an offence under s. 22A of the Road Traffic Act 1988 had also been committed, concerned a motorcyclist injured when he collided in poor visibility on an unlit road with a pile of debris which had been deliberately placed in the road (CICB, 1995, para. 6.4).

5 Defining and Proving a Personal Injury

5.1 DEFINITION OF PERSONAL INJURY

A criminal injury means one or more personal injuries directly attributable to one of
the three victimising events specified in para. 4 of the old and para. 8 of the new
Scheme. Like the Rules of the Supreme Court 1965 and the County Court Rules
1981, the old Scheme contained no definition of 'personal injury'. Paragraph 3 of the
general Guide to the old Scheme provided that the phrase could include mental
injury, while para. 2 of the *Guide to Child Abuse and the Criminal Injuries
Compensation Scheme* (CICB, 1995, App. H) more helpfully provided that personal
injury meant injury 'of a physical or mental nature, including shock or psychological
disturbance'. Paragraph 9 of the new Scheme is explicit:

> For the purposes of this Scheme, personal injury includes physical injury
> (including fatal injury), mental injury (that is, a medically recognised psychiatric
> or psychological illness) and disease (that is, a medically recognised illness or
> condition).

This closely captures the scope of the phrase as interpreted by the Board. However,
para. 9 then specifies four sets of circumstances only under which an applicant who
sustains mental injury but no physical injury directly attributable to a victimising
event will sustain a criminal injury for the purposes of the new Scheme. These four
categories are dealt with in chapter 5.1.3.3.

5.1.1 Physical Injury

The vast majority of applications to the Board have involved physical injuries to the
person, and call for little further comment. Most of them will have been occasioned
directly by the offender striking, head-butting or kicking the victim, using a knife or
hitting her with a weapon or other object used for the purpose — often bottles and

drinking glasses — even setting the victim on fire or shoving a hot pie into his face, burning him (CICB, 1992, paras 27.1–27.2). In some instances the injury may be indirect, for example, where victims injure themselves while making an escape. A common instance is being struck by a vehicle when running into the road (CICB, 1989, para. 25.9), perhaps to avoid the threat of rape (CICB, 1988, para. 10.1).

In an unusual application the Board awarded compensation to a young and simple girl who had been forced into prostitution by threats of violence (CICB, 1983, para. 20; s. 2 of the Sexual Offences Act 1956). Personal injury may also be sustained where, though there is no immediate physical injury arising from the victimising event, the victim subsequently suffers such injury. For example, in *R* v *Dawson* (1985) 81 Cr App R 150, the victim was working at the cash till in a petrol station when he was threatened with a shotgun and robbed. The victim had a weak heart and a short while later suffered a heart attack and died. Assuming this to be directly attributable to the crime of violence, the victim's death was a criminal injury (CICB, 1987, paras 43–4; see also *R* v *Watson* [1989] 1 WLR 684 (CA)). The Board's 1984 Report records a rare instance of an award being made in respect of injuries sustained by a child in the womb following an attack upon its mother, who was also compensable for her own injuries (CICB, 1984, para. 21). However, where the child is unlawfully killed in the womb, while the mother will be compensable for any injury she sustained in the act causing the child's death, no compensation is payable to the mother in respect of her dead child (chapter 6.3.1).

The old Scheme specifically provided that where a woman had become pregnant as a result of being raped, compensation would be payable for 'suffering and shock', together with an additional sum of £5,000 in respect of any child born alive whom she intended to keep (old Scheme, para. 10). That provision is maintained in para. 27 of the new Scheme (chapter 8.4.1.2.4).

5.1.2 Disease

A man or woman who, for example, contracts a venereal disease or becomes HIV positive as a result of rape or another sexual offence, or is infected with hepatitis B or some other disease as the result of being unlawfully touched by an infected needle or knife, will suffer a personal injury even if no other physical harm is caused (new Scheme, para. 9). This injury will be compensable under the tariff as a medically recognised illness or condition (not being psychiatric or psychological, which are dealt with separately; see chapter 5.1.3.2) or a significantly disabling disorder, where the symptoms and disability persist for more than six weeks after the incident or the date of their onset. Thereafter, the injury is compensable at four levels in the tariff, ranging from the lowest (£1,000) in the case of persistence between 6 and 13 weeks, to level 17 (£20,000) in the case of permanent disability.

5.1.3 Mental Injury

The new Scheme provides that mental injury may result directly from a physical injury sustained by the applicant (chapter 5.1.3.2) 'or occur without any physical injury' (chapter 5.1.3.3). In the latter case, compensation will only be payable if the applicant falls within one of the four categories specified in para. 9(a)–(d). In this respect, the new Scheme follows the common law in *Alcock* v *Chief Constable of South Yorkshire Police* [1992] 1 AC 310 by distinguishing, on the one hand, the conditions which need to be met before mental injury alone may become payable, and on the other, the kind of mental injury which is compensable in any case. This second matter is considered in the following section.

5.1.3.1 Meaning of Mental Injury

At common law the normal emotions of grief, distress and anxiety which a person may experience when she is herself the victim of an unlawful act causing physical injury are not compensable as separate heads, but will be taken into account as part of the award for general damages. It is similarly settled law that if the victim is not herself physically injured, but has witnessed death or injury to a relative (or its aftermath), the shock she sustains, if it constitutes no more than the normal emotions of grief and distress, is not actionable (*Page* v *Smith* [1995] 2 All ER 736; *Vernon* v *Bosley The Times*, 4 April 1996). It will be, however, should the shock amount to 'psychiatric damage' or a 'psychiatric illness'; even if, as Dillon L.J. observed in *Attia* v *British Gas plc* [1987] 3 All ER 455, the phrase 'psychiatric illness' is not readily amenable to definition [1987] 3 All ER 455 at p. 457. As Lord Bridge said in *McLoughlin* v *O'Brian* [1983] 1 AC 410 at p. 431:

> The common law gives no damages for the emotional distress which any normal person experiences when someone he loves is killed or injured. Anxiety and depression are normal human emotions. Yet an anxiety neurosis or a reactive depression may be recognisable psychiatric illnesses, with or without psychosomatic symptoms. So, the first hurdle which a plaintiff claiming damages of the kind in question must surmount is to establish that he is suffering, not merely grief, distress or any other normal emotion, but a positive psychiatric illness.

In its 1986 review, the government was emphatic that the old Scheme should reflect this distinction (Home Office, *Criminal Injuries Compensation: A Statutory Scheme*, London: HMSO, 1986, para. 4.12). It introduced a clause in the Bill which became the Criminal Justice Act 1988 which would have provided that where a criminal injury caused by shock consisted of harm to a person's mental condition, it would only be a qualifying injury if it amounted to a 'psychiatric illness'. However, in the face of considerable opposition, it was withdrawn; neither was it included in the 1990 revision. This therefore left the Board to determine what constituted compensable nervous shock according to common law principles. Referring in particular to the introduction of criminal injuries arising from trespass on a railway line as a victimising event, the Board observed:

It is important to note in these cases, as in all others in which the applicant claims to have suffered stress as a result of an incident, that the Board can only make an award if he/she has suffered some recognised medical illness. The normal stress associated with such an incident would not generally amount to such a condition. (CICB, 1993, para. 19.2).

More generally, para. 10 of the Guide to the old Scheme states:

Whilst the Board will take into account shock and emotional disturbance, and will give more weight to this if the victim is elderly, compensation would not normally be awarded for temporary shock, distress or emotional upset alone if no more than the inevitable reaction to an unpleasant experience.

The new Scheme speaks of 'mental injury' as a species of personal injury, mental injury being in turn defined as a medically recognised psychiatric or psychological illness (see Napier, M., and Wheat, K., *Recovering Damages for Psychiatric Injury*, London: Blackstone Press, 1995, ch. 2). In this respect, it follows the common law distinction. However, the phrase 'mental injury' does not itself appear in the tariff of awards, which refers instead to 'shock' as the heading under which compensation is payable. In note 2 to the tariff, this is elaborated as follows:

Shock or 'nervous shock' may be taken to include conditions attributed to post-traumatic stress disorder, depression and similar generic terms covering:
    (a)   such psychological symptoms as anxiety, tension, insomnia, irritability, loss of confidence, agoraphobia and preoccupation with thoughts of guilt or self-harm; and
    (b)   related physical symptoms such as alopecia, asthma, eczema, enuresis and psoriasis. Disability in this context will include impaired work (or school) performance, significant adverse effects on social relationships and sexual dysfunction.

Thus, irrespective of whether it accompanies a physical injury, or is the only injury sustained, 'shock' is a specific heading within the tariff attracting four levels of award. The lowest (£1,000), is payable in respect of a disabling but temporary mental anxiety which has been medically verified. The other three, all of which are described as a disabling mental disorder, of which the highest is level 12 (£7,500), cannot be verified only by the applicant's GP, but must be confirmed by a psychiatrist.

5.1.3.2 Mental Injury Triggered by Physical Injury
Victims who suffer physical injury as a result of a robbery, or a personal or sexual attack, frequently also suffer mental distress in consequence. This may include flashbacks, reactive depression, trauma, insomnia, nightmares, irritability, loss of confidence and a fear of going out. Examples drawn from the Board's reports include

a woman's acute depression consequent upon the knowledge that following her rape she is now pregnant with the offender's child or has contracted AIDS (CICB, 1988, paras 21.2–21.3 and 22), a police officer's anxiety during the six months that he waited for the outcome of an AIDS test following his being cut by a hypodermic needle used in connection with drug offences (CICB, 1994, para. 7.4), the anxiety suffered by the elderly following a physical or sexual attack (CICB, 1988, paras 21.7, 26–27 and 44–45), and the psycho-sexual damage caused to a child sexually abused by a close relative (CICB, 1988, paras. 20, 24–25).

Where this distress amounts to no more than the normal reaction to a physical assault it would be compensable at common law, in Fleming's words, as 'but another part of the scrambled strands composing the conventional item of pain and suffering' (Fleming, J., *The Law of Torts*, 8th edn., Sydney: Law Book Co., 1992, p. 160). Under the old Scheme, the compensation payable for these various conditions would therefore have fallen within the global sum for general damages. This remains the case for the new Scheme, whose tariff 'includes an element of compensation for the degree of shock which an applicant in normal circumstances would experience as a result of an incident resulting in injury' (new Scheme, Guide, para. 4.9).

If the shock is more severe, amounting to level 1 on the tariff, the applicant will be eligible for an award separate from that relating to the physical injury. This second award is subject to the rules in para. 26 governing the payment of compensation for separate multiple injuries (chapter 8.3.1.2.2).

5.1.3.3   Mental injury as the sole injury

These and other symptoms of post-traumatic stress disorder described above will, however, not be compensable where they are the *only* sequelae of the victimising event; in this case, they themselves must constitute a 'mental injury', and the circumstances in which they were sustained must come within one of the four categories in para. 9. In some instances, the conditions set out in these categories reflect common law principles, while others derive from other aspects of the Scheme's compensation philosophy; together they are intended to clarify a difficult aspect of the old Scheme. These four categories are that the applicant:

(a)   was put in reasonable fear of immediate physical harm to his own person; or

(b)   had a close relationship of love and affection with another person at the time when that person sustained physical injury (including fatal injury) directly attributable to conduct within paragraph 8(a), (b) or (c), and

(i)   that relationship still subsists (unless the victim has since died), and

(ii)   the applicant either witnessed or was present on the occasion when the other person sustained the injury, or was closely involved in its immediate aftermath; or

(c)   was the non-consenting victim of a sexual offence (which does not include a victim who consented in fact but was deemed in law not to have consented); or

(d) being a person employed in the business of a railway, either witnessed and was present on the occasion when another person sustained physical (including fatal) injury directly attributable to an offence of trespass on a railway, or was closely involved in its immediate aftermath.

5.1.3.3.1 *Immediate physical harm to the applicant: the applicant as primary victim* This was one of the two categories to which the 1986 Working Party considered that compensation for mental injury alone should be confined. The Scheme should, it recommended, 'restrict compensation to those persons actually present at the scene of a crime of violence and put in fear of immediate physical injury to themselves or another person' (Home Office, *Criminal Injuries Compensation: A Statutory Scheme*, 1986, para. 4.11). The distinction is similar to that between primary and secondary victims of nervous shock made by Lord Lloyd in *Page* v *Smith* [1996] AC 155. Primary victims are those who could reasonably have been foreseen as likely to sustain personal or psychiatric injury as a result of the defendant's negligence; secondary victims are those who could reasonably have been foreseen as likely to sustain psychiatric injury as a result of the personal injury caused to another person by the defendant's negligence.

The courts (and para. 9(b) of the new Scheme, which is dealt with in chapter 5.1.3.3.2) exert a number of control mechanisms as a matter of policy to limit the number of claims by secondary victims. The new Scheme also limits claims by primary victims. Unlike at common law, where, as Lord Wilberforce said in *McLoughlin* v *O'Brian* [1983] 1 AC 410 at p. 418, '. . . a claim for damages for "nervous shock" caused by negligence can be made without the necessity of showing direct impact or fear of immediate personal injuries for oneself', that is indeed what the new Scheme does require.

The kind of incident that would clearly give rise to compensation is one in which the applicant is the victim of an attempted crime of violence. Whether the failure to complete the offence is due to the intervention of a third party, the offender's ineptitude, or the victim's own skill or luck in avoiding physical injury, if he was put in reasonable fear of immediate harm, and the mental injury he suffers is directly attributable to the attempt, he will be compensable if the shock is of sufficient severity to meet at least level 1 of the tariff.

When referring to being put in reasonable fear of physical harm, para. 9(a) is not limited to being put in that state by crimes of violence. An elderly person who is present while the police are attempting to arrest a number of persons who have committed offences under ss. 1–3 of the Public Order Act 1986 could, if physically close to the event, be put in reasonable fear of physical harm to himself directly attributable to the riotous etc. actions of any of the participants, as well as to the actions of the police officers in seeking to restrain the offenders.

Mental injury may also be sustained by rescuers. If a nurse or those in the fire, ambulance or police services are put in reasonable fear of immediate physical harm to themselves while dealing with a victimising event (for example, during a siege in which the offender is armed and has already shot bystanders or others in these services), they will sustain a criminal injury within the Scheme. The mental injury which a rescuer sustains when dealing with the aftermath of the siege (assume the offender shot a number of children whom he was holding as hostages, before he killed himself) is not a criminal injury within para. 9(a). Nor will it fall within para. 9(b) as the rescuer will not be able to demonstrate the requisite close relationship of love and affection with the children (chapter 5.1.3.3.2).

The issue whether the victim was put in reasonable fear is clearly one of fact, having elements both of subjectivity and objectivity. It is not sufficient that the victim himself was afraid that he might be subjected to immediate physical harm when no other person like him and being of reasonable firmness would be so affected. This test is like that which governs the reasonableness of the defendant's use of force in self-defence. It is not a wholly objective test, but one which relies on standards of common sense, 'bearing in mind the position of the appellant' at the moment of the injury that he purportedly inflicted in self-defence (Ormrod L.J., *R* v *Shannon* (1980) 71 Cr App R 192 at p. 194). If this is correct then the question is whether a person who is like the applicant and of average intelligence and strength would, in the circumstances which the applicant knew or believed to exist at the time, be put in fear. A child or a disabled or otherwise vulnerable victim might well be put in reasonable fear of physical harm in circumstances which a claims officer could conclude were, for a fit adult, only transitory (though immediate) or insubstantial. This test would therefore involve a judgment as to whether the applicant's fear was reasonable at the time, rather than one made with the benefit of hindsight.

It will be noted that para. 9(a) speaks of the applicant being put in fear of immediate physical 'harm', rather than 'injury', to his own person. It is not clear from the Scheme or the Guide why 'harm' was chosen for this purpose. It may be that 'harm' embraces a wider range of detrimental effects on the body than does 'injury'. Thus a person pushed to the ground by an offender and who suffers no cuts or bruises may be said to have been harmed, inasmuch as he suffered some minor and transitory shock, but would deny that he had been injured.

It is also possible for a victim to sustain a mental injury which the offender specifically intended to cause, for example, where a burglar threatens a householder with a knife, or a robber threatens a bank cashier with a sawn-off shotgun. An assault which causes psychiatric injury or harm to another is an offence under s. 47 of the Offences against the Person Act 1861 (*R* v *Chan-Fook* [1994] 1 WLR 689). Discharging a firearm behind a victim in order to scare him or threatening him with a firearm (Firearms Act 1968, s. 16A) could likewise be crimes of violence within para. 8(a) of the new Scheme. A threat to kill, intending the victim to be put in fear that it will be carried out, is an offence under s. 16 of the 1861 Act; it could likewise be regarded as a crime of violence although the external elements of the offence do not require that the victim is in fact put in fear. This offence is well illustrated by an application discussed in the Board's 1986 Report (CICB, 1986, para. 15). The applicant was a divorced woman who, between 1981 and 1984, had been the victim of a series of incidents including death threats, burglary involving criminal damage to her furniture and clothing, phone calls to her son's school saying that he was ill, and the fatal poisoning of her dog. During this time she entered a psychiatric hospital on three occasions, the last as the result of a nervous breakdown. The Board concluded that as the offender (who was thought to be her former husband) was committing offences under s. 16, she was the victim of a crime of violence. A similar case is recorded, though in less detail, in CICB, 1993, para. 29.3.

But if these offences do occasion only mental, and not physical injuries, they will be compensable under the new Scheme only if the applicant was put in fear of *immediate* physical harm. It may not always be easy to demonstrate this. In *R* v *Chan-Fook*, the victim was tied up in a first-floor room in a house he occupied with two others, including the offender. He sustained physical injuries when he tried to escape from the window. Were he an applicant under the new Scheme, he could be compensable both for these physical injuries and for the mental injury which he sustained as a result of his imprisonment. If he had sustained mental injury only (thinking that he might be physically attacked at any time while tied up), he would still have a colourable claim within the conditions specified in para. 9(a) of the new Scheme. This would be so also in the case of the firearms offences, but it is not clear whether the applicant to the Board noted above, who had clearly been the victim of threats, was ever in reasonable fear of *immediate* physical harm at the offender's hands.

This issue is of importance in the context of the mental injury caused to the (typically) female victims by men who 'stalk' or otherwise menace them, for example, by making threatening phone calls, including calls where the offender is silent once his victim picks up the receiver. For the purpose of s. 31(1) of the Criminal Justice Act 1991, whether a threat to kill is a 'violent offence', thus justifying the imposition of a longer sentence under s. 2(2)(b) of that Act is a question of fact (*R* v *Ragg* [1995] 4 All ER 155 (CA)). It is therefore open to a court to ask whether threats made over the phone or by mail were intended by their maker to lead to physical injury (*R* v *Richart* (1995) *The Times*, 14 April 1995 (CA)). Similarly, it is for the claims officer to determine, as a matter of fact, whether the victim's reasonable fear of physical harm was a fear that such harm was immediate. This may be demonstrable where, for example, the victim is sent a bullet with her name engraved upon it (*R* v *Richart*), but neither reasonable fear of physical harm nor immediacy are so easily satisfied in such cases as *R* v *Gelder* (1994) *The Times*, 16 December 1994 and *R* v *Burstow* [1996] *Crim LR* 331, where the threats were of a sexual and personally offensive nature.

In *R* v *Gelder*, the victim had been the subject of obscene telephone calls which had caused her severe psychological and physical problems; in *R* v *Burstow*, the offender had sent hate mail, made silent telephone calls, stolen the victim's clothing and had engaged in a variety of other unpleasant and offensive activities, none of which apparently involved threats of physical harm. The victim suffered grievous harm of a psychiatric nature. If, as in *R* v *Gelder*, the victim does suffer physical injury as a result of the offender's behaviour, then she will be able to invoke para. 8(a) without more, assuming his behaviour to amount to a crime of violence. On facts such as *R* v *Gelder* there would be no difficulty since the offender had been convicted of inflicting grievous bodily (including physical) harm on the victim. Nor, in such a case, would it matter whether the victim was put in fear of physical harm; the claims officer would only need to be satisfied that there was a crime of violence and that the victim suffered a physical injury as a result of it. The mental injury would be compensated as a separate injury arising from that injury (chapter 5.1.3.2).

But if an applicant such as the victim in *R* v *Gelder* or, apparently, *R* v *Burstow*, sustained no physical injury as a result of the offender's behaviour, the claims officer would have to be satisfied that the victim was put in reasonable fear of physical harm and that she feared such harm to be immediate. While such fear need not follow from threats of a sexual and personally offensive kind, even where, as was the case in *R* v *Burstow*, the offender committed a s. 18 offence, the Court of Appeal's decision in *R* v *Ireland* [1997] 1 All ER 112 suggests that personally offensive and silent phone calls can come within the Scheme where the victim sustains mental injury as a result. In this case the defendant was convicted of s. 47 offences as a result of making a series of silent telephone calls to three women. Each suffered a variety of psychological symptoms including palpitations, hyperventilation, anxiety, inability to sleep, and stress. The Court of Appeal held that if the Crown could prove that the victims had suffered actual bodily harm, in this case, psychological harm, and that the defendant intended such harm or was reckless as to whether they would be harmed, then it was open to the jury to convict. As to immediacy, Swinton Thomas L.J. said that (at pp. 115 and 118):

> ... by using the telephone the appellant put himself in immediate contact with the victims and when the victims lifted the telephone they were placed in immediate fear.... [The calls] were just as terrifying as if actual threats had been made.

Whether the victim was placed in immediate fear is a question of fact, but immediacy does not require physical proximity between the victim and the offender. That element can be satisfied by visual as well as aural proximity, as in *Smith* v *Chief Superintendent, Woking Police Station* (1983) 76 Cr App R 234, where, for the purpose of a conviction under s. 4 of the Vagrancy Act 1824, it was necessary to prove that when the accused stood in the garden of a private house looking in at the victim through the window intending to frighten her, he committed an assault. The court held that he had put her in fear of then and there being subjected to violence in that the basis of the fear that he had instilled in her was uncertainty about what he would do next and whether that might involve violence directed against her. Were victims such as those in *R* v *Ireland* and *Smith* v *Chief Superintendent Woking Police Station* to apply, a claims officer could readily conclude that they had been put in reasonable fear of physical harm to their own person.

5.1.3.3.2 *Actual physical injury to another: the applicant as secondary victim*
 5.1.3.3.2.1   Introduction   An applicant who suffers mental injury as a consequence of a physical injury being sustained by a third party (the primary victim) will

be compensable only where he satisfies two conditions; what Napier and Wheat describe in the context of the law of negligence as 'event proximity' and 'relational proximity' (Napier and Wheat, *Recovering Damages for Psychiatric Injury*, 1995, p. 81). Relational proximity exists where there was 'a close relationship of love and affection' between the applicant and the primary victim which subsisted at the time of the application (unless the primary victim has died); event proximity exists where the applicant himself was present and witnessed the injury or was closely involved in its immediate aftermath. It will be seen that these conditions follow recent House of Lords decisions concerning the class of persons, and the degree of their proximity to the event, who may succeed in an action for nervous shock against a negligent defendant who causes injury to the primary victim. Before dealing with these criteria some other points about the scope of para. 9(b), should be noted.

First, the primary victim must sustain a physical injury as defined in para. 9 of the Scheme. Accordingly, an applicant whose mental injury is caused by the fact that the primary victim herself sustained a mental injury (or a disease) directly attributable to a victimising event is outside the scope of para. 9(b). What this subparagraph is primarily intended to cover is mental injury sustained by an applicant who is present while a close relative is physically injured, for example, a parent who witnesses the murder of her child or a husband the rape of his wife.

The physical injury sustained by the primary victim does not itself have to be one which is sufficiently serious to qualify for an award under the Scheme, although of course, it may. Where it is sufficiently serious, but the primary victim would, if he were an applicant, be refused an award by virtue of any of the criteria in para. 13 of the new Scheme (old Scheme, para. 6), the person suffering the mental injury would nevertheless remain eligible for compensation, provided that she was not caught by this paragraph. Similarly, should the primary victim die, the person suffering the mental injury (his dependant) will be ineligible for either the standard award in fatal cases or additional compensation arising from any financial dependency (new Scheme, para. 14), but she will retain her eligibility in her own right for the criminal injury she sustained.

Secondly, the causal test for the link between the injury sustained by the primary victim and the victimising event is the same as it is between the mental injury sustained by the applicant and the victimising event: both injuries must be directly attributable to it (chapter 5.2.2). This can be readily demonstrated in connection with the second of the two categories to which the 1986 Home Office Working Party considered the Scheme should, when dealing with mental injury alone, be confined, that is, 'where the applicant is actually present at the scene of a crime of violence and put in fear of immediate physical injury to ... another person' (Home Office, *Criminal Injuries Compensation: A Statutory Scheme*, 1986, para. 4.11). Suppose that the applicant and his partner, who is of Asian origin, are caught up in a race riot. He suffers mental injury when, having been brushed aside by the rioters, but suffering no great physical harm, he sees his partner carried away and assaulted by a group of young men. The parallel between these hypothetical facts and the Home Office's category is not exact, since the new Scheme does not cover cases where the applicant sustains mental injury by being put in fear of immediate injury to the primary victim; the physical injury must occur. But if that and his mental injury are directly attributable to the rioters' behaviour, then he will sustain a criminal injury.

Thirdly, the injury (or death) sustained by the primary victim may be directly attributable to any of the three victimising events in para. 8 of the new Scheme. The obvious case is, as indicated above, a parent who witnesses his child being the victim of crime of violence. Also within the scope of the paragraph would be a parent who witnessed her daughter sustaining physical injury while engaged in an act of law enforcement within para. 8(c) (chapter 4.5). A rarer case within the paragraph would be a parent who witnesses her son sustain physical injury directly attributable to an offence of trespass on a railway (para. 8(b)); for example, as the train on which he is a passenger approaches the station at which she is waiting for him, a suicide runs in front of the train, causing the driver to break suddenly, as a result of which the passengers are thrown against each other, causing injury. But the train driver's husband, who is also waiting on the platform and who sustains mental injury as a consequence of the mental injury which his wife sustains in attending the suicide will fall outside para. 9(b).

5.1.3.3.2.2   Relational proximity   The 'close relationship of love and affection' in para. 9(b) is based on the first of the two conditions established in *Alcock* v *Chief Constable of South Yorkshire Police* [1992] 1 AC 310 for the purpose of a claim by his relatives for the nervous shock they sustained a result of the injuries caused to the primary victim by the defendant's negligence. That case arose from the desperate events which occurred at Hillsborough football ground in April 1989, when, as a result of the police's negligence in allowing an excessive number of spectators to crowd into one end of the stadium, 95 people died and over 400 were injured. In some instances the victims could be seen, in Lord Wilberforce's words, being 'literally crushed to death' against the wire fencing separating the terraces from the pitch. In determining who might be able to sue for the nervous shock they sustained witnessing the deaths of their relatives live on television or hearing of them later, the House of Lords did not prescribe a list of potential plaintiffs, but held that there must be a close and intimate relationship between the plaintiff and the primary victim of the sort generally enjoyed by spouses and parents and children. Brothers, sisters, aunts and uncles, grandparents and in-laws would normally fall outside this relationship, but, as the decision in *Alcock* itself shows, there are exceptions, such as the primary victim's fiancé.

Whether there is relationship such as that specified in para. 9(b) is a question of fact; a grandmother or an uncle who has lived with the primary victim's family and looked after him (in the absence perhaps of one of the natural parents) may well meet the condition. The relationship must subsist at the time of the application, unless the primary victim is dead (para. 9(b)(i)). Assuming that the other conditions in para. 9 are met, a husband who sustains mental injury directly attributable to the homicide of his wife has a claim for compensation in his own right, independent of any claim for fatal injury arising from her death (that is, the standard amount and/or additional compensation for dependency; see chapter 6.3.3).

5.1.3.3.2.3 Event proximity: presence on the occasion when the other person sustained the injury The second condition introduced in *Alcock* requires proximity in space and time between the injury to the primary victim and the mental injury (nervous shock) sustained by the plaintiff. This proximity can be demonstrated first and most clearly by the fact that the plaintiff herself witnessed the event, as in the examples given above where the applicant was present when his wife or child was the victim of a crime of violence. The applicant may witness the injury by sight or by sound, for example, where the parent or spouse is tied up and left in one room of their home from which he or she can hear the child's or spouse's cries of pain from another room in which the crime is being committed.

By contrast, an applicant who, while watching a football match live on television, sees her husband attacked and injured by the other team's supporters or injured as a result of law enforcement activity by the police, thereby sustaining mental injury, falls outside the scope of para. 9(b). This is so because, though present in time, she is not present in space. Her application under the Scheme would be rejected in the same way that the parents who had watched live on television the harrowing events at Hillsborough football ground in which their children died had their claims rejected. Witnessing the victimising event via a media broadcast does not satisfy the requirement that the applicant be 'present on the occasion when the other person sustained the injury', *a fortiori* where the applicant sees, hears or reads the account in the following day's media and so is proximate neither in space nor in time.

5.1.3.3.2.4 Event proximity: close involvement in the immediate aftermath of the occasion on which the other person was injured By way of alternative, para. 9(b)(ii) provides that the applicant may be sufficiently proximate in space and in time where he can show that he was 'closely involved' in the 'immediate aftermath' of the injury to or death of the primary victim. This second phrase echoes the common law, where the plaintiff may recover who sustains nervous shock when he comes upon the immediate aftermath of the defendant's negligence (*Ravenscroft* v *Rederiaktiebolaget Transatlantic* [1992] 2 All ER 470 (CA)). The question which therefore arises is whether the Authority will follow the common law's restrictive interpretation of this kind of event proximity, or adopt a more relaxed approach. If it wished to do so, the justification could lie in the differing policy and causal tests operated at common law and under the Scheme. The common law requires that the injury be reasonably foreseeable; the Scheme, that it be directly attributable to the victimising event. The Divisional Court confirmed in *R* v *Criminal Injuries Compensation Board, ex parte Johnson* (1994) 21 BMLR 48 (DC) that while the foreseeability of injury was a factor which the Board could take into account in determining whether the applicant's mental injury was directly attributable to the victimising event, the Scheme expressly imposes a different causal test to that which governs negligently inflicted nervous shock. Moreover, when considering the preliminary question of the extent of the duty of care, there is no need to ask, in addition to the question whether the plaintiff was sufficiently proximate, whether it is just, fair and reasonable to impose a duty not to cause such injury.

Close involvement. Paragraph 9(b)(ii) requires the applicant to be 'closely involved' in the immediate aftermath to the victimising event. This suggests some physical involvement or engagement on the applicant's part in the aftermath of the event. A clear case is where the applicant himself is engaged in activity, to borrow a phrase from para. 12(b) of the new Scheme, 'directed to containing, limiting or remedying the consequences of a crime' (or other victimising event). This could include giving first aid to the victim or consoling him; accompanying the victim to hospital; or being involved in a search for the primary victim (as in the case of child abduction). Thus an applicant who arrives home from work to discover that her partner is lying unconscious having been physically injured during a burglary, would be closely involved in its aftermath when she endeavours to give him first aid while waiting for the police and ambulance to arrive. The second question in this instance is whether that close involvement occurs in the 'immediate' aftermath of the victimising event, it having occurred some hours earlier. We return to this point below.

The requirement of close involvement suggests, as at common law, that mental injury occasioned by being informed by the police or another third party that the primary victim has been physically injured as the result of a crime of violence will not satisfy the Scheme's requirements. Although such information may be given only a very short time after the occasion on which the primary victim was injured, the applicant would, though arguably proximate in time, not be physically proximate to its aftermath. But, to adapt an example from *Street on Torts* (Brazier, M., ed., 9th ed., London: Butterworths, 1993, p. 201), a mother who, on being told by the police of an injury to her son directly attributable to one of the victimising events in para. 8, on arriving at his bedside in hospital within the hour, then sustains mental injury at the sight of his injuries, would meet this requirement: she would at that point be sufficiently proximate, both physically and temporally. It may be that even where the mother travels some miles to the hospital at which her son is being treated, she would still satisfy the requirement of physical proximity. This would be so because 'close involvement' does not signify physical proximity to the place at which the injury was inflicted on the primary victim, but physical proximity to the place of its aftermath; these may, but need not be, one and the same place. By contrast, her husband who sustains mental injury when she phones him from the hospital, would not satisfy this condition. His mental injury arises not from his close, but his distant (spatial) involvement in the aftermath of the injury.

At common law, sufficent proximity is not established where the plaintiff is asked to identify his relative's dead body (*Alcock* v *Chief Constable of South Yorkshire Police* [1992] 1 AC 310 at 348 (CA)). But the reasoning behind the rejection in *Alcock* v *Chief Constable of South Yorkshire Police* of claims for nervous shock arising from cases such as this, and where the plaintiff is told of a relative's death, was that the plaintiff's injury was not reasonably foreseeable. This is not the causal test employed in the Scheme; accordingly it may be open to a claims officer to conclude that where an applicant satisfies the temporal condition, being asked to identify the body of a person with whom he had the kind of relationship described in para. 9(a) will amount to 'close involvement', that is, physical involvement, in the aftermath of the victimising event causing death, and thus that the mental injury he sustained as a result will be directly attributable to it.

Immediate aftermath. The second requirement of para. 9(b)(ii) is proximity in time between the applicant's close involvement and the aftermath of the occasion giving rise to the primary victim's injury: it must be 'immediate'. This could be satisfied, for example, where a parent leaves her child in her car while she walks the few yards around the car park corner to withdraw money from a bank cash dispenser, and returns a few minutes later to discover that her child has been abducted. Alerting the police, she assists in a search, consoling her child when she is found some hours later. Any mental injury she sustains does not fall within the first limb of para. 9(b)(ii) because she neither witnessed nor was present on the occasion when her child was injured, but would be sufficiently proximate in time to satisfy this element of the second limb.

'Immediacy' implies that the time lag between the initial injury to the primary victim and the mental injury sustained by the applicant be of short duration. In the case of a physical attack, this would normally mean seeing the primary victim within minutes or perhaps a few hours of the victimising event. A clear example is where the applicant's daughter arrives home in an extremely emotional and hysterical condition, to say that she has been raped. A second is provided by the facts in *R* v *Criminal Injuries Compensation Board, ex parte Johnson* (1994) 21 BMLR 48 (DC) (chapter 5.2.2), where the applicant sustained mental injury when she returned home from work to find that her partner had been murdered by an intruder. The Northern Ireland case, *O'Dowd* v *Secretary of State* [1982] NI 210 (CA) is similar to this: the shock sustained by the applicants when they came home to find the dead bodies of three of their close relatives who had been murdered earlier that day was held to be sufficiently proximate to the crime of violence. It may confidently be expected that such facts would warrant an award under the new Scheme. Similarly, if upon arrival at his home, the applicant were to be met by the police who had already arrived in response to a neighbour's phone call that she had heard shots being fired in the house and had seen a man hurriedly drive away, and then be taken at once by them to a hospital where his parents were being treated in an accident and emergency department or on a ward, as was the case in *McLoughlin* v *O'Brian* [1983] 1 AC 410, the mental injury thereby sustained may well be regarded as sufficiently immediate (and his presence at his parents' bedside 'close involvement').

At common law, 'immediacy' need not imply only close temporal proximity. In the context of most cases involving a physical attack on the primary victim, 'immediate' takes its significance in part from the fact that the event itself was of short duration and in part from the lapse of time between the event and the injury to the primary victim. But suppose that the applicant does not discover for some days or even weeks after the incident, that his parents were the victims of a crime of violence, for example, where she returns from a month's holiday or work abroad to find her parents murdered in their home. Unlike the facts in *ex parte Johnson*, the mental injury in this case is not sustained in the immediate aftermath of the crime of violence, if 'immediate' is to be construed in a strictly temporal sense. But it is immediate if, rather than focusing upon the lapse of time between the infliction of the injury and the applicant's discovery of its aftermath, one looks instead at the lapse of time between the applicant's discovery of the aftermath of the injury to the primary victim and her own mental injury. The mental injury which she sustains in the hours following this discovery could satisfy the requirement of immediacy if one took the view that until her return, she could not have been closely involved in the aftermath, but once that opportunity had arisen, she was immediately so involved.

Therefore, if the applicant can establish that he has sustained a mental injury which is directly attributable to his discovery of and physical ('close') involvement in the aftermath of a crime of violence committed against a person of the kind specified in para. 9(b), he may be regarded by a claims officer as satisfying the condition set out in para. 9(b)(ii). This interpretation may meet the following facts. Suppose that the applicant's daughter had, unknown to her, for many months been the victim of sexual abuse at the hands of the applicant's common-law husband, her husband having left the matrimonial home a year earlier. In consequence of her later discovery of this abuse following the abuser's departure, the applicant sustains mental injury. On similar facts the Board has awarded compensation (CICB, 1991, para. 14.5); but would she be successful under the new Scheme? The applicant herself may have been mentally injured immediately upon discovering the facts, but she was not, it seems, closely involved in the immediate aftermath of the offences against her daughter, both because the offences (and the aftermath of each of them) had taken place over a period of time, and because there was a delay between their cessation and their revelation to her. The question of fact for the claims officer will be, after what lapse of time between the injury to the primary victim (in this case, say, the last offence against the daughter) and its discovery by the applicant will the mental injury no longer be directly attributable to its immediate aftermath? If the applicant's mental injury was sustained when she first had the opportunity to become closely involved in the aftermath of the injury to her daughter, and then was so closely involved, for example, accompanying her daughter to a medical examination and to counselling sessions, she may satisfy para. 9(b)(ii). Such a case may be distinguished from one in which her husband, learning of this abuse, visits his daughter but otherwise has no involvement in the counselling or other medical treatments. Any mental injury that he sustained would fall outside the scope of this paragraph.

5.1.3.3.3 *Non-consenting victims of sexual offences*   Mental injury alone which is directly attributable to a sexual offence is not a criminal injury unless 'the applicant was the non-consenting victim of a sexual offence (which does not include a victim who consented in fact but was deemed in law not to have consented)'; in other words, the applicant must, subject to the point below concerning children, in actuality have been a non-consenting victim. In the case of an adult victim, this means, for example, that a woman who consents to sexual intercourse with a man who impersonates her husband is not within the new Scheme if she only sustains mental injury on discovering the truth, notwithstanding that the man commits rape (s. 1(3) of the Sexual Offences Act 1956). Likewise, if she should consent because the man deceives her as to the nature of the act, for which he may be guilty of rape (*R* v *Linekar* [1995] QB 250), or because when marrying her, he committed bigamy. In this latter case, even if there were an indecent assault on each occasion they had 'marital' sexual intercourse (a proposition which may be questioned), the applicant would be unsuccessful because she had consented in fact to the act of intercourse. This would be so also where the man deceived the applicant as to some other characteristic for which, though not guilty of rape, he might be guilty of the offence in s. 3 of the 1956 Act (procuring sexual intercourse by false pretences).

By ss. 14 and 15 of the Sexual Offences Act 1956, victims under the age of 16 cannot in law consent to indecent assault. They are unlike adult victims whose consent in fact was obtained by fraud and therefore of no legal effect who are excluded from para. 9(c): a child can never consent to indecent assault. As indecent assault is the basis of offences under ss. 5 and 6 of the Act (unlawful sexual intercourse with girls under 13 or 16 years of age respectively), incest (ss. 10 and 11), and buggery (ss. 12 and 16), it follows that mental injury alone sustained by such children is compensable notwithstanding that they did in fact consent.

5.1.3.3.4 *Trespass on a railway* Where train drivers come across the bodies of successful or would-be suicides, the injuries they sustain will typically be mental rather than physical. Having limited mental injury to the three categories in para. 9(a)–(c), were it not for para. 9(d), train drivers would be unable to pursue compensation claims for mental injury unless it accompanied a physical injury, such as could occur if the driver braked the train so hard that he injured himself by falling in his cab.

Paragraph 9(d) provides that mental injury alone is a criminal injury where it is sustained by a person employed in the business of a railway, who either witnessed and was present on the occasion when another person sustained physical (including fatal) injury directly attributable to an offence of trespass on a railway, or was closely involved in its aftermath. Though it may seem entirely arbitrary, the nurse, ambulance driver, police or fire brigade officer who answers an emergency call to give assistance to the train driver and who sustains the same (or worse) mental injury will fall outside the Scheme. It might be argued that these rescuers, unlike the drivers, have been trained to cope with the aftermath of such events, but this will not be true of the passenger who assists the driver (*Chadwick* v *British Railways Board* [1967] 1 WLR 912) who is likewise outside the Scheme.

The scope of trespass on a railway was dealt with in chapter 4.4, and it will be seen that para. 9(d) relies on the same proximity conditions as para. 9(b) (chapter 5.1.3.3.2). Paragraph 9(d) provides that the exceptional risk requirement, which applies to accidental injuries sustained while a person was engaged in any activity directed to containing, limiting or remedying the consequences of a crime, does not apply to mental injury sustained as described in para. 9(d). If this were not so, a train driver's mental injury would be a criminal injury only where, for example, he risked his own life moving the suicide out of the path of an oncoming train.

5.2   ESTABLISHING THE CRIMINAL INJURY

For a personal injury to be a criminal injury it must be directly attributable to one of the three victimising events defined in para. 4(a)–(c) of the old Scheme or para. 8(a)–(c) of the new. The two matters considered in this section are first, what will be required to prove to a claims officer's satisfaction that such an event occurred, and secondly, the question of causation.

5.2.1   Proof of a Victimising Event

As it has constituted by far the most common victimising event considered by the Board, the discussion will focus on the need to prove that an injury was sustained as the result of the commission of a crime of violence (old Scheme, para. 4(a); new Scheme, para. 8(a)).

The Scheme has never required a conviction to be recorded against an offender; this is maintained in para. 10 of the new Scheme, which states that 'It is not necessary for the assailant to have been convicted of a criminal offence in connection with the injury'. Neither has the nature of the sentence been relevant to the Board's decision whether the conduct of the alleged offender fell within para. 4(a). Nor, except in the case of applications arising from intra-family violence (chapter 6.4), is a prosecution necessary. What is required is that the alleged offender's conduct can be shown, on the available evidence and on the balance of probabilities (new Scheme, paras 19 and 64), to amount to a crime of violence. Formal evidence of such an offence is essentially supplied by the requirement that the victim report the circumstances to the police.

A conviction for a crime of violence, which has occurred in 40–50% of the applications which the Board has received, will almost invariably constitute compelling proof of this aspect of an application. Nevertheless, both the Board and the Authority must exercise their discretion to determine whether or not the applicant is within the terms of the Scheme. Moreover, even where they are satisfied by the conviction that the injury was a criminal injury, their hands are not tied concerning their discretion to refuse or reduce an award because of the applicant's or, in fatal cases the victim's, conduct or character (old Scheme, para. 6(c); new Scheme, para. 13(d)–(e)). Notwithstanding that a jury has by its verdict rejected evidence of self-defence, the Board or the Authority may reduce the award if it thinks that that is appropriate in view, for example, of the victim's conduct before, during or after the incident. However, it would be incongruous to reject an application altogether on the basis that the victim was entirely to blame in such a case (chapter 7.5.3.1).

A conviction for an offence other than a crime of violence, though obviously not directly to the point, may neverthless assist the claims officer to conclude that the conduct complained of does fall within para. 8(a). Such was the case where the Board held that a crime of violence had occurred when some factory apprentices, as a practical joke, pushed the applicant into a tank of caustic solution causing him 58% burns, and for which they were convicted under s. 7(a) of the Health and Safety at

Work etc. Act 1974 (CICB, 1982, para. 28). Although the Report is not explicit, the Board would have been able to conclude that the apprentices had committed a crime of violence, s. 47 of the Offences against the Person Act 1861 being an obvious possibility. The burns would certainly have constituted actual bodily harm, and it would not be difficult to regard their behaviour as being, on a civil standard of proof, reckless.

Neither is it relevant that the alleged offender is immune from conviction. Until the 1990 revision, the old Scheme provided that 'in considering ... whether any act is a criminal act, any immunity at law of an offender, attributable to his youth or insanity or other condition, will be left out of account'. The scope of this provision was considered in *R* v *Criminal Injuries Compensation Board, ex parte Webb* [1987] QB 74. In one of the applications heard in that case, the deceased was an 84-year-old man who had been run over by a train driven by the applicant, though the coroner's jury evidently considered the deceased was not capable of knowing what he was doing, since they returned a verdict of accidental death rather than suicide. The Board dismissed the train driver's application. It argued that 'immunity' in the Scheme meant immunity from prosecution, and that since there was nothing in the deceased's condition to preclude a prosecution, the fact that he would not have been convicted had he been prosecuted under s. 34 of the Offences against the Person Act 1861 meant that there was no crime of violence. The Board further argued that it could not proceed as though he were in full possession of his faculties.

This reasoning could lead to a difficult problem. The suicide would not have been convicted presumably because his mental state would have precluded him from satisfying the fault element of s. 34. What then of a person of low intelligence who makes a mistake about facts which, if true, would justify his actions? Or indeed, what of any offender who could not be convicted because he had available to him an excuse which, if sufficient to raise a reasonable doubt in the mind of a jury, is incompatible with any one or more of the fault or external elements of a crime of violence? As was suggested earlier (chapter 4.3.2.2), the fact that the defendant in *Director of Public Prosecutions* v *Morgan* [1976] AC 182 honestly believed the victim to be consenting would never stand in the way of the Board's concluding that she was indeed raped, though her 'rapist' may be acquitted. The difficulty in *ex parte Webb* was not that the suicide was immune either from prosecution or conviction, but that he may simply have been unable to form the appropriate fault element of a crime of violence.

On the facts of the particular application the Court of Appeal affirmed the Divisional Court's decision that the words 'or other condition' in that version of the old Scheme were apt to include a lack of mental capacity due to old age. Accordingly the question for the Board was whether a crime of violence had been committed assuming the deceased were in full possession of his faculties. On this basis the Divisional Court held that there was no apparent reason to suppose he would have escaped conviction ([1986] QB 184 at p. 187), but, as we have seen, it also held that there was no criminal injury because s. 34 of the Offences against the Person Act 1861 is not a crime of violence.

The difficulty encountered in *ex parte Webb* is present also in applications by nurses and others working in psychiatric and geriatric hospitals who have been injured by a patient (CICB, 1991, para. 33.7). To remove any doubt about the possibility of concluding that there was a crime of violence in such cases, para. 4 of the old Scheme was revised:

> In considering for the purposes of this paragraph whether any act is a criminal act a person's conduct will be treated as constituting an offence notwithstanding that he may not be convicted of the offence by reason of age, insanity or diplomatic immunity.

The new Scheme is in substantively identical terms (new Scheme, para. 10):

> Moreover, even where the injury is attributable to conduct within para. 8(a) in respect of which the assailant cannot be convicted of an offence by reason of age, insanity or diplomatic immunity, the conduct may nevertheless be treated as constituting a criminal act.

It will be seen that the phrase 'immunity at law' was changed in the 1990 revision, and that the new Scheme maintains the substitution of diplomatic immunity. The phrase 'immunity at law' allowed the Board to treat as criminal injuries, personal injuries caused, apart from those under the age of criminal responsibility, which is eight in Scotland and 10 in England and Wales (and see *C (A Minor) v Director of Public Prosecutions* [1996] AC 1), by alleged offenders who were unfit to plead, or who possessed diplomatic immunity or an immunity offered to a prosecution witness. In *ex parte Webb* the Divisional Court held that 'immunity' meant 'immunity from conviction', a decision which prompted the Working Party to recommend that the Scheme specifically cater for diplomatic immunity (Home Office, *Criminal Injuries Compensation: A Statutory Scheme*, 1986, para. 4.15). Accordingly, in the case of an offender who is, as a matter of fact or law, immune from conviction for one of the reasons specified in para. 10, the claims officer will be required to consider whether, had he not been so, he could, on a balance of probabilities, have been convicted of a crime of violence.

Because it does not include 'or other condition', neither the 1990 revision nor the new Scheme seemingly covers applications in which the alleged offender is offered immunity by the prosecution; but cases of this sort pose no real difficulty. A decision by the Crown Prosecution Service not to prosecute in exchange for the offender giving evidence against others does not deny that an offence was committed or that the offender might be convicted of it. Unlike cases in which the alleged offender has diplomatic immunity, is below the age of responsibility or is in law insane or unfit to plead, such a decision is only an exercise of the CPS's prosecutorial discretion, and that decision, if it results in no prosecution being brought, would not preclude a claims officer from holding that a crime of violence had been committed if the evidence supported such a finding.

Convictions for crimes of violence have figured in approximately half of the applications made to the Board. For the rest, the failure to secure a conviction will principally be due to the fact that the assailant was unknown. In a small number of cases, though known, the alleged offender was not charged. Where there is no conviction, the question for the Board is whether the requisite fault and external elements of a crime of violence can be inferred from the facts as reported to and verified by the police. In such cases, the claims officer must first be satisfied that there is sufficient evidence to warrant a finding that the injury was caused by a crime of violence, rather than being accidentally sustained (CICB, 1993, para. 17.4: applicant sustained injury by inhaling smoke from a fire on board a ship but which could not be attributed to arson), or self-inflicted (CICB, 1991, para. 17.3; 1992, paras 17.4 and 26.14), possibly as a consequence of falling over while drunk (CICB, 1994, para. 6.4; 1995, para. 6.4).

Assuming the injuries to have been caused by another's actions, examples of the kind of reconstruction which the Board has made include: an applicant who cut her arm when pushing her hand through the glass door to her home after being tapped on the shoulder by the offender (CICB, 1979, para. 20: assault occasioning actual bodily harm); a passenger in a light aircraft who was killed when the pilot recklessly attempted a barrel roll (CICB, 1983, para. 19: manslaughter; and see *R* v *Warburton-Pitt* (1990) 92 Cr App R 136); and an applicant who sustained injury to the skin and underlying flesh as a result of sitting on an object to which superglue had been previously applied (CICB, 1983, para. 20: assault occasioning actual bodily harm).

The Board's Reports are also replete with examples of applications which have been dismissed because they did not satisfy these criteria. Sometimes they simply disclose no offence; for example: where the victim alleged that a group of people were using radio equipment to hurt her (CICB, 1986, para. 18); or where the victim cut her arm when pushing her hand through her kitchen window to scare away a man who had been peering in at her (CICB, 1985, para. 22). Sometimes the offender could have been convicted of an offence, but only a crime against property, despite harm being caused to the applicant; as for example where the victim suffered bronchitis by inhaling butane gas fumes emitted by a blowlamp left in the fridge by a burglar (CICB, 1987, paras 19–21).

A third type of case is where the injury could clearly constitute the external elements of a crime of violence, but the question is whether the offender had the requisite fault element. Where that includes recklessness, the question must be determined according to whether the subjective or the objective test is appropriate to the offence which the facts could sustain (chapter 4.3.2.2). Although, as noted earlier, nurses and others may come within the Scheme where they are injured by patients in their care striking them, for example, while in an epileptic fit, the Board concluding that if they had been possessed of their faculties, they could have formed the requisite fault element, some such injuries, for example, being bitten while trying to give sugar to a diabetic suffering a hypoglycemic episode, may amount to no more than an accident (CICB, 1991, para. 17.3).

The need to conclude that the person causing the injury could have the fault elements of a crime of violence has posed some difficulties for the Board, in particular where children injure each other when firing airguns or playing with fireworks (CICB, 1986, para. 17). In its 1990 Report the Board noted that during a six-month period it had received some 130 applications arising from injuries caused by airguns fired by children. The difficulty associated with determining whether the child was subjectively reckless is exacerbated by the fact that many of the injuries are very serious, involving irreparable damage to the victim's eyes, or significant deterioration in his vision; facial scarring is also a common disfiguring injury (CICB, 1990, paras 14.1–14.3). Similar difficulty arises in connection with injuries which are sustained as a consequence of over-robust tackling in football, rugby and other contact sports (CICB, 1986, paras 34–7; 1987, para. 37). If it can be demonstrated that the player causing the victim's injury was, at the time, acting outside the rules of the game, for example, by late tackling (CICB, 1993, para. 17.5) or throwing a punch (CICB, 1989, para. 25.3), the Board has been able to conclude that there was a crime of violence. But if a child under 14 cannot appreciate the seriousness of the offence (*L* v *Director of Public Prosecutions* (1996) *The Times*, 31 May 1996 (CA)), or all that can be inferred is that the children or the participants were negligent, then the injury is not a criminal injury (CICB, 1989, paras 16.3 and 16.5; 1993, para. 28.16).

In a minority of applications heard by the Board a prosecution has resulted in the acquittal of the 'offender'. Where the acquittal follows a successful defence, for example, of alibi, there can be no objection to the conclusion that there was nevertheless a crime of violence, but it was committed by someone else. Likewise where the acquittal is the consequence of the application of evidential or procedural rules particular to the criminal trial, there need be no incompatibility between that verdict and a claims officer's decision that on the balance of probabilities the injury was a criminal injury. Besides operating to the lower standard of proof, neither the Board nor the Authority is constrained by rules precluding, for example, hearsay or opinion evidence; in the case of the offender's prior convictions, however, there is an important difference between the old and new Schemes (chapter 7.5.3.2.1).

There remains a small number of applications which pose a slightly different problem, namely where the application of the substantive criminal law of excuses has led to an acquittal. Instances of such applications were discussed earlier in this chapter. Clearly there does not have to be a conviction for there to have been an offence; yet if someone has been acquitted precisely because he believed in facts which negatived a necessary element of a possible offence under paras 4(a) or 8(a), can we say that the personal injury is a criminal injury? It surely seems perverse that where the offender is never tried the Board or the claims officer is free to determine that there was, though the offender's beliefs are never examined and might indeed have resulted in an acquittal; yet where they were and they did, there would be no criminal injury. Nor need the perversity apply only in respect of a failure to satisfy the fault element of a crime of violence. The injury may have been sustained in circumstances which would support a defence of automatism, thus negativing a necessary aspect of its external elements. Here too, the victim seems better placed if the offender is never prosecuted.

One way out of this apparent dilemma is simply to acknowledge that while there has been an acquittal on one charge, other offences which would satisfy paras 4(a) or 8(a) have, on the balance of probabilities, been committed. Where, on a charge of rape, the accused honestly believes that, despite her physical resistance which he sought to overcome by force, the woman was consenting, there may still be an offence, for example, under s. 47 of the Offences against the Person Act 1861. But this analysis would only hold good so long as there was another possible offence the fault and external elements of which could be attributed to the accused. A second approach is to attend to the differing standards of proof employed by the Scheme and within the criminal trial. A jury must acquit a man accused of rape if the prosecution have not proved beyond a reasonable doubt that he did not believe there was consent, but this doubt is quite compatible with their taking the view, on a balance of probabilities, that he did not. Thus although the facts cannot satisfy the demands of the criminal standard of proof, they may be sufficient to satisfy the civil standard. The conclusion which follows, that there was a criminal injury, is analogous to the Court of Appeal's decision in *Gray* v *Barr* [1971] 2 QB 554, where, notwithstanding the defendant's acquittal, he was said by Lord Denning MR to have committed manslaughter ([1971] 2 QB 554 at p. 568). Only if the Board or the claims officer were to conclude that the facts would not sustain, on a balance of probabilities, the fault and external elements of a crime of violence, can it be said that the personal injury was indeed not a criminal injury.

But this resolution too is essentially flawed, since it is dependent on standards of proof, and if they were to change, then an acquittal would surely also require the conclusion that the victim did not sustain a criminal injury. To maintain the view that a victim may sustain a criminal injury notwithstanding that the offender's beliefs or ability to control his behaviour are wholly inconsistent with the fault and external elements of the offence charged, it is necessary also to adopt the view that, whatever the outcome of the prosecution, the prima facie illegality of the conduct complained of remains. As noted earlier, this was in essence the view taken by the Court of Appeal in *R* v *Cogan* [1976] QB 217.

5.2.2 Causation

The test of causation under the Scheme has been, and continues to be, that the injury is 'directly attributable' to the victimising event. This phrase was considered in *R* v *Criminal Injuries Compensation Board, ex parte Schofield* [1971] 1 WLR 926 and in *R* v *Criminal Injuries Compensation Board, ex parte Ince* [1973] 1 WLR 1334. In *ex parte Schofield*, the applicant was knocked down and injured either by a store detective or the man whom he suspected of theft and was chasing. The Board dismissed the application on the ground that the Scheme was not intended to compensate injuries to bystanders accidentally injured by someone else engaged in law enforcement activity, but Lord Parker C.J. held that the Scheme was not so limited (chapter 4.5.3). As to the question whether the applicant's injuries were directly attributable to the law enforcement activity, his Lordship said that the phrase meant that the victimising event must be a *causa causans* of the injury, and not merely a *causa sine qua non* ([1971] 1 WLR 926 at p. 930; CICB, 1987, para. 17).

The decision on this issue signifies no more perhaps than that a but-for test is a precondition of any test of remoteness. Of much greater significance was the Court of Appeal's decision in *ex parte Ince* that 'directly attributable' did not mean 'solely attributable' but directly attributable in whole or in part to a state of affairs which existed or which the victim believed to exist, even where the intervening cause was the wrongful act of the injured person or of a third party. On the first point Megaw L.J. said ([1973] 1 WLR 1334 at p. 1344):

> ... personal injury is directly attributable to any of the matters [in paragraph 4(a) and (b)], if such matter is, on the basis of all the relevant facts, a substantial cause of personal injury. It does not need to be the sole cause. By the word 'substantial' I mean that the relationship between the particular cause and the personal injury is such that a reasonable person, applying his common sense, would fairly and seriously regard it as being a cause.

As in negligence, an intervening cause will not necessarily extinguish a plaintiff/victim's eligibility if the original cause continues to be operative. The victim noticed an argument between a man and a group of youths in a car park. As he went to assist him, the man briefly escaped the youths and got into his car, reversing it at high speed so as to get away from them. In so doing, he accidentally struck and killed the victim. On the basis of the initial assault on the driver, the Board was able to conclude that the victim's death was directly attributable to a crime of violence (CICB, 1992, para. 25.8). But in the 1986 Working Party's view, Lord Denning's dictum in *ex parte Ince*, that the injury would only cease to be attributable to the original cause where the intervening event was 'so powerful a cause as to reduce the original event to a piece of the history' (p. 1341) went too far, permitting the Scheme 'to cover injuries sustained in a much wider range of circumstances than was originally intended' (Home Office, 1986, para. 4.9). It recommended 'that the statutory scheme should include a more stringent test of remoteness which clearly conveys the need for a very close and immediate link between the offence and the consequent injury' (Home Office, *Criminal Injuries Compensation: A Statutory Scheme*, 1986, para. 4.10).

There was, however, no change in the 1990 revision to the old Scheme. The new Scheme maintains the same test of remoteness, the Guide stating (para. 7.8):

> You will only be compensated for injuries directly resulting from a crime of violence or threat of violence [or either of the other two victimising events]. This means that we must satisfy ourselves, on the basis of all the available facts, that not only was the incident in which you were injured a crime of violence [or either of the other two victimising events], but also that the incident was the substantial cause of your injury.

It is unclear whether the apparent anomaly that arose in *R* v *Criminal Injuries Compensation Board, ex parte Parsons* (1982) *The Times*, 25 November 1982 will recur. There a train driver suffered mental injury when he found a decapitated body of a suicide lying by the railway line. Given that the Board had conceded that the original act of the deceased constituted a crime of violence (chapter 4.3.1), the question which arose was whether the shock suffered by the train driver was directly attributable to that offence. Both the Divisional Court (with some misgivings) and the Court of Appeal disagreed with the Board, and held that it was. The Board considered it anomalous that the Scheme's test could produce a sufficient causal link between the suicide and the shock, but that this would not be so on the foreseeability test applicable in the law of negligence. In *R* v *Criminal Injuries Compensation Board, ex parte Johnson* (1994) 21 BMLR 48 the Divisional Court was invited to reconsider the question whether the offender's foresight of mental injury to the secondary victim was relevant in a case where the primary victim had been killed as a result of his commission of a crime of violence. Observing that its drafter could have very readily incorporated such a test into the Scheme, the court held that *ex parte Parsons* was correctly decided, but added (per Kay J. at p. 53):

> Whilst foreseeability is in no way the test for entitlement to compensation, clearly the less foreseeable a consequence of an event is, the more difficult it may be to establish the necessary causal link. Thus it would not be improper for the Board to have in mind foreseeability in determining whether the evidence established causation in a case such as this.

In any event, it is questionable whether the difference between the two tests of remoteness will lead to anomalous results between what an applicant/plaintiff could receive under the new Scheme by comparison with a successful civil action. Crimes of violence typically require intention or recklessness and are for civil purposes akin to assault, battery and the other intentional torts; their test of remoteness is also one of directness. In addition, para. 8(b) only extends to trespass on a railway, thus excluding the possibility of personal injuries caused by negligent conduct constituting criminal injuries. Accordingly, in most cases there would be no difference in the test applicable to applications under the Scheme and those available in an action in tort.

6 Eligible Persons

6.1 INTRODUCTION

Paragraphs 4, 15 and 16 of the old Scheme and paras 6, 37 and 38 of the new Scheme (Act, s. 1(2)(b)) specify those to whom awards of compensation may be made. The categories of eligible persons are the same under both Schemes. These persons are, with one minor exception, natural persons. The exception is that such legal persons as local authorities may be eligible for compensation for funeral expenses. The heads of compensation payable and the method by which compensation is assessed are the subject of chapter 8. Besides any restrictions mentioned in these paragraphs, there is a further group of persons who may be refused an award, notwithstanding that they have sustained criminal injuries. This group comprises those who, broadly speaking, have been victimised by intra-family violence. Here, too, the old and new Schemes impose similar conditions upon their eligibility. This chapter deals first with the categories of eligible persons, distinguishing between applications concerning personal and fatal injuries, before turning to the category of potentially ineligible persons.

6.2 COMPENSABLE PERSONS: PERSONAL INJURIES

6.2.1 Adult Victims

Paragraph 4 of the old Scheme provides that the Board will entertain applications for *ex gratia* compensation in any case where the applicant sustained a criminal injury. The new Scheme is in virtually identical terms, save for the omission of the reference to compensation being *ex gratia* (new Scheme, para. 6(a)). This paragraph also specifically recognises that the 'applicant' need not be the same person as the victim. In the case of adult victims this contemplates applications made on behalf of those who are incapable, by reason of mental disorder as defined in the Mental Health Act 1983, of managing and administering their property and affairs. Both the old and the new Schemes make special provision for such applications (old Scheme, Guide, para. 47; new Scheme, Guide, para. 3.10).

6.2.2 Child Victims

In cases in which the victim is under 18 years of age, the application will be made by an adult with parental rights over the child. Both the Board and the Authority give guidance to parents wishing to make claims for compensation on behalf of their children (old Scheme, App. H; new Scheme, Guide, para. 3.7). In non-wardship cases, the Official Solicitor makes application in the Chancery Division to be appointed guardian of the child's estate, in order to have the necessary standing to conduct the application and to accept an award (CICB, 1989, para. 26.2). In Scotland a curator or tutor may perform the same function.

Most applications on behalf of children are for physical injuries suffered at school or while the child is otherwise in a public place (CICB, 1989, para. 25.1; 1992, paras 26.23 and 27.1). They may also involve a sexual assault by a stranger (CICB, 1994, para. 5.9) or someone, other than a member of the child's family (see chapter 6.4), who is known to the child — sometimes the child's babysitter (CICB, 1990, para. 22.7; 1992, para. 14.5; 1994, para. 5.9). A less usual application would be one made on behalf of a child born disabled as the result of sustaining a criminal injury while in the womb, the injury being directly attributable to a crime of violence committed against its mother (CICB, 1984, para. 21; compare *Burton* v *Islington Health Authority* [1993] QB 204 where the Court of Appeal held that at common law an unborn child has a cause of action against the defendant for the injuries he negligently inflicted on the child while in the womb). Similarly, if an offender were to give a pregnant woman a drug in circumstances constituting an offence under ss. 23 or 24 of the Offences against the Person Act 1861 and the drug causes no harm to her but causes the child to be born disabled, there would be a criminal injury for the purposes of both Schemes. Applications on behalf of a child injured in the womb are quite separate from any application that the mother may make arising from the offence committed against her, or, where the child was conceived as a result of rape, in respect of her keeping the child (see chapter 8.4.1.2.4).

Where one or both of the parents were responsible for the injuries, with the result that the child is in care, the application will be made by the local authority. A practice direction issued by the Family Division provides that where a child is a ward of court and has a right to make a claim for compensation, application must be made by the guardian *ad litem* for leave to apply and to disclose to the Board such documents on the wardship proceedings as are considered necessary to establish eligibility and quantum. If leave has not been given by the judge at the wardship hearing the guardian may make an application *ex parte* to a registrar or, where no guardian has been appointed, by the local authority's director of social services or by any other person having care and control of the child (*Practice Direction (Ward: Criminal Injury)* [1988] 1 WLR 33). Where an application for leave to apply to the Authority is made by the Official Solicitor acting as the guardian *ad litem*, the court should consider only whether the claim for compensation is arguable and whether it is in the child's interest to pursue it. It is not for the court, but for the Board (now the Authority) to evaluate whether the claim has been made out (*Re G (A Minor) (Ward: Criminal Injuries Compenstion)* [1990] 1 WLR 1120 (CA)). While it would be normal practice for the application for leave to be made *ex parte*, so that the child's assailant (in *Re G*, her father) would have no knowledge of it, even in a case where the assailant did know and strenuously opposed it, the Official Solicitor's special position as guardian *ad litem* means that it would be rare for leave to be refused.

Applications by directors of social services in respect of physical or sexual abuse of children now in their care rose substantially during the 1990s as local authorities became increasingly aware of the Scheme. Both the Board and the Authority publish guidelines on applications relating to child abuse (old Scheme, App. H; new Scheme, *Child Abuse and the Criminal Injuries Compensation Scheme*). In its 1991 Report the Board began to record the overall total of applications made on behalf of children who had suffered abuse, commencing with the figures for 1989–90 (4,825). Within that figure it identified the number of applications arising from sexual abuse (1,318) and, as a further subset, the number of cases of sexual abuse within the family (802). By 1995 these figures had risen to 13,162, 6,787 and 3,025 respectively. The total had increased by 173%. Some of this increase is attributable to applications arising from abuse suffered while the children were themselves in care. During 1993–94 and 1994–95, the Board had some 150 such applications under consideration (CICB, 1994, para. 5.3; 1995, para. 5.3).

Child abuse cases currently comprise some 9% of all applications. Unlike the majority of applications by adult victims, they are typically very time consuming and, as the harrowing examples which the Board give demonstrate (CICB, 1990, para. 22.6; 1991, paras 14.4–12; 1992, paras 14.4, 14.6–10; 1994, para. 5.9; 1995, para. 5.9), call for 'a particularly sensitive and sympathetic approach' (CICB, 1991, para. 1.8). When dealing with these cases the Board has usually sought to minimise any further distress for the child, for example, by not calling the victim of sexual abuse to give evidence at a hearing if there is adequate medical and other evidence.

One of the major difficulties which these applications pose is that they frequently relate to injuries sustained many years before the application is made. Where the abuse occurred before 1979 and was inflicted by a person who was living with the child as a member of the child's family, no compensation is payable under the terms of the Scheme then in force. As we have seen (chapter 1.4.3), the Court of Appeal held in *R v Criminal Injuries Compensation Board, ex parte P* [1995] 1 WLR 845 that, notwithstanding that the 'same roof' rule had been modified from 1979, its continued application to claims arising before that date was lawful. Accordingly, some 16 years on, the Board (as does the Authority) has continued to emphasise the effect of para. 7 of the pre-1979 Scheme, 'to avoid encouraging false expectations' (CICB, 1995, para. 5.8).

Applications arising from child abuse within the family or in a children's home will typically be made after the normal time limit for applications has expired: three years under the old Scheme, two under the new (see chapter 7.2.1). Nevertheless, the

Board has 'invariably' accepted an application made while the victim is still a child (CICB, 1990, para. 16.3: applicant 16, abused between the ages of 8 and 10; 1991, para. 14.10: applicant 16, abused between the ages of 9 and 13; 1992, para. 14.7: applicant 17, abused between the ages of 8 and 13; 1994, para. 5.9: applicant 17, abused between the ages of 7 and 11). The Board has taken a similarly sympathetic approach where victims themselves make an application within a reasonable time of reaching maturity (CICB, 1991, para. 14.4: applicant 19, abused between the ages of 8 and 16; para. 16.5: applicant 18, abused by her father between the ages of 7 and 11 and threatened at the time that the police would not believe her if she told them; para. 16.6: applicant 30, abused by her father between the ages of 9 and 19, father recently convicted of offences against her), but would refuse the application where it is now impossible to verify the abuse (chapter 7.2.2).

Where the offence against the child was committed by a stranger, the Board would normally require a prosecution to have taken place, though it has always recognised the particular difficulties which will be encountered in connection with the giving of evidence by a child. In the case of intra-family abuse, where no prosecution has taken place, the Board would require an explanation on the child's behalf. In the absence of a conviction, what the Board has looked for is opinion evidence from the police that the incident occurred; a finding of fact by a judge in a wardship hearing will be conclusive. Medical reports indicating vaginal or anal interference, psychological and school reports may also provide sufficient evidence when taken in conjunction with police reports.

Assuming the injury is made out, both the old and the new Schemes impose two further conditions: first, that an award will not be made where it is likely that an assailant will benefit (old Scheme, para. 7; new Scheme, para. 15(a)), and second, that an award will not be made if it would not be in the child's interest (old Scheme, para. 8(c); new Scheme, para. 15(b)). The first of these conditions is not restricted to the proven or suspected offender, but extends to any assailant whom the Board or the Authority considers will benefit; this could, for example, include a party to the assault against whom no proceedings were taken. Neither the old nor the new Scheme gives discretion to make a reduced award if it appears that there is a possibility (old Scheme) or a likelihood (new Scheme) that an assailant would benefit. If such benefit is possible, then no award can be made.

The award must also not be against the child's interest. Commenting on this condition, Denyer suggests that 'relevant circumstances would include consideration of factors such as whether an award might exacerbate family tensions, whether a family reconciliation might be hindered and whether the child might have to undergo distressing medical examinations or suffer the distress of giving oral evidence' (Denyer, R., *Children and Personal Injury Litigation*, London: Butterworths, 1993, para. 9.7). Some of these points are illustrated by Board decisions. In one case an application was made by a local authority on behalf of two children aged three years and six months respectively who had been injured by their parents. They had both recovered well from their injuries, and the Board member 'declined to make any awards as he felt that receipt, at a later stage, of somewhat minor awards could lay the children open to unpleasant and potentially dangerous revelations of their natural parents' treatment of them' (CICB, 1990, para. 22.8; new Scheme, Guide, para. 9.2). Similarly, where the applicant had been sexually abused by her brother from the age of 6 to 13 and had been taken into care, the Board considered that it would be against her interest to make an award as she had since returned to the parental home. There was, moreover, the possibility that the brother might have benefited from it (CICB, 1994, para. 6.14).

Where the award is less than £1,000, it will normally be paid to those having parental responsibility for the child, who may now be the child's foster or adoptive parents (CICB, 1993, para. 28.14), unless the claims officer considers that the assailant would benefit from it. This provision applies irrespective of the age of the applicant, though in the case of a child, it is of greater significance inasmuch as the child has no status to accept an award. Where the child continues to live in the same household as the assailant, the Board, 'conscious of the need to ensure that children who have suffered abuse are fully and properly compensated for their suffering' (CICB, 1995, para. 5.5), would invest the money, to be released with the interest upon the child's majority. The Authority will adopt the same practice. The condition which precludes an award where the victim and the offender are still living together in the same household (chapter 6.4) does not apply to cases where the victim is a child (old Scheme, para. 8(b); new Scheme, para. 16(b) and Guide, para. 9.5). Where the child is in care, the local authority will normally be expected to be responsible for the investment and management of the award (CICB, 1993, para. 29.4).

6.3   COMPENSABLE PERSONS: FATAL INJURIES

6.3.1   Fatal Injuries Sustained in the Womb

The intentional or reckless killing of a child in the womb is neither murder nor manslaughter (*Attorney-General's Reference (No. 3 of 1994)* [1996] 2 WLR 412 (CA)). Accordingly, no compensation is payable in such circumstances to its dependants. On the other hand, such killing may amount to the offence of child destruction under the Infant Life (Preservation) Act 1929 or an abortion offence under s. 58 of the Offences against the Person Act 1861. In that event, if the mother sustained a personal injury as a result of the offender's commission of either of these offences, she may be eligible for compensation in her own right (CICB, 1991. para. 33.9).

If a child should survive a criminal injury inflicted on its mother and be born alive but later die as a substantial result of injuries sustained while in the womb, the assailant may be guilty of either murder or manslaughter (*Attorney-General's Reference (No. 3 of 1994)*). In this event, the mother would be eligible for compensation in respect of her child's death (which would be limited to the standard award of £10,000 for a single claimant) as well as for any compensation for the injury she sustained.

6.3.2 Non-survival of Compensation

In tort law, s. 1 of the Law Reform (Miscellaneous Provisions) Act 1934 provides that any cause of action possessed by an individual on his or her death survives for the benefit of his or her estate whether death was caused by the defendant's tort or otherwise. Independently of this, the Fatal Accidents Act 1976 provides that if an individual's death was caused by tort, the deceased's dependants may sue the tortfeasor for compensation for loss of support and, under s. 1A, a limited class will be eligible for a fixed bereavement award. At common law the primary significance of the survival of the victim's cause of action was to give the estate the benefit of the conventional sum for loss of expectation of life, abolished by s. 1(1)(a) of the Administration of Justice Act 1982.

When the Scheme was first devised, it was thought inappropriate that this award should be payable from public funds and so it was excluded, limiting compensation in fatal cases to dependants (though this class was then more narrowly drawn than under the Fatal Accidents Act 1976 or the Damages (Scotland) Act 1976) and to those non-dependants who incurred reasonable funeral expenses (old Scheme, para. 15). The new Scheme is in similar terms: 'Where the victim has died in consequence of the injury, no compensation other than funeral expenses will be payable for the benefit of his estate' (new Scheme, para. 37). Thus, even if compensation for pre-death injury had been payable to the benefit of the deceased's estate in *Hicks* v *Chief Constable of the South Yorkshire Police* [1992] 2 All ER 65 (HL), it would not, if the victim's death by asphyxiation were intentionally caused so as to lead to criminal liability, survive under either the old or the new Scheme.

6.3.3 Qualifying Claimants

Paragraph 4 of the old Scheme provides that the Board will entertain applications for *ex gratia* payments of compensation from a spouse or dependant of a person who sustained a criminal injury and who later died. Under the new Scheme, compensation may be paid in such cases to applicants who are 'qualifying claimants' (see para. 7 of the Authority's *Guide to Applicants for Compensation in Fatal Cases*, Issue Number One 4/96; reproduced in Appendix 5). Both Schemes then distinguish between cases in which the victim died in consequence of the injury (old Scheme, para. 15; new Scheme, para. 37), and those in which she died from other causes (old Scheme, para. 16; new Scheme, para. 38). Even where the victim sustained a criminal injury in respect of which the Board did not exercise its discretion under para. 6(c) of the old Scheme, it could nevertheless refuse or reduce compensation if it considered the dependant(s) to be undeserving as defined in those ways (chapter 7.5.2.1). The new Scheme likewise provides that para. 13, under which an award may be refused or reduced on the grounds, *inter alia*, of non-cooperation, conduct or character, 'will apply in relation both to the deceased and to any applicant' (new Scheme, para. 14), and that compensation may be payable to a 'qualifying claimant' subject to the application of para. 14 (new Scheme, para. 38).

For the purpose of paras 15 and 16 of the old Scheme, the words 'dependant' and 'relative' have the same meaning as they are given respectively by s. 1(3) of the Fatal Accidents Act 1976 and sch. 1 to the Damages (Scotland) Act 1976. This includes the deceased's spouse or former spouse, brothers, sisters, aunts and uncles, the deceased's children and parents, and a person who was living with the deceased immediately before his death and who had been living with him in the same household for the past two years as his spouse. A change made in the 1990 revision was that cohabitees could make an application for loss of support. When the Administration of Justice Act 1982 extended the class of dependants in the Fatal Accidents Act 1976 to persons who had been living with each other as husband and wife for at least two years immediately before the death, the Scheme was amended so as to maintain their non-eligibility. The 1986 Working Party, which recommended that the conditions attaching to applications arising from domestic violence (chapter 6.4) should apply also to cohabitees, did not believe that the factors which had prompted the imposition of those conditions 'justify the exclusion of people who have enjoyed a stable relationship as unmarried husband and wife of which there is ample evidence' (Home Office, *Criminal Injuries Compensation: A Statutory Scheme*, London: HMSO, 1986, para. 5.6). However, as in tort law under the 1976 Act, cohabitees are not eligible for the bereavement award.

In order to dissociate itself from the resonance of a fatal accident action, the new Scheme deliberately does not refer to dependants or to relatives, but to 'qualifying claimants'. This is a term of art in the new Scheme which is defined in para. 38 as meaning:

(a)   the deceased's spouse or a former spouse who was financially dependent on the victim immediately before the date of death;

(b)   a parent, whether or not the natural parent, provided that the parent was accepted as such by the deceased; and

(c)   a child (who may be of any age), whether or not the natural child, provided that the child was accepted as such by, or was dependent on, the deceased.

Like the old Scheme, the definition of 'spouse' also includes:

(d)   'a person who was living with the deceased as husband and wife in the same household immediately before the date of death and who, if not formally married to him, had been so living throughout the two years before that date' (para. 38(a)(i)).

The new Scheme is thus limited to (*Guide to Applicants for Compensation in Fatal Cases*, para. 7): the deceased's husband or wife, parents, children, or a former spouse who was financially dependent on the deceased at the time of death though they were not living together. A former spouse living apart from, and not financially dependent on the deceased is not a qualifying claimant. A child or a parent may be the deceased's natural child or parent, or one accepted by the deceased as a member of the family. The definition of child is not restricted to persons under 18 years of age. Uncles, aunts, grandparents and siblings are excluded. Included are long-term partners in heterosexual relationships. Though not formally married, a person who lived with the deceased as husband and wife in the same household immediately before the date of death and had been so living for at least two years is a qualifying claimant. But long-term partners in a homosexual relationship are, not as was the case under the old Scheme (HC Debs, Standing Committee A, col. 172, 20 June 1995).

6.3.3.1 Death caused by the criminal injury

Those who are dependants within s. 1(3) of the Fatal Accidents Act 1976 (or relatives under the equivalent Scottish law) can, under para. 15 of the old Scheme, be awarded compensation assessed on the basis of the principles that apply to fatal accident actions. This includes compensation for bereavement, and, in Scotland, loss of society. Compensation for bereavement in England and Wales is payable to any person falling within s. 1A(2) of the Fatal Accidents Act 1976, which, as just noted, excludes cohabitees. Their compensation is otherwise assessed on the same principles as apply to actions under the 1976 Act, which principally concern loss of support.

Under para. 38 of the new Scheme, compensation is payable to qualifying claimants in respect of the 'standard amount of compensation, dependency, and loss of parent', save that the 'standard amount of compensation' is not payable to a former spouse of the deceased, even though the spouse may be a qualifying claimant for the purposes of loss of dependency (new Scheme, para. 39). The 'standard amount of compensation' in these cases is the new Scheme's equivalent of the bereavement award (new Scheme, para. 39; chapter 8.5.2). 'Dependency', known elsewhere in the new Scheme as 'additional compensation', is calculated in essentially the same manner as loss of dependency under the 1976 Act (new Scheme, para. 41; chapter 8.5.3.1). 'Loss of parent' is a new ground of compensation, based on loss of society in Scots law, applicable where the claimant is under 18 years of age at the time of the victim's death (new Scheme, para. 42; chapter 8.5.4). The 1996 tariff Scheme thus substantially meets the criticisms made of its unlawful predecessor, which provided only for a bereavement award in cases where the victim died as a result of the criminal injury. Both the old and the new Schemes also provide that a reasonable amount of compensation for funeral expenses may be awarded to any person incurring them, 'even where the person bearing the cost of the funeral is otherwise ineligible to claim under this Scheme' (old Scheme, para. 15; new Scheme, para. 37). The phrase 'otherwise ineligible' is apt to cover a local authority (chapter 8.5.3.2).

Occasionally the victim may survive the immediate injuries caused by the victimising event and die from them some time later. If, while he was still alive, he became entitled to compensation from the Board or the Authority, an application may nevertheless be made for the payment of any of the heads of compensation payable under the applicable Scheme (old Scheme, para. 15; new Scheme, para. 43). In both cases, such applications are subject to the time limits applicable to the reopening of cases: three years in the case of the old Scheme, two in the case of the new (chapter 2.3.4). Any award payable in response to such an application will be reduced by the amount of the compensation paid to the victim while he was alive, save for the standard amount of compensation (or bereavement), and funeral expenses (new Scheme, para. 43). The total of compensation payable to the victim and any qualifying claimants under the new Scheme in respect of the same injury is £500,000 (new Scheme, paras 23 and 43).

6.3.3.2   Death from Other Causes

By para. 16 of the old Scheme, where the victim died otherwise than in consequence of the injury, the Board could make an award to a dependant (or relative) for loss of wages, expenses and liabilities incurred by the victim before his death. It is implicit in para. 16 that if the victim had made a successful application for compensation during his lifetime, no compensation would be payable to the dependants since the award to him would have fully covered these items up to the time of death. If an interim award only was made prior to the victim's death, a dependant may be made an award under the terms of para. 16, though it too will be reduced by the amount of the interim award.

The new Scheme makes similar provision. 'Where the victim has died otherwise than in consequence of the injury, compensation may be payable to a qualifying claimant only under para. 44 (supplementary compensation)' (new Scheme, para. 38). 'Supplementary compensation' is limited to loss of earnings and special expenses; this may be payable to a qualifying claimant who was financially dependent on the deceased within the terms of para. 40 of the Scheme (chapter 8.5.1.2), whether or not any application was made by the victim prior to her death (new Scheme, para. 44). As with the old Scheme, no compensation is therefore payable in these cases in respect of funeral expenses or bereavement.

Whereas in the case where the victim died as a result of the criminal injury, loss of dependency is calculated from the date of death, if the victim died from other causes, loss of earnings is calculated only after the first 28 weeks of loss. This is so, of course, because where the victim survives her injuries, compensation for loss of earnings is payable only after this time (chapter 8.4.2.1). Special expenses are those expenses incurred by the victim or someone caring for her, where the victim 'has lost earnings or earning capacity for longer than 28 weeks as a direct consequence of the injury (other than injury leading to his death), or, if not normally employed, is incapacitated to a similar extent' (new Scheme para. 35), in connection with the purchase, for example, of special equipment or adaptations to the victim's accommodation (chapter 8.4.2.2.3). An award may be reduced or refused because of the action, conduct or character of either the deceased or the applicant (new Scheme, para. 14); if made, the total payable to the victim (if he made an application during his lifetime) and the qualifying claimants shall not exceed £500,000 (new Scheme, para. 44).

6.4 POTENTIALLY UNCOMPENSABLE PERSONS: DOMESTIC VIOLENCE

When first established, the old Scheme excluded applications arising from incidents of domestic violence. The factors which were then persuasive — the difficulty of establishing the facts and of distributing blame, the possibility of fraud, and the administrative problem of ensuring that the offender does not benefit — were reviewed by the Home Office in 1978 (Home Office, *Review of the Criminal Injuries Compensation Scheme, Report of an Inter-departmental Working Party*, London: HMSO). As counsel argued in *R v Criminal Injuries Compensation Board, ex parte P* [1994] 1 All ER 80 at p. 83 (DC), this rule 'sweeps too broadly in its exclusions; it discriminates arbitrarily and unfairly between different classes of citizen, bearing in mind that girls are more commonly than boys the victims of sexual abuse; and it lacks any rational nexus or proportionality between the Secretary of State's legitimate aims and the means employed to achieve those aims'. The Working Party recommended that the rules be changed to permit such applications, subject to strict qualifications. These are contained in para. 8 of the old Scheme. They provide that compensation will not be paid unless:

(a) the person responsible has been prosecuted in connection with the offence, except where there are practical, technical or other good reasons why a prosecution has not been brought; and

(b) in the case of violence between adults in the family, the Board is satisfied that the person responsible and the applicant stopped living in the same household before the application was made and seem unlikely to live together again.

For the purposes of para. 8, 'a man and a woman living together as husband and wife shall be treated as members of the same family'. 'Living together' was interpreted by the Divisional Court in *R v Criminal Injuries Compensation Board, ex parte Staten* [1972] 1 WLR 569 by giving that phrase its 'ordinary sensible meaning', without reference to divorce law. In this case relations between the husband and wife were bad, and following the husband's release from prison, having been convicted of cruelty to his wife, they slept apart and had no sexual relations. Neither did the wife undertake any cleaning or cooking for her husband. But they were in other respects living together as a family, and on the facts of the case, Lord Widgery C.J. found that they were 'living together as members of the same household', and upheld the Board's rejection of the wife's application arising from an assault committed by her husband. Similarly, an applicant divorced from the victim but living with him when he was murdered was not entitled to compensation under the Scheme, the Board on this occasion applying *Payne-Collins v Taylor Woodrow Construction Ltd* [1975] QB 300 (CICB, 1980, para. 22). The scope of the phrase was taken further in *R v Criminal Injuries Compensation Board, ex parte Fox* (unreported, 8 February 1972) where the applicant was assaulted by the brother of the man with whom she was living, the brother also living in the same house. While there was clearly no familial relationship between them, the court upheld the Board's rejection of the applicant's claim on the ground that she was living together with her assailant in the same household.

When first introduced there was a further condition, that the injury met a higher (£500) minimum loss than the normal case, and, as noted (chapter 6.2.2), para. 8(c) of the old Scheme provides that an award will not be made to a minor if it is against her interest. Though regarded as an 'important advance' by the Board (CICB, 1980, para. 9), there was a limited response to this change to the Scheme. Given the preconditions to compensation and the circumstances of much family violence, there was, not surprisingly perhaps, a very high proportion of rejected applications. The main reasons for rejection were (and often more than one reason might apply): a failure to reach the £500 threshold, the victim and offender continuing to live together, a failure to report without delay, and want of prosecution. A notable feature of the rejected applications to which the Board drew attention was the role played in these cases by the excessive consumption of alcohol; the applications also often disclosed a history of violence. The 1986 Working Party was satisfied with the approach taken by the Board, and saw little scope for amendment (Home Office, *Criminal Injuries Compensation: A Statutory Scheme*, 1986, para. 8.1).

Paragraph 16 of the new Scheme makes the same provision for these applications. Where 'at the time when the injury was sustained, the victim and any assailant (whether or not that assailant actually inflicted the injury) were living in the same household as members of the same family', an award will be withheld unless the conditions in para. 16(a) and (b) are met. As under the old Scheme, a man and a woman living together as husband and wife will be treated as members of the same family. The two conditions are:

(a)   that the assailant has been prosecuted, except where the claims officer considers 'that there are practical, technical or other good reasons why a prosecution has not been brought' (para. 16(a)); and

(b)   that the claims officer 'is satisfied that the applicant and the assailant stopped living in the same household before the application was made and are unlikely to share the same household again' (para. 16(b)).

Paragraph 16(a) is in virtually identical terms to para. 8(a) of the old Scheme, and it must expected that claims officers will exercise their discretion according to the same criteria as members of the Board. There is no guidance from the Board's Reports on the exercise of this discretion, but the 1978 Working Party identified the inability of the victim to give evidence, lack of corroborative evidence, and the possibility that the offender might be dead or could not be traced as factors which might justifiably explain why a prosecution had not been brought.

The second condition is, similarly, substantively the same as para. 8(b) of the old Scheme. The exercise of this discretion can be exemplified from the Board's reports. Thus an award was made where the victim and the assailant had been living apart for 14 days prior to the attack (CICB, 1989, para. 21.2); and where, though the assailant lived in the same house, this was at the applicant's mother's invitation and against the applicant's wishes, the applicant spending most of her spare time in the company of her fiancé and his family (CICB, 1993, para. 28.15). But an award was not made where the victim indicated on her application form that she and her assailant might live together again 'if things work out' (CICB, 1991, para. 25.2); or having been raped or otherwise injured by him, she later married her assailant (CICB, 1991, para. 25.3; 1994, para. 24.2) or resumed living with him (CICB, 1994, para. 24.3), or attempted a reconciliation (CICB, 1995, para. 6.14); or she invited him to stay the night in breach of his bail condition not to go within a mile of the applicant's house (CICB, 1991, para. 25.4); or she simply continued to live with her assailant (CICB, 1991, paras 25.5–6). An award was withheld even where the victim, being registered blind and partially disabled, continued to live with the assailant (her husband) upon whom she was wholly dependent (CICB, 1990, para. 22.2). While recognising that it may work harshly in some circumstances, the government was not disposed to amend the 'same roof' rule for the new Scheme (HL Debs, vol. 566, col. 1393, 31 October 1995):

> ... there can be occasions when it is difficult for, let us say, the woman to leave the home where she has been subjected to violence. I fully understand that. Nonetheless, if she is someone who is subjected to violence and a domineering husband, and she remains in the home, those are precisely the circumstances — and there is no getting away from it — where it is likely that any award which she obtained would not go to benefit her, but would be liable to be taken over and used by the man whose violence caused the award to be made in the first place.

Neither the Board nor the Authority will make an award where there is a likelihood that the assailant will benefit from it (old Scheme, para. 7; new Scheme, para. 15(a)). Thus even where the applicant had her own flat, the fact that her assailant (her former boyfriend) had a key to it raised the possibility that he might benefit from any award made to her (CICB, 1994, para. 6.14). Nor, where the application is made by or on behalf of a child, will an award be made if it is against the child's interest (old Scheme, para. 8(c); new Scheme, para. 15(b)). As the Authority observes in para. 9.3 of the Guide to the new Scheme, these considerations, 'while they apply to all cases, are particularly relevant to the situation where the victim and the offender were living together in the same household as members of the same family'.

7   *Eligibility*

7.1   INTRODUCTION

Assuming that the victim has sustained a criminal injury which falls within the scope of the Scheme (chapter 4), there are a number of conditions which he or his dependants (or relatives) must satisfy if an application for compensation is to succeed. Section 3(1)(a) of the Act permits the new Scheme to make provision for 'the circumstances in which an award may be withheld or the amount of compensation reduced'. The provision which has been made is 'largely based on the equivalent provisions of the earlier tariff scheme and of the existing scheme, where discretion is provided and is routinely exercised' (HC Debs, Standing Commmittee A, col. 198, 20 June 1995). Some of the conditions of eligibility have been alluded to in previous chapters; this chapter will examine them in detail. These conditions are:

    (a)   that the application must be made within two years (three under the old Scheme) of the date of the incident which gave rise to the injury (new Scheme para. 17; old Scheme, para. 4);

    (b)   that the compensation payable must be not less than the minimum amount (new Scheme, para. 24; old Scheme, para. 5);

    (c)   that the applicant must without delay take all reasonable steps to inform the police or an appropriate authority of the circumstances of the injury, co-operate with them in bringing the offender to justice, and give them (in particular the Board or the Authority) all reasonable assistance in connection with the application (new Scheme, para. 13(a)–(c); old Scheme, para. 6(a)–(b)); and

    (d)   that the applicant's conduct before, during or after the events giving rise to the application, or his character as shown by his criminal convictions or by evidence available to the claims officer (or, in the case of the old Scheme, instead of this latter formulation, by his unlawful conduct), do not make an award inappropriate (new Scheme, para. 13(d)–(e); old Scheme, para. 6(c)–(d)).

Whereas non-compliance with either the limitation period (assuming it has not been waived) or the financial minimum means that no award will be made, failure to comply with the other conditions may lead either to no award or to a reduced award. There are also other provisions designed to prevent a person responsible for causing the injury from benefiting from an award to the victim and affecting intra-family violence; these were dealt with in chapter 6.4. As will become clear, the eligibility rules of the new Scheme will in the main operate on the same lines and with the same criteria as the 1990 Scheme, a point on which the government gave one of its golden assurances (HC Debs, Standing Commmittee A, col. 208, 22 June 1995).

7.2 LIMITATION OF ACTIONS

7.2.1 Time Limit

There has always been a time limit on the making of an application. Under the original Scheme applications had to be made 'as soon as possible', but it was thought more appropriate that the same limitation period as is applicable to civil actions for personal injury should be required (Home Office, *Review of the Criminal Injuries Compensation Scheme: Report of an Interdepartmental Working Party*, London: HMSO 1978, ch. 9; HC Debs, Standing Commmittee A, col. 193, 20 June 1995).

But if harmony with analogous areas of law is what was sought, *Stubbings* v *Webb* [1993] AC 498 (HL) suggests that the appropriate period is six years, not three. The respondent in this case issued a writ in 1987 when she was over 30 years of age, claiming damages for mental injury allegedly caused by the sexual and physical abuse committed by the respondents, her stepbrother and stepfather, against her as a child between the ages of two and 14. The question was whether her action was an 'action for damages for negligence, nuisance or breach of duty' within s. 11(1) of the Limitation Act 1980 or was 'an action founded on tort' within s. 2 of that Act. If it were the former the three-year period of limitation for personal injury actions ran from the date on which the appellant 'first had knowledge . . . (a) that the injury was significant' (s. 14(1)), whereas if it were the latter, the absolute limit of six years specified in s. 2 ran from the date on which she reached her majority (s. 28). The House held that the injuries which she alleged had been caused by the respondents were not personal injuries as defined in s. 11(1), which carried with them 'the implication of a breach of duty of care not to cause personal injury, rather than an obligation not to infringe any legal right of another person' (per Lord Griffiths at p. 508). His Lordship continued, 'If I invite a lady to my house one would naturally think of a duty to take care that the house is safe but would one really be thinking of a duty not to rape her?' His Lordship concluded that 'cases of deliberate assault such as we are concerned with in this case [the allegations included rape and indecent assault] are not actions for breach of duty within the meaning of [s. 11(1)] of the 1980 Act)'. It follows from this that all offences against the person, if they give rise to a civil action, will be actions founded on tort (trespass to the person) to which the six-year limitation period will apply (the European Court of Human Rights subsequently confirmed that this limit entails no violation of Article 14 of the Convention; *Stubbings* v *United Kingdom, The Times*, 24 October 1996).

Be that as it may, the three-year limitation period was introduced in 1969 'because of the difficulties involved in investigating late claims, in many of which the original documentation is no longer available ... police involvement and medical evidence at the time can often not be confirmed because records have been destroyed' (CICB, 1995, para. 3.4; para. 7.3 of the Guide to the new Scheme is in virtually identical terms). As Lord Carlisle of Bucklow observed during the debates on the Bill (HL Debs, vol. 566, col. 693, 17 October 1995):

A person who puts in a claim two years nine months after the event may not remember the exact date when the assault occurred. He may not even remember the month in which it occurred. One then starts numerous cross-correspondence with the police force — the applicant having claimed that he reported the incident at the time — to try to chase down a criminal offence about which the applicant has no clear recollection. . . . a great deal of time is taken up in pursuing claims that are put in shortly before the end of the three-year time limit.

Initially, the Board was also mindful of the possibility of being unable to verify alleged evidence of criminal injuries arising in connection with the commission of sexual offences. Paragraph 7 of the pre-1990 revision to the old Scheme provided that it would 'have special regard' to any delay in the reporting of such offences where the relationship between the victim and the alleged offender was such that it might be difficult to establish the facts. In these cases simple compliance with the three-year limit could have been insufficient.

While the 1986 Working Party saw no need to alter the three-year limit (Home Office: *Criminal Injuries Compensation: A Statutory Scheme*, London: HMSO, 1986, para. 4.14), the Home Office's initial tariff proposals contemplated a reduction to one year: 'this will help the scheme administrators predict the work flow and the future costs of administration and compensation more readily' (Home Office, *Compensating Victims of Violent Crime: Changes to the Criminal Injuries Compensation Scheme*, Cm 2434, London: HMSO, 1993, para. 27(i)). During the first year of its short life, the Authority's staff automatically waived the one-year limit in the unlawful tariff Scheme, and continued to exercise the discretion to accept applications under the old Scheme beyond the three-year limit in accordance with the established criteria (CICB, 1995, para. 3.7).

Under s. 3(1)(e) of the Act, the Scheme may include provision 'requiring claims under the Scheme to be made within such periods as may be specified by the Scheme'. 'In the light of experience' (HC Debs, Standing Committee A, col. 193, 20 June 1995), the period was reduced by one year only in the new Scheme to two years. Even this was controversial, with attempts being made during the debates to reinstate the three-year time limit. Concern was expressed that applicants would be disadvantaged where their claims arose from sexual offences committed against them in childhood. In the Commons, the Minister's response was to confirm that the discretion then operated by the Board to waive the time limit would be incorporated into the new Scheme (HC Debs, Standing Committee A, col. 194, 20 June 1995). As we shall see, that is indeed what has happened. Also influential in this debate were Lord Carlisle of Bucklow's remarks during the committee stage in the Lords. Welcoming the change, the Chairman of the Board observed that the reduction to two years would be an improvement in the Scheme: 'It will encourage people to make application at a time when incidents can be more easily investigated' (HL Debs, vol. 566, col. 694, 17 October 1995). The Chairman also observed that in practice the reduction will make little difference since the vast majority of claims are made very shortly after the injury.

7.2.2 Implementation

By para. 4 of the old Scheme, 'Applications for compensation will be entertained only if made within three years of the incident giving rise to the injury, except that the Board may in exceptional cases waive this requirement'; and by para. 17 of the new, an application:

> ... should be made as soon as possible after the incident giving rise to the injury and must be received by the Authority within two years of the date of the incident. A claims officer may waive this time limit where he considers that, by reason of the particular circumstances of the case, it is reasonable and in the interests of justice to do so.

It will be seen that both the old and new Schemes give a discretion to waive the time limit. In 1994 the Board received 3,704 applications out of time, of which it allowed 2,715 (CICB, 1994, para. 3.7); in the previous year the comparable figures were 2,183 and 1,633 (CICB, 1993, para. 4.5). These applications have typically posed difficulties for the Board by virtue of the delay, and the new Scheme is explicit in providing that it will be for the applicant to make out his case for a waiver of the time limit (new Scheme, para. 18(a)). Paragraph 7.2 of the Guide to the new Scheme reiterates the discretion in para. 17 of the Scheme, but gives no further indication of the circumstances in which it could be exercised in the applicant's favour save in the case of those who were under 18 at the date of the injury (Guide, para. 7.4; chapter 6.2.2). It may therefore be expected that the Authority will draw upon decisions made over the years by previous Board Chairmen.

Applications received out of time from or on behalf of victims of low intelligence, who are deaf and dumb, who are suffering from mental disability or, in the words of para. 7.4 of the Guide to the new Scheme, 'whose ability to help themselves is or was impaired', have traditionally been treated sympathetically (CICB, 1981, para. 39; 1983, para. 25). It may also be just and reasonable to waive the limit where an application is received one week outside the time limit (CICB, 1994, para. 6.3) or where an applicant is raped by her marriage guidance counsellor, but takes no action for four years because she felt that no one would believe her, given the counsellor's position of authority (CICB, 1990, para. 16.7).

It was noted in chapter 6.2.2 that the Board has 'invariably' waived the three-year time limit where an application is made on behalf of a child (CICB, 1995, para. 3.3, repeating observations in earlier Reports). This is subject to the application to incidents arising before 1979 of the 'same roof' rule whose effect is to preclude compensation to children abused by members of their family living in the same household (CICB, 1994, para. 6.3; chapter 1.4.3). In cases where this rule does not apply, and the victim was under 18 at the time of the incident but did not make a claim until after attaining her majority (as in *Stubbings* v *Webb* [1993] AC 498), the Chairman's practice has been to waive the limit where it was received 'within a reasonable time of the victim reaching 18' (new Scheme, Guide, para. 7.4).

The exercise of this discretion is of particular importance in cases where the applicant had been the victim of physical or sexual abuse as a child, 'in which a complaint is not made to the police, often because of family circumstances, until some considerable time after the original incident' (CICB, 1995, para. 3.4); indeed, in Popplewell J.'s view, the Board has been generous in what it regards as an exceptional case (*R* v *Criminal Injuries Compensation Board, ex parte Wilson* (1991) LEXIS, 5 February 1991 (DC)). In such cases, the Board would consider the waiver of the time limit 'where the applicant is in his or her early twenties and the Board is satisfied that enough information can readily be made available to allow ... a fair decision on the case' (CICB, 1995, para. 3.4). Such information is best provided where there has been a recent conviction (CICB, 1991, para. 16.6: applicant then 30, sexually abused from the age of nine by her father who was not reported to the police for some 11 years but was then convicted of an offence; 1994, para. 6.3: applicant then 24, sexually abused between 1976 and 1984 by her mother's boyfriend who was convicted of an offence in 1993) or other corroborative evidence (CICB, 1993, para. 16.4); and where there are exceptional reasons why a prosecution has not been taken, the Chairman could still accede to the request to waive the time limit. Even then, the time limit may be waived *in extremis*. The Board's 1991 Report contains an account of an application made by a woman, then 39, who had suffered physical, sexual and mental abuse at the offender's hands over some 20 years. When she was 12 she went to live with the man who was to become the offender, his wife and their children, after her own mother had been evicted from her house. The sexual abuse began shortly afterwards, with the applicant having his child when she was 17. Two years later the offender's wife left him, and the applicant became his common-law wife. During this time he tried twice to kill her, and made numerous threats to kill her and the further four children she had by him. After several unsuccessful attempts, she finally left him, changing her name so that he could not trace her. Her application was made four years after the date of the last incident; the Chairman waived the time limit (CICB, 1991, para. 16.7).

In the absence of evidence to substantiate it, the application will be refused (CICB, 1991, para. 16.9: applicant then 34, alleged that she had been sexually abused between the ages of three and 13 by her stepfather, application refused because of the

24-year delay; 1993, para. 16.2: applicant then 27, alleged that she had been sexually abused between the ages of five and 10, application refused because the police could offer no corroborative evidence; 1994, para. 6.3: applicant then 50, alleged that she had been raped by her brother in 1989, application refused because of her age and because she had not reported the offence until 1992). On occasion, the time limit may be waived, but ultimately the application may fail because it proves impossible to substantiate the applicant's claim that she is the victim of a crime of violence (CICB, 1995, para. 6.3).

There have also been cases in which an application has been submitted late because the victim did not know that his injury was attributable to a criminal offence (CICB, 1981, para. 39; 1983, paras 22 and 24; 1988, paras 15.4–15.6). In such cases the Board has considered accepting the application if it was made 'within a reasonable time of the applicant discovering that the injury was attributable to a crime of violence' (CICB, 1986, para. 7). The Board has also looked sympathetically upon late applications 'where the physical or psychological effects of the incident have only just become apparent' (CICB, 1995, para. 3.6). If it was the case that the applicant did not apply earlier because at that time the injuries were apparently minor or even non-existent, the Board would accept a late application if it was made within a reasonable time of their appearance and if confirmatory details of the incident were available (CICB, 1995, para. 3.6). An example of this was an application determined some 19 years after appalling injuries were inflicted upon the victim when she was two years old, whose full extent had only by then become apparent (*The Times*, 24 March 1989). The new Scheme provides that the Authority will give careful consideration to claims in which the applicant's injuries only become apparent some time after the incident, but only if it can investigate and verify the details of the incident, and the application is made 'as soon as possible' after discovering the cause (new Scheme, Guide, para. 7.5).

On the other hand, simple ignorance of the Scheme's existence will not constitute grounds for waiving the limitation period (CICB, 1991, para. 16.8: applicant raped, her statement that she would have made a claim earlier than five years after the event had she known of the Board's existence was discounted). To condone ignorance would introduce an infinite regress 'since to apply any time limit at all would simply result in imposing another limitation period in place of that specified in the Scheme' (CICB, 1988, para. 15.1). Delay beyond the three-year limit caused by the pursuit of a civil action will not avail an applicant (CICB, 1985, para. 8), even where the victim's legal advisers have given negligent advice about the Scheme (CICB, 1988, para. 15.5). In that event, the applicant may wish to obtain advice about any rights of action against her solicitors (CICB, 1990, para. 16.5).

Under the old Scheme the Chairman's decision whether or not to waive the time limit was final, though subject to judicial review. In *R* v *Criminal Injuries Compensation Board, ex parte A* (1992) LEXIS, 20 February 1992 (DC), for example, the court held that the Chairman should have given consideration to additional evidence concerning the severity of the impact of a sexual offence as well as to other possible explanations for the applicant's delay in making the application.

But the fact that the Board is generous in some cases is not a good reason for saying that it has behaved unreasonably in a case where it has refused to waive the time limit (*R* v *Criminal Injuries Compensation Board, ex parte Wilson* (1991) LEXIS, 5 February 1991 (DC)).

Under the new Scheme, the applicant may request that the claims officer's decision be reviewed (new Scheme, para. 58(a); chapter 3.2.2), which in turn may be the subject of an appeal (new Scheme, para. 66(a); chapter 3.2.3).

7.3 THE FINANCIAL MINIMUM

7.3.1 The Policy

There has always been a financial threshold. At first, the sole expressed justification was a bureaucratic one: to eliminate applications whose administrative costs would exceed the compensation payable. Prompted by inflation, the increases in 1977 and 1981 were necessary 'to ensure that trivial cases of a kind never intended to be eligible for compensation continue to be excluded' (HC Debs, vol. 2, col. 52, 31 March 1981). Of more recent origin has been the use of the financial limit as an explicit means of controlling expenditure on awards. In 1983 the lower limit was increased above the rate of inflation in order to fund payments made under the bereavement provision introduced in that year. This and other increases during the 1980s were intended to concentrate resources on cases most deserving of compensation, that is, those who sustain 'an appreciable degree of injury' (Home Office, *Criminal Injuries Compensation: A Statutory Scheme*, 1986, para. 52). Why these were regarded as the most deserving cases raised questions of social policy which were never fully addressed.

As a fiscal device, the lower limit was also used to control the experimental power introduced in the 1979–80 revisions to include victims of intra-family violence within the Scheme; ten years later it was considered as a means of holding its costs within government spending limits and of cutting the Board's workload (House of Commons Home Affairs Committee, *Compensating Victims Quickly: the Administration of the Criminal Injuries Compensation Board*, House of Commons Paper 92, Session 1989–90, London: HMSO, 1990, para. 37).

7.3.2 The Provision

The Schemes impose their lower limit of compensation in different ways.

7.3.2.1 The Old Scheme
In the old Scheme, para. 5 provides:

> Compensation will not be payable unless the Board are satisfied that the injury was one for which the total amount of compensation payable after deduction of social security benefits, but before any other deductions under the Scheme, would not be less than the minimum amount of compensation.

In the version applying to applications made between 6 January 1992 and 1 April 1996, this minimum is £1,000. Paragraph 5 further provides that the lower limit shall not apply either to the payment of funeral expenses under para. 15 (thus an application for such expenses in which a dependant can show no actual dependency on the victim's income will not fail for this reason) or para. 16, which permits the Board to make an award to the dependants for pecuniary losses incurred by the victim prior to his death from a cause other than the criminal injury.

Paragraph 5 requires the Board not to make an award unless it is satisfied that the total amount of compensation payable after the deduction of social security benefits, but before any other deductions under the Scheme, will be more than the lower limit. By para. 19, social security payments are deducted in full and without limitation of time. They are also deducted from the total award that might be payable and not merely from that item of special damage to which the benefit may be taken as referring (chapter 9.2.3). If, therefore, an applicant would have received a total award (that is, comprising elements both of pecuniary and non-pecuniary loss) in excess of £1,000, but which, after the deduction of any social security benefits to which he was entitled reduced that total to less than the threshold, para. 5 has meant that no award at all will be made, not even of the balance that is left.

The paragraph is specific in requiring the prior deduction only of social security benefits. Thus, even though the Board were to apply para. 6(c) so as to reduce an award to less than £1,000, or the victim is in receipt of a compensation order which, since its value has to be deducted under the terms of para. 21, would bring the compensation payable to less than £1,000, the applicant would still be compensable. In other words, the financial minimum does not mean that awards of less than £1,000 could not be made; its effect is to preclude those applications which can be predicted to be worth less than £1,000 on the basis of the prior deduction of the specified benefits.

7.3.2.2 The New Scheme
The new Scheme provides that 'The injury must be sufficiently serious to qualify for an award equal at least to the minimum amount payable under this Scheme in accordance with para. 25' (new Scheme, para. 24). This in turn provides that level 1 (£1,000) 'represents the minimum amount payable under this Scheme ... for any single description of injury'. Where social security benefits are to be deducted from an award, the deduction does not affect the tariff award, but only 'those categories or periods of loss or need for which additional or supplementary compensation is payable' (new Scheme, para. 45; chapter 9.3.1). An applicant who sustains a broken jaw and is off work for a month will receive a tariff award of £5,000 (level 5) unaffected by any payments he receives by way of social security benefits or insurance.

Like the old Scheme, the new in effect disapplies the lower limit in the circumstances described in para. 15 of its predecessor: where the victim dies, funeral expenses up to an amount which a claims officer considers reasonable (which may therefore be less than £1,000) may be payable even where the person bearing the cost of the funeral is otherwise ineligible under the Scheme (new Scheme, para. 37).

Although para. 25 states that level 1 is the minimum amount payable under the new Scheme, the Authority, like the Board, can make awards which amount to less than £1,000. A clear case is where the applicant receives damages or a payment under a compensation order made upon the offender's conviction (new Scheme, para. 48; Guide, para. 4.10). The award will be reduced by the full amount of these sums which, in the case of a compensation order, is very likely to be less than the applicable tariff level, since the court making the order is bound to take into account the offender's means; Home Office research shows that orders tend to be for small sums (Newburn, T., *The Use and Enforcement of Compensation Orders in Magistrates' Courts*, Home Office Research Study 102, London: HMSO, 1988).

It is not quite so clear what will happen where the claims officer considers that the applicant has not wholly satisfied the eligibility criteria in para. 13. The Guide to the new Scheme indicates that once the Authority has the information it needs, it will first decide whether the application is acceptable, a process which, amongst other factors, will require the claims officer 'to consider whether an award should be withheld or reduced under any of the provisions of paras 13–16' (Guide, para. 4.5). These concern not only the conditions discussed in chapter 7.4 (co-operation with the authorities) and 7.5 (undeserving claimants), but also such matters as whether it is against the interest of an applicant under 18 years of age for an award to be made (new Scheme, para. 15(b); chapter 6.2.2), or whether an award should be withheld in an application arising from domestic violence (para. 16; chapter 6.4).

The claims officer may decide that the application is unacceptable, and make no award; in that case, the decision may at once be reviewed (new Scheme, para. 58(c); chapter 3.2.2). If, however, the application is acceptable, but the claims officer is minded to reduce any award by 75% on the basis of the applicant's convictions (new Scheme, Guide, para. 8.16; chapter 7.5.3.2.1), the question arises whether that reduction is to be made before or after the assessment of the injury as being 'serious enough to qualify for at least the minimum award payable under the tariff' (new Scheme, Guide, para. 4.6). One interpretation is that the claims officer should apply the reduction at the same time as determining what amount is payable. If, leaving aside the effect of the reduction, the injury would be valued at the minimum, then no award would be made, since it would clearly be less than £1,000. The effect of this would be to equate some reductions with a complete withholding of an award. Even an injury which would, but for this 75% reduction, attract a tariff award of £3,000 would still not result in an award because only £750 would be payable after the reduction; the injury would have to be valued at level 8 (£3,500) to be compensable. This interpretation must be irrational, since it confuses two different judgments: the severity of the injury and the eligibility of the applicant.

The alternative is that the claims officer should first determine what tariff is applicable to the injury, and then make the 75% reduction. In this way, even the lowest level of injury on this example would ultimately result in an award of £250. The purpose of para. 24 is to exclude from the Scheme injuries defined in financial terms as minor: level 1 represents the minimum amount payable 'for any single description of injury'; it is not to preclude the making of awards below £1,000.

Likewise the wording of the Guide indicates that once the application is acceptable (even with reservations), 'we will assess whether or not your injury is serious enough to qualify for at least the minimum award payable under the tariff' (new Scheme, Guide, para. 4.6). This suggests that only when that judgment is made (which may involve placing the injury in a higher tariff level: Guide, para. 4.7), will the claims officer then make the appropriate reduction.

7.3.3 Implementation

The lower limit 'will usually apply when the injuries are of a minor nature, e.g., cuts, bruises or sprains where there has been no more than minor medical treatment and where there is no remaining visible scarring, or which have not necessitated more than three to four weeks absence from work' (Guide, old Scheme, para. 10). The Board's Reports give instances of applications disallowed because the applicants sustained only bruising, scratches, black eyes, bloody noses, cut lips and similar injuries requiring little or no medical attention (CICB, 1990, paras 19.2–19.4; 1991, paras 21.2–21.5).

Criticism of the lower limit invariably draws attention to the plight of elderly victims for whom an injury, though valued less than £1,000, is often not trivial, especially where they have only a limited income. Such injury can also turn a self-reliant and outgoing person into one who withdraws from social life. In practice the Board has been prepared to make at least a minimum award to the elderly applicant who, though sustaining neither pecuniary loss nor physical injury, has been put in fear by an assault upon him or upon another standing nearby (CICB, 1987, para. 24). Remarks made by the present Chairman to the Home Affairs Committee in 1989 (House of Commons Paper 92, 1989–90, para. 38) envisage that further increases in the lower limit would not prevent such injuries from being compensated.

The new Scheme maintains the approach evident in the Board's Reports: 'Minor injuries such as scratches or bruises alone will not qualify you for an award' (new Scheme, Guide, para. 7.6). But the new Scheme also indicates that a combination of minor injuries may be sufficient. This possibility is provided for in para. 26 of the Scheme and note 1 to the tariff:

Minor multiple injuries will only qualify for compensation where the applicant has sustained at least three separate injuries of the type illustrated below, at least one of which must still have had significant residual effects six weeks after the incident. The injuries must also have necessitated at least two visits to or by a medical practitioner within that six-week period. Examples of qualifying injuries are:

    (a)   grazing, cuts, lacerations (no permanent scarring)
    (b)   severe and widespread bruising
    (c)   severe soft tissue injury (no permanent disability)

- (d)   black eye(s)
- (e)   bloody nose
- (f)   hair pulled from scalp
- (g)   loss of fingernail.

The qualifying injuries are all physical injuries. It is thus not open to an applicant to argue that he should be compensated where he has sustained two of the illustrated injuries, together with mental injury in the form of anxiety or loss of confidence (two of the forms of psychological symptoms of nervous shock given in note 2 to the tariff; chapter 5.1.3.1). This is so in part because the tariff 'includes an element of compensation for the degree of shock which an applicant in normal circumstances would experience as a result of an incident resulting in injury' (new Scheme, Guide, para. 4.9). Thus an (elderly) applicant who sustains three minor injuries and who satisfies the other criteria in note 1 will receive an award for those injuries and (implicitly) for her mental injury. But if she sustains mental injury alone as the result of an assault (or together with physical injuries that do not satisfy the criteria in note 1), she will be compensable only if it is sufficiently severe to meet the criteria for a tariff award for shock, that is, disabling and medically verified, though of a temporary nature and the shock was sustained in one of the sets of circumstances specified in para. 9 (chapter 5.1.3.3).

7.3.4   Impact of Increases in the Threshold

Increases in the lower limit have a variety of implications for the Scheme; most obviously, those which significantly exceed the rate of inflation will and may be intended to lead to a decrease in the number of applications, at least for a while, but there has been disagreement whether increases which only reflect the rate of inflation will have that effect. The Board was never convinced that modest increases in the lower limit would have anything but a marginal impact upon the application rate (CICB, 1988, para. 2.2); its critics regularly deplored them as disentitling substantial numbers of formerly eligible victims.

The difficulty lies in trying to gauge how many victims are indeed so disentitled. It is tempting, but wrong, to conclude, for example, that because 37.2% of awards (10,312) made in 1988–89 were for sums less than £800 (CICB, 1989, para. 8.1; £750, which was then the lower limit, is not used in the table), the total of eligible victims was cut by about a third when the increase to £1,000 was introduced in February 1990. Nor can much assistance be obtained simply by noting the number of awards made in 1988–89 which fell between the old and the new lower limits (5,700, or 20.6% of all awards). As has already been noted, the lower limit does not mean that awards less than that figure cannot be made; one only has to look at the table in the 1988–89 Report to see that 5.6% of awards were for sums less than £499, and 12.6% were for sums between £500 and £599. Even in 1994–95, 8.2% of awards were for less than £1,000 (CICB, 1995, para. 3.14).

It is also important to be clear what is meant by 'disqualify' in this context. On the assumption that compensation for injuries rises in line with inflation, increases in the lower limit which did not exceed the rate of inflation would disqualify no one who would not, in the normal course of events, have been disqualified if, instead of being adjusted every few years, the limit were index-linked and adjusted annually. It is only because there has been a delay in catching up with the effect of inflation that the numbers of those disqualified looks so substantial. In reality, of course, the effect of the delayed adjustments was progressively to qualify for compensation more victims than the lower limit would admit if it had been adjusted annually.

7.4   CO-OPERATION WITH THE AUTHORITIES

Both versions of the Scheme provide that the applicant must report the incident without delay to the police, and thereafter co-operate with them in bringing the offender to justice, and with the Board or the Authority in the processing of the application. The Board always regarded compliance with these requirements as crucial to establishing the applicant's *bona fides*: 'Even where the circumstances of a particular incident are fully known and disclose no blameworthy conduct on the part of the applicant, the Board will only rarely excuse an applicant's failure in his obvious duty to report crimes of violence to the police with a view to bringing the offender to justice' (CICB, 1983, para. 27); *a fortiori* where the circumstances of the incident were obscure and there was no corroboration of the applicant's version of events. The 1986 Working Party proposed no change to these requirements. In 1994–95, 4,806 of the nil-award applications were rejected for failure to comply with one or other of the requirements in para. 6(a) and (b) of the old Scheme (CICB, 1995, App. B).

The new Scheme likewise emphasises the importance of these requirements:

> Payment of compensation for injury as a result of a crime of violence is intended to be an expression of public sympathy and support for innocent victims. The original Scheme, introduced in 1964, envisaged that it would be inappropriate for those with significant criminal records or whose own conduct led to their being injured, to receive compensation from public funds. It was also felt that people who failed to co-operate in bringing the offender to justice should not benefit from such payments. These provisions continue in this Scheme (new Scheme, Guide, para. 8.1)

The relevance of the applicant's criminal record is considered in chapter 7.5.3.2.1.

The provisions in the old Scheme concerning co-operation with the authorities are therefore to be found in virtually identical terms in the new. Paragraph 6 of the old Scheme provided that the Board could withhold or reduce compensation where:

> (a)   the applicant has not taken, without delay, all reasonable steps to inform the police, or any other authority considered by the Board to be appropriate for the

purpose, of the circumstances of the injury and to co-operate fully with the police or other authority in bringing the offender to justice; or

(b)   the applicant has failed to give all reasonable assistance to the Board or other authority in connection with the application.

These two paragraphs create three separate requirements, which is how the new Scheme deals with them.

7.4.1   Reporting the Circumstances of the Injury

By para. 13(a) of the new Scheme, a claims officer may withhold or reduce an award where he considers that 'the applicant failed to take, without delay, all reasonable steps to inform the police, or other body or person considered by the Authority to be appropriate for the purpose, of the circumstances giving rise to the injury'. This decision, should it go against the applicant, may be the subject of a review under para. 60 of the new Scheme, then of an appeal and finally, of a judicial review. In *R v Criminal Injuries Compensation Board, ex parte Jobson* (1995) LEXIS, 4 May 1995 (DC), Dyson J. held that in approaching para. 6(a) of the old Scheme, the Board should ask itself three questions:

(a)   Did the applicant take without delay all reasonable steps to inform the police of the circumstances of the injury and co-operate with the police in bringing the offender to justice;

(b)   If so, should compensation be withheld or reduced;

(c)   What award, if any, should the applicant consequently receive?

In *R v Criminal Injuries Compensation Board, ex parte Cook* [1996] 1 WLR 1037 the Court of Appeal referred to this formulation without comment. In *ex parte Jobson*, Dyson J. found that the Board had indeed asked itself the very questions required of it; its failure was in not giving the applicant adequate reasons for the answers it reached.

Noting that it is unnecessary for an offender to have been convicted before an award can be made, and that many offenders are never identified, the Guide to the new Scheme confirms the Board's long-held view that the reporting requirement is the primary safeguard against fraudulent applications (CICB, 1990, para. 20.1; new Scheme, Guide, para. 8.4). The Authority attaches 'great importance to the duty of every victim of crime to inform the police of all the circumstances without delay . . . [thus] if you have not reported the circumstances of the injury to the police and can offer no reasonable explanation for not doing so, you should assume that any application for compensation will be rejected' (new Scheme, Guide, para. 8.4). It goes virtually without saying, that the applicant must report all the relevant circumstances (new Scheme, Guide, para. 8.6).

In some cases, an application will be rejected simply because the applicant did not himself report the incident to the police (*R v Criminal Injuries Compensation Board, ex parte Aston* (1994) LEXIS, 9 May 1994 (DC): application for review dismissed; *R* v *Criminal Injuries Compensation Board, ex parte Pearce* (1993) LEXIS, 5 December 1993 (DC): application for review dismissed; *R* v *Criminal Injuries Compensation Board, ex parte Powell* (1993) LEXIS, 16 July 1993 (DC): remitted to the Board for its failure to exercise its discretion properly and to give reasons for its rejection of the application), or the police have no record of the report which the applicant alleges he made (CICB, 1989, para. 20.4; 1992, para. 15.7). In other cases, the Board has rejected the claim because the applicant refused to confirm, when the police arrived at the scene or shortly thereafter, that any offence might have occurred (CICB, 1990, para. 20.5; 1991, para. 22.2; 1994, para. 6.11). In some such instances the applicant may be seen in hospital but was not able to confirm what had happened or make a formal complaint because he was disoriented. This was so in *R* v *Criminal Injuries Compensation Board, ex parte Jobson*, in which the court found that the Board had failed to give adequate reasons, and in *R* v *Criminal Injuries Compensation Board, ex parte Cobb* (1994) LEXIS, 26 July 1994 (DC) where the Board rejected the application because the applicant did not attend a police station until five days after the incident. This decision too was remitted because the Board had failed to give adequate reasons following the hearing for its rejection of the application.

Likewise, the Board will reject an application where the applicant delayed making a report to the police but offered no explanation for the delay (CICB, 1991, para. 22.4; 1992, paras 26.15 and 26.18; 1995, para. 6.9). More common are cases where the applicant does offer an explanation for the delay in informing the police which the Board does not accept, for example: because the applicant thought that in the circumstances of the assault he might himself be suspected of having committed an offence, and so delayed for two days before reporting it (CICB, 1989, para. 19.3); because the applicant was vague about the date of the offence and could narrow it down only to a period of two months (CICB, 1989, paras 19.4–19.6); because the applicant was shocked, did not know the identity of his assailants and could not give a description of them (CICB, 1989, para. 19.1; new Scheme, Guide, para. 8.4); because the applicant had been drinking and did not want to go to the police station smelling of alcohol (CICB, 1992, para. 26.16); or because the applicant only reported the assault in order to make a claim (CICB, 1990, para. 20.3; 1992, para. 26.17; new Scheme, Guide, para. 8.8). The Guide also confirms (para. 8.4) that a failure to inform the police is unlikely to be excused because the applicant was afraid of reprisals (CICB, 1991, para. 22.3) or saw no point in reporting it (CICB, 1990, para. 20.2). It adds, 'Reporting such incidents can help the police prevent further offences against others'.

The Guide insists that 'You should report to the police at the *earliest possible opportunity*' (new Scheme, Guide, para. 8.7; original emphasis). But like the Board, it also recognises some circumstances in which delay may be excusable. The Authority 'will take a sympathetic view where the delay in reporting the incident to the police is clearly attributable to youth, old age, or to some physical or mental incapacity or psychological effects of the crime; for example, where the impact of the crime upon an elderly victim restricts her movements and makes her fearful about going out' (CICB, 1988, paras 33.1–33.4). In *R* v *Criminal Injuries Compensation Board, ex parte S* (1995) LEXIS, 24 March 1995 (DC), the victim was raped and sexually assaulted with a screwdriver. She was so traumatised by the attack that it was only with great reluctance that she disclosed the fact to her friends at work, and six weeks elapsed before she reported the offence to the police. A man was proceeded against, but her identification was uncertain; together with the impossibility of any forensic evidence, the Board dismissed her application. Sedley J., remitting the case to the Board, held that the major deficit in the Board's reasoning was that it had proceeded from the acknowledgement that the applicant had been traumatised by the event to an inspection of the impact of her delay on the criminal process, and thence directly to its conclusion to reject her application, 'omitting the crucial step of weighing the significance of the delay against the reason for it'.

Delay may be excused where the applicant was, by reason of the injuries sustained, unable to contact the police herself (new Scheme, para. 8.5), for example, because she was concussed or unconscious in hospital. In such a case it is the applicant's duty to contact the police as soon as she can. This is so even where the police were present at or after the incident in which she was injured. In the past, the Board has indicated that in the case of a large-scale incident such as a riot, the applicant's explanation that he thought that he did not personally have to report what the police had obviously seen (CICB, 1987, para. 28) or that she did not have to make a complaint because she could not identify anyone in the crowd who pushed her (CICB, 1992, para. 26.22), might suffice; but para. 8.5 of the Guide suggests otherwise: 'It is not sufficient to assume that the incident will have been reported by someone else because, even if it has, that person may not have known the full circumstances'.

Under the old Scheme, the report could only be made to the police; the Board would normally regard reports to employers, trade union officials, social workers and the like as unacceptable. The new Scheme continues this policy. Paragraph 8.9 of the Guide states: 'Crimes of violence must be reported to the police' and reiterates the Board's approach to these other groups. Similarly, reports by friends, relatives or workmates will not be sufficient unless there is a good reason why the applicant himself did not inform the police (new Scheme, Guide, para. 8.7). Again in line with the Board's practice, exceptions may be made in the case of injuries sustained in mental hospitals or prisons, 'where a prompt report to the appropriate person in authority represents a willingness that the matter should be formally investigated'.

In the case of an injury to a child, the 'appropriate authority' will normally be her parents, whose own failure to report to the police will not prevent the claim from proceeding if the claims officer considers it unreasonable to expect the child to pursue the claim herself. Nevertheless, the Guide does emphasise the importance of the parent reporting to the police, since without such a report, it may be difficult to verify the incident and the alleged injuries. For example, the Board received in 1991 an application from a 22-year-old who claimed that he had sustained injury to his eye when aged seven as the result of the reckless discharge of a firearm. The applicant could produce no evidence showing that the incident had been reported to the police, nor did the police have any record. At a hearing the Board concluded that the injury had been sustained in circumstances which were unlikely to admit of any explanation other than a crime of violence; notwithstanding that there were no police records, an interim award was made pending further ophthalmic investigation (CICB, 1993, para. 29.1). Where the injury is minor and was sustained at school, the Authority may be prepared to accept the parent's report to the school authorities, where police intervention might be thought unnecessary.

7.4.2 Co-operating in Bringing the Offender to Justice

By para. 13(b) of the new Scheme, a claims officer may withhold or reduce an award where he considers that 'the applicant failed to co-operate with the police or other authority in attempting to bring the assailant to justice'.

Throughout its lifetime the Board maintained an uncompromising approach towards this requirement: 'If the rising tide of crime is to be stemmed ... [and] if we are to walk our streets free from fear and injury ... [then] victims should co-operate fully and fearlessly in the process of justice' (CICB, 1983, para. 27). Likewise, the Authority may withhold or reduce compensation if the applicant fails to co-operate with the police, even where the incident was promptly reported (new Scheme, Guide, para. 8.10). An application from someone who deliberately misled the police, either by withholding or giving false information (CICB, 1991, para. 22.6), or who refused to co-operate with them would, unless there were strong reasons to explain the refusal, be rejected. In a case reported in 1993, the victim, a male homosexual who had been diagnosed HIV positive, reported that he had been assaulted by an unknown assailant. Later he indicated that because of his condition, he could not endure the continuation of the investigation, and withdrew his complaint. In normal circumstances, the Board observed, such retraction would result in the rejection of the application, but in this case it was prepared to make an exception, reducing the award by 50% (CICB, 1993, para. 21.1).

Drawing on the Board's decisions, para. 8.11 of the Guide to the new Scheme distinguishes two sets of circumstances. The first includes cases in which the applicant refuses to make a statement either at the time or later at the station (CICB, 1990, para. 20.6; 1994, para. 6.11), to attend court (CICB, 1991, para. 22.5) or makes a statement which he later withdraws (CICB, 1990, para. 20.3; 1994, para. 6.11). In all of these cases, the Authority will normally make no award (new Scheme, Guide, para. 8.11(a)). A similar outcome could be expected where the applicant refuses to attend an identification parade, to name the assailant where he is clearly known to the victim, or to give evidence. As in the case of non-reporting, the fact that he has been threatened by reprisals will not excuse an applicant (CICB, 1985, para. 27; new Scheme, Guide, para. 8.12). This paragraph also indicates that an applicant who initially failed to co-operate for fear of retaliation but who later assists the police, may be made a reduced award.

The second set of circumstances covers those cases where, despite the applicant's co-operation, the police or the prosecuting authority decide to take no further action. In these circumstances, assuming that no other issues of eligibility are in question, an award will normally be made (new Scheme, Guide, para. 8.11(b)). The same outcome could be expected where it is now impossible for any further action to be taken, because the alleged offender has died (CICB, 1994, para. 7.2). In the past the Board has drawn a distinction between cases where the applicant refused to co-operate in the senses described above, from a refusal to press charges. Provided that a victim had fully co-operated with the authorities (CICB, 1986, para. 20), his express wish that there should be no prosecution or his refusal to make a formal complaint has not necesarily precluded him from compensation. It is not clear from the Guide whether an applicant would be refused an award in these circumstances. Clearly, it would almost certainly be fatal to an application arising from domestic violence (new Scheme, para. 16(b); chapter 6.4). But even if she has a general social or moral duty to assist the police, the citizen has no duty to initiate a prosecution; the issue is whether it is appropriate that she should be penalised if she does not.

7.4.3   Assistance in Connection with the Application

By para. 13(c) of the new Scheme, a claims officer may withhold or reduce an award where he considers that 'the applicant has failed to give all reasonable assistance to the Authority or other body or person in connection with the application'.

The rejection of an application on the ground of non-compliance with para. 6(b) of the old Scheme was a rare event. Under the new Scheme failure to give all reasonable assistance will include persistent failure to comply with requests for information from the Authority (CICB, 1991, para. 23.2; 1994, para. 6.12; 1995, para. 6.10) unless the failure is due to the applicant's solicitors (CICB, 1992, para. 26.21), including a failure to attend medical examinations or inspections which the claims officer considers necessary to determine the application (CICB, 1991, para. 23.3; 1993, para. 22.1; new Scheme, Guide, para. 8.13). It will also include the applicant's failure to give reasonable assistance to such other authorities who may be involved in the determination of the claim as his GP, a hospital out-patients' clinic (CICB, 1987, para. 38), the DSS or his employer, all of whom may be approached by the Authority to verify details connected with the application.

The reasonable assistance required by the claims officer may relate to matters other than the immediate circumstances giving rise to the injury. For example, failing to disclose details of a prior conviction, or failing to give a convincing explanation of why a claim for pecuniary loss includes a holiday in the West Indies on which the applicant has taken his girlfriend (CICB, 1978, para. 18) may amount to failure to give all reasonable assistance.

7.5   UNDESERVING APPLICANTS

7.5.1   The Policy

As noted earlier, the original Scheme 'envisaged that it would be inappropriate for those with significant criminal records or whose own conduct led to their being injured, to receive compensation from public funds' (new Scheme, Guide, para. 8.1). Indeed, the 1961 Working Party noted that while a person's character is not normally taken into account in determining eligibility for State benefits, the matter is different where crime is concerned. Not all victims are 'innocents', and where his mode of life, the company he keeps or the undesirable activities in which he engages are connected with the incident in which he is injured, then, it argued, the State may owe him no moral obligation, at least in the form of compensation for that injury (Home Office, *Compensation for Victims of Crimes of Violence*, Cmnd 1406, London: HMSO, 1961, para. 31 et seq.). It is of course true that many victims have themselves been offenders, a point which has been amply demonstrated in victimisation surveys (Walklate, S., *Victimology*, London: Unwin Hyman, 1989, ch. 2). Thus para. 6(c) of the old Scheme provided that the Board could withhold or reduce compensation if it considered that:

> having regard to the conduct of the applicant before, during or after the events giving rise to the claim or to his character as shown by his criminal convictions or unlawful conduct — and, in applications under paras 15 and 16 below, to the conduct or character as shown by the criminal convictions or unlawful conduct of the deceased and of the applicant — it is inappropriate that a full award, or any award at all, be granted.

The continuation of 'a wide power enabling the Board to reduce or refuse compensation on the grounds of the relevant conduct of the victim' was specifically recommended by the Home Office review in 1978 (Home Office, *Review of the Criminal Injuries Compensation Scheme Report of an Interdepartmental Working Party*, 1978, para. 61), and it will continue to play a significant role in the new Scheme. Both the formulation and the implementation of this paragraph have occasioned criticism; many of the applications for judicial review of the Board's decisions have concerned the exercise of the discretion given by para. 6(c). The central issue turns on the varying conceptions of relevance that have been held by the Board, its supporters and its critics, in particular, concerning what the Board should be able to take into account when considering the relevance to his application of the applicant's biography.

The Board has always regarded 'clean hands' as being of primary importance. In the event of a hearing, the old Scheme imposed on the applicant the obligation to make out his case, and where appropriate this extended, by para. 25, 'to satisfying the Board that compensation should not be withheld or reduced under the terms of para. 6'. This obligation is present in the new Scheme, para. 18(b) of which provides that it is for the applicant to satisfy the claims officer dealing with his application (including an officer reviewing a decision under para. 60) that an award should not be withheld or reduced under para. 13(d) or (e), equivalent to para. 6(c) of the old Scheme. The new Scheme also provides for the reconsideration of a decision before the award has been paid, which envisages the possibility of its being withheld or reduced (chapter 2.3.5) and, where the application comes before the Panel, the applicant must satisfy the adjudicator responsible for determining his appeal, that the award 'should not be reconsidered, withheld or reduced' under this paragraph.

Though quantitatively small (of the 56,869 applications resolved in 1994–95, 4,723 were rejected on this basis: CICB, 1995, App. B), this issue is qualitatively of the first importance. It is the one facet of a compensation scheme which most strikingly brings into focus the assumptions which lie behind the notion of the innocent, and hence deserving victim (Miers, D., 'Compensation and Conceptions of Victims of Crime', *Victimology*, 1983, vol. 8, p. 204). The source of the puzzlements which this issue generates goes well beyond the causal problems which may arise in the analogous context of contributory negligence in personal injury actions. Whether damages should be payable to those who are victimised while they are intoxicated by alcohol, solvents or hallucinatory drugs, or who were at the time engaged in unlawful activity, are questions that rarely trouble the courts (e.g., *Hegarty* v *Shine* (1878) 14 Cox CC 145; *Ashton* v *Turner* [1981] QB 137; *Pitts* v *Hunt* [1991] 1 QB 24), even though in recent years retaliatory action by victims of crime has prompted their 'victims' into taking civil action (*Revill* v *Newbery* [1996] QB 567 (CA)).

The first problem is that because delinquent victims resemble offenders too closely, and may indeed have been formally so defined in the past, the possibility of their receiving compensation threatens the stereotype of the 'innocent' victim for whom such schemes are created. A former Chairman of the Board, Sir Michael Ogden QC, observed (CICB, 1985, para. 19):

It is sometimes useful to consider extreme examples. Suppose that Peter Sutcliffe ('The Yorkshire Ripper') had been awarded compensation by the Board for an injury which was wholly unrelated to his crimes, or that an award had been made to the criminal who put a bomb on a coach containing women and children, or made an award to the man who is at the time of writing being hunted by the police in the Dunstable area in connection with extremely nasty offences of rape and other crimes. I would expect that there would be a howl of public outrage; in my view rightly so.

Despite these observations, the Board has made a full award to a prisoner who sustained severe injuries when attacked in his cell (CICB, 1990, para. 26.1: the victim was later pardoned). Public hostility is often expressed about decisions taken by legal bodies; a measure of compatibility between popular sentiment and what the law decides, permits or punishes, is an important factor in the success of any legal system to command the support of those affected by it, but it would be a poor system which used public approval or disapproval of its activities as the determining factor in its decisions. The question is whether it is defensible to refuse compensation to a person because he has a criminal record, but one which is unconnected with the injury complained of. Thousands of people remain eligible for State benefits notwithstanding prior convictions, and if those who are injured in incidents unconnected with their criminal history have been convicted and punished by due process of law, is it right that they should be so disqualified in the future? The Scheme's simple answer to date has been that it is: where offenders commit serious offences, they put themselves, so to speak, beyond the pale of criminal injury compensation. But as the Court of Appeal held in *Revill* v *Newbery*, a burglar is not to be treated as an outlaw for the purpose of a civil action for damages (chapter 7.5.3.2.2); nor should a court reduce exemplary damages where a plaintiff with serious convictions was badly injured by police officers seeking his confession to a series of armed robberies (*Treadaway* v *Chief Constable of West Midlands* (1994) *The Times*, 25 October 1994).

Secondly, the possibility that 'offenders' might, as victims, be eligible for compensation, subverts a prime objective of criminal injury schemes, which is to distinguish victims of crime from offenders where penal regimes are perceived to be too forgiving and too neglectful of the victim. The politicisation of the victim of crime requires that the taxpayer be asked to compensate only those victims who present 'deserving' characteristics, so it therefore becomes necessary to exclude the delinquent victim (however defined) from the Scheme's beneficial provisions. This consideration was instrumental in the 1986 Working Party's recommendation that the Board's discretion in this matter be unchanged (Home Office, *Criminal Injuries Compensation: A Statutory Scheme*, 1986, para. 6.2):

> It is important to remember ... that the justification for compensation by the State is that it is paid on behalf of the community as a practical expression of public feeling reflecting the sense of responsibility for and sympathy with the innocent victim which is felt by the public at large. Clearly it would not reflect this public feeling to make awards from public funds to those who have themselves led a life of serious crime, preying upon persons and property of fellow citizens, irrespective of whether their injuries are attributable to their own offences.

7.5.2 The Provision

7.5.2.1 The terms of the two Schemes

Earlier versions of the old Scheme permitted the Board to take into account, in addition to his criminal record and his conduct before, during or after the incident giving rise to the injury, the victim's 'way of life'. Many critics considered this power to be wholly objectionable, permitting the intrusion of judgments bearing an inappropriately moralist slant. For example, the Board rejected an application from a man who had been attacked while on bail pending trial on charges of buggery with his wife and six-year-old son. He 'had been the subject of considerable publicity regarding attendance at orgies, and local feeling ran high against him' (CICB, 1989, para. 20.3). It was also objectionable because, as the Court of Appeal confirmed some years ago, its scope was 'not limited to matters relevant in some way to the particular incident' (*R* v *Criminal Injuries Compensation Board, ex parte Thompstone* [1984] 1 WLR 1234). This element was removed in the 1990 revision, with the result that para. 6(c) permitted the Board to reduce or withhold compensation either because of the applicant's conduct before, during or after the events giving rise to the claim, or because of his character as shown by his criminal convictions or unlawful conduct. However, this second alternative continued to permit the Board to exercise its discretion against the applicant irrespective of any causal connection between those convictions or the unlawful conduct and the incident giving rise to the criminal injury.

The new Scheme effects some further changes. While the first alternative is maintained in para. 13(d), the Scheme also introduces rehabilitation limits on the effect of those convictions (chapter 7.5.3.2.1). The second alternative, set out in para. 13(e), omits any reference to the applicant's 'unlawful conduct', but includes instead 'evidence available to the claims officer' which makes it inappropriate that a full award or any award at all be made (chapter 7.5.3.2.3).

It should also be noted that these provisions in both the old and the new Schemes apply not only where the applicant survives his injuries, but also where he dies and his dependants make a claim. In such a case, the Board or the Authority can refuse or withhold compensation to wholly respectable dependants where their deceased relative is judged to come within their scope (old Scheme, para. 6(c); new Scheme, para. 14; CICB, 1993, para. 27.5: applicant's award for loss of society reduced by 50% because the deceased was a prostitute and dealt in drugs), whether he died in consequence of the criminal injury (old Scheme, para. 15; new Scheme, paras 39–42) or merely subsequent to it (old Scheme, para. 16; new Scheme, para. 44). Similarly, where the victim died as a result of the injury, both schemes provide that any funeral expenses incurred by his relatives can be withheld on account of his bad character (chapter 8.5.3.2).

The relevance of the applicant's good character, by contrast with the bad character of the deceased, was considered in *R v Criminal Injuries Compensation Board, ex parte Cook* [1996] 1 WLR 1037 (CA) (chapter 1.5.2). In this case the applicant, who was wholly innocent of her husband's criminal activities (for which he was serving a substantial prison sentence), applied under para. 15 of the old Scheme when he was shot and killed in a contract killing. The Board rejected her application because of her husband's criminal record. In the Divisional Court Potts J. held that the word 'and' between the words, 'the deceased' and 'the applicant', did not mean that both the applicant and the deceased had to be of bad character for the application to fail. This was accepted by the applicant who argued in the Court of Appeal that the Board should have taken her good character into account and weighed that against the deceased's bad character. Giving the leading judgment, Aldous L.J. held that Board had no duty to consider the applicant's good character (p. 150):

In the present case there was one main issue, namely whether the applicant was entitled to an award under the Scheme in the light of the bad character of the deceased and the good character of the applicant. If the Board had decided she was entitled to an award, it had to go on to decide whether it should be a full compensatory award or a reduced one. The decision of the Board was that no award out of public funds was appropriate because of the character of the deceased. The reasons given were in my view adequate. They did not refer to the character of the applicant and there was no need to do so.

These eligibility criteria will not, however, exclude a dependant who suffers a criminal injury separate from that which caused the victim's death and in respect of which he makes an application for compensation for personal injuries. For example, the para. 15 application made by a woman whose husband had been killed in a fight arising from a long-standing dispute with his killers was rejected because of his conduct; but the nervous shock which she sustained as a result of his killing constituted a wholly independent criminal injury in respect of which an application might succeed (CICB, 1992, para. 21.4). Conversely, compensation may be withheld or reduced where it is the dependants, not the deceased, who fall within the scope of para. 6(c) or para. 13(d)–(e) (new Scheme para. 14).

It will be seen that there is some overlap between these conditions. A victim injured in a fight which he initiated can be disentitled in whole or in part under either of them. In the case of the old Scheme, such behaviour could either be regarded as inappropriate because of his 'conduct . . . before . . .the events giving rise to the claim' or because of his 'character as shown by his . . . unlawful conduct'. Under the new Scheme, such behaviour could likewise be regarded as disentitling of compensation under para. 13(d) because of his 'conduct . . . before . . . the incident giving rise to the application', or, conceivably, under para. 13(e), as it is 'evidence available to the claims officer' making it inappropriate to make an award. However, although the scope of this element of para. 13(e) is unclear, it is probably not intended to cover such facts, which readily fall within para. 13(d).

Following the next section, we deal in turn with the implementation of the discretion given by para. 13(d) (chapter 7.5.3.1) and (e) (chapter 7.5.3.2) of the new Scheme.

7.5.2.2 The Scheme's Relationship with the Common Law

It will also be seen that, though cast in different terms, these disentitling conditions bear obvious similarities to those defences in tort which may preclude a claim for personal injuries or under the Fatal Accidents Act 1976, or result in a reduction in the damages ordered to be paid. A victim/plaintiff who was engaged in illegal conduct may be barred by the rule, *ex turpi causa non oritur actio*, and one who was engaged in risky, though not necessarily unlawful conduct, may be barred by the defence, *volenti non fit injuria*. Likewise the victim/plaintiff will fail where the defence can show that his conduct amounted to a *novus actus interveniens*. If his conduct did not break the causal link between the defendant's negligence and his injury, but nevertheless contributed to it, the court shall, by s. 1(1) of the Law Reform

(Contributory Negligence) Act 1945, reduce his damages to such extent as it thinks just and equitable. Though there are similarities between the old and new Schemes and these aspects of tort law, there are also important differences between them. These differences may be summarised as follows:

(a)   Both Schemes give a discretion to refuse or to reduce an award irrespective of which of the two conditions it invokes to disentitle the applicant. In tort law, on the other hand, only the defence of contributory negligence permits reduction in the amount of compensation (and it only permits this); the other defences completely bar any recovery.

(b)   Where the application is made by the deceased victim's dependants, both conditions apply to the victim's conduct or biography. If, for example, the victim had a conviction for a serious offence, though it was unconnected with the attack on him, there may be no award if the Board or the claims officer think that it would be inappropriate to make one. In a fatal accident action, however, such a background would not bar the dependants. It is probably otherwise where the deceased lived a life of crime, as the dependants' claim arises *ex turpi causa* (*Burns* v *Edman* [1970] 2 QB 541); but it would almost certainly be refused under the Scheme. Likewise, compensation may be reduced or denied to the dependant because of the victim's conduct before, during or after the injury.

(c)   Where the claim is made by dependants, both conditions also apply to them. A dependant with criminal convictions or who had engaged in unlawful conduct may be refused compensation, and the Board and the claims officer can also take into account his conduct before, during or after the events giving rise to the victim's death. This would not be the case in a fatal accident action.

(d)   The Schemes permit the Board or a claims officer to take into account the applicant's convictions whenever they occurred (subject, in the case of the new Scheme, to the rehabilitation periods on convictions), including a time after the injury or death, and irrespective of the absence of any connection between them and the injury. The fact that the victim had a conviction for an offence is immaterial to a personal or fatal injury action, whenever that conviction was returned.

(e)   The Schemes also give a discretion to consider the applicant's conduct before, during and after the events giving rise to the claim. In negligence a defendant takes his victim as he finds him, and will not escape liability for the actual extent of injury where the plaintiff, being a Jehovah's witness for example, refuses medical treatment (likewise his criminal liability: *R* v *Blaue* [1975] 1 WLR 1411). It is not clear whether such a person would succeed in an application under the Scheme, but the tenor of the Board's implementation of para. 6(c) suggests that both it and a claims officer would take a more sceptical view of post-event conduct on the applicant's part which aggravated her injuries.

(f)   Both Schemes give a discretion to refuse or reduce an award because the applicant was at the time he sustained the criminal injury, engaged in a criminal act.

In tort law, the maxim *ex turpi causa* will probably only disbar the victim/plaintiff when the injury was so closely interwoven in the illegal act as to be virtually a part of it (*Pitts* v *Hunt* [1991] 1 QB 24); but merely because the plaintiff was engaged in a criminal act at the time will not be a complete defence (*Revill* v *Newbery* [1996] QB 567 (CA)).

(g) In tort law, the defences *ex turpi causa* and *volenti* appear not to apply in the case of an unlawful fight initiated by the victim where the defendant's response is disproportionate to the provocation (*Lane* v *Holloway* [1968] 1 QB 379 (CA)); for the Scheme, however, proportionality is not the determining factor.

(h) In invoking these two conditions, similar though aspects of them are to the defence of contributory negligence, neither the Board nor a claims officer is obliged to apply the common law's interpretation of that notion. This follows from the decision of the Court of Appeal in *R* v *Criminal Injuries Compensation Board, ex parte Ince* [1973] 1 WLR 1334. This case concerned the question, what characteristics of the applicant's conduct prior to the victimising event should the Board take into account? One possibility was that it should reduce or refuse compensation commensurate with the degree to which the applicant's conduct contributed to the occurrence of the events or to the severity of the injuries he sustained. The court emphatically rejected this approach, which reflects the operation in tort law of the defences of *volenti* and contributory negligence.

The facts were that the applicant's husband, who was on duty in a police car, was killed when, in answer to a general police message, he ignored a set of traffic lights en route to the scene of the suspected offence, and collided with another police car (travelling in response to the same message) crossing with the lights. Subsequently it was discovered that this was a false alarm. The Board rejected the application on the grounds first, that he was not at the material time actually engaged in the prevention of a crime, and second, that his death was attributable to his own foolhardiness.

The Court of Appeal was firmly of the view that the analogy which the Board drew between contributory negligence (which it held was applicable to the policeman's driving — albeit at 20 m.p.h. — across a set of traffic lights set at red) and the terms of the Scheme, was mistaken. Scarman L.J., whose judgment is confined to this point said ([1973] 1 WLR 1334 at pp. 1345–6):

> There is no limitation upon the sort of conduct that may be taken into consideration and the clause places upon the Board the responsibility to decide whether the conduct of the victim is such that a reduction or rejection would be appropriate.
>
> Nevertheless, it is important that the Board should not think in terms of contributory negligence when acting under the clause. Clearly a police officer may have to take great risks often with his own safety, and sometimes with the safety of others, in the pursuit of a criminal and in the suppression of violent crime. If he subsequently becomes a claimant for criminal injuries compensation, he is entitled to have his conduct viewed in all the circumstances of his case and the Board must

have a complete discretion, unhampered by any concepts borrowed from another part of the law, to determine whether or not it is appropriate to make a full award or to diminish the amount of his compensation or to reject his claim altogether.

The importance of this judgment in the development of the Board's interpretation of para. 6(c) cannot be exaggerated. It both justifies the broad view the Board has taken of an applicant's conduct (and, in fatal cases, the conduct of the deceased) and indicates what has characterised the Board's attitude to it: whether it is appropriate to withhold or reduce compensation has depended on the Board's perception of its social value. Paragraph 21 of the old Scheme, referring to cases in which the applicant has successfully pursued the offender in a civil action, specifically provides that in its consideration of his application, '. . . the Board will not be bound by any finding of contributory negligence by any court, but will be entirely bound by the terms of the Scheme'.

The Board's Reports disclose a continuum of conduct from the delinquent to the altruistic. Some conduct is so socially valueless, such as initiating or agreeing to a fight, that the Board would seldom compensate the loser, even where the injuries were quite disproportionate to what the victim did or said. There is then a range of conduct, such as being intoxicated or engaging in other risky activity, whose social value is questionable, which may result in refusal or reduction; sometimes, though questionable, conduct which is only the consequence of stupidity or carelessness may be ignored, but only after careful consideration by the Board. An applicant who knowingly walked into an area in which a riot had recently taken place, or a terrorist bomb had recently exploded, might well have his award substantially reduced if he should suffer injury as a result of such victimising events, especially if he has ignored police warnings to keep clear. On the other hand, a stranger who inadvertently wanders into a notoriously dangerous area and who is beaten and robbed of the large sum of money which he displayed (but not carelessly) while buying a drink in a pub, could, depending on the circumstances, suffer no such reduction. Some conduct, though it undoubtedly contributes to the severity of the victim's injury, for example, where he refuses medical treatment, would be discounted if the Board perceived the social value of the victim's choice to outweigh his contribution to the injury. At the positive end of the continuum is helping behaviour. In tort the question whether a negligent defendant should be liable for the injuries suffered by a rescuer will largely turn on the foreseeability of someone attempting a rescue and of the kind of injury he sustains when carrying it out (*Ogwo* v *Taylor* [1988] AC 431); as *ex parte Ince* emphatically demonstrates, the question for the Board turns on the social value of the (exceptional) risk taken by the rescuer/victim. Lord Denning MR thought that the unarmed police officer who tackled an armed robber and was shot dead 'might be said to be foolhardy: but his widow should not be deprived of compensation' (p. 1342).

7.5.3 Implementation

7.5.3.1 Conduct before, during or after the Incident

By para. 13(d) of the new Scheme, a claims officer may withhold or reduce an award where he considers that: 'the conduct of the applicant before, during or after the incident giving rise to the application makes it inappropriate that a full award or any award at all be made'.

This wording is, as we have seen, substantively identical to that in para. 6(c) of the old Scheme. Though the Board's decisions on this element often speak of a causal connection between the victim's conduct and the incident in which he was injured, such a relationship is not the determining factor; it is as much a moral as a causative judgment. The Board, and a claims officer, can regard as disentitling of compensation conduct which has no causal connection with the incident giving rise to the application, provided only that the conduct occurred 'before, during or after' it. So far as any conduct occurring during the incident is concerned, the only question is whether the Board considers it disentitling of compensation, but in the case of conduct occurring before or afterwards, the prior question arises, what is the limit to the lapse of time between that conduct and the incident?

As to conduct occurring after the incident, the limit under the old Scheme would have been the final decision upon the application, including the determination of any hearing. Because of the increasing delay in processing applications during the late 1980s, this limit would have moved further in time from the events giving rise to the claim. Thus it would have been open to the Board to take into account conduct occurring many months or even years after the events giving rise to the claim. Suppose that one year subsequent to his sustaining a criminal injury in an unprovoked assault, the applicant, whose claim has yet to be determined, is party to a revenge attack on his assailant. The Board would almost certainly reject his application. It would also be able to do so if the revenge attack took place after it had determined the application but before the hearing concerning, for example, quantum, which the applicant had requested, had been determined. The hearing could well take place two or more years after the disentitling revenge attack. Under the new Scheme, the claims officer may, at any time before the award has been paid, reconsider her decision (new Scheme, paras 57–58; chapter 2.3.5), with the possibility of reducing or withholding it. However, it it is less easy to identify a temporal limit to the question, how long *before* the incident may the Board or the claims officer go to find conduct for taking into consideration? Subject to its duty when determining a question of fact and degree not to reach a conclusion which no reasonable tribunal could reach, it seems clear that temporal proximity may shift according to the Authority's view of the social value of the conduct in question. The Guide to the new Scheme suggests a closer rather than a more distant connection: 'In this context "conduct" means something which can fairly be described as bad conduct or misconduct and includes provocative behaviour and offensive language' (new Scheme, Guide, para. 8.14). These instances contemplate conduct by the victim which, within a relatively short time, precipitates violence by the offender. They may also be illustrated by reference to earlier decisions taken by the Board.

The decisions which most vividly illustrate the development of the Board's conception of the social value of the victim's conduct and its relevance to the subsequent application concern injuries sustained in fights in which the victim was, at least initially, a willing participant. In tort law, a plaintiff who picks a fight in which he comes off worse may be denied a remedy either because of the application of the *volenti* doctrine, or because his claim arises *ex turpi causa*. Their application is, however, substantially tempered where the defendant's response is disproportionate to the plaintiff's conduct. In *Murphy* v *Culhane* [1977] QB 94, the Court of Appeal, on an interlocutory appeal, thought that notwithstanding a guilty plea by a defendant, it would still be open to him to raise the defences of *ex turpi causa*, *volenti*, or possibly contributory negligence in civil proceedings by a victim (or his dependants) where the victim initiated the incident that resulted in his injury (or death); but as *Lane* v *Holloway* [1968] 1 QB 379 shows, a trivial assault by the victim will not preclude full damages where the retaliation is savage. Moreover, as Lord Denning MR observed in *Murphy* v *Culhane*, the plaintiff's conduct would have to be serious before he could be regarded as even partly responsible for his injury. This suggests that these defences would only be applicable in cases of well-matched fighting (Hudson, A., 'Contributory Negligence as a Defence to Battery', *Legal Studies*, 1984, vol. 4, p. 332).

The Board's initial response to such applications was very similar: if a 'fair fight' ensued from the victim's conduct the application was to be rejected, but where the offender's response was out of the ordinary a reduced award was appropriate (CICB, 1966, para. 25). At that time, para. 6E of the Statement read, 'The Board may consider how the amount of provocation offered by the victim compares with the amount of violence used by the offender'. By the late 1970s the 'fair fight' approach had been replaced by one in which the actions of the victim became the determining factor:

Our experience leads us to believe that there is seldom such a thing as a fair fight, particularly where the participants are inflamed by drink, passion, greed or aggression, and unless we adopt a realistic approach we could well end by making a full or reduced award to the one who comes out of the incident with injuries. (CICB, 1980, para. 26)

This 'realistic approach' is well exemplified by *R* v *Criminal Injuries Compensation Board, ex parte Comerford* (CICB, 1981, para. 20(a)), where the victim, who had been annoying other customers in a public house, was butted by a man who had been singled out by the victim's provocative and offensive behaviour, and who thought that the victim was about to attack him. The victim fell, and sustained severe head injuries. The Divisional Court confirmed the Board's decision, which was that notwithstanding the extent of the injuries sustained, the victim had initiated the incident; and that compensation should be refused. *Ex parte Comerford* gave expression to a corollary of the well-established principle of both tort and criminal law, that the defendant must take his victim as he finds him: the victim must take his offender as he finds him. A negligent or reckless defendant cannot complain if the plaintiff/victim has a particular sensitivity which aggravates the injury; a fortiori where some injury was intended. Neither it seems can the provocative victim complain if the offender has a particular sensitivity which aggravates the severity of his reaction, or merely reacts disproportionately to the provocation offered.

On the basis of decisions concerning voluntary fights in which the victim emerged the loser (note also the decision in *Attorney-General's Reference (No. 6 of 1980)* [1981] QB 715 in which the Court of Appeal held that fights between consenting adults were nevertheless unlawful), the Guide to the old Scheme gave a list of examples which would normally result in an award being reduced or withheld (old Scheme, App. F, para. 30). That list is reproduced, with some minor amendments, in para. 8.14 of the Guide to the new Scheme. Illustrative examples from Board decisions have been added:

(a)   If your injury was caused in a fight in which you had voluntarily agreed to take part [CICB, 1992, para. 21.3: victim challenged assailant to a fight; 1994, para. 6.13]. This is so even if the consequences of such an agreement go far beyond what you expected [CICB, 1991, para. 24.3: victim went, at her assailant's request, to her house where a fight developed during which the assailant produced a knife, slashing the victim's head; 1992, para. 26.18: victim agreed to a fight with one assailant who was then joined by his family]. If you invited someone 'outside' for a fist fight, we will not usually award compensation even if you ended up with the most serious injury [CICB, 1989, para. 20.4: victim asked his assailant if he was going to 'do anything' about an argument they were having; he did, hitting him with a beer glass]. The fact that the offender went further and used a weapon will not normally make a difference.

(b)   If without reasonable cause you struck the first blow, regardless of the degree of retaliation or the consequence [CICB, 1989, para. 20.4].

(c)   If the incident in which you were injured formed part of a pattern of violence in which you were a voluntary participant; for example, if there was a history of assaults involving both parties where you had previously been the assailant [CICB, 1993, para. 23.2: victim involved in a long-standing dispute in which he was injured by an assailant against whom he had, on a previous occasion, used violence; 1994, para. 6.13: 50% reduction].

(d)   Where you were injured whilst attempting to obtain revenge against the assailant [CICB, 1994, para. 7.14: victim armed himself in order to attack the person who had reportedly been offensive about him; as the victim got the upper hand in the ensuing fight, one of his opponent's allies stabbed and killed him].

(e)   If you used offensive language or behaved in an aggressive or threatening manner which led to the attack which caused your injuries [CICB,1989, para. 20.5: victim brandished an iron bar at and struck his assailant; 1990, para. 21.4: victim initiated an argument with his assailants, raising his hand against one of them; 1991, para. 24.2: victim had been making a nuisance of himself in a queue, annoying other customers and pulling a girl's hair; 1994, para. 16.13: victim drunk, tried to board a bus, abusive and offensive to the driver and passengers; 1995, para. 6.11: victim involved in a dispute in a nightclub; *R v Criminal Injuries Compensation Board, ex parte Williams* (1993) LEXIS 7 April 1993: victim involved in a physical dispute with his assailant].

These guidelines both give effect to the realistic approach developed by the Board and signal powerfully the difference between the standards expected of applicants for taxpayer-funded compensation and those required by the law of tort. They give effect to the criminal law's approach to the liability of parties to a joint venture whose consequences were unforeseen (*Davies v Director of Public Posecutions* [1954] AC 378), but not to that aspect of accessorial liability which excludes liability for actions which go beyond the scope of the agreement (*R v Anderson* [1966] 2 QB 110 (CCA); *Chan Wing-Siu v The Queen* [1985] AC 168). Similarly, in their conscious discounting of any notion of proportionality, these examples are in marked contrast to a primary principle of sentencing (Ashworth, A., *Sentencing and Criminal Justice*, London: Weidenfeld & Nicolson, 1995, ch. 4). The example in para. 8.14(c) of the Guide also indicates that 'a history' of assaults in which the applicant was then the assailant may amount to 'conduct of the applicant before . . . the incident' which is disentitling of compensation. The question which remains unanswered is how far into the past consideration of this pattern of violence may extend.

A second form of conduct which the Board has regarded as capable of disentitling the applicant is intoxication, whether through drink, drugs or other substances. In many of the applications it has rejected in which the victim provoked the assailant or was willing to fight, drink clearly played a significant part; intoxication thus has an aggravating effect. But merely being drunk need not result in rejection. Unlike its approach to cases where the victim initiated a fight, the Board made a full award to an applicant who was severely brain damaged when he was pushed against a wall by the taxi driver with whom he was disputing the fare. Although the applicant had been drinking, and had been a nuisance, that did not, the Board held, justify what had happened to him (CICB, 1992, para. 26.3). In its 22nd Report, the Board set out at length what it then regarded as the relevant considerations in these cases (CICB, 1986, para. 23; the points made in the quotation can be found in shorter form in paras 31 and 32 of the Guide to the old Scheme).

The Board continues to receive a large number of applications in which drink, drugs or solvent abuse, or a combination thereof, have been a substantial cause of the victim's misfortune. Many of the incidents occur at weekends and often in places and situations which the victim might have avoided had he been sober or not willing to run some kind of risk. Occasionally it is plain that the incident occurred solely as a result of the victim's own aggressive behaviour. In these cases the Board will make no award. In other cases the most that can be levelled at the victim is his or her own lack of judgment or stupidity. In this situation the Board may make an award but only after looking very carefully at all the surrounding circumstances to establish whether the applicant's conduct 'before, during or after the events giving rise to the claim' was such that it would be appropriate to make a payment from public funds, In particular the Board will look critically at any provocative, annoying or loutish behaviour which can clearly be seen to be attributable to the applicant's own over-indulgence in alcohol or the misuse of drugs. Such conduct will often be grounds for complete rejection of the application or at the least some reduction in the amount of compensation awarded.

If the 'provocative, loutish or annoying behaviour' constituted an offence under s. 5 of the Public Order Act 1986, or more simply constituted a common assault, then some of this conduct would be disentitling because it is unlawful (CICB, 1995, para. 6.11; one-third reduction for provocative conduct). Other aspects are disentitling because, as the quotation clearly shows, the Board has regarded such conduct as socially valueless. Judging by its initial remarks in para. 8.1 of the Guide to the new Scheme, the Authority is likely to maintain this view. Paragraph 8.14(e) of the Guide clearly covers the applicant who provokes the attack by the use of offensive language or threatening behaviour.

Not all questionable conduct has resulted in the refusal or reduction of compensation: what the Board might regard as immoral conduct has not of itself been a reason for reducing an award, but may be where it is provocative (CICB, old Scheme, Guide, para. 34). The issue has appeared to centre on what the applicant risked by his conduct. Where the Board has perceived it as being of low social value, its Reports suggest that it applied a robust sense of justice involving an equation between the risky conduct (broadly conceived) of the victim, and the injury he sustained. For example, it denied an award to a 15-year-old boy who, having been asked to give a talk to his class about a favourite pastime, described various ways of torturing cats, the result of which was that one of his classmates who took objection to this punched him in the face (CICB, 1988, para. 36.1).

The low social value exhibited in this application is present also in cases where children sustain injuries caused by playing dangerous games, in particular, by the use of air rifles and pistols. As we saw in chapter 5.2.1, where the victim is entirely innocent, the question will be whether the child, if under 14, could, if of full age, be regarded as having acted at least recklessly. In tort, the question would be whether an ordinary child of the victim's age would have taken any greater care, but this is clearly more difficult to answer where both victim and perpetrator are children. The Board's approach was to make no award if there was nothing to choose between the conduct of the child who inflicted the injury and that of the victim in the context of their respective understanding of the risks involved. This approach is maintained in the new Scheme. Under the heading, 'Children Playing Dangerous Games', para. 7.22 of the Guide, which repeats para. 36 of the Guide to the old Scheme, states:

These cases present two problems. We must first of all be satisfied that a crime of violence has been committed and the fact that a game was dangerous will not of itself be sufficient. Secondly, even if a crime of violence is established, we will not make an award where there is little to choose between the conduct of the child who inflicted the injury and the victim. To do so would merely be compensating the loser. In a case, for example, where 11 and 12-year-old boys fired stones from catapults at each other, and one boy received a serious eye injury, this could technically be an assault and therefore a crime of violence. The application would, however, be rejected.

This is a reference to *R* v *Criminal Injuries Compensation Board, ex parte Cragg* (unreported, 23 April 1982). The Guide continues, 'In cases where children are of different age groups or take unequal parts in the game, a full or reduced award may be made depending on the degree of participation and understanding of the risks involved'. This is illustrated by an application in which the victim, who was 13, fired an air pistol at his friend, who in turn fired a high-powered air rifle at the applicant. The friend suffered no injury; the applicant lost his sight in one eye: he received an award reduced by 25% because of his own conduct (CICB, 1978, para. 29).

7.5.3.2   The Applicant's Character
Paragraph 6(c) of the old Scheme and para. 13(e) of the new are similar in that both give a discretion to reduce or deny compensation because the applicant (or, in fatal cases, the victim) had a criminal record. They differ, however, in that the old Scheme extended the discretion to include 'unlawful conduct', a criterion omitted from para. 13(e) but replaced by a reference to 'evidence available to the claims officer'. This section deals first with the common criterion, criminal convictions. We then turn to these two alternatives.

7.5.3.2.1   *Criminal convictions*   As with the other disentitling conditions, the convictions may be those either of the victim, or, where the victim died, of a dependant. Where the application is made on behalf of the victim, such as a child or an adult unable to manage his own affairs, the applicant's convictions will not be taken into account (though the victim's might); but the Board and the claims officer would have to be satisfied that any award it made will not benefit anyone responsible for the injury, as might occur, for example, where a parent with a criminal record brings an application on behalf of his child who has been injured by someone else living in the same household (new Scheme, para. 15(b); chapter 6.4).

It was an article of faith throughout the Board's lifetime that it should have discretion to refuse or reduce an award where applicants had convictions which it regarded as being qualitatively or quantitatively 'serious', irrespective of the absence of any causal connection between those offences and the injury sustained. This was so notwithstanding that the victim's assailant is himself convicted of an offence arising from the incident in which the victim is injured (CICB, 1990, para. 21.2). It is also clear that in determining the salience of the applicant's criminal record, the

Board has been able to take account of the circumstances surrounding a given conviction. In *R* v *Criminal Injuries Compensation Board, ex parte Maxted* (1994) LEXIS, 8 July 1994, the applicant argued that the Board had treated his conviction for indecent assault on a prosecution for attempted rape as though it were the full offence, notwithstanding that the court had accepted that there was no physical contact between the applicant and the girl. Rejecting the application for judicial review Schiemann J. held that the Board was entitled to take the view that a five-year-old conviction for indecent assault was a matter which should cause it to withhold compensation.

One conviction for a serious crime of violence such as murder, manslaughter, rape or sexual abuse, or an offence under the Offences against the Person Act 1861, s. 18 or s. 20 would be sufficient to reject an application outright, as would such 'other very serious crime' as drug smuggling or dealing, kidnapping or treason (old Scheme, Guide, para. 38(a)–(b)). This category would presumably also include such offences as aggravated burglary, arson, poisoning, robbery and firearms offences.

More than one recent conviction for less serious crimes or crimes of violence such as assault, burglary or criminal damage, or numerous convictions for dishonesty of a serious nature, likewise could be sufficient (old Scheme, Guide, para. 38(c)–(d); CICB, 1989, para. 20.2: the victim's application was rejected because he had been involved in 12 burglaries; 1990, para. 21.3; 1992, paras 21.1–21.2: victim had 13 convictions; 1993, para. 23.4: five recent convictions; para. 23.5: five convictions over 10 years, including two for assault). Offences of dishonesty could include, as in *R* v *Criminal Injuries Compensation Board, ex parte Evans* (1995) LEXIS, 17 May 1995 (DC), offences under s. 55 of the Social Security Act 1986 (obtaining DSS benefits by deception). As Donaldson MR observed in *R* v *Criminal Injuries Compensation Board, ex parte Thompstone* [1984] 1 WLR 1234 at p. 1239, 'The public servant who before or after the event embezzles public funds might well not be thought to be an appropriate recipient of public bounty, although that would depend upon the circumstances and be a matter to be considered by the Board'.

The Scheme has permitted the Board to reduce rather than reject the application altogether (CICB, 1991, para. 24.5: victim raped but her compensation was reduced by 50% because of her criminal record; CICB, 1993, para. 23.3: victim's award reduced by a third for having three recent convictions; 1995, para. 6.11, award reduced by 50%); thus petty offences, for example, of drunkenness or minor breaches of the peace, are likely to prompt only the reduction of an award. Paragraph 8.15 of the Guide to the new Scheme states that 'We have discretion to withhold or reduce an award on the basis of an applicant's character as shown by his criminal convictions, even when these are unrelated to the incident for which the claim is made', and then proceeds to illustrate how this discretion might be exercised in particular cases (see further below).

As this makes clear, there continues to be no requirement that the convictions be causally connected with the injury. This matter was considered in the early 1980s by the Divisional Court and the Court of Appeal in *R* v *Criminal Injuries Compensation Board, ex parte Thompstone*, which was confirmed in *R* v *Criminal Injuries*

Compensation Board, ex parte Cook [1996] 1 WLR 1037 (CA). In *ex parte Thompstone*, the Board had denied compensation to two applicants, both of whom had long lists of previous convictions. The attacks were unprovoked, and had no connection with these convictions. The applicants sought judicial review, contending that the Board had no jurisdiction to withhold compensation where there was no connection between the injury complained of and their 'character'. Following an extensive review of the history of the Scheme and in particular of para. 6(c) and its earlier variants, Stephen Brown J. said [1983] 1 All ER 936, 943:

> ... the Scheme, as published, is intended to afford the widest possible discretion to the Board in its administration of the Scheme. Paragraph 6(c) gives the Board discretion to withhold or reduce compensation, both having regard to the conduct of the applicant in relation to the incident and, furthermore, having regard to his character and way of life. In my judgment, this latter consideration is not limited to matters relevant in some way to the particular incident.

He dismissed the application, and his decision was affirmed, in arguably more forceful language, by the Court of Appeal ([1984] 1 WLR 1234). The Master of the Rolls was quite unable to accept the appellants' submissions. The Scheme gave the Board a wide discretion to reject applications where it would be inappropriate to compensate the applicant from public funds, and was in no way limited to a consideration of those convictions only that might be connected with the injury in respect of which the compensation was sought. Lord Donaldson's characterisation of the Scheme has been regularly relied upon by the Divisional Court, for example, in *R v Criminal Injuries Compensation Board, ex parte Maxted* (1994) LEXIS 8 July 1994, *R v Criminal Injuries Compensation Board, ex parte Thomas* (1994) LEXIS 18 October 1994 and *R v Criminal Injuries Compensation Board, ex parte Evans* (1995) LEXIS 17 May 1995, and more recently by the Court of Appeal. In *R v Criminal Injuries Compensation Board, ex parte Cook* [1996] 1 WLR 1037 an application by the widow of a man who had been murdered was refused because of his criminal convictions. The primary issue in the Court of Appeal turned on the question whether the Board should have considered her good character (chapter 7.5.2.1). Though no point was taken concerning the Board's ability under the old Scheme to take into account convictions having no causal relationship with the criminal injury, Hobhouse L.J. quoted at length from the Master of the Rolls's judgment in *ex parte Thompstone*, concluding (at p. 1052), that, 'The character of the scheme and of the decisions of the Board which implement it is as stated by Donaldson MR'.

A useful illustration of the application of para. 6(c) is recorded in the Board's 22nd Report (CICB, 1986, para. 22). The applicant and his girlfriend were unexpectedly visited by two friends of hers whom she had not seen for two years. There was much celebration accompanied by much alcohol; later an inebriated argument developed between the applicant and one of the visitors. The visitor's boyfriend arrived, and there were some verbal exchanges between him and the applicant, but no violence. The following morning three men called at the applicant's house, attacked him with knives and an iron bar and, as they were leaving, shot him with a sawn-off shotgun. The victim, who had to have his right leg amputated, had nine previous convictions, including possessing offensive weapons and controlled drugs. The single member made an interim award and decided that the final award should be reduced by 20% on account of these convictions. Under the provisions in para. 22 of the old Scheme, he referred the claim to a hearing, which agreed with his decision.

The 1978 Review was slightly critical of the Board's somewhat unforgiving response to an applicant's criminal record (Home Office, *Review of the Criminal Injuries Compensation Scheme: Report of an Interdepartmental Working Party*, 1978, para. 17.9). It considered that the Board should take into account any meritorious conduct on the applicant's part. This is reflected in para. 39 of the Guide to the old Scheme, and is now included in para. 8.17 of the Guide to the new Scheme. This indicates that the claims officer 'will consider any relevant mitigating factors such as where the injury resulted from the applicant's assistance to the police or in upholding the law or from genuinely helping someone who was under attack' (CICB, 1991, para. 24.4: victim injured when going to another's assistance, but denied compensation because of his criminal convictions; 1995, para. 6.11: victim having a substantial list of convictions made a full award who assisted the prevention of an armed robbery).

A key difference between the old and new Schemes which was signalled in the 1993 White Paper (Home Office, *Compensating Victims of Violent Crime: Changes to the Criminal Injuries Compensation Scheme*, Cm 2434, London: HMSO, 1993, para. 27(iii)) is that whereas the Board was able to take account of spent convictions if it considered that it could not reach a just decision without that information, the new Scheme provides that convictions which are spent under the Rehabilitation of Offenders Act 1974 are to be ignored (new Scheme, Guide, para. 8.15). The new Scheme further provides for a system of 'penalty points' for live convictions, based in part upon the rehabilitation periods in the 1974 Act and in part on the period of time between the imposition of the sentence and the receipt of the application (new Scheme, Guide, para. 8.16). Although the calculation of the applicable penalty points in any case may prove difficult, the intended transparency of the new Scheme in this regard is a clear improvement on its predecessor, where research (admittedly on a small sample) showed a disquieting variation in the Board's exercise of this controversial discretion (Newburn, T., *The Settlement of Claims at the Criminal Injuries Compensation Board*, Home Office Research Study 112, London: HMSO, 1989).

The table setting out the penalty points which is to be found in para. 8.16 of the Guide to the new Scheme is reproduced in substance in Table 7.1.

Table 7.1   Penalty Points

Case	Sentence of the Court	Period between sentence and application	Penalty points
1	30 months' imprisonment or more	(a) sentence or less	10
		(b) more than sentence but less than sentence plus 5 years	9
		(c) more than sentence plus 5 years but less than sentence plus 10 years	7
		(d) more than sentence plus 10 years	5
2	Between 6 and 30 months' imprisonment	(a) sentence or less	10
		(b) more than sentence but less than sentence plus 3 years	7
		(c) more than sentence plus 3 years but less than sentence plus 7 years	5
		(d) more than sentence plus 7 years	2
3	6 months' imprisonment or less	(a) sentence or less	10
		(b) more than sentence but less than sentence plus 2 years	5
		(c) more than sentence plus 2 years	2

Case	Sentence of the Court	Period between sentence and application	Penalty points
4	Fine, community service order, probation or supervision order, combination order, attendance centre order, bind-over, conditional discharge, compensation order	(a) less than 2 years (b) 2 years or more	2 1
5	Absolute discharge, admonishment	(a) less than 6 months (b) 6 months or more	1 0

For the purposes of the table, 'imprisonment', whether suspended or not, means the sentence imposed by the court, not the actual time spent in prison. It includes a sentence of detention in a young offender institution, borstal or borstal training, or other custodial sentence. Any sentence other than those provided for will be placed by the Authority into one of the table's five categories according to its seriousness as measured by the rehabilitation period(s) in the 1974 Act. Any sentence imposed by a court after the application has been sent in will be treated as if it had been imposed on the day before the Authority received the application.

The table does not specify whether the date of a deferred sentence runs from the date of conviction, as in the Rehabilitation of Offenders Act 1974, or from the date on which such a sentence was in fact imposed. This will not, however, affect its impact because, even where the sentence was deferred, if at the date on which the application was received the conviction was spent by virtue of the 1974 Act, the claims officer would be bound to ignore it. Suppose the applicant had been convicted on 1 February 1990 and his sentence deferred for four months. When imposed, it was three months' imprisonment. Under the 1974 Act this conviction will be spent, in the case of an adult, on 1 February 1997. If the Authority were to receive his application on 1 March 1997, it would be bound to ignore it, notwithstanding that it is two months less than the seven-year rehabilitation period when counted from the date of the sentence (1 May 1990).

Depending on the number of penalty points appropriate in any case, para. 8.16 provides a scale of reduction in any award which is reproduced in Table 7.2. However, this must be read subject to the Authority's discretion to determine what ought to be the appropriate reduction in any case.

Table 7.2   Reduction in Award

Penalty points	*Percentage reduction*
0–2	0%
3–5	25%
6–7	50%
8–9	75%
10 or more	100%

In general terms, increasing credit is given as the period of time between the original sentence and the application to the Authority increases; in this way the new Scheme formalises the Board's recognition of an applicant's efforts to go straight (old Scheme, Guide, para. 37). Conversely, the shorter the lapse of time between the sentence and the application, the greater the degree of reduction. Subject to what is said below concerning the Authority's exercise of its discretion, applications made during the currency of a sentence of imprisonment (cases 1(a), 2(a) and 3(a)) will attract a 100% reduction, that is, be rejected, irrespective of its length and, in line with note 1 to para. 8.16, whether or not the applicant might, for example, at that time be on release on licence.

Because of the provisions of the 1974 Act (under which sentences of more than 30 months' imprisonment can never be rehabilitated), sentences falling within cases 2–5 in table 7.1 will in due course be spent, and thus will have no bearing upon an application (new Scheme, Guide, paras 8.15 and 8.16, note 3). For example, the 1974 Act provides that sentences of imprisonment between six and 30 months may be rehabilitated, in the case of an adult, after 10 years. Suppose that the applicant had been sentenced to two years' imprisonment in 1984; that conviction will be spent by the date of his application to the Authority in 1996 and will be ignored by the claims officer. If, however, the date of conviction were 1990, his application would attract five penalty points because (case 2(c)) the period (six years) between the date of the sentence (1990) and the date of the application (1996) is more than the sentence plus three years (five years) but is less than the sentence plus seven years (nine years). If the sentence had been nine months' imprisonment and had been imposed in 1987, an application made in 1996 would attract two penalty points because (case 2(d)) the period (nine years) between the date of the sentence (1987) and the date of the application (1996) is more than the sentence plus seven years (seven years and nine months). This sentence will continue to attract two penalty points for one more year after which the conviction will be spent. Similar examples can be drawn from case 4. The 1974 Act provides that the rehabilitation period for a fine is five years in the case of an adult. Thus a conviction and fine imposed on the applicant in 1990 will be spent in 1995 and will have no bearing on his application in 1996. If the fine had been imposed in 1995, it would attract two penalty points in the case of an application received by the Authority during 1996 or 1997 (case 4(a)); thereafter, and until 2000, when it would be spent, it will attract one point (case 4(b)).

The 1974 Act provides that a conviction against an offender who was under 18 on the date of the conviction will, in the case of terms of imprisonment under 30 months, fines and community service orders, be spent in half the time that would apply had he been an adult. It is not necessary for the table to make any further adjustment to the penalty points applicable in cases 2–4 because their impact will inevitably be reduced by the operation of the shorter rehabilitation periods. Suppose therefore that an applicant who was a juvenile in 1984 had been sentenced to two years' youth custody then; his conviction would have been spent in 1989 and would be ignored by a claims officer dealing with his application received in 1996. Were the date of conviction 1990, the table would likewise have no impact on his application; in his case, penalty points would only begin to bite where the conviction occurred after 1991. Had he been fined in 1990, the conviction would have been spent after two and a half years and would have no bearing on his 1996 application.

However, where the conviction imposed on a juvenile is not spent, the penalty points affecting the application will be the same as if the applicant were an adult. The rehabilitation periods governing an offender who, in 1994, was sentenced to two months' imprisonment are, for an adult, seven, and for an offender who was a juvenile at the date of conviction (and who would have been sentenced to detention in a young offender institution), three and a half years. If either should apply in 1996, their applications will attract five penalty points because (case 3(b)) the period (two years) between the date of the sentence (1994) and the receipt of the application (1996) is more than the period of the sentence (two months) but is less than the sentence plus two years (two years and two months).

The operation of these rehabilitation periods also suggests that there may be instances in which, if the applicant delays making the application (but of course keeping within the two-year limitation period (chapter 7.2)), she may be able to render spent a conviction which, if her application were received by the Authority a year earlier, would have attracted penalty points. Suppose an applicant had been convicted and sentenced to 18 months' imprisonment in 1987. That conviction will be spent in 1997. Now suppose she sustains a criminal injury in 1996. If she applies during 1996, her sentence will attract two penalty points, because (case 2(d)) the period (nine years) between the date of the sentence (1987) and the receipt of the application (1996) is more than the sentence plus seven years (eight years and six months). By themselves, two penalty points will effect no reduction in the compensation which would otherwise be awarded. But now add a further conviction and a fine imposed in 1994. This will attract one penalty point. Taken alone this would again effect no reduction in the award, but when added to the other two penalty points, there may be a 25% reduction. Since the conviction and fine will not be spent until 1999, if the applicant delays her application so that it is received in 1997 after her 1987 conviction is spent, the penalty points which a year earlier it would have attracted will no longer bite.

If an applicant has been convicted more than once, each conviction that is not spent will attract the appropriate penalty points, which will be aggregated. Thus the table gives effect to the Board's approach under the old Scheme that a series of minor offences may, in their impact on the applicant's eligibility for an award, be as cumulatively disentitling as one very serious offence. For example, an applicant who was, as an adult, convicted and sentenced in 1992 to nine months' imprisonment and who makes an application in 1996, will suffer five penalty points because (case 2(c)) the period (four years) between the date of the sentence (1992) and the receipt of the application (1996) is more than the period of the sentence plus three years (three years and nine months) but is less than the sentence plus seven years (seven years and nine months). The same total of penalty points will apply to an applicant who makes an application in 1996, having been convicted and fined for offences twice in 1995 (case 4(a): the period (one year) between the date of sentence (1995) and the receipt of the application is less than two years, so two penalty points each) and once in 1993 (case 4(b): the period (three years) between the date of sentence (1994) and the receipt of the application (1996) is more than two years, so one penalty point), giving five penalty points in all.

By contrast, and in common with the Rehabilitation of Offenders Act 1974, sentences of imprisonment falling within case 1, that is, those exceeding 30 months (as well as similar sentences concerning young offenders, such as detention in a young offender institution or under s. 53 of the Children and Young Persons Act 1933), will continue to be relevant to the applicant's position throughout his lifetime, even though the Scheme does, as can be seen from the table, provide for a partial rehabilitation. An application made in 1996 by someone who had been sentenced in 1980 to eight years' imprisonment will attract seven penalty points because (case 1(c)) the period (16 years) between the date of the sentence (1980) and the receipt of the application (1996) is more than the sentence plus five years (13 years) but is less than the sentence plus 10 years (18 years). If the sentence had been four years it would attract five penalty points because (case 1(d)) the period (16 years) between the date of the sentence (1980) and the receipt of the application (1996) is more than the sentence plus 10 years (14 years). If, in each case, the offender had, since the date of that sentence, committed no further offences, then the reduction would normally be 50% and 25% respectively.

But the most rehabilitation which a sentence of imprisonment exceeding 30 months will normally attract is 75%. The table makes no provision for a further reduction as the period between the date of sentence and the receipt of the application increases beyond the year in which the total of the sentence plus 10 years falls. It will be noted that the table does specify zero penalty points in the case of an application made six months after an absolute discharge or an admonishment (case 5(b)); the omission of any zero option in cases 2, 3 and 4 follows from the fact that the operation of the 1974 Act will eventually mean that the convictions in these cases will be spent. But a conviction whose sentence falls within case 1 of the table can never be spent under the 1974 Act, which is why it continues to have an impact on the offender's application, whenever it is made. For example, an application made by an offender who, at the age of 25, had been sentenced in 1985 to 16 years for armed robbery, will:

(a)   attract 10 penalty points if it is made during the currency of the sentence (case 1(a));

(b)   attract nine penalty points if it is made between 16 and 21 years after the sentence was imposed (case 1(b));

(c)   attract seven penalty points if it is made between 21 and 26 years after the sentence was imposed (case 1(c)): and

(d)   attract five penalty points whenever it is made 26 years or more after the sentence was imposed (case 1(d)).

In this last case, the applicant would, if the application were made in the 26th year after the sentence was imposed, be 51. Indeed, the sentence would continue to attract five penalty points should (like the deceased in *R v Criminal Injuries Compensation Board, ex parte Cook* [1996] 1 WLR 1037) he be murdered and his widow apply for compensation.

The continuation of penalty points throughout the victim's lifetime in this case gives effect to the policy of ensuring that applications concerning those who have pursued a life of crime, or otherwise reoffend, will always be subject to the scale of percentage reductions. Thus where the offender commits further offences, those penalty points will be aggregated with the subsisting points to effect a more substantial reduction in any award. For example, in case 1(d) above, where an applicant has five penalty points subsisting from an earlier sentence of imprisonment exceeding 30 months, the commission in the year preceding the year in which the application is made of even a minor offence attracting a fine upon conviction will mean a total of seven penalty points (five for the case 1(d) sentence, plus two for a fine imposed within two years of the date on which the application is received (case 4(a)), which in turn suggests a 50% reduction in the award.

The Guide therefore indicates, first, that there are some circumstances in which no award will be made, and, second, that there are some cases in which penalty points will subsist thoughout an offender's life and will result in the reduction (say, by 25%) in an award, even if he has never reoffended. But these propositions must be subject to the Authority's exercise of its discretion under the Scheme; it would act unlawfully if it determined the outcome of individual applications on the basis of the application of rules of its own making which deprived the claims officer of the power to make the judgment required by para. 13(e). This was the case in *R v Criminal Injuries Compensation Board, ex parte RJC (An Infant)* [1978] Crim LR 220, where the Divisional Court held that an earlier version of the old Scheme which provided that, in certain circumstances, the applicant 'will not receive' an award, deprived the Board of its discretion in such cases. The Scheme was amended to read, 'will rarely receive' an award. The Board has made an award to a prisoner badly injured following an attack in his cell (CICB, 1990, para. 26.1).

Assuming that the penalty point procedure describes what will normally, but not inevitably, be the outcome of an application made by a person with criminal convictions (who, in fatal cases, may be the victim or the dependant), some further examples may be used to explain the application of the procedure as it affects cases 1–3. Cases 4 and 5 are relatively straightforward.

Case 1: Suppose that the applicant was sentenced to 10 years' imprisonment under the Offences against the Person Act 1861, s. 18, in 1980. Under the 1974 Act, that sentence cannot be rehabilitated. If she were to make an application in 1996, she would attract seven penalty points because (case 1(c)) the period (16 years) between the date of the sentence (1980) and the date on which the application was received by the Authority (1996) is more than the period of the sentence plus five years (15 years) but is less than the period of the sentence plus 10 years (20 years). If the sentence had been imposed in 1985, then she would attract nine penalty points because (case 1(b)) the period (11 years) between the date of the sentence (1985) and the date on which the application was received by the Authority (1996) is more than the period of the sentence (10 years) but is less than the sentence plus 5 years (15 years). She will attract five penalty points only where the sentence was imposed at any time before 1976 (case 1(d)).

Case 2: Suppose that the applicant was sentenced to two years' imprisonment in 1980. That sentence would have been spent in 1990 and will be ignored. Such a sentence will therefore be 'live' for the purposes of the table if, the application being made in 1996, it were imposed in any year after 1986. Suppose therefore that it was imposed in 1990. In this case the application will attract five penalty points because (case 2(c)) the period (six years) between the date of the sentence (1990) and the date on which the application was received by the Authority (1996) is more than the period of the sentence plus three years (five years) but is less than the period of the sentence plus seven years (nine years). But if the sentence had been imposed in 1992, then it would attract seven penalty points because (case 2(b)) the period (four years) between the date of the sentence (1992) and the date on which the application was received by the Authority (1996) is more than the period of the sentence (two years) but is less than the sentence plus three years (five years).

Case 3: Suppose that the applicant was sentenced to six months' imprisonment in 1990. That sentence will be spent in 1997 in the case of an adult, and will already be spent (in three and a half years) if the applicant was under 18 when it was imposed. An application received in 1996 from the adult offender will therefore attract two penalty points (case 3(c)) because the period (six years) between the date of the sentence (1990) and the receipt of the application (1996) is more than the sentence plus two years (two years and six months). Had the application been made at any time within two years and five months after the sentence was imposed in 1990, that is, sometime during 1993, then (assuming that this table were part of the old Scheme) it would have attracted five penalty points because the period (two years and five months) between the date of the sentence (1990) and the receipt of the application (1993) would have been more than the sentence (six months) but less than the sentence plus two years (two years and six months).

To summarise: where the applicant (or, in fatal cases, the deceased) had criminal convictions, the position is:

(a) If the conviction is spent, then it will be ignored by the Authority; but if the sentence was to imprisonment for more than 30 months, then it will continue to attract penalty points throughout the offender's lifetime (and beyond).

(b) If the conviction is live and the application is received during the period of sentence, irrespective of whether the applicant has earned remission or is on early release, the sentence will attract 10 penalty points.

(c) If the application is received after the period of sentence, the penalty points which it will attract can be calculated, in cases where the applicant was sentenced to imprisonment (cases 1–4) from Table 7.3 where:

P = the period between date of sentence and receipt of application
S = period of sentence

Table 7.3   Penalty points

Case	Period (P) between sentence and application	Penalty points
$S > 30$ months		
1(a)	$P < S$	10
(b)	$S < P < S + 5$	9
(c)	$S + 5 < P < S + 10$	7
(d)	$S + 10 < P$	5
6 months $< S < 30$ months		
2(a)	$P < S$	10
(b)	$S < P < S + 3$	7
(c)	$S + 3 < P < S + 7$	5
(d)	$S + 7 < P$	2
$S < 6$ months		
3(a)	$P < S$	10
(b)	$S < P < S + 2$	5
(c)	$S + 2 < P$	2

(d) Non-custodial sentences attract a maximum of two penalty points where the application is made within two years of their imposition; thereafter they attract one point until the conviction is spent.

(e) The penalty points for all live convictions must be calculated and aggregated to give the total affecting the application.

(f) A total of two or less penalty points will normally effect no reduction in the award.

7.5.3.2.2 *Unlawful conduct* The second condition under which the Board has been able to refuse or reduce compensation because of the applicant's character is where an applicant has engaged in unlawful conduct. This part of para. 6(c) of the old Scheme overlaps with the Board's power to disentitle an applicant because of his conduct before, during or after the events giving rise to the claim. An applicant who strikes the first blow may be refused compensation under either provision, as may an applicant who, having made one genuine application yet not finalised, subsequently makes one that is fraudulent (CICB, 1988, para. 36.1). Under the new Scheme, such an applicant could similarly be caught by the alternative criterion in para. 13(e) (chapter 7.5.3.2.3) or, if the second application were made before the first award had been paid, following a reconsideration under paras 56–57 (chapter 2.3.5).

Whereas the phrase 'before, during or after' implies a temporal relationship, though not necessarily a causal one, between the applicant's conduct and the events giving rise to the application, there is no requirement of any relationship, however tenuous, between those events and the applicant's 'unlawful conduct'. Like his criminal convictions, what this demonstrates is the applicant's lack of personal worth to be a recipient of public money. This disentitling condition can therefore be seen as an important supplement to that just discussed. It permits the Board to take into account findings of guilt following proceedings in a juvenile court or in a Scottish children's hearing, or admissions of guilt, as typically in a caution. Since the Board can take hearsay evidence into account, it has also been able to disentitle an applicant whom the police have for years suspected of committing serious offences, but against whom no convictions for these offences have been secured.

While this provision has permitted the Board to refuse or reduce compensation whether the unlawful conduct was connected with the injury or not, its wording clearly covers applications in which the injury arose while the victim was indeed engaged in such conduct (old Scheme, Guide, para. 35). The Board's practice has been to reject claims from victims injured in the course of committing a serious crime, for example, dealing in drugs (CICB, 1984, para. 34). What constitutes a 'serious' crime is not explicit for the purpose of this element of para. 6(c), but may be taken as having the same connotation as in its approach to an applicant's convictions (old Scheme, Guide, para. 37). Such conduct would likewise almost always preclude a plaintiff from recovering in a personal injury action should he be injured during its commission (*Pitts* v *Hunt* [1991] 1 QB 24 (CA)), but as *Revill* v *Newbery* [1996] QB 567 shows, where the assailant's response to the victim's illegal behaviour was unreasonable, the victim may yet recover damages in a civil action against him.

The facts of *Revill* v *Newbery* were that the defendant, a 76-year-old man, was sleeping in the brick shed on his allotment in order to protect his gardening equipment. His shed had been burgled on previous occasions. He was awoken in the night by the sound of the plaintiff attempting to break in. He loaded his shotgun, and without being able to see whether there was anybody directly in front of the door, fired a shot through a small hole in the door, wounding the plaintiff in the arm and chest. The plaintiff was subsequently prosecuted for other offences he had committed that night, pleading guilty. The defendant was prosecuted on a charge of wounding and was acquitted. These facts are materially similar to a number of other instances during the mid 1990s in which victims of burglary and personal violence took retaliatory action, injuring their offender, and which atttracted widespread publicity.

The plaintiff succeeded in an action for breach of the duty of care in s. 1 of the Occupiers' Liability Act 1984, Rougier J. rejecting the defendant's submission that the claim arose *ex turpi causa*. He also held the plaintiff two-thirds responsible for his injuries. Dismissing the defendant's appeal, the Court of Appeal held (Neill L.J., p. 577) that notwithstanding the plaintiff's status as a trespasser, '... by enacting s. 1 of the 1984 Act, Parliament has decided that an occupier cannot treat a burglar as an outlaw', and has imposed a duty of care whose particular application will depend on the facts of the case. In this case, the defendant was shooting blind, at body height, on the horizontal, and in the direction of the noise which had alerted him. On these facts, the Court held that the defendant owed the plaintiff *some* duty (Neill L.J., p. 578, original emphasis). It also agreed with the finding of contributory negligence. Millett L.J. put the principles very shortly (p. 580):

> For centuries the common law has permitted reasonable force to be used in defence of the person or property. Violence may be returned with necessary violence. But the force used must not exceed the limits of what is reasonable in the circumstances. Changes in society and in social perceptions may have meant that what might have been considered reasonable at one time would no longer be so regarded; but the principle remains the same. The assailant or intruder may be met with reasonable force but no more; the use of excessive violence against him is an actionable wrong.

But it is not a basis for compensation under the Scheme. Although it is an early decision, the Board did reject an application from a burglar who had been peppered with shot by the irate householder (CICB, 1970, para. 5(4)). If a plaintiff such as in *Revill* v *Newbery* were to make an application under the new Scheme, it would surely be rejected. The fundamental justification for the continuation of this approach is that the taxpayer should not be called upon to compensate offenders who happen to become victims at the time of their offending. Such cases are distinguishable first from the criminal liability of the 'victim's' assailant, since the State properly has a general interest in punishing offences against the person where these cannot be justified as instances of the reasonable use of force in the prevention of crime or in self-defence, and secondly from the civil liability of the assailant, since this will amount to a charge on private, and not public, funds. There is also, no doubt, an element of just deserts in the rejection of such applications.

Although the discussion has centred on criminal conduct, the old Scheme was not so restricted. A landlord who persistently failed to comply with his statutory or contractual obligations and is criminally injured by one of his tenants may have his application refused or may receive a reduced award, notwithstanding the criminal liability of the tenant; likewise an employer or co-employee who persists in racial or sexual harassment of an employee who one day, in desperation, assaults him. However, the Board certainly looked askance at such attempts by the tenant and the employee to take the law into their own hands if they, in turn, should come off worse. So, where an applicant attempted to reprimand a schoolboy who had thrown an aerosol can into the road, and then slapped his face when the boy swore at him, the Board reduced his award by 20% when one of the boy's friends who had gathered round the two of them punched the applicant in the face, causing lacerations and subsequent numbness on his right side (CICB, 1988, paras 37.1–37.3).

The discussion has centred on the unlawful conduct of the victim as applicant. Where the victim is killed as a result of his unlawful conduct then, as has been noted earlier, his dependants, though blameless, could be refused compensation (CICB, 1986, para. 27: application by the victim's father rejected, the victim having injected a fatal quantity of heroin). Similarly it would be open to the Board to refuse or reduce an award, for example, to the widow of a murdered terrorist or gang member (old Scheme, Guide, para. 33). A life of crime may therefore preclude compensation both for the victim, or in the event of his death, his dependants (*Burns* v *Edman* [1970] 2 QB 541).

Conversely, though the victim could not be in any way blamed for his death, the unlawful conduct (at any time) of the applicant may bar or reduce compensation. This would clearly be so, for example, if a wife had taken out a contract on her husband's life, so that she would be free to marry someone else. Similarly, suppose, in a dispute between terrorist or other violent gangs, the innocent child of one of the protagonists were killed in a kidnap attempt; even though the applicant had been once acquitted on a charge under the Prevention of Terrorism (Temporary Provisions) Act 1989, his application might well be refused. Like the Court of Appeal in *Gray* v *Barr* [1971] 2 QB 554, the Board has not been bound to take an acquittal as indicating that the plaintiff/victim was acting lawfully at the time. In permitting the refusal or reduction of compensation in such a case, the 1990 revision of the old Scheme provided no less than did the earlier version of para. 6(c), for it would have been open to the Board to reach a similar decision on the basis of the terrorist applicant's 'way of life'. That phrase, however, allowed the Board to take into account any aspect of the victim's or the applicant's way of life, whether lawful or unlawful; the 1990 revision did therefore impose one significant limitation here: the conduct had to be unlawful.

7.5.3.2.3 *Evidence available to the claims officer* By comparison with the relatively complex provisions in the Guide to the new Scheme which specify the penalty points attaching to an applicant's convictions (new Scheme, para. 13(e); Guide, para. 8.16) and with the Guide's illustrations of 'conduct before, during or after' the incident giving rise to the application (new Scheme, para. 13(d); Guide, para. 8.14), no guidance whatever is given about this second, wide discretionary power contained in para. 13(e) of the new Scheme. Allowing for the requirement that the Authority must act in accordance with the Scheme and with the principles of rationality and reasonableness required by *Associated Provincial Picture Houses Ltd* v *Wednesbury Corporation* [1948] 1 KB 223, it seems that the claims officer will indeed be at liberty to take account of any evidence available to her which she considers make it inappropriate that the applicant should receive a full or any award.

That evidence will almost always emanate from the police, a source which the Board would almost always regard as impeccable. This will mean that the Authority will, as now, be able to consider hearsay evidence which would be inadmissible at trial and allegations against the applicant which the police have been unable to verify, or which the CPS or a Procurator Fiscal has decided not to prosecute, because they were not persuaded that there was a reasonable prospect of a conviction. Likewise, the Authority would be able to take into account cautions and findings of guilt in respect of juveniles.

The scope of this discretion is also broad enough to permit the reintroduction of the kind of consideration which was associated with the power the Board had under the pre-1990 version of para. 6(c) of the old Scheme, to take into account the applicant's 'way of life'. As we saw earlier (chapter 7.5.2.1), this discretion was widely criticised in that it permitted the Board to reach judgments about the applicant's moral worth, and hence eligibility for compensation. It was objectionable too, because, as the Court of Appeal confirmed in *R* v *Criminal Injuries Compensation Board, ex parte Thompstone* [1984] 1 WLR 1234, its scope was 'not limited to matters relevant in some way to the particular incident'. This is also the case under the new Scheme: para. 13(e) does not require that the evidence which makes it inappropriate that the applicant should be compensated should be in any way connected with the incident giving rise to the application. With such a power, the more specific provisions in para. 13(d) and (e) appear almost superfluous. Either the applicant's conduct before, during or after the incident, or his criminal convictions, could as well be described as 'evidence available to the claims officer'.

8   Assessment of Compensation

8.1   BACKGROUND: THE COMMON LAW BASIS OF ASSESSMENT

With the exception of the survival of a deceased victim's action, and a number of other variations, the assessment of compensation under the old Scheme has been based on the principles applicable to an action under the Fatal Accidents Act 1976 or to a personal injury action. These variations are in large measure attributable to the fundamental distinction in the source of funding for the two systems of compensation: the taxpayer on the one hand and the wrongdoer (or his insurance company) on the other. As we saw in chapter 1.2.2, the common law basis of assessment was the preferred model; this was so because it was considered to be 'the closest to providing the type of compensation which is required' (Home Office, *Review of the Criminal Injuries Compensation Scheme: Report of an Interdepartmental Working Party*, London: HMSO, 1978, para. 10.3), that is, compensation based neither on a criterion such as need, as can be found in a welfare context, nor on the full measure of damages in a civil action, but which otherwise comes as close as the prevailing political judgment will allow to restoring the victim to his position prior to the injury. As the introduction of the tariff Scheme clearly shows, that judgment may in time entail the proposition that it is either too expensive, or the expenditure patterns too unpredictable, to continue to allow such restoration.

Unquestioning acceptance that the loss to the victim or his dependants ought to be compensated could not disguise some real difficulties. One of these concerns how victims earning high salaries should be dealt with. Though the adoption of the common law model necessarily implied that high earners should be compensated to the full extent of their loss, the Scheme's supporters thought it inequitable that this should be met from the public purse (Home Office, *Compensation for the Victims of Crimes of Violence*, Cmnd 1406, London: HMSO, 1961, para. 49), a sentiment echoed by the 1986 Working Party (Home Office, *Criminal Injuries Compensation: A Statutory Scheme*, London: HMSO, 1986, para. 14.1; see also Cane, P., *Atiyah's*

Accidents, Compensation and the Law, 5th ed., London: Weidenfeld and Nicolson, 1993, pp. 127–131):

> Public feeling demands that innocent victims should be able to maintain a reasonable standard of living compared with that which they enjoyed previously, but this does not extend to compensating in full from public funds the loss of earnings incurred by very highly paid employees.

The Working Party further endorsed its predecessor's view that high earners are more likely to make some provision against the possibility that their earnings or earning capacity will be interrupted by injury, whether accidental or otherwise. Accordingly, the solution to this matter was the imposition of an arbitrary ceiling on compensable loss of earnings and earning capacity, a ceiling which is maintained in the new Scheme.

A rather different approach canvassed before the 1986 Working Party was that compensation under the Scheme should be assessed according to a tariff reflecting not merely the harm to the victim, but also its 'seriousness' as evidenced by the offender's degree of fault. Such a tariff would reflect the difference between negligently and intentionally (or recklessly) inflicted injuries, a difference frequently relied on, for example, by Victim Support as the factor which makes criminal injuries more injurious to their victims than simply the physical harm caused (Home Office, *Criminal Injuries Compensation: A Statutory Scheme*, 1986, para. 12.2):

> The 'criminal scale' would be based on a concept of the seriousness of the offence from the point of view of the typical victim, taking into account not only the actual consequences to the victim, but also the symbolic gravity of the offence and the fact that the victim has been the victim of a crime rather than an accident.

Under this proposal the victim of a given injury would receive greater compensation than is available at common law where it was inflicted in the commission of an offence of high seriousness, and conversely less where the offence was of low seriousness. Such a proposal clearly faces formidable objections. Devising a matrix which would permit distinctions to be drawn in one dimension according to the offender's degree of fault (representing, though very crudely, the seriousness of the offence), and in the other according to the actual impact of the injury, would be profoundly controversial. Let us suppose, as is demonstrated by the Board's 23rd Report (CICB, 1987, para. 41), that a victim having his two front teeth knocked out would receive an award of £2,000 (the current tariff level). What multiplier could be used to distinguish an intentional from a reckless blow or to distinguish a 70-year-old from a 20 or 10-year-old, or a male from a female victim? Or to show that the injury was not caused by a crime of violence but was accidentally sustained while the victim was taking an exceptional risk, justified in all the circumstances, in an act of law enforcement? If he should therefore receive less because it was of low symbolic gravity, we should hardly be surprised if the Scheme came under a torrent of criticism. And then how would the Board have any way of judging the seriousness of a criminal injury caused by a crime of violence when the offender is unapprehended? The Working Party rightly rejected this proposal while favouring the retention of common law damages as the preferred model.

While the heads of damage and the maximum payable for loss of earnings and of earning capacity under the old Scheme have always been restricted by comparison with the private remedy, the virtually complete parallel between the old Scheme and the common law in the matter of the assessment of general damages has meant that awards for pain and suffering and loss of amenity in particular have been comparable; indeed, the awards made by the Board and the civil courts have for many years been regarded as generally interchangeable. Apart from the shared basis of assessment, this follows both from the fact that the Board's members are for the most part themselves personal injury practitioners, and from the fact that the number of monetary awards made each year by the Board (34,570 in 1994–95; CICB, 1995, para. 3.8) exceeds the number of personal (and fatal) injury cases which come to trial by a ratio of about 10 : 1. Conversely, where such figures have been laid down by the courts for particular injuries, the Board has always regarded itself as being bound by them, subject to the particular facts of each application. Moreover, in the case of an applicant earning at or below the average weekly wage, there would be no difference at all between public and private compensation save, in the former case, for the full deduction of virtually all collateral benefits. In this respect, the changes introduced by the Social Security Act 1989 brought the common law very much closer to the arrangements under the old Scheme; arrangements which, for the most part, survive in its successor (chapter 9.1).

However, while para. 12 of the old Scheme provided that 'Subject to the other provisions of this Scheme, compensation will be assessed on the basis of common law damages', this did not mean, in Hutchinson J.'s words in *R v Criminal Injuries Compensation Board, ex parte Cummins* (1992) LEXIS, 17 January 1992 (DC) that 'there was being imposed upon the Board an obligation slavishly to follow the conventional methods of assessment'. Thus in determining the compensation payable for the applicant's future care the Board was able to take a round sum which was not reached by means of the application of a multiplier to a multiplicand (although in this case the court held that the reasons given by the Board for its choice of that sum were inadequate). Nor did the Board compensate a train driver for the loss of a holiday which had been 'ruined' by the stress caused to him when he was unable to stop the train he was driving from hitting and severely injuring a man lying with his head on the track (CICB, 1991, para. 19.3), though such loss would probably be recoverable in a personal injury action.

In general, the principles upon which quantum has been assessed have depended on whether the application fell to be determined under the law of Scotland or of England and Wales. One major difference between the two jurisdictions is that in the case of fatal injuries, the law in England and Wales provides for the conventional sum of £7,500 for bereavement, whereas in Scotland compensation for loss of society is to be assessed in each case. To the extent that it appears anomalous that different provisions should apply to the same injury depending upon where it was sustained, the Working Party did not think that the anomaly required rectification; in any event it was unable to find any acceptable common method of assessment to be followed throughout Great Britain (Home Office, *Criminal Injuries Compensation: A Statutory Scheme* 1986, paras 12.6–12.9, 15.3–15.4). One consequence of the new Scheme is the elimination of this anomaly: the tariff provides that all qualifying claimants (except for a former spouse of the deceased) are eligible for an award at level 13 (£10,000) or at level 10 if there is more than one qualifying claimant (new Scheme, para. 39; chapter 8.5.2), and that an award for loss of services may be payable to any qualifying claimant who was under 18 at the time of the deceased's death (new Scheme, para. 42; chapter 8.5.4).

As the assessment of compensation has been based on the principles applicable in personal injury and fatal accident actions, the Board has, for example, expected the victim to mitigate his loss where it would be reasonable for him to do so (CICB, 1987, para. 46). The old Scheme's variations upon those principles have concerned such matters as what is compensable (for example, no exemplary or punitive damages), what is deductible (for example, all moneys accruing from occupational pensions), and the finality of an award (the Board may reconsider cases in the event of deterioration; chapter 2.3.4). There have also been other differences, such as the upper limit on loss of earnings, the power to make interim awards (and therefore no power to make awards of provisional damages under s. 32A of the Supreme Court Act 1981), and in fatal cases, the requirement that the applicant (and not just the deceased) should himself not fall within the terms of para. 6(c) disentitling him from any or full compensation. Nor, since the applicant's loss is determined at the date of assessment, has interest been payable on awards as in a personal injury action (Supreme Court Act 1981, s. 35A; see Law Commission, *Damages for Personal Injury: Non-Pecuniary Loss*, Consultation Paper No.140, London: HMSO, 1995).

8.2 SIZE OF AWARDS

Table 8.1 shows the distribution of final monetary awards under the old Scheme for the three years ending in March 1995 (CICB, 1995, para. 3.14). It is unsurprising that, reflecting increases in common law damage awards and the effects of inflation, the underlying trend of awards is upwards.

Table 8.1   Distribution of Awards 1992–93 to 1994–95

	1994–95	%	1993–94	%	1992–93	%
Up to £999	2,835	8.2	2,753	6.8	7,796	21
£1,000–£4,999	26,031	75.3	32,345	79.6	23,829	65
£5,000–£9,999	3,284	9.5	3,398	8.4	2,952	8
£10,000 and over	2,420	7.0	2,139	5.2	2,061	6

8.3   THE TARIFF SCHEME

Driven by its concerns that decisions should be speedy and consistent, that the basis of the awards made should be clearer to applicants, and that expenditure on the Scheme should be more closely controlled, the government published its proposals for a tariff-based Scheme in late 1993 (Home Office, *Compensating Victims of Violent Crime: Changes to the Criminal Injuries Compensation Scheme*, Cm 2434, London: HMSO, 1993, para. 9):

> ... a scheme based on common law damages [is] inherently incapable of delivering the standard of service claimants now reasonably expect — that is a service which produces awards reasonably quickly, and in an understandable and predictable manner. Accordingly [the government] decided to introduce a new scheme, based on a tariff or scale of awards for injuries of comparable severity. There would no longer be a link with common law damages, making the new scheme more straightforward and easier for claimants to understand.

As noted in chapter 1.4.1, this first, unlawful tariff scheme, specifying 25 levels of award covering 186 injuries, an upper limit of £250,000, no compensation for loss of earnings or of earning capacity or, in fatal cases, no compensation for loss of support, and no compensation for future medical care, was bitterly opposed. The Scheme now in force, described in the Lords debates by the government as the 'enhanced tariff Scheme' and by the opposition as as the 'tariff plus' Scheme (HL Debs, vol. 566, col. 298, 19 July 1995) reintroduced some elements of the old Scheme, though in most cases subject to stringent conditions. The tariff itself was extended to 310 injuries and the maximum award payable doubled to £500,000. In summary, the 1995 Act provides for payment of three kinds of compensation for personal injuries: the standard amount (s. 2(2)(a)); an additional amount for loss of earnings (s. 2(2)(b)); and an additional amount for special expenses (s. 2(2)(c)). More specifically, para. 22 of the new Scheme provides that compensation payable under an award will be:

    (a)   a standard amount of compensation determined by reference to the nature of the injury in accordance with paragraphs 25–29;

    (b)   where the applicant has lost earnings or earning capacity for longer than 28 weeks as a direct consequence of the injury (other than an injury leading to his death), an additional amount in respect of such loss of earnings, calculated in accordance with paragraphs 30–34; and

    (c)   where the applicant has lost earnings or earning capacity for longer than 28 weeks as a direct consequence of the injury (other than an injury leading to his death) or, if not normally employed, is incapacitated to a similar extent, an additional amount in respect of any special expenses, calculated in accordance with paragraphs 35–36.

In providing compensation for loss of earnings and for special expenses the new Scheme maintains the common law principles governing its predecessor. These principles are, however, subject to the important qualification that such additional compensation only becomes payable where the applicant meets the relevant time condition. In the case of loss of earnings this is 28 weeks' loss of earnings or earning capacity (new Scheme, para. 30). In the case of special expenses, the condition is met where the applicant has either sustained such a loss or, if not normally employed, has been or is likely to be incapacitated for 28 weeks (new Scheme, para. 35).

    In the case of fatal injuries, there are, similarly, three kinds of compensation: the standard amount (s. 2(2)(a); new Scheme, para. 39); an additional amount for loss of dependency (s. 2(2)(d); new Scheme, paras 40-1); and an additional amount for loss of a parent's services (s. 2(2)(d); new Scheme, para. 42). In this case, the additional amount for loss of dependency or of a parent's services runs from the date of death.

    Although there are differences between them, the remainder of this chapter sets out, in the case of pecuniary loss, the provisions in both the old and the new Schemes using these and associated headings drawn from the common law assessment of damages. This approach is adopted both because there continue to be similarities between the two Schemes and because it is useful to compare the way in which each Scheme deals with the same issue. Attention is also drawn to the differences between these Schemes and personal injury or fatal accident actions where appropriate, but no particular attention is paid to those aspects of the common law assessment of damages which go beyond the immediate concerns of the two Schemes.

    One major difference between the old and new Schemes which should be noted before turning to their details is that unlike its predecessor, the new Scheme imposes a 'total maximum amount payable in respect of the same injury' of £500,000 (s. 2(7)(a); new Scheme, para. 23). This applies both to personal and to fatal injury applications; in the latter case, '... any application made by the victim before his death and any application made by any qualifying claimant or claimants after his death will be regarded as being in respect of the same injury' (para. 23). The

Authority's *Guide to Applicants for loss of Earnings and Special Expenses* puts this differently in the case of personal injuries: the total maximum payable in respect of the *claim as a whole* (emphasis added) (covering standard (tariff) amount, loss of earnings and for special expenses) is £500,000 (para. 3.3). This suggests that where the claim includes multiple injuries, they are to be held within the financial limit. But where two claims arise from the same event (for example, an injury to a pregnant woman which also affects the child who is born deformed), the limit will apply to each claim separately.

The fact that the £500,000 maximum is double the figure stipulated in the unlawful Scheme was welcomed during the debates. Nevertheless the point was made that while it is likely to affect only a very small number of applicants, some of those whom it does affect will receive significantly less than they would at common law (where awards over £3 million have been made), but at very little saving to the taxpayer. In 1994–95 there were 13 cases in which the applicant received more than £500,000, the highest award that year being £722,450 (CICB, 1995, para. 3.15). The government's answer to an amendment which would have removed this maximum was to reiterate its wish to dissociate the Scheme from the common law basis for the measure of damages:

> The State attempts to pay some compensation as an expression of society's concern for and sympathy with the victim. I do not think it reasonable to expect the scheme to make good each and every loss — to the fullest absolute extent — that a victim may have suffered (HC Debs, Standing Committee A, col. 175, 20 June 1995).

The point was also made that an applicant who takes the award in the form of a structured settlement may be able to satisfy the full cost of his long-term care from the income though the capital is less than £500,000 (HL Debs, vol. 566, col. 647, 16 October 1995).

8.4 PERSONAL INJURIES

8.4.1 General Damages

8.4.1.1 The Old Scheme

8.4.1.1.1 *Common law damages* Being based on the common law, the Board has been able to award compensation for pain and suffering (depending on the applicant's personal awareness of pain and capacity for suffering: *Lim Poh Choo* v *Camden and Islington Area Health Authority* [1980] AC 174; Law Commission, *Damages for Personal Injury: Non-Pecuniary Loss*, Consultation Paper No. 140, London: HMSO, 1995, paras 2.10-2.12, 4.11–4.22), and for loss of amenity, irrespective of the applicant's subjective awareness of her condition (*Wise* v *Kay* [1962] 1 QB 638; *H. West and Son Ltd* v *Shephard* [1964] AC 326; Law Commission, Consultation Paper No. 140, paras 2.14–2.20). It could also take into account under pain and suffering the victim's awareness of his loss of expectation of life which, before it was abolished by the Administration of Justice Act 1982, was dealt with as a separate element of general damages (Law Commission, Consultation Paper No. 140, paras 2.6–2.9). Excluded by para. 14(b) of the old Scheme has been any element comparable to exemplary or punitive damages, being matters inappropriate to a State-funded compensation scheme (Home Office, *Criminal Injuries Compensation: A Statutory Scheme*, 1986, para. 14.7). By contrast, aggravated damages are intended to be compensatory, reflecting the injury to the plaintiff's feelings which arises from the defendant's particularly malicious conduct or from the unusually distressing circumstances of the injury (*Rookes* v *Barnard* [1964] AC 1129). The old Scheme was silent on this matter, and it is not clear whether the Board did incorporate into its awards additional amounts of compensation to reflect particularly offensive conduct towards the victim, for example, gross indignities forced upon a female victim of a sexual offence. We return to this point below (chapter 8.4.1.1.2).

In common with judicial practice, the Board has routinely expressed the award for general damages as a global sum, and thus only limited assistance can be gleaned from its Reports as to how this was made up in any particular case. Guidance can be obtained from the Judicial Studies Board's *Guidelines for the Assessment of General Damages in Personal Injury Cases*, 3rd ed. (1996), Butterworths *Personal Injury Litigation Service* and Kemp and Kemp, *The Quantum of Damages*, which contain reports of CICB awards, and from the specimen awards given in the Board's Reports. However, as its more recent reports have contained fewer of these, and the summary of the applicant's injuries has tended to be brief, they are of limited value. The Reports do contain the Board's Guide to the Level of Awards, which are guideline figures for pain and suffering in common cases, drawn in part from the compensation exercises its members conduct with judges and other experienced personal injury silks. The last two sets of figures are contained in App. G to the Annual Reports published in 1991 and 1995. These are set out in table 8.2.

Table 8.2   The Board's Guide to the Level of Awards

Injury	*1991*	*1995*
Undisplaced nasal fracture	£650	£750
Displaced nasal fracture	£1,000	£1,000
Loss of two front upper teeth (plate or bridge)	£1,170	£1,750
Elevated zygoma (following injury to cheekbone)	£1,750	£1,750
Fractured jaw (wired)	£2,500	£2,750
Simple fracture of the tibia, fibula, ulna or radius with complete recovery	£2,500	£2,500
Laparotomy (exploratory stomach operation and scar)	£3,000	£3,500
Scar, young man, from join of lobe of the left ear and his face across his cheek to within one inch of the left corner of his mouth	£6,000	£6,000
Scar, young woman, running from left corner of her mouth backwards and downwards ending just beneath the jawbone	£9,000	£9,000
Total loss of hearing in one ear	£11,500	£11,500
Total loss of taste and smell as result of a fractured skull	£12,000	£12,000
Total loss of vision in one eye	£15,000	£17,500
Loss of one eye	—	£20,000

These are guideline figures only. They did not, and could not, displace the Board's discretion under the old Scheme to assess the appropriate compensation in each case. Reflecting Lord Halsbury LC's observations in *The Mediana* [1900] AC 113, at pp. 116–17 that, 'Nobody can suggest that you can by any arithmetical calculation establish what is the exact sum of money which would represent such a thing as the pain and suffering which a person has undergone by reason of an accident', the Guide states:

There is no 'right' or 'exact' figure for all cases involving the same injury because no two victims suffer in exactly the same way. The figures below are therefore only a very general guide and may be increased or decreased according to the medical evidence, the victim's sex, age and any other factors which appear to the Board to be relevant in a particular case.

The Board also used to indicate that in each case the figure was a starting point, but this was evidently taken by some practitioners to mean a minimum. Any ambiguity is surely dispelled by the Board's clear statement that 'They are not minimum figures for an award'. Such cautionary remarks were frequently accompanied by an illustration, again in fairly general terms, of its application to particular injuries: 'For example, most broken noses recover completely, but if there is any significant permanent disability or cosmetic defect, the award will be more, and perhaps substantially more, than the guideline figure' (CICB, 1987, para. 41). Similarly, an elderly victim sustaining a minor assault may well be made an award higher than if the victim were young: 'in particular, handbag snatching cases frequently turn a self-reliant, confident, elderly person into one who is frightened and nervous' (CICB, 1987, para. 41).

8.4.1.1.2 *Compensation for rape and its aftermath* The regular iteration of this cautionary advice did not diminish the level of criticism directed at earlier indications of a guideline award for rape (CICB, 1987, para. 41). The figure given (£5,000) was, according to the Board, appropriate for cases leading to no serious physical or psychological damage, and where it was assured that the applicant had made a complete recovery from the experience. Nevertheless, critics regarded this to be an insufficient recognition of the impact of the offence, comparisons being drawn between rape and other injuries attracting similar monetary values but which they argued had a less serious impact on the victim. Criticism was particularly heightened by the outcome of the claims for compensation, both to the Board and in civil proceedings, which arose from the injuries Christopher Meah sustained when a passenger in a negligently driven car, and from the injuries he in turn caused to two women as a consequence of the personality change he suffered (*Meah* v *McCreamer* [1985] 1 All ER 367). Meah was awarded £45,750 general damages for the personality change and for his classification as a category A prisoner following his violent rape and sexual assaults upon his two victims who, in their civil action against him, received respectively £6,750 and £10,250 (*W* v *Meah, D* v *Meah* [1986] 1 All ER 935). In a separate application to the Board, W was awarded £1,000 and D £3,600. Many were critical of the discrepancies between these figures, discrepancies aggravated by the requirement that the victims would either have to repay to the Board the awards from their civil action, or have those damages deducted in advance of the award being made. Some of this criticism was no doubt uninformed: unlike the Board, the court was able to include in its judgment a specific amount for aggravated damages (as was also the case with Miss S, a third of Meah's victims (*S* v *Meah* [1986] CLY 1049)); but two substantial points remained. First, while the Board always relied on High Court judges and barristers with experience of personal injury litigation for its guideline figures, civil actions such these are very rare and thus only a handful of practitioners will ever have had direct experience of them. Secondly, and given the paucity of cases, it may be that the level suggested by the compensation exercises simply does not, if attempts are to be made to translate such injuries into money terms, adequately value the pain and suffering experienced by a rape victim (as was urged, for example, during the debates on the 1995 Act; HC Debs, Standing Committee A, cols. 156–8, 15 June 1995). At any rate, the Board omitted from its 1990 guidelines any figure for rape.

Against the background of the remarks made by its predecessor, that the element of pain and suffering will implicitly take into account the injury to the applicant's feelings, 'and that it is therefore unnecessary for awards by the Board to allow for such injury explicitly' (Home Office, *Review of the Criminal Injuries Compensation Scheme*, 1978, para. 14.8), the 1986 Working Party was particularly conscious of the sensitivity of this matter. It observed that it would expect the pain and suffering award in claims arising from rape to make exceptional provision for that offence (Home Office, *Criminal Injuries Compensation: A Statutory Scheme*, 1986, para. 14.8):

> An exception [to the normal assessment of pain and suffering which will take into account the injury to the victim's feelings] must be made for offences where injury to feelings caused by an abhorrent act might be of greater importance than any actual physical or mental injuries. Such an exception is in our view essential in the case, for example, of sexual offences as the Board's current assessment of compensation for rape starts from a figure which would be awarded where there were no long-lasting physical or psychological injuries, and such an award must contain a substantial element in respect of injury to feelings.

Whatever the earlier position concerning the award by the Board of an element of compensation equivalent to aggravated damages, the Board did, during the late 1980s, seek to reflect in its awards any particularly distressing features of a sexual attack. This was so in the case of attacks on children (*Re E, J, K and D (Minors)* [1990] CLY 1596; *Re AP (Female)* [1991] CLY 1363; *Re C* [1991] CLY 1367; Denyer, R., *Children and Personal Injury Litigation*, London: Butterworths, 1993, ch. 9.11) and on older women (CICB, 1988, paras 26 and 27), and in the case of attacks accompanied by severe physical injury (*Re H* [1988] CLY 1104). In 1987 the Board also indicated that it would include in an award for rape, a sum designed to recognise the victim's inevitable fear that she had become HIV positive (CICB, 1987, para. 41).

The pain and suffering associated with the pregnancy and any expenses associated with the birth of a child conceived as a result of rape were always compensable under the old Scheme. The 1986 Working Party also recommended that while the Scheme should not provide for its maintenance, there should be a fixed sum payable where the woman bears and keeps the child. Introduced in the 1990 revisions, para. 10 of the old Scheme provided for the payment of an additional sum of £5,000 for each child conceived as a result of the rape and born alive, whom the mother, at the time of the award, intends to keep provided that she herself had been awarded for the offence. This figure was reached by the application of a multiplier of 10 to 17 years' maintenance of the child. This award has not been recoverable by the Board should she later seek to have the child adopted, nor has it been subject to any deductions by virtue of paras 19 and 20 (chapter 9.2.3.2).

8.4.1.2 The New Scheme

8.4.1.2.1 *The tariff* By s. 2(3)(a) of the 1995 Act, 'Provision shall be made for the standard amount to be determined in accordance with a table ('the Tariff') prepared by the Secretary of State as part of the Scheme and such other provisions of the Scheme as may be relevant'. The government's philosophy, which in part reflects the systemic character of damages for non-pecuniary loss as being incapable of measurement in money terms (Law Commission, Consultation Paper No. 140, 1995, paras 2.1–2.3), was articulated by Baroness Blatch during the committee stage in the Lords (HL Debs, vol. 566, col. 637, 16 October 1995):

> As the government have sought repeatedly to explain, there is no right figure that can compensate the blameless victim for the pain and hurt that he or she has suffered as a result of a crime of violence. Under the enhanced tariff scheme we do not try to make a finely judged assessment of compensation, in the sense of attempting to put the individual back into the position in which he or she would have been had the attack not occurred. What we aim to do is to make a generous payment in recognition of society's concern for the blameless victim of a violent crime. In our view, a simple, transparent system, where the awards are based on the most typical award for the injury concerned — the median award — is the right way to do that.

The Act requires the tariff to show, in respect of each description of injury, the standard amount of compensation payable in respect of that description of injury (s. 2(4)). Descriptions of the injury sustained by the victim were chosen as the principal defining characteristic for the tariff because it was thought that references to the offence committed by the offender (though there are some such references) could produce uncertainty where the law of Scotland differs from that of England and Wales, and because offences defined in their legislative terms might confuse applicants as to their potential eligibility for an award (HL Debs, vol. 566, col. 620, 16 October 1995).

Paragraph 25 of the new Scheme thus provides that:

> The standard amount of compensation will be the amount shown in respect of the relevant description of injury in the Tariff appended to this Scheme, which sets out:
> (a)   a scale of fixed levels of compensation; and
> (b)   the level and corresponding amount of compensation for each description of injury.

The tariff of 310 descriptions of injury is reproduced in Appendix 3 of this book. There are 25 levels of compensation, from £1,000, the minimum payable, to £250,000, the maximum payable for any single description of injury. As was the case with the unlawful Scheme, the tariff was widely criticised for its inflexibility, anomalies and unfairness in making no distinction between individuals, 'each victim of crime with the same injury being treated in the same way as another' (HL Debs, vol. 566, col. 321, 19 July 1995; HC Debs, vol. 260, cols. 753 ff., 23 May 1995). The Act gives the Secretary of State the discretion to describe an injury in the tariff by reference to its nature, severity or the circumstances in which it was sustained (s. 2(5)). While the descriptions of injury do make some distinctions between injuries according to their impact on the victim (for example, whether the victim has made a full or a partial recovery from an injury to a limb, or whether an injury to the hand involves the thumb or the index finger), they do not permit many of the standard factors to be taken into account. Lord Broadbridge continued (HL Debs, vol. 566, col. 321, 19 July 1995):

> It cannot be right, for example, that a young child who loses an eye should receive the same compensation as an elderly person. The disability suffered by the child will last for much longer; in fact for decades. The effect of a facial scar on a young woman is likely to be far greater than on an elderly man. No distinction is made between injuries to the dominant or non-dominant hand or arm.

Without seeking to generalise from one instance, in 1996 the Board made an award of £7,000 general damages to an applicant, two of whose fingers had been dislocated in the assault and one of which was subsequently amputated at the proximal metacarpal joint because of the deformity caused by the dislocation. The injury, which was to her non-dominant hand and to her middle and ring fingers, resulted in continued discomfort during cold weather, and her grip had been reduced (*New Law Journal*, 1996, vol. 146, p. 990). The tariff award for the loss of part of a finger (other than the thumb or the index finger) is £2,500. The applicant would also be eligible for 10% of the standard amount for the second most serious injury, that is, the second, dislocated finger, with full recovery (£125); total: £2,625.

The inflexibility, insensitivity and, indeed, impracticality of a system which offers no opportunity to those assessing compensation to respond to applicants' individual circumstances were singled out by Lord Carlisle in the Lords committee stage as fundamental objections to the tariff Scheme. Referring in particular to cases involving scarring, mental shock, sexual abuse and child abuse, the then Chairman of the Board argued a powerful case for an amendment creating bands rather than fixed amounts of compensation. In the case of child abuse, for example, the Chairman observed that the proposed distinction in the tariff is based in part on the length of time over which the child had been victimised. But just as important are 'the relationship with the abuser, the type of abuse [some distinctions are made on this issue], and the effect on and the age of the individual child and its emotional development' (HL Debs, vol. 566, col. 616, 16 October 1995). Not only was the lack of discretion objectionable, but the differences in levels of award were, in Lord Carlisle's view, in some instances unhelpfully wide. In the case, for example, of mental injury, a disabling mental disorder lasting more than a year but not permanent attracts £7,500; the next, and most serious of such injuries attracts £20,000. Substantial and inflexible differences between adjacent descriptions of injury lead inevitably to injustices between victims and to administrative difficulties. One of these is that awards will be made 'which are far more substantial than were being given under the Board and far more substantial than we would have recommended in those cases' (HL Debs, loc. cit.).

The government resisted this and other attempts to introduce bands of compensation such as those published in the Judicial Studies Board's *Guidelines* and recommended by Victim Support (*Compensating the Victim of Crime*, London: Victim Support, 1994), within which the claims officer would have discretion to respond to the applicant's own circumstances. To introduce such discretion:

would undermine the whole rationale of the tariff system. In effect, it would reintroduce a common law damages scheme ... with the associated delays and complexity. The whole point of a tariff system is that it provides a quicker, simpler and more transparent arrangement (HL Debs, vol. 566, col. 619, 16 October 1995).

For the same reasons the government resisted an amendment which would have permitted a claims officer to increase the standard amount of compensation payable by no more than 20% to reflect special factors relating to the applicant including but not limited to sex, occupation or intended occupation, or dominant limb, in the case of injury to the upper limb (HC Debs, Standing Committee A, col. 183, 20 June 1995; HL Debs, vol. 566, cols. 633–9, 1366–71, 16 and 31 October 1995). Making the particular point that the median level of award in the case of injury to the hand and arm is based on the dominant limb (HL Debs, vol. 566, col. 337, 19 July 1995), the government also argued that this amendment, permitting cumulative additional amounts, could result in a 70% increase in the compensation payable in any one case, and would inevitably encourage incremental drift, as applicants sought additional amounts of compensation reflecting these and other special factors.

The Secretary of State has the power to add to or to remove from the tariff any description of injury, to increase or reduce the amount shown as the standard amount of compensation for any given injury, or to alter the tariff in such other way as he considers appropriate (s. 2(6)). In answer to concerns that the power to reduce awards might encourage the government to introduce real reductions in the amount of compensation payable for particular descriptions of injury, the Minister indicated that it was as likely to be used to permit the consolidation of several broadly similar injury descriptions 'if experience showed that the tariff could better describe injuries of the relevant type, or the introduction of a new more serious injury description, while reserving an existing one for less serious injuries for which a lower amount was appropriate' (HC Debs, Standing Committee A, col. 159, 15 June 1995).

The government also resisted attempts to introduce an annual review of the tariff, arguing that this would impose unnecessary bureaucratic burdens on the Authority, and that in any event the initial determination of the standard amounts had increased the levels of award by more than the rate of inflation. It agreed to a three-year review, commencing in 1999 (HC Debs, Standing Committee A, col. 153, 15 June 1995).

Where a criminal injury exacerbates or accelerates an existing condition, the compensation to be awarded for it will reflect only the degree of exacerbation or acceleration (new Scheme, para. 25). In this the Scheme follows the common law (*Jobling* v *Associated Dairies Ltd* [1982] AC 794).

Table 8.3   Tariff Awards Compared with the Board's Guide

Injury	*1995*	*Tariff*
Undisplaced nasal fracture	£750	£1,000
Displaced nasal fracture	£1,000	£1,500
Loss of two front upper teeth (plate or bridge)	£1,750	£2,000
Elevated zygoma (following injury to cheekbone)	£1,750	£2,000
Fractured jaw (wired)	£2,750	£3,000
Simple fracture of the tibia, fibula, ulna or radius with complete recovery	£2,500	£3,000
Laparotomy (exploratory stomach operation and scar)	£3,500	£3,500
Scar, young man, from join of lobe of the left ear and his face across his cheek to within one inch of the left corner of his mouth	£6,000	£7,500
Scar, young woman, running from left corner of her mouth backwards and downwards ending just beneath the jawbone	£9,000	£7,500
Total loss of hearing in one ear	£11,500	£15,000
Total loss of taste and smell as result of a fractured skull	£12,000	£15,000
Total loss of vision in one eye	£17,500	£20,000
Loss of one eye	£20,000	£25,000

Table 8.3 lists the tariff awards against the figures given by the Board in its 1995 guide to the level of awards. While care must be taken when comparing them (for example, there are three levels of award applicable to scarring, distinguishing minor (£1,500), significant (£3,500) and serious (£7,500) disfigurement, none of which exactly matches the description given in the Board's guide), it does seem, as the government repeatedly claimed during the debates, that in some instances, and before inflation erodes them, the general level of awards for the equivalent of general damages will, notwithstanding the claims officer's lack of discretion to adjust the tariff figure in the light of the applicant's own circumstances, be at least as high as the equivalent common law figures (Lord Carlisle, HL Debs, vol. 552, col. 1084, 2 March 1994). Indeed this ought to be so given that, when conducting its exercise to determine the median level for specified injuries, the government used, as was described earlier (chapter 1.4.1), the full award payable to the applicant, thus including compensation for both special and general damages. This tentative conclusion does not square with the criticisms made by the Association of Personal Injury Lawyers when the White Paper was published (APIL, *Changes to the Criminal Injuries Compensation Scheme Leading to Hardship and Inconsistency for Victims*, London: Robin Thompson and Partners, 1993). But the comparative figures which APIL gave indicating that some applicants would receive substantially less under the proposed tariff were based on the initial unlawful Scheme, which made no provision for loss of dependency in fatal cases or for special expenses in the case of serious disabling injuries, both of which are now provided for. It is difficult at this early stage in the operation of the tariff to be confident about how levels of compensation will work out in individual cases.

It also seems that this exercise means that there will be instances where the tariff payments will be significantly higher than the general damages that would be assessed at common law. This is so, for example, in the case of paraplegia and quadriplegia, where the tariff figures of £175,000 and £250,000 are very much higher than the maxima of £100,000 and £130,000 indicated in the Judicial Studies Board's 1996 Guidelines (see also Law Commission, 1995, paras 4.38 and 4.43; *Housecroft* v *Burnett* [1986] 1 All ER 332). The calculations on which these figures were based were made when the government had no intention of introducing into the tariff Scheme compensation either for loss of earnings or earning capacity, or for the special expenses associated with the long-term care of victims disabled in this way. But once the decision was taken to include these heads of damage, the question was then 'whether it is right to leave figures in the tariff which roughly are double the amount being paid by the civil courts at the moment without any apparent consideration of the effect this may have on inflation' (HL Debs, vol. 566, col. 643, 16 October 1995). Lord Carlisle received no answer to his question.

It was also argued that the levels of award for some injuries, in particular concerning sexual abuse of children and mental injury, were too low. In part this criticism was linked with Lord Carlisle's objections concerning the inflexibility of the tariff (for example, the tariff awards for facial scarring do not distinguish, as did the Board, between male and female victims), but the overall levels of the standard amounts were of themselves considered inadequate. Efforts to exclude them from the tariff and to apply the common law's measure of damages to them inevitably foundered on the government's insistence that any dilution of the tariff principle was fundamentally objectionable ((HL Debs, vol. 566, cols. 656–60 (child abuse), 660-62 (mental injury), 16 October 1995).

8.4.1.2.2 *Multiple injuries* An applicant may have sustained a number of separate injuries as a result of the commission of a crime of violence. Where these are minor, that is, injuries none of which alone meets the minimum level, the applicant may nevertheless be compensated where she sustains at least three separate injuries of the type illustrated in the notes to the tariff, one of which must have had significant residual effects six weeks after the incident (new Scheme, para. 26). The rules governing the compensation of minor injuries were discussed in chapter 7.3.3. If the applicant meets the criteria specified in the note she will be made an award at level 1 of the tariff (£1,000).

Where two or more of the injuries sustained by the applicant would each attract an award at least at level 1, it is provided in para. 26(a)–(c) of the new Scheme that she will receive the tariff amount for the highest-rated description of injury plus 10% of the second highest-rated and 5% of the third highest-rated description of injuries. To use the example given in the Guide: 'Where the injuries are a depressed fracture of the skull (£6,000), loss of two front teeth (£2,000) and a broken nose (£1,500), the combined award would be £6,000 + £200 + £75 totalling £6,275' (new Scheme, Guide, para. 4.8).

Recognising, as the Introduction to the second edition of the Judicial Studies Board's *Guidelines* put it (1994, p. 3), that it is 'axiomatic that it is not appropriate separately to value the individual elements of a multiple-injury case and to aggregate the figures thus achieved', it was argued in debate that the tariff awards will, where the injuries are unrelated and each one is itself severe, be significantly less than the comparable common law awards. There were 641 applications (from a total of 71,734) made under the unlawful Scheme which involved multiple injuries. It is impossible to predict what the impact on such cases will be of the limits introduced by para. 26; but the following examples of the potential unfairness of the effect of para. 26 are taken from the Lords committee stage (HL Debs, vol. 566, col. 651, 16 October):

(a)   Applicant suffering a right-sided haematoma in the head with evidence of confusion of the brain; epilepsy over a number of years following the injury; right-sided headaches and tinnitus; a tendency to become depressed and irritable with attendance at a psychiatric hospital; speech incapacity; marital breakdown: common law damages of £50,000. 'Under the tariff scheme he would have received £20,000 for the psychiatric injury, only 10% of £12,500 for the epilepsy and only 5% of £7,500 for tinnitus. That is a total award of £22,000.'

(b)   Applicant (aged 23) 'lost the sight of her left eye, she has a traumatic cataract and severe retinal damage and is left with double vision in her left [?right] eye. She is unable to wear an occlusive contact lens, she has a shrunken eye, a shattered eyebrow, a fixed dilated pupil and divergent squint and she cannot close her eye because of the tethering of the skin'; unsuccessful plastic surgery; depression. She was awarded £33,500 under the old Scheme. Under the tariff, 'she would have received £20,000 for the loss of sight, only 10% of £7,500 for scarring and only 5% of £7,500 for psychiatric injury'; a total of £21,000.

Supporting an amendment which would have reintroduced the common law's assessment of multiple injuries, Lord Carlisle observed that 'When you have injuries which are totally distinct, it seemed to those of us on the Board who looked at those cases [that is, the ones decided under the unlawful Scheme which therefore had to be reassessed under the terms of the old Scheme] to be unfair to limit the award for the second injury to 10 per cent'. The government resisted this and similar amendments, in each case relying on two familar arguments; first, that to allow an element of common law assessment would be to undermine the central purpose of the tariff Scheme; and second that the result of its assessment exercise showed that since in assessing damages for multiple injury, almost the whole amount awarded was related to the most serious injury, the tariff proposals broadly correspond to the common law position (HC Debs, Standing Committee A, col. 240, 27 June 1995; HL Debs, vol. 566, cols. 654 and 1386, 16 and 31 October 1995). In general terms, the government's response was correct; the Introduction to the second edition of the Judicial Studies Board's *Guidelines* continued, 'An overall view must be taken in which the largest single element will usually be the most serious of those injuries'. The Lord Advocate stressed that the government had taken care to consider the Judicial Studies Board's approach to multiple injuries (HL Debs, vol. 566, col. 1386, 31 October 1995), and had concluded that it was 'even possible to say, in the light of the analysis, that the formula errs on the side of generosity'.

The government also resisted an amendment which would have increased to 50% and 25% the award for the the second and third highest-rated injuries where each of the injuries would individually attract an award at level 12. Its purpose was to deal with cases where applicants sustain more than one unrelated serious injury. The government's response was that cases where there are two very disparate and serious injuries are very rare, but added that if a rare combination of injuries arose which the Authority or the Panel considered ought to be specifically provided for, it would be open to them to use the procedures in para. 28 of the new Scheme, described in the following section.

8.4.1.2.3 *Unprovided-for injuries* Notwithstanding the list of injuries, it is possible that the applicant will sustain an injury for which the tariff makes no provision. The Act provides that in such cases the Scheme may make such provision for a standard amount of compensation to be paid 'as may be relevant' (s. 2(3(b)). Where the Authority considers that any description of injury for which no standard amount is specified in the tariff is nevertheless sufficiently serious to qualify for the minimum amount payable, it will, after consultation with the Panel, refer the injury to the Secretary of State with a recommendation as to the appropriate description and amount of compensation (new Scheme, para. 28). This recommendation must not refer to the circumstances of any individual application save the relevant medical evidence. At the same time, the Authority may make an interim award to the applicant of not more than half the amount of the recommended amount of compensation. The applicant will keep the award notwithstanding that the standard amount finally agreed for inclusion in the tariff is less than the interim award, or even if it is not included in the tariff at all (new Scheme, para. 29; HL Debs, vol. 566, col. 676, 17 October 1995).

8.4.1.2.4 *Compensation for rape and its aftermath* As with its predecessor, the new Scheme provides an additional amount of compensation for each child conceived as a result of rape who is born alive and whom the woman intends to keep (new Scheme, para. 27). Provided that she has been made an award in respect of non-consensual vaginal intercourse, an additional sum at level 10 (£5,000) is payable to her for each child. This award is not subject to any reduction to reflect her receipt of, or eligibility for, social security benefits or insurance payments (new Scheme, para. 45). An amendment designed to introduce additional amounts payable where the pregnancy has ended in a miscarriage or abortion, or where the mother bore the child but gave it for adoption was withdrawn (HL Debs, vol. 566, cols. 1371–4, 31 October 1995).

Non-consensual vaginal sexual intercourse itself is compensable at any of three levels: £7,500 (level 12), £10,000 (level 13) where two or more attackers are involved, or £17,500 (level 16) where other serious bodily injuries are also sustained. But, as noted earlier, there was a strongly held view during the debates on the Bill that the proposed figures lamentably undervalue the impact of rape upon its victims. A victim whose rape attracts the highest-rated of these three descriptions will, should she also suffer trauma amounting to a disabling mental disorder lasting more than a year though not permanent, be eligible for a second award of compensation. But this award will, by virtue of para. 26(b), amount only to 10% of the standard amount for that description of injury, so that she would receive a further £750. This total of £18,250 is, however, substantially less than the £44,000 awarded under the old Scheme to a woman who was assaulted for over an hour and raped in a public lavatory (HC Debs, Standing Committee A, cols. 156–8, 15 June 1995). As noted earlier, critics of the tariff were also dissatisfied by the lack of any discretion in the making of awards for rape.

8.4.2 Special Damages

8.4.2.1 Loss of Earnings and Earning Capacity

8.4.2.1.1 *Calculation of the loss* Under the old Scheme, as at common law, the applicant has been entitled to damages for loss of earnings to the date of the assessment, and for future loss of earnings. Where the applicant had two jobs, only one of which was affected by the injury, an award could be made to compensate for that loss, as it could for the loss of a fringe benefit (CICB, 1986, paras 9 and 30). Where the victim's life expectancy has been reduced the assessment would include compensation for the lost years (*Pickett* v *British Rail Engineering Ltd* [1980] AC 136; *Gammell* v *Wilson* [1982] AC 27; *Harris* v *Empress Motors Ltd* [1984] 1 WLR 212).

Compensation for this head of special damage was excluded from the unlawful Scheme and when included in the new Scheme was subject to the time condition specified in para. 30:

Where the applicant has lost earnings or earning capacity for longer than 28 weeks as a direct consequence of the injury (other than an injury leading to his death), no compensation in respect of loss or earnings or earning capacity will be payable for the first 28 weeks of loss. The period of loss for which compensation may be payable will begin 28 weeks after the date of commencement of the applicant's incapacity for work and continue for such period as a claims officer may determine.

In short, as para. 4.13 of the Guide to the new Scheme puts it, 'Compensation is *not* payable for the first 28 full weeks of lost earnings or earning capacity' (original emphasis). The Authority will send the applicant a separate Guide on how this element of additional compensation is calculated (*Guide to Applicants for Loss of Earnings and Special Expenses*; hereafter, *Guide to Earnings and Expenses*, reproduced in Appendix 4).

The 28-week period was chosen because it coincides with the period of time for which statutory sick pay is payable. It was inevitably the object of sustained criticism during the debates on the 1991 Act, with a number of unsuccessful attempts being made to re-establish the common law position under the old Scheme (HC Debs, vol. 260, col. 753, 23 May 1995; Standing Committee A, cols. 92–128, 13 June 1995; HL Debs, vol. 566, cols. 648–51, 16 October 1995). The point was repeatedly made that there are many potential victims of crime who will be unable to continue work as a result of their injuries but who will not be eligible for statutory sick pay. Prime among this group are the estimated 3 million self-employed and some 3 million low-paid employees earning below the threshold for national insurance contributions. There will, in addition, be many employees eligible under occupational sick pay arrangements, but these often do not become payable until after a number of years' service. Taken together with those employees on short-term contracts or whose employers have no occupational sick pay schemes, critics reckoned that some 12 million people currently in work would be ineligible either for statutory or occupational sick pay, and thus would be adversely affected by the 28-week time condition (HL Debs, vol. 566, cols. 648–51, 16 October 1995). Neither were the critics impressed by the argument that a victim ineligible for statutory sick pay might be eligible for invalidity benefit (incapacity benefit from 1 April 1995; Social Security (Incapacity for Work) Act 1994). Qualification for this benefit is dependent on the applicant satisfying a number of tests which many who are temporarily unable to work will not be able to meet. Qualification for income support is similarly tested; victims with capital in excess of £8,000 would be ineligible, while those with capital between £3,000 and £8,000 would lose £1 a week for each £250 or part thereof between those limits. In short (HC Debs, Standing Committee A, col. 99, 13 June 1995):

> ... the following categories of people are likely to experience particular financial hardship: low-paid workers, temporary workers, employees who have no contractual rights for sick pay and who have to rely on statutory sick pay, incapacity benefit or income support, self-employed people, and employees of small businesses.

Observing that 'A great deal of the time of the board's staff is taken up in inquiring as to the loss of wages claimed by someone who may not have been off work for three or four weeks but for, say, two or three days', Lord Carlisle was prepared to accept the pragmatic argument that some limit should be introduced. The Board's proposal was three months (HL Debs, vol. 566, col. 649, 16 October 1995). However, the government resisted amendments moved in both the Commons and the Lords to remove or reduce the 28-week threshold. In the standing committee, the Minister observed that there will, at least for a few years, be an element of loss of earnings in every award of the standard amount of compensation. This is so because, when it determined what was the median award under the old Scheme for particular descriptions of injury, the government did not deduct compensation for loss of earnings. The figures were reflated by 19% prior to their introduction in the unlawful 1994 Scheme, but since inflation over the period in question was only 11%, it followed that the operative award levels were better than would otherwise have been the case (HC Debs, Standing Committee A, col. 99, 13 June 1995; chapter 1.4.1). This point is subject to four qualifications: first, for any one application the element of loss of earnings in the standard amount of compensation can only be nominal and thus not reflect actual loss since that figure is averaged from past applications; secondly, the government is also relying on the element of loss of earnings to support its argument that because of its inclusion in the standard amount, most applicants will receive the same or more compensation for general damages than would have been the case had it stripped out that element when determining median awards; thirdly, the inflated level is a diminishing one; and fourthly, the question which remains unanswered is by how much the government of the day will increase the levels when the first review of the tariff takes place in 1999.

There are some groups of workers who are particularly susceptible to personal victimisation; those who work in sub-post offices and in the retail trade being prime examples. In an effort to ameliorate the 28-week rule for applicants such as these, an amendment was moved in the Lords which would have provided for the aggregation of the weeks of lost earnings or earning capacity where the applicant had sustained more than one injury in separate incidents within two years; in this way two 15-week periods of lost earnings, for example, would bring the applicant within para. 30. This was resisted by the government, observing that (HL Debs, vol. 566, cols. 678–9, 17 October 1995):

> The purpose of the qualifying period is to distinguish between the more serious cases which merit special consideration and the less serious ones which can reasonably be settled on the basis of a straight tariff payment. We do not consider that two less serious injuries can be regarded as more serious for these purposes, bearing in mind that the victim will receive two separate tariff awards.

The main rules for the payment of additional compensation for loss of earnings are that the injury must have been the direct cause of the applicant's loss of earnings or of earning capacity, and that the loss must have lasted longer than 28 full weeks. That period will normally run from the date of injury. Where the applicant returned to work immediately following the injury but was subsequently admitted to hospital for treatment or convalescence, the period runs from the date of admission (*Guide to Earnings and Expenses*, paras 7 and 8). The calculation of loss will commence from the first day of the 29th week out of work to the applicant's return to work, or for such period of time as the Authority considers reasonable on the information it has. Where the applicant was unemployed at the date of the injury, the Authority may take into account an offer of employment which the applicant was unable to take up because of it (*Guide to Earnings and Expenses*, paras 8 and 9). As indicated, the loss must be the direct result of the criminal injury. Accordingly the Authority will take into account the extent to which the applicant's extant health problems or a previous injury (*Jobling* v *Associated Dairies Ltd* [1982] AC 794), or the insecurity of his employment or self-employment contributed to his loss of earnings. Like the Board, the Authority will also expect the applicant to mitigate his loss if he could reasonably be expected to take another job within his physical or intellectual capacity (*Guide to Earnings and Expenses*, para. 15).

Apart from the introduction of the 28-week time condition, the method by which the new Scheme is to calculate an applicant's loss of earnings will be as was the position under the old Scheme; this was a matter on which the government gave one of its 'golden assurances' (HC Debs, Standing Committee A, col. 186, 20 June 1995). Paragraphs 31 and 32 of the new Scheme specify the factors which the claims officer will take into account when determining the applicant's loss, first, prior to or at the date on which the claim is assessed, and, second, subsequent to that date. So far as the former is concerned, para. 31 provides:

> For a period of loss ending before or continuing to the time the claim is assessed, the net loss of earnings or earning capacity will be calculated on the basis of:
>
> (a)   the applicant's emoluments (being any profit or gain accruing from an office or employment) at the time of the injury and what those emoluments would have been during the period of loss; and
>
> (b)   any emoluments which have become payable in respect of the whole or part of the period of loss, whether or not as a result of the injury; and

(c)   any changes in the applicant's pension rights; and

(d)   in accordance with paragraphs 45–47 (reductions to take account of other payments), any social security benefits, insurance payments and pension which have become payable to the applicant during the period of loss; and

(e)   any other pension which has become payable to the applicant during the period of loss, whether or not as a result of the injury.

Put more shortly:

> The calculation is based on a comparison of your earnings or other income before and after the injury. If there is a loss to you as a *direct result of the injury*, we take that figure and deduct from it any financial benefits you have received which also result from the injury. (*Guide to Earnings and Expenses*, para. 13; original emphasis)

In the standard case of an applicant in regular employment there will generally be little difficulty in calculating loss of earnings by reference to wage or salary slips. Applicants to the Board have been required to state their average net earnings after tax, that figure being routinely checked with the employer. The matter can of course be more complicated: salary may depend in part on commission, on turnover or profits declared over given periods of time. There may also be a loss of emoluments attributable to the lost opportunity for promotion. Where the applicant is self-employed, or has income from some other source, such as a share of a firm's profits, he will be asked to produce a set of accounts or a tax assessment.

A second element of loss is the impact, if any, on the applicant's pension rights as a result of the reduction in his income. Such reduction may come about because the injured applicant has to give up work or take less well-paid work, with the result that he loses his entitlement to a pension, or becomes entitled to a less valuable pension on reaching pensionable age. This reduction may become particularly acute where there is a continuing loss of earning capacity (new Scheme, para. 32). But if, notwithstanding the reduction in his income, the applicant would suffer no diminution in his pension because the employer was obliged to maintain its contributions at their original level, there would be no loss under this heading (*Dews* v *National Coal Board* [1988] AC 1).

From the loss represented by these items, the claims officer will deduct any social security benefits, insurance payments or pension which the applicant has received as a result of the injury. Paragraph 45 of the new Scheme requires this reduction to be applied to those periods of loss for which additional compensation is payable, that is to say, from the beginning of the 29th week (chapter 9.3.4).

An example of the implementation of para. 31 of the new Scheme is given in para. 17 of the *Guide to Earnings and Expenses*; see Appendix 4.

So far as future loss of earnings or of earning capacity are concerned, para. 32 of the new Scheme provides:

Where, at the time the claim is assessed, a claims officer considers that the applicant is likely to suffer continuing loss of earnings or earning capacity, an annual rate of net loss (the multiplicand) or, where appropriate, more than one such rate will be calculated on the basis of:

(a) the current rate of net loss calculated in accordance with the preceding paragraph; and

(b) such future rate or rates of net loss (including changes in the applicant's pension rights) as the claims officer may determine; and

(c) the claims officer's assessment of the applicant's future earning capacity; and

(d) in accordance with paragraphs 45–47 (reductions to take account of other payments), any social security benefits, insurance payments and pension which will become payable to the applicant in future; and

(e) any other pension which will become payable to the applicant in the future, whether or not as a result of the injury.

This calculation begins with the rate of net loss determined under para. 31 as applying to the period of loss at the date of assessment. The determination of the applicant's future rate of loss and of earning capacity can, as the Board observed in its 25th Report (CICB, 1989, paras 23.3–23.9), be protracted, especially where the applicant has had to change employment or been medically retired (*Guide to Earnings and Expenses*, paras 18 and 19). This could be further complicated where, for example, because he must take medical retirement, the applicant no longer enjoys the possibility of being able to purchase at a discount the house of which he is, by virtue of his employment, a tenant (CICB, 1994, para. 7.4). Extensive enquiries may have to be made to determine salary increases, promotion prospects and pension rights (CICB, 1989, para. 23.9). In the case of a manual worker, for example, Kemp suggests that the following contingencies be examined: the security of the applicant's job; any periods during which he was laid off; promotion prospects and consequent increases in earnings; incremental increases in earnings attributable to further training or years of experience; normal age of retirement; the risk of personal injury normally associated with the job; and post-retirement employment (Kemp, D., 'Damages for Future Pecuniary Loss', in Kemp, D., ed., *Damages for Personal Injury and Death*, 5th ed., London: Longman, 1993, ch. 5).

From the loss represented by these items, the claims officer will deduct any social security benefits, insurance payments or pension which the applicant has received as a result of the injury. As noted in connection with loss of earnings before or continuing at the time when the claim is assessed (new Scheme, para. 31), para. 45 of the new Scheme requires this reduction to be applied to those periods of loss for which additional compensation is payable, that is, from the beginning of the 29th week of loss (chapter 9.3.4).

To the figure reached by this process, the multiplicand, the claims officer applies an appropriate multiplier. A table given in note 3 to the tariff gives illustrations of multipliers applicable to periods from five to 40 years of loss (Appendix 3); this table is reproduced, with an explanation in para. 22 of the *Guide to Earnings and Expenses* (Appendix 4). These multipliers reflect those used at common law. As the Authority stresses in a number of its Guides, these illustrative multipliers are just that: it is for the claims officer to select that which best reflects the applicant's loss. In order to refine the selection of the multiplier, the claims officer may refer to the Actuarial Tables for use in Personal Injury and Fatal Accident Cases published by the Government Actuary's Department (*Guide to Earnings and Expenses*, para. 24; HL Debs, vol. 566, col. 1350, 31 October 1995). This possibility represents a change in practice inasmuch as the 'Ogden tables' were not used by the Board, notwithstanding that their author was for many years its Chairman (see Prevett, J., 'Actuarial Assessment of Damages' in Kemp, D., ed., *Damages for Personal Injury and Death,* 5th ed., 1993, ch. 7; Civil Evidence Act 1995). In selecting the multiplier, the claims officer may also take account of any other factors and contingencies which appear relevant. Such ordinary risks as illness, redundancy, temporary unemployment or accident will normally be reflected in a reduction of 10% in the multiplier. A further reduction may be made to reflect special factors reducing the applicant's loss of earnings, for example, that he might not have been in full employment until retirement (*Guide to Earnings and Expenses*, para. 25).

An example of the operation of para. 32 of the new Scheme is given in para. 26 of the *Guide to Earnings and Expenses* (Appendix 4).

Like personal injury actions, the assessment of compensation under the Scheme has not been and is not specifically linked to the retail price index (*Cookson* v *Knowles* [1979] AC 556; *Wright* v *British Railways Board* [1983] 2 AC 773). This does not imply any erosion of awards greater than would occur in a personal injury action, since the multipliers used in the old and new Schemes, being those approved by the courts, assume a net rate of return on investment of about 4.5% after the effects of tax and inflation have been taken into account (*Mallett* v *McMonagle* [1970] AC 166; HL Debs, vol. 566. col. 659, 17 October 1995); but, as with common law damages, the Board's awards were necessarily affected when the rate was higher. In the case of loss of earnings and of earning capacity, the upper limit specified under para. 14 of the old Scheme and para. 34 of the new is self-adjusting, being based upon the weekly average published by the Department of Employment (chapter 8.4.2.1.2).

Similarly, no further adjustment to the multiplier should be made to take account of the fact that in a very serious case where the multiplicand is substantial, it is likely that the income generated by the investment of the award will attract a higher rate of tax. It should ordinarily be assumed that the future incidence of tax will be dealt with by the conventional assumption of an interest rate applicable to a stable currency and the selection of a multiplier appropriate to that rate (*Hodgson* v *Trapp* [1989] AC 807).

Should the claims officer consider that the approach specified in para. 32 is impracticable, 'the compensation payable in respect of continuing loss of earnings or earning capacity will be such other lump sum as he may determine' (new Scheme para. 33).

8.4.2.1.2 *Ceiling on loss of earnings* Both the old and new Schemes impose the same limit on the net rate of current and future loss of earnings and earning capacity which is to be used for the purpose of determining the multiplicand. An upper limit was included in the original Scheme not so much as an economic measure, as was argued in connection with the minimum limit, but rather, as noted earlier (chapter 8.1), to prevent the perceived inequity of the very high earner being sustained at the taxpayer's expense. In practice, this entirely arbitrary limit does not appear to have adversely affected applications made under the old Scheme. By para. 14(a) of the 1990 revision to the old Scheme:

> the rate of net loss of earnings or earning capacity to be taken into account shall not exceed one and a half times the gross average industrial earnings at the date of assessment (as published in the *Department of Employment Gazette* and adjusted as considered appropriate by the Board).

For applications received before 1 February 1990, the limit was twice the gross average industrial earnings. 'Gross' average industrial earnings means earnings before deductions for income tax and national insurance contributions (*R* v *Criminal Injuries Compensation Board, ex parte Richardson* [1974] Crim LR 99; CICB, 1974, para. 4). This means therefore that the applicant's net loss of earnings or of earning capacity, that is, his employment income less deductions for income tax, superannuation or NIC, is controlled by a figure which takes no account of such deductions. Conversely, the upper limit applies before any deductions are made to take account of social security benefits, occupational pensions and the like. If it were otherwise, the multiplicand would be lower and thus the applicant would lose the value of those benefits, since they would have been deducted twice.

Paragraph 34 of the new Scheme provides:

> Any rate of net loss of earnings or earning capacity (before any reduction in accordance with this Scheme [i.e., under paras 45–7]) which is to be taken into account in calculating any compensation payable under paras 30–33 must not exceed one and a half times the gross average industrial earnings at the time of assessment according to the latest figures published by the Department of Education and Employment.

In February 1996 that figure was of the order of £28,500 a year.

8.4.2.2 Compensation for Special Expenses

Paragraph 35 of the new Scheme provides for an additional amount of compensation to be paid in respect of loss or damage to certain kinds of property, costs associated with National Health Service and private health treatment, and costs associated with the applicant's long-term care. To qualify for additional compensation under any of these headings, the applicant must satisfy the 28-week time condition; that is, that at the date of the application he has either sustained or is likely to sustain 28 weeks' loss of earnings or of earning capacity, or, in the case, for example, of someone retired from work, has been or is likely to be incapacitated for more than 28 weeks. The Authority's application form for personal injuries indicates that 'incapacitated' includes injuries which prevent the applicant from working, attending school or, if retired, from following his normal lifestyle to a significant extent (see also, *Guide to Earnings and Expenses*, para. 11). That being so, compensation is payable for such expenses *from the date of the injury* (new Scheme, Guide, para. 4.14; original emphasis). An applicant who sustains a criminal injury from which she makes an initial recovery but whose circumstances subsequently change, may, if she has already completed the application form, apply for additional compensation giving details of that change (new Scheme, Guide, para. 4.15). An applicant who applies for this element of additional compensation will be sent the *Guide to Earnings and Expenses* (reproduced in Appendix 4).

8.4.2.2.1 *Loss or damage to property*   Under para. 17 of the 1990 version of the old Scheme:

> Compensation will not be payable for the loss of or damage to clothing or any property whatsoever arising from the injury unless the Board are satisfied that the property was relied upon by the victim as a physical aid.

Physical aids were the sole exception to the general position under the old Scheme, that awards could only be made in respect of personal injury. Compensation has always been payable for the cost of replacing such lost or damaged personal adjuncts as spectacles, dentures, hearing aids and artificial limbs, the reasoning being that damage or loss to such items is, because of the applicant's dependence on them, akin to personal injury. By contrast, compensation has not been payable for such items as jewellery, watches (other than talking watches where required) or rings which were lost or damaged at the time of or after the incident, or in the course of medical or other treatment. Neither is lost or damaged clothing a compensable item under the 1990 revision (though it was under the version which it replaced).

   Paragraph 35(a) of the new Scheme provides that an additional amount of compensation may be payable for 'loss of or damage to property or equipment belonging to the applicant on which he relied as a physical aid, where the loss or damage was a direct consequence of the injury'. If the applicant meets the time condition, expenses incurred by her from the date of injury in respect of, for example, the repair or replacement of such physical aids as those mentioned above will be compensable. The applicant will be required to produce the relevant receipts (*Guide to Earnings and Expenses*, para. 28).

8.4.2.2.2 *Medical expenses*   On the assumption that the applicant could verify each item, the Board would routinely include in its award compensation for such out-of-pocket expenses as dental costs, fares to hospital and the cost of any prescribed treatment (old Scheme, Guide, para. 56). This will be the case also under para. 35(b) of the new Scheme, which provides for an additional amount to be paid in respect of 'costs (other than by way of loss of earnings or earning capacity) associated with National Health Service treatment for the injury', provided that the applicant meets the time condition (*Guide to Earnings and Expenses*, para. 29).

The old Scheme assumed that the medical treatment sought by, and provided to, the victim would fall within the NHS. Where the victim sought private medical treatment, para. 18 provided that:

> The cost of private medical treatment will be payable by the Board only if the Board consider that, in all the circumstances, both the private treatment and the cost of it are reasonable.

The Guide to the old Scheme is perhaps more emphatic about the presumption in favour of the NHS: 'The Board will not compensate for the cost of private treatment unless satisfied that it was reasonable to obtain treatment privately. Where the Board are so satisfied compensation will not exceed a reasonable amount' (old Scheme, Guide, para. 57). The reference to reasonable expense reflects the common law (*Cunningham* v *Harrison* [1973] QB 942); but by contrast with s. 2(4) of the Law Reform (Personal Injuries) Act 1948, which provides that in an action for damages for personal injuries there shall be disregarded, in determining the reasonableness of any expenses, the possibility of avoiding those expenses by taking advantage of NHS facilities, the burden will be on the applicant to show why he did not use them. Where they are used, the Board could reduce the award for pecuniary loss which would otherwise be payable, to reflect 'any saving to the injured person which is attributable to his maintenance wholly or partly at public expense in a hospital, nursing home or other institution' (Administration of Justice Act 1982, s. 5; see further the Law Commission, *Damages for Personal Injury: Medical, Nursing and Other Expenses*, Consultation Paper No. 144, London: HMSO, 1996).

The 1986 Working Party thought that the statutory Scheme should not normally pay for medical (which includes dental) expenses unless, in addition to their being of reasonable cost, they were essential (Home Office, *Criminal Injuries Compensation: A Statutory Scheme*, 1986, para. 18.1). This was provided for in para. 9 of sch. 7 to the Criminal Justice Act 1988, but what might constitute 'essential' treatment was a matter of some debate during the Bill's parliamentary stages. The typical case used in support of amendments to return to a test of reasonableness was that of a young woman waiting for many months or even years for plastic surgery to correct the facial scars left by a criminal injury.

The new Scheme provides that additional compensation may be paid in respect of the cost of private health treatment, 'but only where a claims officer considers that, in all the circumstances, both the private treatment and its cost are reasonable' (new Scheme, para. 35(c)). Subject to the applicant's compliance with the time condition, it can be seen that this discretion is identical to that given to the Board. It can be assumed that the discretion will be similarly exercised; comments made during the debates on the Criminal Justice Bill 1986 by Lord Morton of Shuna, a member of the

Board, made it clear that in the example of facial scarring, the Board would consider private treatment entirely reasonable, even essential (HL Debs, vol. 489, col. 756, 29 October 1986). Paragraph 30 of the *Guide to Earnings and Expenses* indicates that private treatment may be acceptable where the treatment required by the applicant — such as cosmetic or dental work — is not routinely available on the NHS in his area; but the burden is on the applicant to show that private treatment is a reasonable option.

8.4.2.2.3 *Long-term care*   Concern was voiced during the debates on the Bill that the new Scheme should make adequate provision for the care of victims seriously disabled by their injuries (HC Debs, Standing Committee A, col. 50, 13 June 1995; HL Debs, vol. 566, cols. 625–30, 16 October 1995). Responding to these concerns, the government gave repeated assurances that the expenses associated with the provision of long-term care would continue to be compensable under the new Scheme (HC Debs, Standing Committee A, cols. 57 and 93, 13 June 1995; HL Debs, vol. 566, cols. 294 and 627, 19 July and 16 October 1995). Paragraph 35(d) of the new Scheme provides that an applicant who has been or is likely to be incapacitated for more than 28 weeks may be paid additional compensation for the reasonable cost (to the extent that it falls to her) of any one or more of (i) special equipment, (ii) adaptations to her accommodation or (iii) care, whether in a residential establishment or at home, where these 'are not provided or available free of charge from the National Health Service, local authorities or any other agency'.

Special equipment.   This 'covers aids to mobility whether at home or outside, including specially adapted vehicles, wheelchairs, walking aids, and kitchen implements designed to help those with weakened grip' (*Guide to Earnings and Expenses*, para. 31). These items were routinely dealt with under the old Scheme; the Board's Reports show awards covering the cost of rehabilitation courses (CICB, 1977, para. 30); blind aids, talking watches and home assistance for victims blinded by an attack (CICB, 1984, para. 36); and the provision of an adapted car for victims handicapped by paralysis (CICB, 1979, para. 6; *Povey* v *Governors of Rydal School* [1970] 1 All ER 841).

Adaptations to accommodation.   These 'can include both internal and external works to improve mobility and access' (*Guide to Earnings and Expenses*, para. 31). Here again, where his injuries have required alterations to the applicant's house, reasonable expenses thus incurred have been compensable under the old Scheme as at common law (*Roberts* v *Johnstone* [1989] QB 878). These have included changes to the structure and layout of a house (CICB, 1981, paras 14–15; 1982, para. 18; 1985, para. 11; 1986, para. 9), including the provision of additional heating (CICB, 1987, para. 11).

Care.   The costs of care 'are assessed on the basis of what is reasonably necessary in your case. We will consider your circumstances carefully, taking account of the services which may be provided to you free of charge from other sources, such as the NHS or local authority' (*Guide to Earnings and Expenses*, para. 31). This last point may, as in the case of medical treatment, be contrasted with the position at common law by virtue of s. 2(4) of the Law Reform (Personal Injuries) Act 1948 (chapter 8.4.2.2.2). The claims officer must also be satisfied that the expense is necessary as a direct consequence of the injury.

Under the old Scheme 'care' has included nursing care (CICB, 1982, para. 18; 1985, para. 11; 1986, para. 9; 1987, para. 11) and expenses or losses incurred by a spouse or parent who gives up a job to nurse the victim (*Donnelly* v *Joyce* [1974] QB 454; *Roberts* v *Johnstone* [1989] QB 878; *Hunt* v *Severs* [1994] 2 AC 350; CICB, 1981, paras 14–15; 1983, para. 11; 1984, para. 10; 1986, para. 9). Paragraph 35 of the new Scheme makes similar provision for what the Law Commission identified as the significant burden of unpaid care provided at home by relatives or friends of injured victims (Law Commission, *Personal Injury Compensation: How Much is Enough?*, Law Com. No.225, London: HMSO, 1994; HL. Debs, vol. 566, col. 1395, 31 October 1995); possibly some 6.5 million people (HC Debs, Standing Committee A, col. 53, 13 June 1995). 'If you are being looked after at home by a relative or friend we will consider what the costs are to the carer in question and the level of care provided' (*Guide to Earnings and Expenses*, para. 31); the unpaid care provided by the relative or friend will attract additional compensation whether or not the carer him- or herself quits employment for the purpose. This was clarified during the report stage in the Lords by the inclusion of the phrase 'earning capacity' in para. 35, the approach being 'to take account of the time which the relative or friend is devoting to the care of the victim and make an assumption about how much that may represent in loss of earning capacity' (HL Debs, vol. 566, col. 1606, 6 November 1995). It may be assumed that this care is not being provided by the offender, and thus that that aspect of *Hunt* v *Severs* is dealing with care provided by the negligent defendant is inapplicable to the new Scheme; generally, see the Law Commission *Damages for Personal Injury: Medical, Nursing and Other Expenses*, Consultation Paper No. 144, London: HMSO, 1996.

This expense will therefore be compensated by assessing the carer's loss of earnings or earning capacity, including any additional personal and living expenses, as calculated on such basis as the claims officer considers appropriate in all the circumstances. Where the lost earnings are high, the common law's approach has been to assess the commercial cost of supplying a nurse, less a discount (around 25%) because the carer is untrained. If this is inappropriate, the compensation payable will be such sum as the claims officer determines having regard to the level of care provided (compare *Housecroft* v *Burnett* [1986] 1 All ER 332). However, it may be that the new Scheme will not cover all of the expenses incurred by a carer. In response to a Lords amendment which would have included as an additional amount of compensation, 'the reasonable cost of housework, childcare, maintenance of the applicant's home, garden or means of transport to the extent that the applicant cannot perform such maintenance he did before the injury and as a consequence of it', the Minister said (HL Debs, vol. 566, col. 627, 16 October 1995):

In general the new scheme will cover the 'core' losses which are covered under the present arrangements. However, the scheme is not intended to cover each and every item which might be allowable under common law damages either now or in the future. That is because the scheme is no longer based on common law damages, and it is not the function of a scheme funded by the taxpayer to make good each and every potential loss which a victim might conceivably suffer.

Accordingly, while care, in the sense of looking after the applicant's daily needs for food, washing and bathing, toilet and sleeping arrangements, housework, and the administration of prescribed medications, will attract an additional amount of compensation calculated as provided in para. 35, the loss of earnings incurred by the carer in looking after what the government described as more peripheral matters will not (HL Debs, vol. 566. cols. 1606–7, 6 November 1995). What constitutes the periphery will be for claims officers and, on appeal, adjudicators, to determine.

In line with the common law, the Board has endeavoured to make provision for any increases in such expenses that are foreseeable at the date on which the application is determined (CICB, 1986, para. 29). The new Scheme provides that a claims officer, if satisfied that the need for any special expenses is likely to continue, shall, in calculating the additional compensation, determine the annual cost of those expenses and select the appropriate multiplier in accordance with para. 32 (chapter 8.4.2.1.1), taking account of any other relevant factors and contingencies (new Scheme, para. 36; *Guide to Earnings and Expenses*, para. 32).

8.4.2.3   Other Expenses Associated with the Application

As noted in chapter 2.4, legal expenses incurred by the applicant in the preparation of an application to the Board or to the Authority are not compensable. Neither are they compensable where they have been incurred for the purpose of representation at a hearing (even at one requested by a single member), though para. 25 of the old Scheme and para. 74 of the new permit the reimbursement of reasonable expenses incurred by the applicant and any person who attends to give evidence at a hearing.

Like the Board, the Authority may require applicants to attend a specified venue for an inspection of their injuries. Under the old Scheme, these inspections have been carried out on hearing days (CICB, 1995, para. 4.16). Paragraph 4.7 of the Guide to the new Scheme indicates that the Authority will pay reasonable travelling expenses for this purpose including, where appropriate, both the applicant's and a carer's expenses.

8.5   FATAL INJURIES

8.5.1   Cause of Death

8.5.1.1   The Old Scheme
As we saw in chapter 6.3.3, the old Scheme drew a distinction between a victim who died as a consequence of the injury (old Scheme, para. 15), and one who died from some other cause (old Scheme, para. 16).

In the case of death which is not a consequence of the criminal injury, para. 16 of the old Scheme confined compensation to 'loss of wages, expenses and liabilities incurred by the victim before death as a result of the injury whether or not the application for compensation in respect of the injury has been made before the death'. If the victim had made a successful application, any amount to which he had become entitled would be deducted from any further award payable to the dependants. If the application had been submitted but not determined by the Board, it would lapse, and the dependants would have to pursue their own application (CICB, 1991, para. 29.1). Under para. 16, an award for the pecuniary losses mentioned would be payable to a dependant (or relative) in respect, for example, of the victim's reasonable medical treatment following the victimising event and for her loss of earnings. However, any loss suffered by a reduction in the deceased's prospective earnings was by implication excluded from para. 16. Likewise any expenses or liabilities incurred by the dependant concerning the victim's death, for example, funeral expenses, were not compensable.

By para. 5 of the old Scheme, the lower limit did not apply to applications under para. 16 (CICB, 1991, para. 29.2: award of £182 payable to the deceased's father). However, para. 6(c) of the old Scheme did apply, so that any 'loss of wages, expenses' etc. would not be reimbursed if the Board considered that the applicant's or the deceased's conduct or character made an award inappropriate (CICB, 1993, para. 27.9).

Also excluded from the old Scheme in such cases was any compensation for non-pecuniary loss to which the victim would have been entitled had he made an application before his death. In this respect the old Scheme differed from the law of England and Wales, which allows for the deceased's estate 'to recover the full value of any pre-death pain, suffering and loss of amenity, whether or not the death was caused by the injury itself and whether or not the deceased had commenced an action for damages while alive', but only where there was a reasonably prolonged period of suffering (s. 1 of the Law Reform (Miscellaneous Provisions) Act 1934; Law Commission, Consultation Paper No. 140, 1995, para. 4.126; *Hicks* v *Chief Constable of the South Yorkshire Police* [1992] 2 All ER 65). By virtue of the Damages (Scotland) Act 1993, this is now also the case in Scotland, where, between 1976 and 1992, the Damages (Scotland) Act 1976 provided that actions for non-pecuniary loss did not survive for the benefit of the victim's estate (see the Law Commission, Consultation Paper No. 140, 1995, paras 4.126–4.127). Neither did para. 16 of the old Scheme give those dependants specified in s. 1A(2) of the Fatal Accidents Act 1976 the fixed award for bereavement; nor, in Scotland, relatives, the award for loss of society.

By contrast, where the victim did die as a result of the criminal injury, para. 15 of the old Scheme provided that compensation would be assessed as though it were an action by a dependant (or relative) under the Fatal Accidents Act 1976 (chapter 6.3.3). This paragraph also explicitly provided that no compensation would be payable for the benefit of the victim's estate. Where an application had been made by the victim before he died as a result of the criminal injury, his dependants could make their own application under this paragraph, subject to the conditions for the reopening of cases set out in para. 13 of the old Scheme. This meant that such an application would have to be made within three years of the victim's death, and that the Board would have to be satisfied that this new application 'can be considered without a need for extensive enquiries'. Any award made to the victim during his lifetime would be deducted from the award, if any, to the dependants.

8.5.1.2   The New Scheme

The distinction between deceased victims of criminal injuries who died as a result of their injuries and those who died from other causes is maintained in the new Scheme. Where the victim has died otherwise than as a result of the criminal injury, para. 22(e) provides that supplementary compensation is payable to a qualifying claimant (see below) who was financially dependent on the victim within the terms of para. 40 of the new Scheme. Supplementary compensation is confined by para. 44 to cases in which the victim would have qualified for additional compensation for loss of earnings or earning capacity (new Scheme, para. 22(b)) or for special expenses (new Scheme, para. 22(c)): no compensation is payable, therefore, for the first 28 weeks of loss. If the victim did apply before his death, but his application was rejected, no supplementary compensation is payable under this paragraph (Guide, para. 24).

It follows, therefore, that no supplementary compensation will be payable where the victim did not live for a further 28 weeks after sustaining the criminal injury. If he did, then the additional amount payable for special expenses is payable from the date on which they were first incurred; but the first 28 weeks' loss of earnings is not compensable. It is not necessary for the victim to have made an application for compensation prior to death, but if he did and an award was made, the total payable to the victim and the qualifying claimant(s) must not exceed £500,000.

Where the victim died as a result of the criminal injury, para. 22(d) provides for three possible awards of compensation: a standard amount of compensation (para. 39), an additional amount to reflect loss of dependency (para. 40), and an additional amount for the loss of a parent's services (para. 42). The first two categories broadly reflect the existing distinction between the bereavement award payable in England and Wales, and damages for loss of support. The third is, however, a novel head of compensation, having elements both of conventional and of assessed compensation. If, prior to his death, the victim successfully applied for compensation under the Scheme, the amount of the award will be deducted from any amount payable to a qualifying claimant (Guide, para. 23).

These heads of compensation are payable to 'qualifying claimants' who are, at the time of the victim's death (new Scheme, para. 38; *Guide to Applicants for Compensation in Fatal Cases* (hereafter, *Guide to Fatal Cases*, reproduced in Appendix 5, para. 7). Qualifying claimants are:

(a)   the victim's spouse who was formally married to and living with the victim as husband and wife in the same household (but not a spouse who was living apart from and not financially dependent on the victim);

(b)   the victim's spouse or former spouse who was financially dependent on the victim at the date of death;

(c)   the victim's parent or child (of any age), whether natural or accepted by the deceased as a parent or child of the family, or, in the case of a child only, was dependent on the victim;

(d)   a person who, though not formally married to the victim, had at the date of death been living with the victim as husband and wife for at least two years.

The three heads of compensation will now be considered in more detail. In order to draw upon relevant parallels with the old Scheme and at common law, the discussion is grouped under the more familiar fatal accident action headings. An application arising from a fatal injury will fail in whole or in part either because the deceased's conduct or character make it inappropriate that a full or any award should be made (CICB, 1990, para. 25.5; 1991, paras 28.1–28.4; 1993, para. 27.5; 1994, para. 6.18), or because the applicant is similarly disqualified (CICB, 1992, para. 25.3).

8.5.2   General Damages: the Standard Amount of Compensation

In England and Wales (Law Reform (Miscellaneous Provisions) Act 1934) and, following the reversal of policy in the Damages (Scotland) Act 1993, in Scotland, any action for non-pecuniary loss which the victim had at the time of death survives for the benefit of his estate. As noted, the survival of this cause of action was expressly excluded from the old Scheme, and it likewise has no place in the new (new Scheme, para. 37).

In England and Wales, general damages for dependants have only been available since the introduction of the bereavement award in the Administration of Justice Act 1982. This is currently a fixed sum of £7,500, payable to a more narrowly defined range of dependants than are eligible for special damages, namely the husband or wife of the deceased, and, where the deceased was a minor who never married, his parents if he was legitimate or his mother if illegitimate, and divisible between the parents (CICB, 1990, para. 25.4). Where the deceased leaves a widow and children, the award is payable to the widow (Fatal Accidents Act 1976, s. 3(2)). As noted earlier, s. 1A(2) of the Fatal Accidents Act 1976 provides that 'common law' wives and husbands are ineligible for this award.

The new Scheme's equivalent to the bereavement award is a standard amount of compensation at level 13 of the tariff (£10,000) where there is only one qualifying claimant, and, where there is more than one, at level 10 each (£5,000). There are therefore two immediate differences between the tariff Scheme and the bereavement award: as a single payment it is of greater value, and it is payable (at the lower level) to all qualifying claimants. In providing that they would receive a standard amount of compensation (at the higher or lower level), the government sought to meet the criticisms made of the unlawful Scheme. This provision would mean, first, that all qualifying claimants would receive some financial support, and secondly, that 80%

of claimants would be better off than under the bereavement award payable under the old Scheme (HC Debs, Standing Committee A, cols. 163–73, 15 June 1995). It remains to be seen whether these forecasts are accurate, though Lord Carlisle did acknowledge that the government had 'gone a long way towards meeting the major objections' to the earlier Scheme (HL Debs, vol. 566, col. 305, 19 July 1995). A former spouse of the deceased is not a qualifying claimant for this purpose (new Scheme, para. 39), although a former spouse who was financially dependent on the victim may be eligible for additional compensation.

8.5.3 Special Damages

8.5.3.1 Loss of Support: Additional Compensation
The new Scheme provides that 'Additional compensation ... may be payable to a qualifying claimant where a claims officer is satisfied that the claimant was financially dependent on the deceased' (new Scheme, para. 40). Paragraph 41 goes on to provide that the amount of compensation payable in respect of dependency will be calculated on the same basis as paras 31–4, that is, the paragraphs dealing with the calculation of loss of earnings and of earning capacity (chapter 8.4.2.1). Unlike additional compensation in cases where the victim survives the injury, which does not take effect for the first 28 weeks of loss, 'The period of loss will begin from the date of the deceased's death and continue for such period as a claims officer may determine' (compare *Graham* v *Dodds* [1983] 1 WLR 808).

The calculation to be adopted is basically the same as under the old Scheme, which was in turn based on the assessment of the value of the lost dependency in a fatal accident action. This, as Lord Wright said in *Davies* v *Powell Duffryn Associated Collieries Ltd* [1942] AC 601 at p. 617, 'is a hard matter of pounds, shillings and pence'. Lord Wright's description of a three-stage process entailing the determination of the deceased's loss of earnings from which his or her own living expenses are deducted, to give a datum figure (the multiplicand) to be converted into a lump sum by the selection of a number of years' purchase (the multiplier) was differently described by Lord Diplock in *Mallett* v *McMonagle* [1970] AC 166 at p. 174 as necessitating the court to take a view on three uncertain matters: (a) the value of the material benefits which the deceased would have provided but for his or her death; (b) the value of any material benefits which the dependants will acquire as a result of the death; and (c) the amount of the capital sum which, with prudent management would generate an annual income equivalent to the difference between (a) and (b) (see further Lord Pearson in *Taylor* v *O'Connor* [1971] AC 115 at p. 143). This is, in essence, the approach described in the Authority's *Guide to Fatal Cases*.

Paragraph 12 of the *Guide to Fatal Cases* describes the process as beginning with the assessment of the total net annual loss to the qualifying claimant. In a case where the deceased was the principal source of income, this will involve a determination of the victim's earnings and earnings prospects at the date of death. Adapting paras 31–4 of the new Scheme to fatal cases, the claims officer will be required to consider any changes to the annual rate of loss which may have arisen, for example, by the loss of the victim's prospects of promotion (*Guide to Fatal Cases*, para. 15). Where the deceased provided a secondary income, or was primarily responsible for looking after the domestic arrangements, including any children of the marriage, the claims officer will have to calculate the value of those services in addition to the loss of the income. This evaluation may involve the cost of employing a housekeeper or nanny to look after the children while the surviving parent is at work, or to pay for an outside contractor to undertake gardening which the deceased would have undertaken had he or she been alive (CICB, 1991, para. 28.11). Where, alternatively, the surviving parent gives up work to look after the children, it is appropriate to value the loss to the parent of the deceased's services not by reference to the cost of employing a housekeeper, but to the direct loss of the parent's earnings (*Mehmet* v *Perry* [1977] 2 All ER 529). In fatal accidents actions, the courts have also recognised the loss of the constant presence and guidance which such a parent — typically the mother — brings to the children's upbringing (*Spittle* v *Bunny* [1988] 1 WLR 847). Where the surviving parent — say the father — gives up his job to provide services in replacement for the loss of the children's mother, the children may still sustain a loss so far as their mother's services have not been replaced by their father (*Hayden* v *Hayden* [1992] 1 WLR 986), which will be part of the dependency apportioned to them. In addition, the children may also pursue a separate application under para. 42 (loss of parental services) as qualifying claimants in their own right (chapter 8.5.4).

In addition to the victim's gross earnings before tax, the claims officer will take into account any income or emoluments from an office or employment accruing to the applicant (new Scheme, para. 41). From the total of earnings, the new Scheme gives the claims officer discretion, when determining the multiplicand in cases where the victim and applicant were living together in the same household at the date of death, to 'make such proportional reduction as he considers appropriate to take account of the deceased's own personal and living expenses' (new Scheme, para. 41). Where the claim for dependency is made in such cases by an adult, and there were no children, the normal division is one third to each of the couple, and one third as common living expenses. Where the couple had children, the victim's personal expenses will normally be set at 25% (*Guide to Fatal Cases*, para. 14; *Harris* v *Empress Motors* [1984] 1 WLR 212).

The Scheme also requires that any income received by the applicant by way of pensions or social security benefits resulting from the death (*Guide to Fatal Cases*, para. 16) be taken into account. In the words of para. 45, 'The reduction [to take account of such payments made for the same contingency] will be applied to those categories or periods of loss or need for which additional or supplementary compensation is payable, including compensation calculated on the basis of a multiplicand or annual cost'. The point is to preclude double compensation. Under the old Scheme, the Board has proceeded, as s. 4 of the Fatal Accidents Act 1976 requires, by disregarding any 'benefits which have accrued or will accrue to any person from his estate or otherwise as a result of his death'. The purpose of s. 4, though broader than its predecessors in not confining 'benefits' to 'social security benefits' is, like them, intended 'to produce an exception to the common law rules for calculating *quantum* of damages, namely to prevent the deduction of a benefit which otherwise would have to be deducted in order to arrive at the true loss on a common law basis' (*Pidduck* v *Eastern Scottish Omnibuses Ltd* [1990] 1 WLR 993 at p. 998). However, the old Scheme produced the same effect as the new, since it also provided that certain kinds of benefit were to be deducted from the award which would otherwise be payable for the lost dependency. This is dealt with in chapter 9.2.3.

The old Scheme necessarily imported into the Board's assessment of the loss of support sustained by the dependants, s. 3(3) and (4) of the Fatal Accidents Act 1976. These subsections mean, first, that in assessing the compensation payable to a widow in respect of the death of her husband, the Board could take no account of her remarriage or the prospects thereof. This provision does not apply where the applicant was a woman living with the deceased as his wife; nor, possibly, does it apply to a widower's chances of remarriage (*Stanley* v *Saddique* [1992] QB 1). However, where the dependant was not married to the deceased but was living with the deceased as husband or wife, the Board has, by s. 3(4) of the 1976 Act, been required to take into account the fact that the applicant had no enforceable right to financial support. In the new Scheme, para. 41 provides that '... no account [shall be] taken, where the qualifying claimant was formally married to the deceased, of remarriage or prospects of remarriage'.

If there was no dependency, then no compensation is payable. The new Scheme expressly provides that a dependency will not be established if the deceased's normal income comprised only social security benefits, whether their source was the United Kingdom or another country (new Scheme, para. 40(a) and (b)). This reflects the Board's practice (CICB, 1992, para. 25.3). Similarly, there will be no loss of dependency if, as in a case such as *Burns* v *Edman* [1970] 2 QB 541, the victim's earnings were the proceeds of criminal activity.

Paragraph 34 imposes the same limit on the multiplicand in fatal cases as it does where the victim is the applicant. As para. 25 of the *Guide to Fatal Cases* puts it, take-home pay above one and a half times gross average industrial earnings cannot be considered.

To this net loss the claims officer applies the multiplier he considers appropriate, normally using the the date on which the victim would have retired. This process is 'even less precise' than the computation of the multiplicand (Saunt, T., 'Damages on Death', in Kemp. D., ed., *Damages for Personal Injury and Death*, 5th ed., 1993, para. 2.22). As in the case of applications by the victim, the Authority may use the illustrative multipliers in note 3 to the tariff, or use the Actuarial Tables, 'to refine our selection of the multiplier' (*Guide to Fatal Cases*, para. 19). The Guide also indicates that a claims officer will normally reduce the multiplier by 10% to take account of the vicissitudes of life (which are already accounted for in the Ogden Tables). A further reduction may be made if the deceased would not always have been in full employment to the normal retirement age (*Guide to Fatal Cases*, para. 19; *Graham* v *Dodds* [1983] 1 WLR 808). The *Guide to Fatal Cases* gives a lengthy example of how the Authority will calculate the dependency in an application made by a widow having two children of the marriage (Appendix 5). For examples of the Board's approach, see CICB, 1989, paras 24.3–24.5; 1990, para. 25.4 (England and Wales) and 1989, paras 24.6–24.9 (Scotland).

Where there are children of the family, the award has, in line with judicial practice, been apportioned so that the surviving parent has ready access to the funds which will have to be expended on them. But this apportionment has the potential for an improper deduction from the children's share (when determining the multiplicand) of collateral benefits payable only to the parent. As at common law, where a genuine estimate of the children's share might be undertaken (*Robertson* v *Lestrange* [1985] 1 All ER 950), the Board has been required to ensure that collateral benefits are only deducted from their recipient's income (*R* v *Criminal Injuries Compensation Board, ex parte Barrett* [1994] 1 FLR 587).

8.5.3.2 Funeral Expenses

Where the victim died as a result of the injury, compensation for reasonable funeral expenses has been payable under the old Scheme to anyone who incurred them. This has been so notwithstanding that the expense is less than the minimum limit specified in para. 5 or that the applicant was otherwise ineligible. However, funeral expenses have not been payable to his dependants or relatives where the Board could apply para. 6(c) because of either the victim's or their unlawful conduct or character (CICB, 1993, para. 27.9).

The position is the same under the new Scheme. Paragraph 37 provides that funeral expenses will be payable to anyone who incurs them, even where that person is otherwise ineligible under the Scheme. However, they will not be payable if the claims officer considers that the deceased's or the applicant's actions, conduct or character make an award inappropriate (new Scheme, para. 14).

Where funeral expenses are reimbursed by the Authority, they must be reasonable. This reflects the position under the old Scheme. Earlier statements by the Board have indicated in some detail what it has regarded as a reasonable expense. It includes the cost of a tombstone and of conveying family mourners to the funeral but excludes memorials (if they are part tombstones, that cost has been met), newspaper announcements, wreaths and funeral breakfasts (though reflecting the more generous provision under Scots law, awards have been made for the costs incurred for these three, where the expenditure was apt and reasonable). The 1986 Working Party further indicated that the Board would be very unlikely to meet the cost of burial overseas of a victim resident in this country; by contrast, if satisfied that the expenditure is justified, it may be more prepared to meet the cost of a burial in his own country of a visitor here (Home Office, *Criminal Injuries Compensation: A Statutory Scheme*, 1986, para. 15.11). Paragraph 21 of the *Guide to Fatal Cases* indicates briefly that the Authority 'will take account of the religious and cultural background of the victim and his/her family'.

8.5.4 Loss of Parental Services

A new head of compensation is provided in para. 42 of the new Scheme which is not conditional upon the claimant demonstrating financial dependence on the deceased.

This award may be made whether or not the claimant makes a successful application under para. 41. As para. 13 in the *Guide to Fatal Cases* puts it: 'Unlike assessments under the Fatal Accidents Act, the Scheme recognises the services contributed by both mothers and fathers to the upbringing of children'. This head extends to any qualifying claimant under 18 years of age at the time of his or her parent's death, where the claimant was dependent on the victim — mother or father — for parental services, and provides additional compensation by way of:

    (a)   a payment for loss of that parent's services at an annual rate of level 5 of the tariff; and
    (b)   such other payments as a claims officer considers reasonable to meet other resultant losses.

This is based in part on the award under the Damages (Scotland) Act 1976 for loss of the deceased's society, which is payable to any person who was, immediately prior to the deceased's death, a parent or child of the deceased, or any person accepted by the deceased as a child of his family. Unlike bereavement, loss of society is not a conventional sum, but was interpreted by Lord Jauncey in *Dingwall* v *Walter Alexander and Sons (Midland) Ltd* 1980 SC 64 (CICB, 1985, paras 40–1) as requiring an amount representing proper compensation 'for the loss of a father's help as a member of the household and of his counsel and guidance as a husband and father and for similar, unquantifiable loss in relation to the death of a wife and mother or of a child'. Such an award may be made even though the applicant was not living with the deceased because of his mental or physical disabilities (CICB, 1993, para. 27.2). It follows that such an award may vary considerably: it may well be quite substantial, or it may be small (CICB, 1990, para. 25.6). Where the applicant had had very little recent contact with the deceased, it may be nil (CICB, 1992, paras 25.4, 25.6). The award may also be reduced by virtue of the applicant's own convictions (CICB, 1994, para. 6.18).

Each of the payments under para. 42 is to be multiplied by an appropriate multiplier selected by a claims officer in accordance with para. 32 of the Scheme, which deals with future loss of earnings. The years of loss are the period remaining before the claimant reaches 18. The multiplicand in the case of para. 42(a) is fixed at £2,000. It is therefore unnecessary to gauge whether the parent's services were of good or poor quality, as in the dependency cases *Spittle* v *Bunny* [1988] 1 WLR 847 and *Stanley* v *Saddique* [1992] QB 1. In the case of para. 42(b), it will depend on the exact nature of the pecuniary loss in that application, the claims officer being able to take into account any factors and contingencies she considers appropriate.

The reference to 'other resultant losses' in para. 42(b) will permit compensation to be awarded, for example, to cover 'any additional costs of childcare or loss of earnings suffered by an adult in looking after the child' (*Guide to Fatal Cases*, para. 13). An example is provided by *R* v *Criminal Injuries Compensation Board, ex parte McGuffie* [1978] Crim LR 160. The applicants were two aunts who had given up their jobs to foster the three children left when their father was imprisoned for the murder of their mother. They applied on behalf of the children, and on their own behalf. The Board decided that they themselves were not entitled to an award, any pecuniary loss being sustained not by them but by the children. However, in determining the children's loss by reference to the aunts' loss of earnings, the Board, wrongly in the Divisional Court's opinion, deducted from that loss the full amount of the boarding-out allowance they received from the local authority. Peter Pain J. held that while it was correct to deduct so much of the allowance as was attributable to the actual cost of materials used in looking after the children, there should be no deduction in respect of any amount attrributable to the cost of providing emotional care for the children. Commenting on its approach upon reconsidering the application, the Board said:

> Where a fostering allowance is being paid, the financial element of the allowance intended to pay for the cost of feeding, clothing and maintaining the child is to be set against any claim for dependency, and any element there may be in a fostering allowance which is intended to compensate for the loss of care which the mother bestowed on the child is to be set against any claim for the loss of the mother's services.

Under the new Scheme, the three children would each receive £2,000 multiplied by an appropriate multiplier, while the aunts would be eligible for a payment under para. 42(b), taking into account any income received by them in connection with their fostering (compare *Cresswell* v *Eaton* [1991] 1 WLR 1113; *Hayden* v *Hayden* [1992] 1 WLR 986).

9 Deductions

9.1 INTRODUCTION

A feature of both Schemes is that almost all collateral benefits are to be deducted from any compensation payable. Benefits to be deducted include all social security benefits which accrue as a result of the injury or death without limitation of time, insurance or pension moneys payable otherwise than upon a policy subscribed to by the victim (or his parents if under 18), and any award payable by the offender to the applicant under a compensation order or a court order for damages. There can be no controversy about the last of these; so far as the Schemes seek to substitute for the offender, it must be right that where he can be pursued to judgment, the taxpayer's burden be correspondingly reduced. Deduction of social security benefit has been 'based on the sound principle that there should be no duplication of payments from public funds' (Home Office, *Criminal Injuries Compensation: A Statutory Scheme*, London: HMSO, 1986, para. 19.1), while the deduction of any benefits payable by an employer by way of insurance, gratuity or pension has been justified on the basis that State compensation should not provide an income which is in effect higher than the victim or those financially dependent on him enjoyed before the injury.

In these respects the rules governing the deduction of collateral benefits under the old Scheme were, from its inception, radically different to those which have obtained in personal injury or fatal accident actions. However, the differences between the old Scheme and a personal injury action lessened significantly — at least with regard to the receipt of social security payments — following the enactment of s. 22 of the Social Security Act 1989, now ss. 81 and 82 of the Social Security Administration Act 1992 ('the 1992 Act'). These provide that from any compensation payment made on or after 3 September 1990 in respect of an accident or injury occurring on or after 31 January 1989 or, in respect of a disease, where the first claim for a 'relevant benefit' is made after that earlier date (s. 81(7)), the 'compensator' (s. 82(1)) will be required to withhold the compensation payable under a court order or in pursuance of a settlement, until the Secretary of State has provided him with a certificate stating the value of the benefits to be deducted from the payment. The 'relevant benefits' are listed in the Act, each being aggregated for the 'relevant period'.

Nevertheless, some important differences between the new Scheme and a civil action for damages remain. For the purposes of the 1992 Act, the 'relevant period' is five years, in the case of a disease, from the date of the first claim for a relevant benefit and in any other case, from the day following the accident or injury to the date of final settlement if that occurs at an earlier date (s. 81(1)), whereas both the old and new Schemes continue to require the deduction of these benefits without limitation of time. They also require the deduction of benefits that would, under s. 81(3) qualify as 'exempt payments', such as payments made under compensation orders, or under contracts of insurance. By s. 88(1)(f), a payment by the Board is an exempt payment. This is so because, where the applicant has succeeded in obtaining damages or other compensation from the offender, the Board will deduct that amount from the award it has assessed, and because the applicant is required to reimburse the Board (or the Authority) should he make any similar future recovery (chapter 9.5.1). By analogy, this ought to be so also in the case of awards made by the Authority, but the 1995 Act does not amend the 1992 Act accordingly.

These provisions do not apply to compensation payments made in consequence of an action under the Fatal Accidents Act 1976, which are, by s. 81(3)(c) of the 1992 Act, 'exempt payments'. Accordingly, the several major differences which have prevailed between such actions and applications made under the old Scheme will continue. As the old and new Schemes are very similar in their treatment of collateral benefits, their provisions are considered together.

9.2 BASIC OPERATION OF THE TWO SCHEMES

9.2.1 Deductible Benefits and Payments

The provisions governing the deduction of collateral benefits are contained in paras 19–21 of the old Scheme and paras 45–9 of the new. These distinguish the following benefits:

(a) social security benefits (old Scheme, para. 19(a) and (c); new Scheme, para. 45(a) and (b); chapter 9.3);

(b) personal and non-employer insurance (old Scheme, para. 19(d); new Scheme, para. 45(c); chapter 9.4.1);

(c) occupational pension and insurance arrangements (old Scheme, para. 20; new Scheme, para. 47; chapter 9.4.2);

(d) payments made by way of damages or under a compensation order (old Scheme, para. 21; new Scheme, para. 48(c); chapter 9.5.1); and

(e) other criminal injury compensation awards (old Scheme, para. 19(b); new Scheme, para. 48(a) and (b); chapter 9.5.2).

9.2.2   Non-deductible Payments

There are some payments which may be made to a victim or his dependants as the result of the criminal injury which do not have to be deducted. These include payments made under a privately financed insurance policy (*Bradburn* v *Great Western Railway Co.* (1874) LR 10 Ex 1) (except those relating to special expenses: chapter 9.4.1) or pension plan (chapter 9.4.2). In addition, payments from charitable sources (*Redpath* v *Belfast and County Down Railway* [1947] NI 167), perhaps as a reward for an act of law enforcement, are not deductible unless they are made by the victim's employer. These are consistent with the two 'well-established' exceptions to the rule that receipts accruing to the applicant in consequence of the injury are to be set against his loss (*Hussain* v *New Taplow Paper Mills Ltd* [1988] AC 514). A payment made by a court in recognition of a victim's attempts to enforce the law should also escape.

9.2.3   Impact of the Deduction on the Award

The benefits and payments which are to be taken into account should, where there is more than one applicant, be properly allocated to the applicant who receives them. This is of particular importance in fatal cases where the applicant is claiming on behalf of herself and her children. In *R* v *Criminal Injuries Compensation Board, ex parte Barrett* [1994] 1 FLR 587, the Board had followed the normal practice of apportioning the bulk of the compensation to the parent (CICB, 1991, para. 28.11). In assessing the value of the loss of dependency, the Board had deducted the payments made to the father under the insurance contract to which he and his murdered wife had jointly subscribed. The effect of this was to reduce the children's loss of dependency, as well as their father's. Since 'Neither the common law nor the Scheme sanctions such a deduction', Latham J. allowed the application for judicial review.

Of greater significance, since the following remarks apply to personal injury as well as to fatal applications, these provisions operate under the old Scheme to deduct the benefit accruing to the applicant from the *full* amount of any compensation payable, and not merely from that element of loss to which they may substantially relate. By contrast, under the new Scheme, payments other than those falling into categories (d) and (e) in the list in chapter 9.2.1 (offender or other State criminal injury compensation) will, in essence, only affect any additional or supplementary compensation payable, having no impact on the tariff award payable in any case.

The operative paragraphs in the old Scheme speak of compensation being reduced, in the case of para. 19, 'by the full value' of the benefit, in the case of para. 20, 'to take into account' any pension, and in the case of para. 21, 'by the amount of any payment received' under an order of the court. Whereas the common law position was to exempt non-pecuniary loss from deductions, the Board has never made any attempt to match deductible benefits to particular losses: once it has established the aggregate value of these various benefits it has quite simply deducted that sum, first from any heads of special damage and secondly from any heads of general damage, until it is exhausted. In the case of a personal injury application, the deduction from the award of general damages mirrors what is required by s. 81 of the 1992 Act (*Hassall* v *Secretary of State for Social Security* [1995] 1 WLR 812 (CA)). In the case of an application made by dependants under para. 15, this has meant, unlike a fatal accidents action, deduction from the conventional award for bereavement or from the assessed award for loss of society (CICB, 1987, para. 44).

The 1986 Working Party considered the argument, discussed by the Pearson Commission in relation to all collateral benefits (*Royal Commission on Civil Liability and Compensation for Personal Injury, Report*, Cmnd 7054, London: HMSO, 1978, ch. 13), that these sums should be deducted only from the part of the award for special damage to which they apparently relate, as s. 2(1) of the Law Reform (Personal Injuries) Act 1948 provided, for example, in the case of unemployment benefit, to loss of earnings. The Pearson Commission had distinguished earnings, the cost of care and non-pecuniary losses, and had proposed that offsets be deducted so far as they corresponded to these headings. However, because they do not relate exclusively to pecuniary loss, and thus to allow them to go undeducted would permit some duplication of payment from public funds, the Working Party did not endorse these proposals in the particular case of social security benefits (Home Office, *Criminal Injuries Compensation: A Statutory Scheme*, 1986, para. 19.2). In the case of payments received by way of damages or compensation orders, it would be inappropriate to permit the applicant to recover twice for the same injury, since by definition these orders will have made some allowance for general damages. Similarly payments made under pension or insurance arrangements executed by someone other than the victim or his parent need not be wholly confined to loss of earnings, and even where the payment may be expressly related only to loss of earnings or of earning capacity, the Working Party could see no way in which the Scheme could draw a workable distinction between these and other collateral benefits which may be intended to meet, to some extent, the general damage suffered by the victim. In any event, to allow such differentiation would, in its view, have cut across the government's acceptance of the proposition that, in the context of personal injury actions, the State should not subsidise the tortfeasor, and the victim should not get the windfall of double compensation.

In a major departure both from the requirements of the 1992 Act and from para. 19 of the old Scheme, the new Scheme does indeed differentiate, in the impact of these various collateral benefits, between the pecuniary and non-pecuniary losses sustained by the applicant. It does so, in short, by providing, first, that social security benefits and personal insurance payments shall not be deducted from the standard amount of compensation, but only from those amounts of additional or supplementary compensation to which they relate (new Scheme, para. 45); and, second, that payments under occupational insurance and pension arrangements shall only be deductible from any compensation for loss of earnings or earning capacity (new Scheme, para. 47). Payments made by the offender or under other criminal injury compensation arrangements are deductible in full from the award, including standard amounts of compensation. This is so because, as noted earlier, such payments will include elements of general damage. Thus, para. 45 provides:

> All awards payable under this Scheme, except those payable under paras 25, 27, 39 and 42(a) (tariff-based amounts of compensation), will be subject to a reduction to take account of social security benefits or insurance payments made by way of compensation for the same contingency. The reduction will be applied to those categories or periods of loss or need for which additional or supplementary compensation is payable, including compensation calculated on the basis of a multiplicand or annual cost.

An award payable under para. 25 is the standard amount of compensation for personal injury; an award under para. 27 is the specific award at level 10 for a woman who keeps a child conceived as the result of rape (chapter 9.2.3.2); an award under para. 39 is the standard amount of compensation for qualifying claimants in fatal cases; and the award under para. 42(a) is the specific amount at level 5 which forms the basis of one of the two elements of additional compensation payable for the loss of parental services. The benefits and payments which are to be deducted are those which relate 'to the same contingency' as the award being made, that is, in personal injury applications, benefits and payments compensating for loss of earnings or earning capacity (paras 30-4) or special expenses (paras 35–6); and in fatal injury applications, either loss of dependency (para. 41) and 'other resultant losses' arising from the loss of parental services(para. 42(b)) or, where the victim died otherwise than as a result of the criminal injury, supplementary compensation (para. 44).

9.2.3.1   Funeral Expenses

Compensation for funeral expenses was, under the old Scheme, one of two exceptions to the general operation of the principle of full deduction. Where an application under para. 15 of the old Scheme was made by a person other than the dependant who was in receipt of the specified benefits, the applicant would receive an award irrespective of the value of those benefits (and irrespective of whether the funeral expenses exceeded the lower limit: old Scheme, para. 5). This would be so simply because there would be nothing to deduct from the applicant's claim. However, the Board has also made awards for such expenses where the applicant himself was in receipt of the deductible benefits specified in paras 19(a) and 20. In a case reported in 1986, though the value of the DSS benefits and employer's pension totalled £17,267 as against £16,647 for the value of the lost dependency and thus no award was payable in respect of it, the Board did compensate the applicant for her funeral expenses. These amounted to £412, which was less than the £620 excess of benefits over the lost dependency (CICB, 1986, para. 28).

The basis for this exception to the general principle of deduction lies in para. 15 of the old Scheme, which provides that an award for funeral expenses may be made to an applicant who is otherwise ineligible. But this is not altogether satisfactory, since eligibility usually relates to the question whether an applicant has a cause of action, not to the question of *quantum*, which necessarily supposes that he has. Moreover, if ineligibility includes cases where the applicant's para. 19 and para. 20 benefits exceed the compensation payable, then why should it not equally include para. 21 benefits? The question arises whether the Board would have made an award for funeral expenses if the dependant had succeeded in obtaining a court order for damages against the person responsible for the deceased's death, which order specifically included the cost of the funeral. That would be unlikely.

Nevertheless, as para. 37 of the new Scheme is cast in virtually identical terms to para. 15 of the old, it may be expected that funeral expenses will be payable notwithstanding that the person who incurred them will otherwise receive no compensation (other than the standard amount, if applicable to the qualifying claimant in question) because the value of any deductible benefits or payments exceeds the loss of dependency.

9.2.3.2 Compensation for Children Born as a Result of Rape

The second exception concerns the additional sum payable under para. 10 of the old Scheme. A woman who has been raped and who has suffered a loss of earnings in consequence would have the value of any social security benefits or payments made under occupational insurance arrangements deducted from the compensation payable for this head of damage and, if these exceeded that loss, from her general damages. Though not explicit, the use of the phrase 'additional sum' in para. 10 suggested that whatever the outcome of the application of paras 19–21 to the compensation otherwise payable, the applicant would still be awarded £5,000 in respect of each qualifying child.

Paragraph 45 of the new Scheme specifically provides that no reductions will be made from an award under para. 27 in respect of social security benefits or insurance payments.

9.2.4 Payments Received, Present and Future Entitlements

Paragraph 19 of the old Scheme and paras 45 and 48 of the new refer to benefits to which the applicant's entitlement, whether present or future, can be established at the date upon which the application is determined. Should the applicant subsequently become entitled to another benefit resulting from the criminal injury which would fall to be deducted if the assessment were then to be made, the Board has been unable to do anything to recover the sum payable. The 1986 Working Party recommended that the Board should 'be able to recover any other payments subsequently received which the Board would have been obliged to take into account if they had already been made' (Home Office, *Criminal Injuries Compensation: A Statutory Scheme*,

1986, para. 21.2), but no amendment was made in the 1990 revision of the old Scheme, nor to the new Scheme.

The exception to this has been a subsequent entitlement arising in pursuance of a judgment or settlement of damages, or under a compensation order. Paragraph 21 of the old Scheme expressly required the applicant 'to undertake to repay [the Board] from any damages, settlement or compensation he may subsequently obtain in respect of his injuries.' This is maintained in the new Scheme, para. 49 of which provides:

> Where a person in whose favour an award under this Scheme is made subsequently receives any other payment in respect of the same injury in any of the circumstances mentioned in the preceding paragraph [that is, any other criminal injury compensation award, a compensation order or civil damages], but the award made under this Scheme was not reduced accordingly, he will be required to repay the Authority in full up to the amount of the other payment.

9.3   SOCIAL SECURITY BENEFITS

9.3.1   Scope of the Old and New Schemes

Prior to the changes introduced by the Social Security Act 1989, the value of the benefit to be deducted in a personal injury action varied. Some were fully deductible: unemployment benefit (*Nabi* v *British Leyland (UK) Ltd* [1980] 1 WLR 529); income support (formerly supplementary benefit) received before trial (*Plummer* v *P.W. Wilkins and Son Ltd* [1981] WLR 831); attendance allowance (*Hodgson* v *Trapp* [1989] AC 807); family credit (formerly family income supplement) (*Gaskill* v *Preston* [1981] 3 All ER 427); statutory sick pay (*Palfrey* v *Greater London Council* [1985] ICR 437); and redundancy payments (which are 'exempt payments' under s. 88(1)(j) of the 1992 Act) that would not have been paid but for the injury (*Colledge* v *Bass Mitchells and Butlers Ltd* [1988] 1 All ER 536). Some were deductible under s. 2 of the Law Reform (Personal Injuries) Act 1948 to the extent of half their value over the five years following the accident: sickness and invalidity benefits (now short and long-term incapacity benefit under the Social Security (Incapacity for Work) Act 1994); industrial injury, disablement benefit (*R* v *Criminal Injuries Compensation Board, ex parte Lazzari* (1993) LEXIS, 14 May 1993) and severe disablement benefit (formerly non-contributory invalidity pension) (*Denman* v *Essex Area Health Authority* [1984] QB 735). Some benefits were not deductible at all: constant attendance allowance and the State retirement pension (*Hewson* v *Downs* [1970] 1 QB 73). In the case of an application made by a dependant or a qualifying claimant, death grant and widow's benefits have been, unlike a fatal accidents action, fully deductible (CICB, 1982, para. 19; 1984, paras 40 and 41; and see the example in the *Guide to Fatal Cases*, which is reproduced in Appendix 5).

By contrast, para. 19 of the old Scheme simply provided that compensation would be reduced by the full value of any present or future entitlement to '(a) United

Kingdom social security benefits, and ... (c) social security benefits .... from the funds of other countries' (CICB, 1990, para. 24.3). When the 1979 revised Scheme was introduced, the words 'as a result of injury or death' were positioned so as to refer only to payments falling under para. 19(d), that is, insurance payments, and not to the benefits mentioned in para. 19(a)–(c). This was a typographical error. The equivalent paragraph of the 1969 Scheme (para. 14) makes it clear (as does the Guide to the Scheme) that the words 'as a result of injury or death' apply to all the para. 19 benefits and payments as they do to the payments referred to in para. 20 of the 1990 Scheme. It had therefore been the practice for the first 15 years of the Scheme, which it was the Home Office's intention to continue in the 1979 revision, to take these benefits into account only where their payment accrued by virtue of the criminal injury. Thus, a benefit to a police officer wholly unrelated to the criminal injury which was accelerated by it, would not fall to be deducted from the award (*R v Criminal Injuries Compensation Board, ex parte Withington* (1993), application conceded by the Board).

If, having deducted the full value of any social security benefits accruing to the applicant as a result of the injury or death, the resultant figure was less than the lower limit, no award was payable under the old Scheme (para. 5; chapter 7.3.2.1).

Paragraph 45 of the new Scheme deals with the same benefits and payments. It provides that all awards (except those relating to standard amounts of compensation) will be subject to a reduction, which will be the full value of any payment or present or future entitlement to '(a) United Kingdom social security benefits; (b) social security benefits or similar payments from the funds of other countries' which have been made for the same contingency. As noted in chapter 9.1, whereas the value of the benefits to be deducted under the 1992 Act is determined over five years from the day following the day on which the injury occurred, for both the old and the new Schemes, the value of the benefits payable to the applicant are assessed over his lifetime by the application of an appropriate multiplier; see the examples in paras 17 and 26 of the *Guide to Earnings and Expenses* (Appendix 4) and at the end of the *Guide to Fatal Cases* (Appendix 5).

If the Board considered that an applicant might be eligible for social security benefits, it could refuse to make an award until he had made reasonable efforts to claim them (old Scheme, para. 19). The new Scheme is in virtually identical terms:

Where, in the opinion of a claims officer, an applicant may be eligible for any of the benefits and payments mentioned in the preceding paragraph, an award may be withheld until the applicant has taken such steps as the claims officer considers reasonable to claim them (new Scheme, para. 46).

9.3.2 Incidence of Income Tax

In assessing the applicant's entitlement to the specific benefits and payments, both the Board and the Authority are required to take account of any income tax liability that is likely to reduce their value (old Scheme, para. 19; new scheme, para. 45). This permits the Board or the claims officer to adjust (upwards) an award where the unadjusted payment of it would result in the applicant losing some or all of the value of the benefit to which he is entitled. However, it does not assist applications in which the award itself has an impact upon the entitlement, as may be the case where a rape victim receiving income support will lose that upon being compensated by the Board, since the award is almost always going to be more than the current £8,000 limit above which such benefit ceases to be payable.

9.3.3   Prospects of Remarriage

Under the old Scheme, the Board has been required by para. 19 not to take any account of the prospects of remarriage when calculating the value to the surviving spouse of benefits and payments to be deducted from an award. This maintains a provision introduced in the 1979–80 amendments, which reversed the earlier 'strange anomaly' identified by the 1978 Working Party, whereby, while her prospects of remarriage were to be discounted when determining the value of the lost dependency (in conformity with s. 4 of the Law Reform (Miscellaneous Provisions) Act 1971), any social security benefits payable to a widow were to be reduced in value by the prospects of remarriage (CICB, 1974, para. 6). This gave the applicant both the benefit of not having the value of the lost dependency reduced by the prospect of remarriage and the benefit of having a smaller sum (representing any appropriate social security payments) deducted from that dependency precisely because of her prospects of remarriage. Thus, since 1979, the Board has ignored the applicant's prospects of remarriage 'in assessing both the gross amount of her compensation and the amount of any deductions to be made from it' (Home Office, *Review of the Criminal Injuries Compensation Scheme, Report of an Interdepartmental Working Party*, London: HMSO, 1978, para. 14.2). It will be noted that para. 15 of the old Scheme refers only to the prospects, and not to the actuality, of remarriage. Accordingly, where the applicant has remarried, the Board is required to take into account the loss of the widow's pension when calculating the value of her future entitlement to social security benefits.

As noted in chapter 8.5.3.1, para. 41 of the new Scheme provides that when calculating the value of the dependency, no account is to be taken of the qualifying claimant's 'remarriage or the prospects of remarriage'. This makes it clear, first, that the rule applies both to widows and widowers. Beyond that, the claims officer is required to deduct the value of any social security benefits to which the claimant is entitled, to which an appropriate multiplier is applied (see the example at the end of the *Guide to Fatal Cases*, which is reproduced in Appendix 5).

9.3.4   Impact of the Provisions

Since many applicants will be in receipt of social security benefits, these rules continue to be of considerable importance, and indeed may have a very substantial impact upon the amount of compensation payable. Of particular importance is the deduction of disablement benefit payable to those criminally injured at work, notably the police and occasionally firemen, hospital workers and nurses (CICB, 1983, para. 30). The impact of full deduction for these particular victims has for many years been a controversial aspect of the old Scheme. The Board was often criticised where this has occurred, unfairly perhaps considering that it was here interpreting rules which gave it no discretion.

As noted earlier, the total of all deductible benefits has been deducted not just from the element of special damages but from the entire award. Accordingly, where the victim was seriously disabled as a result of the criminal injury and was entitled to disablement benefit (formerly industrial injury benefit), or to the disability living allowance dealing with mobility (CICB, 1979, para. 6) or blindness (CICB, 1977, para. 30), it would be quite likely that the Board would be unable to make any award at all, or at least one that was not substantially reduced by the aggregated value of these benefits (CICB, 1985, para. 32; 1986, para. 9).

Under the new Scheme, no compensation is payable for loss of earnings or earning capacity for the first 28 weeks of loss (chapter 8.4.2.1.1). Paragraph 30 refers to 'the period of loss' for which compensation may be payable as commencing in the 29th week after the date on which the applicant became incapable of work. None of the social security benefits received by the applicant during that first 28 weeks which relate to his loss of earnings are to be taken into account by the claims officer when determining his net loss of earnings or of earning capacity. Accordingly, neither statutory sick pay nor lower-rate short-term incapacity benefit, both of which are payable only for the first 28 weeks of loss of income, are deductible, since neither comes within the 'period of loss' for which compensation is payable under the new Scheme. But higher-rate short-term incapacity benefit, which is payable after 28 weeks and for the next 24 weeks, and long-term incapacity benefit, which is payable after 52 weeks until pensionable age, are.

By contrast, where an applicant is eligible for additional compensation for special expenses, that is, has sustained 28 weeks' loss of earnings, earning capacity or incapacity (chapter 8.4.2.2.3), any compensation to be awarded under this heading is payable from the date of injury. Since in this case the period of loss commences with the injury, any social security benefits that were received during that first 28 weeks and which related to the same contingency as the claim for special expenses (such as the mobility or care components of the disability living allowance) will be taken into account (new Scheme, para. 45).

9.4 INSURANCE AND PENSIONS

9.4.1 Personal and Non-employer Insurance

Both Schemes provide for the deduction of payments made under life and personal accident insurance contracts, though there are some differences between the two concerning personally effected insurance arrangements. As has been noted (chapter 9.2.3), where deductible, these payments are deducted only from non-standard awards of compensation; that is, in personal injury applications, from loss of earnings or earning capacity (paras 30–4) or special expenses (paras 35–6); and in fatal injury applications, either from loss of dependency (para. 41) and 'other resultant losses' arising from the loss of parental services (para. 42(b)) or, where the victim died otherwise than as a result of the criminal injury, from supplementary compensation (para. 44).

The old Scheme was straightforward. It provided for the reduction 'by the full value of any present or future entitlement to ... payments under insurance arrangements except as excluded below which may accrue, as a result of the injury or death, to the benefit of the person to whom the award is made' (old Scheme, para. 19(d)). The exclusions later in the paragraph are of contracts 'personally effected, paid for and maintained by the personal income of the victim or, in the case of a person under the age of 18, by his parent'. This exclusion reflects the common law position established in *Parry* v *Cleaver* [1970] AC 1, and reiterated by Lord Bridge in *Hussain* v *New Taplow Paper Mills Ltd* [1988] AC 514. Payments made under a privately effected personal accident policy will not, therefore, be deductible (*Bradburn* v *Great Western Railway Co.* (1874) LR 10 Ex 1; these are also exempt payments under s. 88(1)(i) of the 1992 Act). However, para. 19 of the old Scheme further provided that this exclusion was subject to para. 18 of the Scheme. This provides that the Board shall only compensate for private medical treatment where the necessity for and cost of such treatment are reasonable (chapter 8.4.2.2.2). Accordingly, the Board has been required to take into account payments towards the cost of private health or dental treatment which an applicant receives under BUPA or a similar scheme.

This is also the case under the new Scheme. Paragraph 45(c) provides that the claims officer will reduce any award for pecuniary loss by the full value of any present or future entitlement to:

> payments under insurance arrangements, including, where a claim is made under para. 35(c) and (d) and 36 (special expenses), insurance personally effected, paid for and maintained by the personal income of the victim or, in the case of a person under 18 years of age, by his parent. Insurance so personally effected will otherwise be disregarded.

A claim under para. 35(c) is a claim for the cost of private medical treatment. A claim under para. 35(d) is a claim for the reasonable cost, to the extent that it falls to the applicant, of special equipment, adaptations to accommodation and long-term care, where the criminal injury is disabling. The cost may not fall to the applicant precisely because it is met, in whole or part, by insurance. Where she is satisfied that the need for special expenses is likely to continue, the claims officer must also take these insurance payments into account when determining the net loss and the appropriate multiplier (para. 36).

Both para. 19(d) of the old Scheme and para. 45(c) of the new are intended to lead to the deduction from the award of any payments made under insurance arrangements effected by a third party. Where that is the victim's employer, and the payment accrues to the victim by virtue of his employment, the deduction is covered by para. 20 in the old Scheme and para. 47 of the new (chapter 9.4.2).

The rules which apply to the evaluation of the impact of social security benefits concerning the incidence of income tax (chapter 9.3.2), the applicant's prospects of or actual remarriage (chapter 9.3.3), and the requirement that the applicant should take reasonable steps to claim the payments to which he may be entitled (chapter 9.3.1) all apply to the evaluation of the impact on the award of payments under these insurance arrangements.

9.4.2 Occupational Pension and Insurance Arrangements

The two Schemes make identical provision for the deduction from the award of any payments which are payable under a pension plan or an occupational insurance policy effected by the victim's employers. The text of para. 47 of the new Scheme set out below is, apart from its internal references and some grammatical changes, in exactly the same terms as para. 20 of the old:

> Where the victim is alive, any compensation payable under paras 30–4 (loss of earnings) will be reduced to take account of any pension accruing as a result of the injury. Where the victim has died in consequence of the injury, any compensation payable under paras 40–1 (dependency) will similarly be reduced to take account of any pension payable, as a result of the victim's death, for the benefit of the applicant. Where such pensions are taxable, one half of their value will be deducted, but they will otherwise be deducted in full (where, for example, a lump-sum payment not subject to income tax is made). For the purposes of this paragraph, 'pension' means any payment payable as a result of the injury or death in pursuance of pension or any other rights connected with the victim's employment, and includes any gratuity of that kind and similar benefits payable under insurance policies paid for by the victim's employers. Pension rights accruing solely as a result of payments by the victim or a dependant will be disregarded.

Under both Schemes, any pension payable as a result of his injury or death under arrangements connected with the victim's employment is fully deductible (CICB, 1989, paras 23.4–23.6), unless the contributions to the funds were made wholly by the victim. For the purpose of both Schemes, 'pension' means 'any payment payable as a result of the injury or death, in pursuance of pension or other rights whatsoever connected with the victim's employment, and includes any gratuity of that kind and similar benefits payable under insurance policies paid for by [the victim's — these words are not included in the old Scheme] employers' (old Scheme, para. 20). They both provide that where the pension is taxable, for example, as an 'approved scheme' which falls to be taxed as earned income, one half of its value will be deducted, but where it is not so taxable, for example, a lump sum payable upon death or injury in service, or where it is commuted for a proportion of the victim's final salary, it will be deducted in full.

The 1986 Working Party recommended the retention of the deduction for pension payments accruing as a consequence of the victim's employment, but saw little justification for the continuation of the variable rate of deduction based on whether the income from the pension is chargeable to tax (Home Office, *Criminal Injuries Compensation: A Statutory Scheme*, 1986, para. 20.5). The Working Party's objection was that the effect of the distinction was to make an allowance for the pension contributions if the income were taxable, irrespective of whether those contributions were subscribed to by the victim. As there is little difference in practice between contributory and non-contributory schemes (since in the latter the fact will be reflected in the rate of pay), the Working Party thought it simpler to take 'an uncomplicated approach', and recommended that where such benefits are taxable, the allowance should be made at the basic rate. A further objection to para. 20 of the old Scheme was that the 'rough and ready' means of taking account of liability to income tax would in fact mean that the income is treated as being taxed at 50%, whereas some victims would have been retaining, in 1995–96, not 50% but 76% of the income after payment at the basic rate.

Paragraph 20 of the old Scheme and para. 47 of the new are intended to cover first insurance and pension arrangements made by an employer and payable to the victim or her dependants if death should occur while she is in that employment. In line with the common law position, pension rights accruing solely as a result of payments by the victim or a dependant will be disregarded. Payments made to a plaintiff under occupational insurance, whether contributory or not, are deductible if they have reduced the loss she has sustained; but both Schemes would probably go further than the common law in requiring the deduction of a disablement pension even where, and again whether contributory or not, it is provided by the employer/defendant (*Smoker* v *London Fire and Civil Defence Authority* [1991] AC 502 (HL)).

These deductions must be made notwithstanding that the employer provides, in addition to the pension or insurance scheme, a further sum designed to reflect the risk of criminal injury when the victim is acting in the course of his employment. The British Security Industry Association has argued that the blanket deduction rule has acted as a disincentive to its members who have routinely provided additional lump-sum benefits in the event of their employees being killed or injured as a result of a robbery. In its evidence to the 1986 Working Party, it suggested that the statutory Scheme should seek to distinguish these (Home Office, *Criminal Injuries Compensation: A Statutory Scheme*, 1986, para. 20.1). However, the Working Party could devise no formula which would permit a severance of the sums payable to an applicant in these circumstances, and indeed took the view that even if it could, such discrimination would conflict with the general principle which underlies this and the associated provisions, that State compensation should not enrich the victim (Home Office, *Criminal Injuries Compensation: A Statutory Scheme*, 1986, para. 20.2):

The fact remains that in determining an applicant's loss of income it is relevant and reasonable to take account of moneys which accrue as a result of his employment and, if special benefits related to criminal injury on duty are provided as an entitlement under conditions of employment, it is appropriate that these should be taken into account. Accordingly, like the previous Working Party, we favour the retention of the wide definition of 'pension'.

The two Schemes further require the deduction of any other payments payable 'in pursuance of ... other rights whatsoever connected with the victim's employment'. This is apt to cover wages or sick pay paid for by an employer as a matter of contractual obligation, which are fully deductible at common law (*Hussain* v *New Taplow Paper Mills Ltd* [1988] AC 514). However, they both also go on to require the deduction of gratuitous payments made by an employer, which are probably not deductible at common law (*Cunningham* v *Harrison* [1973] QB 94; *McCamley* v *Cammell Laird Shipbuilders Ltd* [1990] 1 WLR 963).

On the matter of *ex gratia* payments made by employers, the 1986 Working Party would have liked to have been able to differentiate from a truly gratuitous sum, such as an award for bravery paid by the victim's employer, those which arise from some expectation on the part of the victim, but was unable to devise a satisfactory test. Thus it reluctantly reached the conclusion 'that the only practical means of dealing with payments by employers is to regard all such payments as benefits arising out of employment which should be taken into account in assessing compensation' (Home Office, *Criminal Injuries Compensation: A Statutory Scheme*, 1986, para. 20.3). That has always been, and continues to be, the position under the Scheme.

9.5 OFFENDER AND OTHER STATE COMPENSATION

9.5.1 Recovery of Damages or of Compensation from the Offender

Both Schemes provide that the full value of any financial recompense which the applicant succeeds in obtaining from the offender (or a third party) in respect of the same injury must be deducted in full from any award, *including any award of standard compensation*. Paragraph 21 of the old Scheme says:

When a civil court has given judgment providing for payment of damages or a claim for damages has been settled on terms providing for payment of money, or when payment of compensation has been ordered by a criminal court, in respect of personal injuries, compensation by the Board in respect of the same injuries will be reduced by the amount of any payment received under such an order or settlement.

The new Scheme makes similar provision, but stated as follows (para. 48(c)):

An award payable under this Scheme will be reduced by the full value of any payment in respect of the same injury which the applicant has received by way of:

...

(c)   any award where:

(i)   a civil court has made an order for the payment of damages;

(ii)   a claim for damages and/or compensation has been settled on terms providing for the payment of money;

(iii)   payment of compensation has been ordered by a criminal court in respect of personal injuries.

It is of course rare that civil proceedings can be successfully pursued against an offender, and as the Board's Reports have, since 1977–78, ceased to publish figures indicating the recovery of damages, it is not possible to judge their contemporary significance.

When a civil court has assessed damages, as opposed to giving judgment for damages agreed by the parties, but the person entitled to such damages has not yet received the full sum awarded, he will not be precluded from applying to the Board, but the Board's assessment of compensation will not exceed the sum assessed by the court.

There is no equivalent in the new Scheme to this provision in para. 21 of the old. That is because of the different basis of assessment adopted by the tariff Scheme. It reflects the provisions in ss. 37 and 38 of the Powers of Criminal Courts Act 1973 which deal with the relationship between compensation orders and the award of damages in civil proceedings (see Miers, D., *Compensation for Criminal Injuries*, London: Butterworths, 1990, pp. 248–55).

On the other hand, while the number of compensation orders made by courts in respect of personal injuries compares very badly with the number made in respect of criminal damage and theft (see Miers, D., op. cit., ch. 12), such orders figure in about 4% of applications to the Board. In the three years to March 1995, the Board's Reports show that 3,418, 2,566 and 2,060 applicants had such orders made in their favour following a conviction, at face value amounting to £271,995, £286,429 and £289,335 respectively (CICB, 1995, para. 2.14). In 1991–92 4,282 compensation orders had been made to applicants; it is not clear why this figure should since have declined by some 50%.

There may be instances where an applicant does receive under a compensation order exactly the compensation which the Board would award (CICB, 1992, para. 27.8), but if entitlement were to be treated as reducing the loss for which compensation is to be assessed, some victims would in fact fail to receive their full award then (since there might be some delay in the offender's compliance with the order) or at all (since he might default). The Board's 1995 Report shows that at the time when these applicants received their awards, the amounts received under the compensation orders totalled about 75% of their face value, but this does not of course indicate how individual applicants fared. In order to deal with the possibility of delay and default in the payment of compensation orders, arrangements have for some time been in existence whereby the award paid to the victim will be for the full sum less only so much of the compensation order as has been received by him; the outstanding instalments paid by the offender have then been forwarded to the Board by the magistrates' court responsible for their enforcement (CICB, 1984, para. 55). The Authority will presumably continue with these arrangements.

The 1986 Working Party received evidence from a number of bodies proposing that the Board should be given a statutory power to recover directly from the offender, either by applying to the court before which the offender was convicted for a compensation order, or by subrogation of the victim's civil action against him (Home Office, *Criminal Injuries Compensation: A Statutory Scheme*, 1986, para. 21.6). It rejected the former, largely because of the inappropriateness of the court having to reconsider an issue designed to be settled at the sentencing stage, 'a compensation order being part (sometimes the whole) of the sentence imposed for the offender's crime'. It also took the view that it was unnecessary for the Board to assume the victim's right of action, but that it was sufficient that it has a power of recovery where it has reasonable cause to believe that the offender has the means to reimburse the whole or a substantial part of the compensation paid. Both Schemes provide that the applicant will be required to pay to the Board (old Scheme, para. 21) or the Authority (1995 Act, s. 3(1)(c); new Scheme, para. 49) any sums subsequently received in respect of the same injury (chapter 9.2.4). The Act provides that such repayments are debts due to the Crown (s. 3(3)).

9.5.2 Other Criminal Injury Compensation Payments

It is possible, though unlikely, that an applicant could be eligible under both the Northern Ireland compensation arrangements and the Scheme. Paragraph 19(b) of the old Scheme and para. 48(a) of the new provide for the reduction by the full value of any payment under those arrangements, including any present or future entitlement.

Some countries have compensation schemes that provide for the compensation of their own nationals who sustain criminal injuries abroad. Many more, and in particular those which are signatories to the Council of Europe's Convention on the Compensation of Victims of Violent Crime, have, or propose to have, reciprocal arrangements whereby a signatory State will compensate the nationals of co-signatories who sustain criminal injuries within its jurisdiction, if the co-signatories will likewise compensate its nationals who sustain criminal injuries in their jurisdictions. It is also the case that such arrangements, where they are made by member States of the European Union, may be enforceable by nationals of other member States who are injured while engaged in conduct falling within the Treaty (chapter 4.2). Paragraph 19(c) of the old Scheme and para. 48(b) of the new prevent double recovery under these arrangements.

Appendix One   The Old Scheme

The following amendments to the Scheme were announced by the Home Secretary on 27 July 1993.

(a) *New* Paragraph 4A

'The Board will entertain applications under Paragraph 4 arising from injury or death caused by or to officers of the United Kingdom — but not of any other state — in the exercise of their functions in the Channel Tunnel or control zones, within the meaning of the Channel Tunnel (International Arrangements) Order 1993'.

(b) *New* Paragraph 28A

'Paragraph 4A will take effect from the date (sic) of the Channel Tunnel (International Arrangements) Order 1993 comes into force'.

The order came into force with effect from 2 August 1993.

1990 SCHEME

A Scheme for compensating victims of crimes of violence was announced in both Houses of Parliament on 24 June 1964 and in its original form came into force on 1 August 1964.

The Scheme has since been modified in a number of respects. The 1990 revision below applies to all applications for compensation received by the Board on or after 1 February 1990 subject to the exceptions set out in Paragraph 28. The 1990 Scheme also applies to applications received by the Board before 1 February 1990 to the extent set out in Paragraph 29.

THE SCHEME

Administration

1.   The Compensation Scheme will be administered by the Criminal Injuries Compensation Board, which will be assisted by appropriate staff. Appointments to the Board will be made by the Secretary of State, after consultation with the Lord

Chancellor and where appropriate, the Lord Advocate. A person may only be appointed to be a member of the Board if he is a barrister practising in England and Wales, an advocate practising in Scotland, a solicitor practising in England and Wales or Scotland or a person who holds or has held judicial office in England and Wales or Scotland. The Chairman and other members of the Board will be appointed to serve for up to five years in the first instance, and their appointments will be renewable for such periods as the Secretary of State considers appropriate. The Chairman and other members will not serve on the Board beyond the age of 72, or after ceasing to be qualified for appointment, whichever is the earlier except that, where the Secretary of State considers it to be in the interests of the Scheme to extend a particular appointment, beyond the age of 72 or after retirement from legal practice, he may do so. The Secretary of State may, if he thinks fit, terminate a member's appointment on the grounds of incapacity or misbehaviour.

2.   The Board will be provided with money through a Grant-in-Aid out of which payments for compensation awarded in accordance with the principles set out below will be made. Their net expenditure will fall on the Votes of the Home Office and the Scottish Home and Health Department.

3.   The Board, or such members of the Board's staff as the Board may designate, will be entirely responsible for deciding what compensation should be paid in individual cases and their decisions will not be subject to appeal or to Ministerial review. The general working of the Scheme will, however, be kept under review by the Government, and the Board will submit annually to the Home Secretary and the Secretary of State for Scotland a full report on the operation of the Scheme together with their accounts. The report and accounts will be open to debate in Parliament.

Scope of the Scheme
4.   The Board will entertain applications for ex gratia payments of compensation in any case where the applicant or, in the case of an application by a spouse or dependant (see Paragraphs 15 and 16 below), the deceased, sustained in Great Britain, or on a British vessel, aircraft or hovercraft or on, under or above an installation in a designated area within the meaning of section 1 sub-section (7) of the Continental Shelf Act 1964 or any waters within 500 metres of such an installation, or in a lighthouse off the coast of the United Kingdom, personal injury directly attributable—

   (a)   to a crime of violence (including arson or poisoning); or

   (b)   to the apprehension or attempted apprehension of an offender or a suspected offender or to the prevention or attempted prevention of an offence or to the giving of help to any constable who is engaged in any such activity; or

   (c)   to an offence of trespass on a railway.

Applications for compensation will be entertained only if made within 3 years of the incident giving rise to the injury, except that the Board may in exceptional cases waive this requirement. A decision by the Chairman not to waive the time limit will be final. In considering for the purposes of this paragraph whether any act is a criminal act a person's conduct will be treated as constituting an offence notwithstanding that he may not be convicted of the offence by reason of age, insanity or diplomatic immunity.

5.   Compensation will not be payable unless the Board are satisfied that the injury was one for which the total amount of compensation payable after deduction of social security benefits, but before any other deductions under the Scheme, would not be less than the minimum amount of compensation. This shall be £1,000*. The application of the minimum level shall not, however, affect the payment of funeral expenses under Paragraph 15 below or, where the victim has died otherwise than in consequence of an injury for which compensation would have been payable to him under the terms of the Scheme, any sum payable to a dependant or relative of his under Paragraph 16.

6.   The Board may withhold or reduce compensation if they consider that—

(a)   the applicant has not taken, without delay, all reasonable steps to inform the police, or any other authority considered by the Board to be appropriate for the purpose, of the circumstances of the injury and to co-operate with the police or other authority in bringing the offender to justice; or

(b)   the applicant has failed to give all reasonable assistance to the Board or other authority in connection with the application; or

(c)   having regard to the conduct of the applicant before, during or after the events giving rise to the claim or to his character as shown by his criminal convictions or unlawful conduct — and, in applications under Paragraphs 15 and 16 below, to the conduct or character as shown by the criminal convictions or unlawful conduct of the deceased and of the applicant — it is inappropriate that a full award, or any award at all, be granted.

Further, compensation will not be payable—

(d)   in the case of an application under Paragraph 4(b) above where the injury was sustained accidentally, unless the Board are satisfied that the applicant was at the time taking an exceptional risk which was justified in all the circumstances.

7.   Compensation will not be payable unless the Board are satisfied that there is no possibility that a person responsible for causing the injury will benefit from an award.

8.   Where the victim and any person responsible for the injuries which are the subject of the application (whether that person actually inflicted them or not) were living in the same household at the time of the injuries as members of the same family, compensation will be paid only where—

(a)   the person responsible has been prosecuted in connection with the offence, except where the Board consider that there are practical, technical or other good reasons why a prosecution has not been brought; and

(b)   in the case of violence between adults in the family, the Board are satisfied that the person responsible and the applicant stopped living in the same household before the application was made and seem unlikely to live together again; and

(c)   in the case of an application under this paragraph by or on behalf of a minor, i.e., a person under 18 years of age, the Board are satisfied that it would not be against the minor's interest to make a full or reduced award.

For the purposes of this paragraph, a man and a woman living together as husband and wife shall be treated as members of the same family.

9.   If in the opinion of the Board it is in the interests of the applicant (whether or not a minor or person under an incapacity) so to do, the Board may pay the amount of any award to any trustee or trustees to hold on such trusts for the benefit of all or any of the following persons, namely the applicant and any spouse, widow or widower, relatives and dependants of the applicant and with such provisions for their respective maintenance, education and benefit and with such powers and provisions for the investment and management of the fund and for the remuneration of the trustee or trustees as the Board shall think fit. Subject to this the Board will have a general discretion in any case in which they have awarded compensation to make special arrangements for its administration. In this paragraph 'relatives' means all persons claiming descent from the applicant's grandparents and 'dependants' means all persons who in the opinion of the Board are dependent on him wholly or partially for the provision of the ordinary necessities of life.

10.   The Board will consider applications for compensation arising out of acts of rape and other sexual offences both in respect of pain, suffering and shock and in respect of loss of earnings due to consequent pregnancy, and, where the victim is ineligible for a maternity grant under the National Insurance Scheme, in respect of the expenses of childbirth. Compensation will not be payable for the maintenance of any child born as a result of a sexual offence, except that where a woman is awarded compensation for rape the Board shall award the additional sum of £5,000 in respect of each child born alive having been conceived as a result of the rape which the applicant intends to keep.

11.   Applications for compensation for personal injury attributable to traffic offences will be excluded from the Scheme, except where such injury is due to a deliberate attempt to run the victim down.

Basis of Compensation

12.   Subject to the other provisions of this Scheme, compensation will be assessed on the basis of common law damages and will normally take the form of a lump sum payment, although the Board may make alternative arrangements in accordance with Paragraph 9 above. More than one payment may be made where an applicant's eligibility for compensation has been established but a final award cannot be calculated in the first instance — for example where only a provisional medical assessment can be given. In a case in which an interim award has been made, the Board may decide to make a reduced award, increase any reduction already made or refuse to make any further payment at any stage before receiving notification of acceptance of a final award.

13.   Although the Board's decision in a case will normally be final, they will have discretion to reconsider a case after a final award of compensation has been accepted where there has been such a serious change in the applicant's medical condition that injustice would occur if the original assessment of compensation were allowed to stand, or where the victim has since died as a result of his injuries. A case will not be

re-opened more than three years after the date of the final award unless the Board are satisfied, on the basis of evidence presented with the application for re-opening the case, that the renewed application can be considered without a need for extensive enquiries. A decision by the Chairman that a case may not be re-opened will be final.

14.   Compensation will be limited as follows:

(a)   the rate of net loss of earnings or earning capacity to be taken into account shall not exceed one and a half times the gross average industrial earnings at the date of assessment (as published in the Department of Employment Gazette and adjusted as considered appropriate by the Board);

(b)   there shall be no element comparable to exemplary or punitive damages. Where an applicant has lost earnings or earning capacity as a result of the injury, he may be required by the Board to produce evidence thereof in such manner and form as the Board may specify.

15.   Where the victim has died in consequence of the injury, no compensation other than funeral expenses will be payable for the benefit of his estate, but the Board will be able to entertain applications from any person who is a dependant of the victim within the meaning of section 1(3) of the Fatal Accidents Act 1976 or who is a relative of the victim within the meaning of Schedule 1 to the Damages (Scotland) Act 1976. Compensation will be payable in accordance with the other provisions of this Scheme to any such dependant or relative. Funeral expenses to an amount considered reasonable by the Board will be paid in appropriate cases, even where the person bearing the cost of the funeral is otherwise ineligible to claim under this Scheme. Applications may be made under this paragraph where the victim has died from his injuries even if an award has been made to the victim in his lifetime. Such cases will be subject to conditions set out in paragraph 13 for the re-opening of cases and compensation payable to the applicant will be reduced by the amount paid to the victim.

16.   Where the victim has died otherwise than in consequence of the injury, the Board may make an award to such dependant or relative as is mentioned in Paragraph 15 in respect of loss of wages, expenses and liabilities incurred by the victim before death as a result of the injury whether or not the application for compensation in respect of the injury has been made before the death.

17.   Compensation will not be payable for the loss of or damage to clothing or any property whatsoever arising from the injury unless the Board are satisfied that the property was relied upon by the victim as a physical aid.

18.   The cost of private medical treatment will be payable by the Board only if the Board consider that, in all the circumstances, both the private treatment and the cost of it are reasonable.

19.   Compensation will be reduced by the full value of any present or future entitlement to—

(a)   United Kingdom Social Security Benefits;

(b)   any criminal injury compensation awards made under or pursuant to statutory arangements in force at the relevant time in Northern Ireland;

(c)   Social Security Benefits, compensation awards or similar payments whatsoever from the funds of other countries; or

(d)   payments under insurance arrangements except as excluded below which may accrue, as a result of the injury or death, to the benefit of the person to whom the award is made.

In assessing this entitlement, account will be taken of any income tax liability likely to reduce the value of such benefits and, in the case of an application under Paragraph 15, the value of such benefits will not be reduced to take account of prospects of remarriage. If, in the opinion of the Board, an applicant may be eligible for any such benefits the Board may refuse to make an award until the applicant has taken such steps as the Board consider reasonable to claim them. Subject to Paragraph 18 above, the Board will disregard monies paid or payable to the victim or his dependants as a result of or in consequence of insurance personally effected, paid for and maintained by the personal income of the victim or, in the case of a person under the age of 18, by his parent.

20.   Where the victim is alive compensation will be reduced to take account of any pension accruing as a result of the injury. Where the victim has died in consequence of the injury, and any pension is payable for the benefit of the person to whom the award is made as a result of the death of the victim, the compensation will similarly be reduced to take account of the value of that pension. Where such pensions are taxable, one half of their value will be deducted; where they are not taxable, e.g., where a lump sum payment not subject to income tax is made, they will be deducted in full. For the purposes of this paragraph, 'pension' means any payment payable as a result of the injury or death, in pursuance of pension or other rights whatsoever connected with the victim's employment, and includes any gratuity of that kind and similar benefits payable under insurance policies paid for by employers. Pension rights accruing solely as a result of payments by the victim or a dependant will be disregarded.

21.   When a civil court has given judgment providing for payment of damages or a claim for damages has been settled on terms providing for payment of money, or when payment of compensation has been ordered by a criminal court, in respect of personal injuries, compensation by the Board in respect of the same injuries will be reduced by the amount of any payment received under such an order or settlement. When a civil court has assessed damages, as opposed to giving judgment for damages agreed by the parties, but the person entitled to such damages has not yet received the full sum awarded, he will not be precluded from applying to the Board, but the Board's assessment of compensation will not exceed the sum assesed by the court. Furthermore, a person who is compensated by the board will be required to undertake to repay them from any damages, settlement or compensation he may subsequently obtain in respect of his injuries. In arriving at their assessment of compensation the Board will not be bound by any finding of contributory negligence by any court, but will be entirely bound by the terms of the Scheme.

Procedure for determining applications

22.   Every application will be made to the Board in writing as soon as possible after the event on a form obtainable from the Board's offices. The initial decision on

an application will be taken by a Single Member of the Board, or by any member of the Board's staff to whom the Board has given authority to determine applications on the Board's behalf. Where an award is made the applicant will be given a breakdown of the assessment of compensation, except where the Board consider this inappropriate, and where an award is refused or reduced, reasons for the decision will be given. If the applicant is not satisfied with the decision he may apply for an oral hearing which, if granted, will be held before at least two members of the Board excluding any member who made the original decision. The application for a hearing must be made within three months of notification of the initial decision; however the Board may waive this time limit where an extension is requested with good reason within the three month period, or where it is otherwise in the interest of justice to do so. A decision by the Chairman not to waive the time limit will be final. It will also be open to a Member of the Board, or a designated member of the Board's staff, where he considers that he cannot make a just and proper decision himself to refer the application for a hearing before at least two members of the Board, one of whom may be the member who, in such a case, decided to refer the application to a hearing. An applicant will have no title to an award offered until the Board have received notification in writing that he accepts it.

23.   Applications for hearings must be made in writing on a form supplied by the Board and should be supported by reasons together with any additional evidence which may assist the Board to decide whether a hearing should be granted. If the reasons in support of the application suggest that the initial decision was based on information obtained by or submitted to the Board which was incomplete or erroneous, the application may be remitted for reconsideration by the Member of the Board who made the initial decision, or where this is not practicable or where the initial decision was made by a member of the Board's staff, by any Member of the Board. In such cases it will still be open for the applicant to apply in writing for a hearing if he remains dissatisfied after his case has been reconsidered and the three month limitation period in Paragraph 22 will start from the date of notification of the reconsidered decision.

24.   An applicant will be entitled to an oral hearing only if—

(a)   no award was made on the ground that any award would be less than the sum specified in Paragraph 5 of the Scheme and it appears that applying the principles set out in Paragraph 26 below, the Board might make an award; or

(b)   an award was made and it appears that, applying the principles set out in Paragraph 26 below, the Board might make a larger award; or

(c)   no award or a reduced award was made and there is a dispute as to the material facts or conclusions upon which the initial or reconsidered decision was based or it appears that the decision may have been wrong in law or principle.

An application for a hearing which appears likely to fail the foregoing criteria may be reviewed by not less than two members of the Board, other than any member who made the initial or reconsidered decision. If it is considered on review that if any facts or conclusions which are disputed were resolved in the applicant's favour it would have made no difference to the initial or reconsidered decision, or that for any other reason an oral hearing would serve no useful purpose, the application for a hearing will be refused. A decision to refuse an application for a hearing will be final.

25.   It will be for the applicant to make out his case at the hearing, and where appropriate this will extend to satisfying the Board that compensation should not be withheld or reduced under the terms of Paragraph 6 or Paragraph 8. The applicant and a member of the Board's staff will be able to call, examine and cross-examine witnesses. The Board will be entitled to take into account any relevant hearsay, opinion or written evidence, whether or not the author gives oral evidence at the hearing. The Board will reach their decision solely in the light of evidence brought out at the hearing, and all the information and evidence made available to the Board Members at the hearing will be made available to the applicant at, if not before, the hearing. The Board may adjourn a hearing for any reason, and where the only issue remaining is the assessment of compensation may remit the application to a Single Member of the Board for determination in the absence of the applicant but subject to the applicant's right to apply under Paragraph 22 above for a further hearing if he is not satisfied with the final assessment of compensation. While it will be open to the applicant to bring a friend or legal adviser to assist him in putting his case, the Board will not pay the cost of legal representation. They will, however, have discretion to pay the expenses of the applicant and witnesses at a hearing. If an applicant fails to attend a hearing and has offered no reasonable excuse for his non-attendance the Board at the hearing may dismiss his application. A person whose application has been dismissed by the Board for failure to attend a hearing may apply in writing to the Chairman of the Board for his application to be reinstated. A decision by the Chairman that an application should not be reinstated will be final.

26.   At the hearing the amount of compensation assesed by a Single Member of the Board or a designated member of the Board's staff will not be altered except upon the same principles as the Court of Appeal in England or the Court of Session in Scotland would alter an assessment of damages by a trial judge.

27.   Procedures at the hearing will be as informal as is consistent with the proper determination of applications, and the hearing (sic) will in general, be in private. The Board will have discretion to permit observers, such as representatives of the press, radio and television, to attend hearings provided that written undertakings are given that the anonymity of the applicant and other parties will not in any way be infringed by subsequent reporting. The Board will have power to publish information about its decisions in individual cases; this power will be limited only by the need to preserve the anonymity of applicants and other parties.

Implementation

28.   The provisions of this Scheme will take effect from 1 February 1990. All applications for compensation received by the Board on or after 1 February 1990 will be dealt with under the terms of this Scheme except that in relation to applications in respect of injuries incurred before that date the following provisions of the 1990 Scheme shall not apply—

(a)   Paragraph 4(c);

(b)   Paragraph 8, but only in respect of injuries incurred before 1 October 1979 where Paragraph 7 of the 1969 Scheme will continue to apply;

(c)   Paragraph 10 but only insofar as it requires the Board to award an additional sum of £5,000 in the circumstances therein prescribed;

(d)   Paragraphs 15 and 16 but only insofar as they enable the Board to entertain applications from a person who is a dependant within the meaning of section 1(3)(b) of the Fatal Accidents Act 1976 or who is a relative within the meaning of Paragraph 1(aa) of Schedule 1 to the Damages (Scotland) Act 1976 other than such a person who is applying only for funeral expenses.

29.   Applications for compensation received by the Board before 1 February 1990 will continue to be dealt with in accordance with Paragraph 25 of the Scheme which came into operation on 1 October 1979 ('the 1979 Scheme') or the Scheme which came into operation on 21 May 1969 ('the 1969 Scheme') except that the following paragraphs of this Scheme will apply in addition to or in substitution for provisions of these Schemes as specified below—

(a)   Paragraph 3 of this Scheme will apply in substitution for Paragraph 4 of the 1969 Scheme and Paragraph 3 of the 1979 Scheme.

(b)   Paragraph 6(c) of this Scheme will apply in substitution for Paragraph 17 of the 1969 Scheme and Paragraph 6(c) of the 1979 Scheme.

(c)   Paragraph 14 of this Scheme will apply additionally to applicants otherwise falling to be considered under the 1969 or 1979 Schemes but only insofar as it allows the Board to require an applicant to produce evidence of loss of earnings or earning capacity.

(d)   Paragraphs 22, 23 and 25 of this Scheme will apply in substitution for Paragraphs 21 and 22 of the 1969 Scheme and Paragraphs 22 and 23 of the 1979 Scheme.

(e)   Paragraph 26 of this Scheme will apply additionally to applications otherwise falling to be considered under the 1969 or 1979 Schemes.

(f)   Paragraph 27 of this Scheme will apply in substitution for Paragraph 23 of the 1969 Scheme and Paragraph 24 of the 1979 Scheme.

30.   Applications to re-open cases received before 1 February 1990 will continue to be dealt with under the terms of Paragraph 25 of the 1979 Scheme. Applications to re-open cases received on or after 1 February 1990 will be considered and determined under the terms of this Scheme.

Appendix Two   Criminal Injuries Compensation Act 1995

Criminal Injuries Compensation Act 1995

ARRANGEMENT OF SECTIONS

Section
1. The Criminal Injuries Compensation Scheme.
2. Basis on which compensation is to be calculated.
3. Claims and awards.
4. Reviews.
5. Appeals.
6. Reports, accounts and financial records.
7. Inalienability of awards.
8. Annuities.
9. Financial provisions.
10. Jurisdiction of Parliamentary Commissioner for Administration.
11. Parliamentary control.
12. Repeal of the 1988 Act scheme and transitional provisions.
13. Short title and extent.

SCHEDULE:
—Repeals.

Criminal Injuries Compensation Act 1995

CHAPTER 53

An Act to provide for the establishment of a scheme for compensation for criminal injuries. [8th November 1995]

Be it enacted by the Queen's most Excellent Majesty, by and with the advice and consent of the Lords Spiritual and Temporal, and Commons, in this present Parliament assembled, and by the authority of the same, as follows:—

1. The Criminal Injuries Compensation Scheme

(1)   The Secretary of State shall make arrangements for the payment of compensation to, or in respect of, persons who have sustained one or more criminal injuries.

(2)   Any such arrangements shall include the making of a scheme providing, in particular, for—

  (a)   the circumstances in which awards may be made; and

  (b)   the categories of person to whom awards may be made.

(3)   The scheme shall be known as the Criminal Injuries Compensation Scheme.

(4)   In this Act—

'adjudicator' means a person appointed by the Secretary of State under section 5(1)(b);

'award' means an award of compensation made in accordance with the provisions of the Scheme;

'claims officer' means a person appointed by the Secretary of State under section 3(4)(b);

'compensation' means compensation payable under an award;

'criminal injury', 'loss of earnings' and 'special expenses' have such meaning as may be specified;

'the Scheme' means the Criminal Injuries Compensation Scheme;

'Scheme manager' means a person appointed by the Secretary of State to have overall responsibility for managing the provisions of the Scheme (other than those to which section 5(2) applies); and

'specified' means specified by the Scheme.

2. Basis on which compensation is to be calculated

(1)   The amount of compensation payable under an award shall be determined in accordance with the provisions of the Scheme.

(2)   Provision shall be made for—

  (a)   a standard amount of compensation, determined by reference to the nature of the injury;

  (b)   in such cases as may be specified, an additional amount of compensation calculated with respect to loss of earnings;

  (c)   in such cases as may be specified, an additional amount of compensation calculated with respect to special expenses; and

  (d)   in cases of fatal injury, such additional amounts as may be specified or otherwise determined in accordance with the Scheme.

(3)   Provision shall be made for the standard amount to be determined—

  (a)   in accordance with a table ('the Tariff') prepared by the Secretary of State as part of the Scheme and such other provisions of the Scheme as may be relevant; or

(b)   where no provision is made in the Tariff with respect to the injury in question, in accordance with such provisions of the Scheme as may be relevant.

(4)   The Tariff shall show, in respect of each description of injury mentioned in the Tariff, the standard amount of compensation payable in respect of that description of injury.

(5)   An injury may be described in the Tariff in such a way, including by reference to the nature of the injury, its severity or the circumstances in which it was sustained, as the Secretary of State considers appropriate.

(6)   The Secretary of State may at any time alter the Tariff—

(a)   by adding to the descriptions of injury mentioned there;

(b)   by removing a description of injury;

(c)   by increasing or reducing the amount shown as the standard amount of compensation payable in respect of a particular description of injury; or

(d)   in such other way as he considers appropriate.

(7)   The Scheme may—

(a)   provide for amounts of compensation not to exceed such maximum amounts as may be specified;

(b)   include such transitional provision with respect to any alteration of its provisions relating to compensation as the Secretary of State considers appropriate.

3.   Claims and awards

(1)   The Scheme may, in particular, include provision—

(a)   as to the circumstances in which an award may be withheld or the amount of compensation reduced;

(b)   for an award to be made subject to conditions;

(c)   for the whole or any part of any compensation to be repayable in specified circumstances;

(d)   for compensation to be held to trusts, in such cases as may be determined in accordance with the Scheme;

(e)   requiring claims under the Scheme to be made within such periods as may be specified by the Scheme; and

(f)   imposing other time limits.

(2)   Where, in accordance with any provision of the Scheme, it falls to one person to satisfy another as to any matter, the standard of proof required shall be that applicable in civil proceedings.

(3)   Where, in accordance with any provision of the Scheme made by virtue of subsection (1)(c), any amount falls to be repaid it shall be recoverable as a debt due to the Crown.

(4)   The Scheme shall include provision for claims for compensation to be determined and awards and payments of compensation to be made—

(a)   if a Scheme manager has been appointed, by persons appointed for the purpose by the Scheme manager; but

(b)   otherwise by persons ('claims officers') appointed for the purpose by the Secretary of State.

(5)   A claims officer—

(a)   shall be appointed on such terms and conditions as the Secretary of State considers appropriate; but

(b)   shall not be regarded as having been appointed to exercise functions of the Secretary of State or to act on his behalf.

(6)   No decision taken by a claims officer shall be regarded as having been taken by, or on behalf of, the Secretary of State.

(7)   If a Scheme manager has been appointed—

(a)   he shall not be regarded as exercising functions of the Secretary of State or as acting on his behalf; and

(b)   no decision taken by him or by any person appointed by him shall be regarded as having been taken by, or on behalf of, the Secretary of State.

4.   Reviews

(1)   The Scheme shall include provision for the review, in such circumstances as may be specified, of any decision taken in respect of a claim for compensation.

(2)   Any such review must be conducted by a person other than the person who made the decision under review.

5.   Appeals

(1)   The Scheme shall include provision—

(a)   for rights of appeal against decisions taken on reviews under provisions of the Scheme made by virtue of section 4; and

(b)   for such appeals to be determined by persons ('adjudicators') appointed for the purpose by the Secretary of State.

(2)   If a Scheme manager is appointed, his responsibilities shall not extend to any provision of the Scheme made by virtue of this section except so far as the provision relates to functions of persons mentioned in subsection (3)(d)(ii).

(3)   The Scheme may include provision—

(a)   for adjudicators to be appointed as members of a body having responsibility (in accordance with the provisions of the Scheme) for dealing with appeals;

(b)   for the appointment by the Secretary of State of one of the members of that body to be its chairman;

(c)   for the appointment of staff by the Secretary of State for the purpose of administering those provisions of the Scheme which relate to the appeal system;

(d)   for specified functions in relation to appeals to be conferred on—

(i)   claims officers; or

(ii)   persons appointed by the Scheme manager as mentioned in section 3(4)(a).

(4)   Any person appointed under this section by the Secretary of State—

(a)   shall be appointed on such terms and conditions as the Secretary of State considers appropriate; but

(b)   shall not be regarded as having been appointed to exercise functions of the Secretary of State or to act on his behalf.

(5)   No decision taken by an adjudicator shall be regarded as having been taken by, or on behalf of, the Secretary of State.

(6)   The Scheme shall include provision as to the giving of advice by adjudicators to the Secretary of State.

(7)   The Secretary of State may at any time remove a person from office as an adjudicator if satisfied that—

(a)   he has been convicted of a criminal offence;

(b)   he has become bankrupt or has had his estate sequestrated or has made an arrangement with, or granted a trust deed for, his creditors; or

(c)   he is otherwise unable or unfit to perform his duties.

(8)   In Schedule 1 to the Tribunals and Inquiries Act 1992 (tribunals under the supervision of the Council on Tribunals), in the entry relating to compensation for criminal injuries substitute, for the second column—

'12.   The adjudicators appointed under section 5 of the Criminal Injuries Compensation Act 1995 (c. 53).'

(9)   The power conferred by section 3(1)(a) to provide for the reduction of an amount of compensation includes power to provide for a reduction where, in the opinion of the adjudicator or adjudicators determining an appeal, the appeal is frivolous or vexatious.

6.   Reports, accounts and financial records

(1)   The Scheme shall include provision—

(a)   for such person or persons as the Secretary of State considers appropriate to make an annual report to him; and

(b)   for the report—

(i)   to be made as soon as possible after the end of each financial year; and

(ii)   to cover the operation of, and the discharge of functions conferred by, the Scheme during the year to which it relates.

(2)   The Secretary of State shall lay before each House of Parliament a copy of every such annual report.

(3)   The Scheme shall also include provision—

(a)   for such person or persons as the Secretary of State considers appropriate—

(i)   to keep proper accounts and proper records in relation to the accounts;

(ii)   to prepare a statement of accounts in each financial year in such form as the Secretary of State may direct;

(b)   requiring such a statement of accounts to be submitted to the Secretary of State at such time as the Secretary of State may direct.

(4)   Where such a statement of accounts is submitted to the Secretary of State, he shall send a copy of it to the Comptroller and Auditor General as soon as is reasonably practicable.

(5)   The Comptroller and Auditor General shall—

(a)   examine, certify and report on any statement of accounts sent to him under subsection (4); and

(b) lay copies of the statement and of his report before each House of Parliament.

(6) In this section 'financial year' means the period beginning with the day on which this section comes into force and ending with the following 31 March and each successive period of 12 months.

7. Inalienability of awards

(1) Every assignment (or, in Scotland, assignation) of, or charge on, an award and every agreement to assign or charge an award shall be void.

(2) On the bankruptcy of a person in whose favour an award is made (or, in Scotland, on the sequestration of such a person's estate), the award shall not pass to any trustee or other person acting on behalf of his creditors.

8. Annuities

After section 329B of the Income and Corporation Taxes Act 1988, insert—

'329C   Annuities: criminal injuries

(1) For the purposes of this section—

(a) "a qualifying award" is an award of compensation made under the Criminal Injuries Compensation Scheme with respect to a person ("A") on terms which provide—

(i) for payments under one or more annuities purchased for A in accordance with the provisions of the Scheme to be received by A or by another person on his behalf; or

(ii) for payments under one or more annuities purchased in accordance with the provisions of the Scheme to be received and held on trust by trustees of a qualifying trust for the benefit of A; and

(b) "a qualifying trust" is a trust under which A is, during his lifetime, the sole beneficiary.

(2) Where a person receives a sum—

(a) as the annuitant under an annuity purchased for him pursuant to a qualifying award,

(b) on behalf of the annuitant under an annuity purchased for the annuitant pursuant to a qualifying award, or

(c) as a trustee to be held on trust for A under a qualifying trust, in a case where the sum is paid under the terms of an annuity purchased pursuant to a qualifying award,

the sum shall not be regarded for the purposes of income tax as income of the recipient, or as A's income, and accordingly shall be paid without any deduction under section 349(1).

(3) In this section "the Criminal Injuries Compensation Scheme" means—

(a) the scheme established by arrangements made under the Criminal Injuries Compensation Act 1995; or

(b)   arrangements made by the Secretary of State for compensation for criminal injuries and in operation at any time before the commencement of that scheme.'

9.   Financial provisions

(1)   The Secretary of State may pay such remuneration, allowances or gratuities to or in respect of claims officers and other persons appointed by him under this Act (other than adjudicators) as he considers appropriate.

(2)   The Secretary of State may pay, or make such payments towards the provision of, such remuneration, pensions, allowances or gratuities to or in respect of adjudicators, as he considers appropriate.

(3)   The Secretary of State may make such payments by way of compensation for loss of office to any adjudicator who is removed from office under section 5(7), as he considers appropriate.

(4)   Sums required for the payment of compensation in accordance with the Scheme shall be provided by the Secretary of State out of money provided by Parliament.

(5)   Where a Scheme manager has been appointed, the Secretary of State may make such payments to him, in respect of the discharge of his functions in relation to the Scheme, as the Secretary of State considers appropriate.

(6)   Any expenses incurred by the Secretary of State under this Act shall be paid out of money provided by Parliament.

(7)   Any sums received by the Secretary of State under any provision of the Scheme made by virtue of section 3(1)(c) shall be paid by him into the Consolidated Fund.

10.   Jurisdiction of Parliamentary Commissioner for Administration

(1)   In the Parliamentary Commissioner Act 1967, insert after section 11A—

'11B   The Criminal Injuries Compensation Scheme

(1)   For the purposes of this Act, administrative functions exercisable by an administrator of the Criminal Injuries Compensation Scheme (''Scheme functions'') shall be taken to be administrative functions of a government department to which this Act applies.

(2)   For the purposes of this section, the following are administrators of the Scheme—

(a)   a claims officer appointed under section 3(4)(b) of the Criminal Injuries Compensation Act 1995;

(b)   a person appointed under section 5(3)(c) of the Act;

(c)   the Scheme manager, as defined by section 1(4) of that Act, and any person assigned by him to exercise functions in relation to the Scheme.

(3)   The principal officer in relation to any complaint made in respect of any action taken in respect of Scheme functions is—

(a)   in the case of action taken by a claims officer, such person as may from time to time be designated by the Secretary of State for the purposes of this paragraph;

(b)   in the case of action taken by a person appointed under section 5(3)(c) of the Act of 1995, the chairman appointed by the Secretary of State under section 5(3)(b) of that Act; or

(c)   in the case of action taken by the Scheme manager or by any other person mentioned in subsection (2)(c) of this section, the Scheme manager.

(4)   The conduct of an investigation under this Act in respect of any action taken in respect of Scheme functions shall not affect—

(a)   any action so taken; or

(b)   any power or duty of any person to take further action with respect to any matters subject to investigation.'

(2)   In Schedule 3 to the Act of 1967 (matters not subject to investigation), insert after paragraph 6B—

'**6C.**   Action taken by any person appointed under section 5(3)(c) of the Criminal Injuries Compensation Act 1995, so far as that action is taken at the direction, or on the authority (whether express or implied), of any person acting in his capacity as an adjudicator appointed under section 5 of that Act to determine appeals.'

(3)   The amendments made by this section do not affect the following provisions of this Act—

(a)   section 3(5)(b);

(b)   section 3(7)(b);

(c)   section 5(4)(b).

11.   Parliamentary control

(1)   Before making the Scheme, the Secretary of State shall lay a draft of it before Parliament.

(2)   The Secretary of State shall not make the Scheme unless the draft has been approved by a resolution of each House.

(3)   Before making any alteration to the Tariff or to any provision of the Scheme as to—

(a)   any additional amount mentioned in section 2(2),

(b)   the circumstances in which compensation may be payable with respect to a criminal injury of a kind for which no provision is made by the Tariff,

(c)   the calculation of compensation in respect of multiple injuries,

(d)   compensation payable in respect of children conceived as a result of rape,

(e)   the circumstances in which an award may be withheld or compensation reduced,

(f)   any limit on compensation imposed by a provision made by virtue of section 2(7)(a),

the Secretary of State shall lay before Parliament a draft of the provision as proposed to be altered.

(4)   Before making any alteration to a provision of the Scheme which—

(a)   gives a right of appeal, or

(b)   specifies the circumstances in which an appeal is to be dealt with by a hearing,

the Secretary of State shall lay before Parliament a draft of the provision as proposed to be altered.

(5)   Where the Secretary of State is required to lay a draft before Parliament under subsection (3) or (4) he shall not give effect to the proposal concerned unless the draft has been approved by a resolution of each House.

(6)   Whenever any other provision of the Scheme is altered, the Secretary of State shall lay a statement of the altered provision before Parliament.

(7)   If any statement laid before either House of Parliament under subsection (6) is disapproved by a resolution of that House passed before the end of the period of 40 days beginning with the date on which the statement was laid, the Secretary of State shall—

(a)   make such alterations in the Scheme as appear to him to be required in the circumstances; and

(b)   before the end of the period of 40 days beginning with the date on which the resolution was made, lay a statement of those alterations before Parliament.

(8)   In calculating the period of 40 days mentioned in subsection (7), any period during which Parliament is dissolved or prorogued or during which both Houses are adjourned for more than 4 days shall be disregarded.

12.   Repeal of the 1988 Act scheme and transitional provisions

(1)   Sections 108 to 117 of, and Schedules 6 and 7 to, the Criminal Justice Act 1988 (the Criminal Injuries Compensation Scheme) shall cease to have effect.

(2)   The arrangements for compensation for criminal injuries in operation immediately before the passing of this Act ('the current arrangements') shall continue in force until the date on which the Scheme comes into force ('the commencement date').

(3)   At any time before the commencement date, the Secretary of State may make such alterations to the current arrangements as he considers appropriate.

(4)   The current arrangements shall cease to have effect on the commencement date.

(5)   The Scheme may include such transitional provisions ('the transitional arrangements') as the Secretary of State considers appropriate in consequence of the replacement of the current arrangements by the Scheme.

(6)   The transitional arrangements may, in particular, provide for the basis on which compensation is to be calculated in cases to which the transitional arrangements apply to differ from that on which compensation is to be calculated in other cases.

(7)   The repeals set out in the Schedule shall have effect.

13. Short title and extent

(1)   This Act may be cited as the Criminal Injuries Compensation Act 1995.

(2)   This Act does not extend to Northern Ireland.

Section 12(7)   SCHEDULE

REPEALS

Chapter	Short title	Extent of repeal
1988 c. 33	Criminal Justice Act 1988.	Sections 108 to 117. In section 171, in subsection (2) the words from 'other than' to the end and subsections (3) and (4). In section 172, in subsection (2) the words 'sections 108 to 115 and 117' and in subsection (4) the words 'section 116'. Schedules 6 and 7.
1992 c. 53.	Tribunals and Inquiries Act 1992.	Paragraph 1 of Schedule 2.

Appendix Three   The New Scheme

The Secretary of State, in exercise of the powers conferred on him by sections 1 to 6 and 12 of the Criminal Injuries Compensation Act 1995 (c. 53), hereby makes the attached Criminal Injuries Compensation Scheme, a draft thereof having been approved by both Houses of Parliament:

Home Office   *Michael Howard*
12 December 1995   One of Her Majesty's Principal Secretaries of State

Criminal Injuries Compensation Authority
Tay House, 300 Bath Street,
Glasgow G2 4JR
Telephone: 0141 331 2726
Fax: 0141 331 2287

THE CRIMINAL INJURIES COMPENSATION SCHEME

TABLE OF CONTENTS

Paragraph   Provision

1.   Preamble.

Administration of the Scheme

2.   Claims officers and Panel.
3.   Decisions and appeals.
4.   Annual report on Scheme.
5.   Advice by Panel.

Eligibility to apply for compensation

6.   Criminal injury sustained since August 1964.
7.   Ineligible cases.
8.   Criminal injury.
9.   Personal injury.
10.   No criminal conviction.
11.   Use of vehicle.
12.   Accidental injury.

Eligibility to receive compensation

13.   Applicant's actions, conduct and character.
14.   Actions, conduct and character in fatal cases.
15.   Beneficiary of award.
16.   Victim and assailant living in same household.

Consideration of applications

17.   Written application within time limit.
18.   Onus on applicant.
19.   Powers of claims officer.
20.   Medical examination of injury.
21.   Guide to Scheme.

Types and limits of compensation

22.   Types of compensation.
23.   Maximum award.
24.   Minimum award.

Standard amount of compensation

25.   Tariff amount for listed injuries.
26.   Multiple injuries.
27.   Child born of rape.
28.   Unlisted injuries.
29.   Interim award for unlisted injuries.

Compensation for loss of earnings

30.   Period of loss.
31.   Loss up to time of assessment.
32.   Loss continuing at time of assessment.

33.   Alternative calculation of future loss.
34.   Limit on rate of loss.

Compensation for special expenses

35.   Types of special expenses.
36.   Special expenses continuing at time of assessment.

Compensation in fatal cases

37.   Funeral expenses.
38.   Qualifying claimants.
39.   Standard amount of compensation.
40.   Dependency.
41.   Calculation of dependency compensation.
42.   Compensation for loss of parent.
43.   Award to victim before death.
44.   Supplementary compensation.

Effect on awards of other payments

45.   Social security benefits and insurance payments.
46.   Refusal of award pending claim.
47.   Pensions.
48.   Compensation and damages from other sources.
49.   Repayment of award.

Determination of applications and payment of awards

50.   Notification of award.
51.   Lump sum and interim payments.
52.   Purchase of annuities.

Reconsideration of decisions

53.   Final payment not yet made.
54.   Decision already notified to applicant.
55.   Decision in accordance with direction by adjudicators.

Re-opening of cases

56.   Change in victim's medical condition.
57.   Time limit.

Review of decisions

58.	Decisions open to review.
59.	Written application within time limit.
60.	Procedure on review.

Appeals against review decisions

61.	Written notice within time limit.
62.	Waiver of time limit.
63.	Procedure for appeals.
64.	Onus on appellant.
65.	Inspection of injury.

Appeals concerning time limits and re-opening of cases

66.	Single adjudicator.
67.	Determination of appeal.
68.	Direction to Authority.

Appeals concerning awards

69.	Referral for oral hearing.
70.	Referral to adjudicator.
71.	Dismissal of appeal.

Oral hearing of appeals

72.	More than one adjudicator.
73.	Notice of hearing and disclosure of documents.
74.	Attendance at hearing.
75.	Procedure at hearing.
76.	Observers.
77.	Determination of appeal.
78.	Failure to attend.

Rehearing of appeals

79.	Written application within time limit.
80.	Waiver of time limit.
81.	Decision on application for rehearing.
82.	Procedure at rehearing.

Implementation and transitional provisions

83.   Scheme in force from 1 April 1996.
84.   Earlier applications dealt with under old Scheme.
85.   Transfer of Board's cases.
86.   Adaptation of Board's powers.
87.   Re-opening of old Scheme cases.

Notes to the Scheme

Note 1.   Definition of Great Britain.
Note 2.   Definition of British craft.
Note 3.   Table of Illustrative Multipliers.

TARIFF OF INJURIES AND STANDARD AMOUNTS OF COMPENSATION

Levels of compensation.
Descriptions of injury.
Notes to the Tariff.

THE CRIMINAL INJURIES COMPENSATION SCHEME

1.   This Scheme is made by the Secretary of State under the Criminal Injuries Compensation Act 1995. Applications received on or after 1 April 1996 for the payment of compensation to, or in respect of, persons who have sustained criminal injury will be considered under this Scheme.

Administration of the Scheme

2.   Claims officers in the Criminal Injuries Compensation Authority ('the Authority') will determine claims for compensation in accordance with this Scheme. Appeals against decisions taken on reviews under this Scheme will be determined by adjudicators. Persons appointed as adjudicators are appointed as members of the Criminal Injuries Compensation Appeals Panel ('the Panel'). The Secretary of State will appoint one of the adjudicators as chairman of the Panel. The Secretary of State will also appoint persons as staff of the Panel to administer the provisions of this Scheme relating to the appeal system.

3.   Claims officers will be responsible for deciding, in accordance with this Scheme, what awards (if any) should be made in individual cases, and how they should be paid. Their decisions will be open to review and thereafter to appeal to the Panel, in accordance with this Scheme. No decision, whether by a claims officer or the Panel, will be open to appeal to the Secretary of State.

4.   The general working of this Scheme will be kept under review by the Secretary of State. The Accounting Officer(s) for the Authority and the Panel must

each submit reports to the Secretary of State as soon as possible after the end of each financial year, dealing with the operation of this Scheme and the discharge of functions under it. The Accounting Officer(s) must each keep proper accounts and proper records in relation to those accounts, and must each prepare a statement of accounts in each financial year in a form directed by the Secretary of State. These statements of accounts must be submitted to the Secretary of State as soon as possible after the end of each financial year.

5.　　The Panel will advise the Secretary of State on matters on which he seeks its advice, as well as on such other matters and at such times as it considers appropriate. Any advice given by the Panel will be referred to by the Accounting Officer for the Panel in his annual report made under the preceding paragraph.

Eligibility to apply for compensation

6.　　Compensation may be paid in accordance with this Scheme:

　　(a)　to an applicant who has sustained a criminal injury on or after 1 August 1964;

　　(b)　where the victim of a criminal injury sustained on or after 1 August 1964 has since died, to an applicant who is a qualifying claimant for the purposes of paragraph 38 (compensation in fatal cases).

For the purposes of this Scheme, 'applicant' means any person for whose benefit an application for compensation is made, even where it is made on his behalf by another person.

7.　　No compensation will be paid under this Scheme in the following circumstances:

　　(a)　where the applicant lodged a claim before 1 April 1996 for compensation in respect of the same criminal injury under any scheme for the compensation of the victims of violent crime in operation in Great Britain before that date; or

　　(b)　where the criminal injury was sustained before 1 October 1979 and the victim and the assailant were living together at the time as members of the same family.

8.　　For the purposes of this Scheme, 'criminal injury' means one or more personal injuries as described in the following paragraph, being an injury sustained in Great Britain (see Note 1) and directly attributable to:

　　(a)　a crime of violence (including arson, fire-raising or an act of poisoning); or

　　(b)　an offence of trespass on a railway; or

　　(c)　the apprehension or attempted apprehension of an offender or a suspected offender, the prevention or attempted prevention of an offence, or the giving of help to any constable who is engaged in any such activity.

9.　　For the purposes of this Scheme, personal injury includes physical injury (including fatal injury), mental injury (that is, a medically recognised psychiatric or psychological illness) and disease (that is, a medically recognised illness or condition). Mental injury or disease may either result directly from the physical injury or occur without any physical injury, but compensation will not be payable for mental injury alone unless the applicant:

(a)   was put in reasonable fear of immediate physical harm to his own person; or

(b)   had a close relationship of love and affection with another person at the time when that person sustained physical (including fatal) injury directly attributable to conduct within paragraph 8(a), (b) or (c), and

(i)   that relationship still subsists (unless the victim has since died), and

(ii)   the applicant either witnessed and was present on the occasion when the other person sustained the injury, or was closely involved in its immediate aftermath; or

(c)   was the non-consenting victim of a sexual offence (which does not include a victim who consented in fact but was deemed in law not to have consented); or

(d)   being a person employed in the business of a railway, either witnessed and was present on the occasion when another person sustained physical (including fatal) injury directly attributable to an offence of trespass on a railway, or was closely involved in its immediate aftermath. Paragraph 12 below does not apply where mental injury is sustained as described in this sub-paragraph.

10.   It is not necessary for the assailant to have been convicted of a criminal offence in connection with the injury. Moreover, even where the injury is attributable to conduct within paragraph 8(a) in respect of which the assailant cannot be convicted of an offence by reason of age, insanity or diplomatic immunity, the conduct may nevertheless be treated as constituting a criminal act.

11.   A personal injury is not a criminal injury for the purposes of this Scheme where the injury is attributable to the use of a vehicle, except where the vehicle was used so as deliberately to inflict, or attempt to inflict, injury on any person.

12.   Where an injury is sustained accidentally by a person who is engaged in:

(a)   any of the law-enforcement activities described in paragraph 8(c), or

(b)   any other activity directed to containing, limiting or remedying the consequences of a crime,

compensation will not be payable unless the person injured was, at the time he sustained the injury, taking an exceptional risk which was justified in all the circumstances.

Eligibility to receive compensation

13.   A claims officer may withhold or reduce an award where he considers that:

(a)   the applicant failed to take, without delay, all reasonable steps to inform the police, or other body or person considered by the Authority to be appropriate for the purpose, of the circumstances giving rise to the injury; or

(b)   the applicant failed to co-operate with the police or other authority in attempting to bring the assailant to justice; or

(c)   the applicant has failed to give all reasonable assistance to the Authority or other body or person in connection with the application; or

(d)   the conduct of the applicant before, during or after the incident giving rise to the application makes it inappropriate that a full award or any award at all be made; or

(e)   the applicant's character as shown by his criminal convictions (excluding convictions spent under the Rehabilitation of Offenders Act 1974) or by evidence available to the claims officer makes it inappropriate that a full award or any award at all be made.

14.   When the victim has died since sustaining the injury (whether or not in consequence of it), the preceding paragraph will apply in relation both to the deceased and to any applicant.

15.   A claims officer will make an award only where he is satisfied:

(a)   that there is no likelihood that an assailant would benefit if an award were made; or

(b)   where the applicant is under 18 years of age when the application is determined, that it would not be against his interest for an award to be made.

16.   Where a case is not ruled out under paragraph 7(b) (injury sustained before 1 October 1979) but at the time when the injury was sustained, the victim and any assailant (whether or not that assailant actually inflicted the injury) were living in the same household as members of the same family, an award will be withheld unless:

(a)   the assailant has been prosecuted in connection with the offence, except where a claims officer considers that there are practical, technical or other good reasons why a prosecution has not been brought; and

(b)   in the case of violence between adults in the family, a claims officer is satisfied that the applicant and the assailant stopped living in the same household before the application was made and are unlikely to share the same household again. For the purposes of this paragraph, a man and woman living together as husband and wife will be treated as members of the same family.

Consideration of applications

17.   An application for compensation under this Scheme in respect of a criminal injury ('injury' hereafter in this Scheme) must be made in writing on a form obtainable from the Authority. It should be made as soon as possible after the incident giving rise to the injury and must be received by the Authority within two years of the date of the incident. A claims officer may waive this time limit where he considers that, by reason of the particular circumstances of the case, it is reasonable and in the interests of justice to do so.

18.   It will be for the applicant to make out his case including, where appropriate:

(a)   making out his case for a waiver of the time limit in the preceding paragraph; and

(b)   satisfying the claims officer dealing with his application (including an officer reviewing a decision under paragraph 60) that an award should not be reconsidered, withheld or reduced under any provision of this Scheme.
Where an applicant is represented, the costs of representation will not be met by the Authority.

19.   A claims officer may make such directions and arrangements for the conduct of an application, including the imposition of conditions, as he considers appropriate in all the circumstances. The standard of proof to be applied by a claims officer in all matters before him will be the balance of probabilities.

20.   Where a claims officer considers that an examination of the injury is required before a decision can be reached, the Authority will make arrangements for such an examination by a duly qualified medical practitioner. Reasonable expenses incurred by the applicant in that connection will be met by the Authority.

21.   A Guide to the operation of this Scheme will be published by the Authority. In addition to explaining the procedures for dealing with applications, the Guide will set out, where appropriate, the criteria by which decisions will normally be reached.

Types and limits of compensation

22.   Subject to the other provisions of this Scheme, the compensation payable under an award will be:

(a)   a standard amount of compensation determined by reference to the nature of the injury in accordance with paragraphs 25–29;

(b)   where the applicant has lost earnings or earning capacity for longer than 28 weeks as a direct consequence of the injury (other than injury leading to his death), an additional amount in respect of such loss of earnings, calculated in accordance with paragraphs 30–34;

(c)   where the applicant had lost earnings or earning capacity for longer than 28 weeks as a direct consequence of the injury (other than injury leading to his death) or, if not normally employed, is incapacitated to a similar extent, an additional amount in respect of any special expenses, calculated in accordance with paragraphs 35–36;

(d)   where the victim has died in consequence of the injury, the amount or amounts calculated in accordance with paragraphs 37–43;

(e)   where the victim has died otherwise than in consequence of the injury, a supplementary amount calculated in accordance with paragraph 44.

23.   The total maximum amount payable in respect of the same injury will not exceed £500,000. For these purposes, where the victim has died in consequence of the injury, any application made by the victim before his death and any application made by any qualifying claimants after his death will be regarded as being in respect of the same injury.

24.   The injury must be sufficiently serious to qualify for an award equal at least to the minimum amount payable under this Scheme in accordance with paragraph 25.

Standard amount of compensation

25.   The standard amount of compensation will be the amount shown in respect of the relevant description of injury in the Tariff appended to this Scheme, which sets out:

(a)   a scale of fixed levels of compensation; and

(b)   the level and corresponding amount of compensation for each description of injury.

Level 1 represents the minimum amount payable under the Scheme, and Level 25 represents the maximum amount payable for any single description of injury. Where the injury has the effect of accelerating or exacerbating a pre-existing condition, the compensation awarded will reflect only the degree of acceleration or exacerbation.

26.   Minor multiple injuries will be compensated in accordance with Note 1 to the Tariff. The standard amount of compensation for more serious but separate multiple injuries will be calculated as:

(a)   the Tariff amount for the highest-rated description of injury; plus

(b)   10 per cent of the Tariff amount for the second highest-rated description of injury; plus, where there are three or more injuries,

(c)   5 per cent of the Tariff amount for the third highest-rated description of injury.

27.   Where a woman has become pregnant as a result of rape and an award is made to her in respect of non-consensual vaginal intercourse, an additional amount will be payable equal to Level 10 of the Tariff in respect of each child born alive which she intends to keep.

28.   Where the Authority considers that any description of injury for which no provision is made in the Tariff is sufficiently serious to qualify for at least the minimum amount payable under this Scheme, it will, following consultation with the Panel, refer the injury to the Secretary of State. In doing so the Authority will recommend to the Secretary of State both the inclusion of that description of injury in the Tariff and also the amount of compensation for which it should qualify. Any such consultation with the Panel or reference to the Secretary of State must not refer to the circumstances of any individual application for compensation under this Scheme other than the relevant medical reports.

29.   Where an application for compensation is made in respect of an injury for which no provision is made in the Tariff and the Authority decides to refer the injury to the Secretary of State under the preceding paragraph, an interim award may be made of up to half the amount of compensation for which it is recommended that such description of injury should qualify if subsequently included in the Tariff. No part of such an interim award will be recoverable if the injury is not subsequently included in the Tariff or, if included, qualifies for less compensation than the interim award paid.

Compensation for loss of earnings

30.   Where the applicant has lost earnings or earning capacity for longer than 28 weeks as a direct consequence of the injury (other than injury leading to his death), no compensation in respect of loss of earnings or earning capacity will be payable for the first 28 weeks of loss. The period of loss for which compensation may be payable

will begin 28 weeks after the date of commencement of the applicant's incapacity for work and continue for such period as a claims officer may determine.

31.   For a period of loss ending before or continuing to the time the claim is assessed, the net loss of earnings or earning capacity will be calculated on the basis of:

(a)   the applicant's emoluments (being any profit or gain accruing from an office or employment) at the time of the injury and what those emoluments would have been during the period of loss; and

(b)   any emoluments which have become payable to the applicant in respect of the whole or part of the period of loss, whether or not as a result of the injury; and

(c)   any changes in the applicant's pension rights; and

(d)   in accordance with paragraphs 45–47 (reductions to take account of other payments), any social security benefits, insurance payments and pension which have become payable to the applicant during the period of loss; and

(e)   any other pension which has become payable to the applicant during the period of loss, whether or not as a result of the injury.

32.   Where, at the time the claim is assessed, a claims officer considers that the applicant is likely to suffer continuing loss of earnings or earning capacity, an annual rate of net loss (the multiplicand) or, where appropriate, more than one such rate will be calculated on the basis of:

(a)   the current rate of net loss calculated in accordance with the preceding paragraph; and

(b)   such future rate or rates of net loss (including changes in the applicant's pension rights) as the claims officer may determine; and

(c)   the claims officer's assessment of the applicant's future earning capacity; and

(d)   in accordance with paragraphs 45–47 (reductions to take account of other payments), any social security benefits, insurance payments and pension which will become payable to the applicant in future; and

(e)   any other pension which will become payable to the applicant in future, whether or not as a result of the injury.

The compensation payable in respect of such continuing loss will be a lump sum which is the product of that multiplicand and an appropriate multiplier. The summary table given in Note 3 illustrates the multipliers applicable to various periods of future loss to allow for the accelerated receipt of compensation. In selecting the multiplier, the claims officer may refer to the Actuarial Tables for use in Personal Injury and Fatal Accident Cases published by the Government Actuary's Department, and take account of any factors and contingencies which appear to him to be relevant.

33.   Where a claims officer considers that the approach in the preceding paragraph is impracticable, the compensation payable in respect of continuing loss of earnings or earning capacity will be such other lump sum as he may determine.

34.   Any rate of net loss of earnings or earning capacity (before any reduction in accordance with this Scheme) which is to be taken into account in calculating any compensation payable under paragraphs 30–33 must not exceed one and a half times

the gross average industrial earnings at the time of assessment according to the latest figures published by the Department of Education and Employment.

Compensation for special expenses

35.   Where the applicant has lost earnings or earning capacity for longer than 28 weeks as a direct consequence of the injury (other than injury leading to his death), or, if not normally employed, is incapacitated to a similar extent, additional compensation may be payable in respect of any special expenses incurred by the applicant from the date of the injury for:

(a)   loss of or damage to property or equipment belonging to the applicant on which he relied as a physical aid, where the loss or damage was a direct consequence of the injury;

(b)   costs (other than by way of loss of earnings or earning capacity) associated with National Health Service treatment for the injury;

(c)   the cost of private health treatment for the injury, but only where a claims officer considers that, in all the circumstances, both the private treatment and its cost are reasonable;

(d)   the reasonable cost, to the extent that it falls to the applicant, of

(i)   special equipment, and/or

(ii)   adaptations to the applicant's accommodation, and/or

(iii)   care, whether in a residential establishment or at home,

which are not provided or available free of charge from the National Health Service, local authorities or any other agency, provided that a claims officer considers such expense to be necessary as a direct consequence of the injury.

In the case of (d)(iii), the expense of unpaid care provided at home by a relative or friend of the victim will be compensated by assessing the carer's loss of earnings or earning capacity and/or additional personal and living expenses, as calculated on such basis as a claims officer considers appropriate in all the circumstances. Where the foregoing method of assessment is considered by the claims officer not to be relevant in all the circumstances, the compensation payable will be such sum as he may determine having regard to the level of care provided.

36.   Where, at the time the claim is assessed, a claims officer is satisfied that the need for any of the special expenses mentioned in the preceding paragraph is likely to continue, he will determine the annual cost and select an appropriate multiplier in accordance with paragraph 32 (future loss of earnings), taking account of any other factors and contingencies which appear to him to be relevant.

Compensation in fatal cases

37.   Where the victim has died in consequence of the injury, no compensation other than funeral expenses will be payable for the benefit of his estate. Such expenses will, subject to the application of paragraph 13 in relation to the actions, conduct and character of the deceased, be payable up to an amount considered reasonable by a claims officer, even where the person bearing the cost of the funeral is otherwise ineligible to claim under this Scheme.

38.   Where the victim has died since sustaining the injury, compensation may be payable, subject to paragraph 14 (actions, conduct and character), to any claimant (a 'qualifying claimant') who at the time of the deceased's death was:

(a)   the spouse of the deceased, being only, for these purposes:

(i)   a person who was living with the deceased as husband and wife in the same household immediately before the date of death and who, if not formally married to him, had been so living throughout the two years before that date, or

(ii)   a spouse or former spouse of the deceased who was financially supported by him immediately before the date of death; or

(b)   a parent of the deceased, whether or not the natural parent, provided that he was accepted by the deceased as a parent of his family; or

(c)   a child of the deceased, whether or not the natural child, provided that he was accepted by the deceased as a child of his family or was dependent on him.

Where the victim has died in consequence of the injury, compensation may be payable to a qualifying claimant under paragraphs 39–42 (standard amount of compensation, dependency, and loss of parent). Where the victim has died otherwise than in consequence of the injury, compensation may be payable to a qualifying claimant only under paragraph 44 (supplementary compensation).

39.   In cases where there is only one qualifying claimant, the standard amount of compensation will be Level 13 of the Tariff. Where there is more than one qualifying claimant, the standard amount of compensation for each claimant will be Level 10 of the Tariff. A former spouse of the deceased is not a qualifying claimant for the purposes of this paragraph.

40.   Additional compensation calculated in accordance with the following paragraph may be payable to a qualifying claimant where a claims officer is satisfied that the claimant was financially dependent on the deceased. A dependency will not be established where the deceased's only normal income was from:

(a)   United Kingdom social security benefits; or

(b)   social security benefits or similar payments from the funds of other countries.

41.   The amount of compensation payable in respect of dependency will be calculated on a basis similar to paragraphs 31–34 (loss of earnings). The period of loss will begin from the date of the deceased's death and continue for such period as a claims officer may determine, with no account being taken, where the qualifying claimant was formally married to the deceased, of remarriage or prospects of remarriage. In assessing the dependency, the claims officer will take account of the qualifying claimant's income and emoluments (being any profit or gain accruing from an office or employment), if any. Where the deceased had been living in the same household as the qualifying claimant before his death, the claims officer will, in calculating the multiplicand, make such proportional reduction as he considers appropriate to take account of the deceased's own personal and living expenses.

42.   Where a qualifying claimant was under 18 years of age at the time of the deceased's death and was dependent on him for parental services, the following additional compensation may also be payable:

(a) a payment for loss of that parent's services at an annual rate of Level 5 of the Tariff; and

(b) such other payments as a claims officer considers reasonable to meet other resultant losses.

Each of these payments will be multiplied by an appropriate multiplier selected by a claims officer in accordance with paragraph 32 (future loss of earnings), taking account of the period remaining before the qualifying claimant reaches age 18 and of any other factors and contingencies which appear to the claims officer to be relevant.

43.   Application may be made under paragraphs 37–42 (compensation in fatal cases) even where an award had been made to the victim in respect of the same injury before his death. Any such application will be subject to the conditions set out in paragraphs 56–57 for the re-opening of cases, and any compensation payable to the qualifying claimant or claimants, except payments made under paragraphs 37 and 39 (funeral expenses and standard amount of compensation), will be reduced by the amount paid to the victim. The amounts payable to the victim and the qualifying claimant or claimants will not in total exceed £500,000.

44.   Where a victim who would have qualified for additional compensation under paragraph 22(b) (loss of earnings) and/or paragraph 22(c) (special expenses) has died, otherwise than in consequence of the injury, before such compensation was awarded, supplementary compensation under this paragraph may be payable to a qualifying claimant who was financially dependent on the deceased within the terms of paragraph 40 (dependency), whether or not a relevant application was made by the victim before his death. Payment may be made in accordance with paragraph 31 in respect of the victim's loss of earnings (except for the first 28 weeks of such loss) and in accordance with paragraph 35 in respect of any special expenses incurred by the victim before his death. The amounts payable to the victim and the qualifying claimant or claimants will not in total exceed £500,000.

Effect on awards of other payments

45.   All awards payable under this Scheme, except those payable under paragraphs 25, 27, 39 and 42(a) (Tariff-based amounts of compensation), will be subject to a reduction to take account of social security benefits or insurance payments made by way of compensation for the same contingency. The reduction will be applied to those categories or periods of loss or need for which additional or supplementary compensation is payable, including compensation calculated on the basis of a multiplicand or annual cost. The amount of the reduction will be the full value of any relevant payment which the applicant has received, or to which he has any present or future entitlement, by way of:

(a) United Kingdom social security benefits;

(b) social security benefits or similar payments from the funds of other countries;

(c)   payments under insurance arrangements, including, where a claim is made under paragraphs 35(c) and (d) and 36 (special expenses), insurance personally effected, paid for and maintained by the personal income of the victim or, in the case of a person under 18 years of age, by his parent. Insurance so personally effected will otherwise be disregarded.

In assessing the value of any such benefits and payments, account may be taken of any income tax liability likely to reduce their value.

46.   Where, in the opinion of a claims officer, an applicant may be eligible for any of the benefits and payments mentioned in the preceding paragraph, an award may be withheld until the applicant has taken such steps as the claims officer considers reasonable to claim them.

47.   Where the victim is alive, any compensation payable under paragraphs 30–34 (loss of earnings) will be reduced to take account of any pension accruing as a result of the injury. Where the victim has died in consequence of the injury, any compensation payable under pargraphs 40–41 (dependency) will similarly be reduced to take account of any pension payable, as a result of the victim's death, for the benefit of the applicant. Where such pensions are taxable, one half of their value will be deducted, but they will otherwise be deducted in full (where, for example, a lump sum payment not subject to income tax is made). For the purposes of this paragraph, 'pension' means any payment payable as a result of the injury or death in pursuance of pension or any other rights connected with the victim's employment, and includes any gratuity of that kind and similar benefits payable under insurance policies paid for by the victim's employers. Pension rights accruing solely as a result of payments by the victim or a dependant will be disregarded.

48.   An award payable under this Scheme will be reduced by the full value of any payment in respect of the same injury which the applicant has received by way of:

(a)   any criminal injury compensation award made under or pursuant to arrangements in force at the relevant time in Northern Ireland;

(b)   any compensation award or similar payment from the funds of other countries;

(c)   any award where:

(i)   a civil court has made an order for the payment of damages;

(ii)   a claim for damages and/or compensation has been settled on terms providing for the payment of money;

(iii)   payment of compensation has been ordered by a criminal court in respect of personal injuries.

In the case of (a) or (b), the reduction will also include the full value of any payment to which the applicant has any present or future entitlement.

49.   Where a person in whose favour an award under this Scheme is made subsequently receives any other payment in respect of the same injury in any of the circumstances mentioned in the preceding paragraph, but the award made under this Scheme was not reduced accordingly, he will be required to repay the Authority in full up to the amount of the other payment.

Determination of applications and payment of awards

50.   An application for compensation under this Scheme will be determined by a claims officer, and written notification of the decision will be sent to the applicant or his representative. The claims officer may make such directions and arrangements, including the imposition of conditions, in connection with the acceptance, settlement, payment, repayment and/or administration of an award as he considers appropriate in all the circumstances. Subject to any such arrangements, including the special procedures in paragraph 52 (purchase of annuities), and to paragraphs 53–55 (reconsideration of decisions), title to an award offered will be vested in the applicant when the Authority has received notification in writing that he accepts the award.

51.   Compensation will normally be paid as a single lump sum, but one or more interim payments may be made where a claims officer considers this appropriate. Once an award has been paid to an applicant or his representative, the following paragraph does not apply.

52.   Where prior agreement is reached between the Authority and the applicant or his representative, an award may consist in whole or in part of an annuity or annuities, purchased for the benefit of the applicant or to be held on trust for his benefit. Once that agreement is reached, the Authority will take the instructions of the applicant or his representative as to which annuity or annuities should be purchased. Any expenses incurred will be met from the award.

Reconsideration of decisions

53.   A decision made by a claims officer (other than a decision made in accordance with a direction by adjudicators on determining an appeal under paragraph 77) may be reconsidered at any time before actual payment of a final award where there is new evidence or a change in circumstances. In particular, the fact that an interim payment has been made does not preclude a claims officer from reconsidering issues of eligibility for an award.

54.   Where an applicant has already been sent written notification of the decision on his application, he will be sent written notice that the decision is to be reconsidered, and any representations which he sends to the Authority within 30 days of the date of such notice will be taken into account in reconsidering the decision. Whether or not any such representations are made, the applicant will be sent written notification of the outcome of the reconsideration, and where the original decision is not confirmed, such notification will include the revised decision.

55.   Where a decision to make an award has been made by a claims officer in accordance with a direction by adjudicators on determining an appeal under paragraph 77, but before the award has been paid the claims officer considers that there is new evidence or a change in circumstances which justifies reconsidering whether the award should be withheld or the amount of compensation reduced, the Authority will refer the case to the Panel for rehearing under paragraph 82.

Re-opening of cases

56.   A decision made by a claims officer and accepted by the applicant, or a decision made by the Panel, will normally be regarded as final. The claims officer may, however, subsequently re-open a case where there has been such a material change in the victim's medical condition that injustice would occur if the original assessment of compensation were allowed to stand, or where he has since died in consequence of the injury.

57.   A case will not be re-opened more than two years after the date of the final decision unless the claims officer is satisfied, on the basis of evidence presented in support of the application to re-open the case, that the renewed application can be considered without a need for further extensive enquiries.

Review of decisions

58.   An applicant may seek a review of any decision under this Scheme by a claims officer:

   (a)   not to waive the time limit in paragraph 17 (application for compensation) or paragraph 59 (application for review); or

   (b)   not to re-open a case under paragraphs 56–57; or

   (c)   to withhold an award, including such decision made on reconsideration of an award under paragraphs 53–54; or

   (d)   to make an award, including a decision to make a reduced award whether or not on reconsideration of an award under paragraphs 53–54; or

   (e)   to seek repayment of an award under paragraph 49.

An applicant may not, however, seek the review of any such decision where the decision was itself made on a review under paragraph 60 and either the applicant did not appeal against it or the appeal was not referred for determination on an oral hearing, or where the decision was made in accordance with a direction by adjudicators on determining an appeal under paragraph 77.

59.   An application for the review of a decision by a claims officer must be made in writing to the Authority and must be supported by reasons together with any relevant additional information. It must be received by the Authority within 90 days of the date of the decision to be reviewed, but this time limit may, in exceptional circumstances, be waived where a claims officer more senior than the one who made the original decision considers that:

   (a)   any extension requested by the applicant within the 90 days is based on good reasons; or

   (b)   it would be in the interests of justice to do so.

60.   All applications for review will be considered by a claims officer more senior than any claims officer who has previously dealt with the case. The officer conducting the review will reach his decision in accordance with the provisions of this Scheme applying to the original application, and he will not be bound by any earlier decision either as to the eligibility of the applicant for an award or as to the

amount of an award. The applicant will be sent written notification of the outcome of the review, giving reasons for the review decision, and the authority will, unless it receives notice of an appeal, ensure that a determination of the original application is made in accordance with the review decision.

Appeals against review decisions

61.   An applicant who is dissatisfied with a decision taken on a review under paragraph 60 may appeal against the decision by giving written notice of appeal to the Panel on a form obtainable from the Authority. Such notice of appeal must be supported by reasons for the appeal together with any relevant additional material which the appellant wishes to submit, and must be received by the Panel within 30 days of the date of the review decision. The Panel will send to the Authority a copy of the notice of appeal and supporting reasons which it receives and of any other material submitted by the appellant. Where the applicant is represented for the purposes of the appeal, the costs of representation will not be met by the Authority or the Panel.

62.   A member of the staff of the Panel may, in exceptional circumstances, waive the time limit in the preceding paragraph where he considers that:

(a)   any extension requested by the appellant within the 30 days is based on good reasons; or

(b)   it would be in the interests of justice to do so.

Where, on considering a request to waive the time limit, a member of the staff of the Panel does not waive it, he will refer the request to the Chairman of the Panel or to another adjudicator nominated by the Chairman to decide requests for waiver, and a decision by the adjudicator concerned not to waive the time limit will be final. Written notification of the outcome of the waiver request will be sent to the appellant and to the Authority, giving reasons for the decision where the time limit is not waived.

63.   Where the Panel receives notice of an appeal against a review decision relating to a decision mentioned in paragraph 58(a) or (b), the appeal will be dealt with in accordance with paragraphs 66–68 (appeals concerning time limits and re-opening of cases). Where the Panel receives notice of an appeal against a review decision relating to a decision mentioned in paragraph 58(c), (d) or (e), the appeal will be dealt with in accordance with paragraphs 68–71 (appeals concerning awards) and may under those provisions be referred for an oral hearing in accordance with paragraphs 72–78. The Panel may publish information in connection with individual appeals, but such information must not identify any appellant or other person appearing at an oral hearing or referred to during an appeal, or enable identification to be made of any such person.

64.   The standard of proof to be applied by the Panel in all matters before it will be the balance of probabilities. It will be for the appellant to make out his case including, where appropriate:

(a)   making out his case for a waiver of the time limit in paragraph 61 (time limit for appeals); and

(b)   satisfying the adjudicator or adjudicators responsible for determining his appeal that an award should not be reconsidered, withheld or reduced under any provision of this Scheme. Subject to paragraph 78 (determination of appeal in appellant's absence), the adjudicator or adjudicators concerned must ensure, before determining an appeal, that the appellant has had an opportunity to submit representations on any evidence or other material submitted by or on behalf of the Authority.

65.   The Panel may make such arrangements for the inspection of the injury as it considers appropriate. Reasonable expenses incurred by the appellant in that connection will be met by the Panel.

Appeals concerning time limits and re-opening of cases

66.   The Chairman of the Panel or another adjudicator nominated by him will determine any appeal against a decision taken on a review:

(a)   not to waive the time limit in paragraph 17 (application for compensation) or paragraph 59 (application for review); or

(b)   not to re-open a case under paragraphs 56–57.

Where the appeal concerns a decision not to re-open a case and the application for re-opening was made more than two years after the date of the final decision, the adjudicator must be satisfied that the renewed application can be considered without a need for further extensive enquiries by the Authority.

67.   In determining an appeal under the preceding paragraph, the adjudicator will allow the appeal where he considers it appropriate to do so. Where he dismisses the appeal, his decision will be final. Written notification of the outcome of the appeal, giving reasons for the decision, will be sent to the appellant and to the Authority.

68.   Where the adjudicator allows an appeal in accordance with the preceding paragraph, he will direct the Authority:

(a)   in a case where the appeal was against a decision not to waive the time limit in paragraph 17, to arrange for the application for compensation to be dealt with under this Scheme as if the time limit had been waived by a claims officer;

(b)   in a case where the appeal was against a decision not to waive the time limit in paragraph 59, to conduct a review under paragraph 60;

(c)   in a case where the appeal was against a decision not to re-open a case, to re-open the case under paragraphs 56–57.

Appeals concerning awards

69.   A member of the staff of the Panel may refer for an oral hearing in accordance with paragraphs 72–78 any appeal against a decision taken on a review:

(a)   to withhold an award, including such decision made on reconsideration of an award under paragraphs 53–54; or

(b)   to make an award, including a decision to make a reduced award whether or not on reconsideration of an award under paragraphs 53–54; or

(c)   to seek repayment of an award under paragraph 49.

A request for an oral hearing in such cases may also be made by the Authority.

70.   Where a member of the staff of the Panel does not refer an appeal for an oral hearing under the preceding paragraph, he will refer it to an adjudicator. The adjudicator will refer the appeal for determination on an oral hearing in accordance with paragraphs 72–78 where, on the evidence available to him, he considers:

(a)   in a case where the review decision was to withhold an award on the ground that the injury was not sufficiently serious to qualify for an award equal to at least the minimum amount payable under this Scheme, that an award in accordance with this Scheme could have been made; or

(b)   in any other case, that there is a dispute as to the material facts or conclusions upon which the review decision was based and that a different decision in accordance with this Scheme could have been made.

He may also refer the appeal for determination on an oral hearing in accordance with paragraphs 72–78 where he considers that the appeal cannot be determined on the basis of the material before him or that for any other reason an oral hearing would be desirable.

71.   Where an appeal is not referred under paragraphs 69 or 70 for an oral hearing, the adjudicator's dismissal of the appeal will be final and the decision taken on the review will stand. Written notification of the dismissal of the appeal, giving reasons for the decision, will be sent to the appellant and to the Authority.

Oral hearing of appeals

72.   Where an appeal is referred for determination on an oral hearing, the hearing will take place before at least two adjudicators. Where the referral was made by an adjudicator under paragraph 70, that adjudicator will not take part in the hearing. Subject to the provisions of the Scheme, the procedure to be followed for any particular appeal will be a matter for the adjudicators hearing the appeal.

73.   Written notice of the date proposed for the oral hearing will normally be sent to the appellant and the Authority at least 21 days beforehand. Any documents to be submitted to the adjudicators for the purposes of the hearing by the appellant, or by or on behalf of the Authority, will be made available at the hearing, if not before, to the Authority or the appellant respectively.

74.   It will be open to the appellant to bring a friend or legal adviser to assist in presenting his case at the hearing, but the costs of representation will not be met by the Authority or the Panel. The adjudicators may, however, direct the Panel to meet reasonable expenses incurred by the appellant and any person who attends to give evidence at the hearing.

75.   The procedure at hearings will be as informal as is consistent with the proper determination of appeals. The adjudicators will not be bound by any rules of

evidence which may prevent a court from admitting any document or other matter or statement in evidence. The appellant, the claims officer presenting the appeal and the adjudicators may call witnesses to give evidence and may cross-examine them.

76.   Hearings will take place in private. The Panel may, however, subject to the consent of the appellant, give permission for the hearing to be attended by observers such as representatives of the press, radio and television. Any such permission will be subject to written undertakings being given:

(a)   that the identity of the appellant and of any other persons appearing at the hearing or referred to during the appeal will be kept confidential and will not be disclosed in any account of the proceedings which is broadcast or in any way published; and

(b)   that no material will be disclosed or in any other way published from which those identities could be discovered.

77.   Where the adjudicators adjourn the hearing, they may direct that an interim payment be made. On determining the appeal, the adjudicators will, where necessary, make such direction as they think fit as to the decision to be made by a claims officer on the application for compensation, but any such direction must be in accordance with the relevant provisions of this Scheme. Where they are of the opinion that the appeal was frivolous or vexatious, the adjudicators may reduce the amount of compensation to be awarded by such amount as they consider appropriate. The appellant and the Authority will be informed of the adjudicators' determination of the appeal and the reasons for it, normally at the end of the hearing, but otherwise by written notification as soon as is practicable thereafter.

78.   Where an appellant who fails to attend a hearing gives no reasonable excuse for his non-attendance, the adjudicators may determine the appeal in his absence.

Rehearing of appeals

79.   Where an appeal is determined in the appellant's absence, he may apply to the Panel in writing for his appeal to be reheard, giving the reasons for his non-attendance. Any such application must be received by the Panel within 30 days of the date of notification to the appellant of the outcome of the hearing which he failed to attend. The Panel will send a copy of the application to the Authority.

80.   A member of the staff of the Panel may waive the time limit in the preceding paragraph where he considers that it would be in the interests of justice to do so. Where he does not waive the time limit, he will refer the application to the Chairman of the Panel or to another adjudicator nominated by the Chairman to decide such applications, and a decision by the adjudicator concerned not to waive the time limit will be final. Written notification of the waiver decision will be sent to the appellant and to the Authority, giving reasons for the decision where the time limit is not waived.

81.   Where a member of the staff of the Panel considers that there are good reasons for an appeal to be reheard, he will refer it for a rehearing. Where he does

not refer it for a rehearing, he will refer the application to the Chairman of the Panel or to another adjudicator nominated by the Chairman to decide such applications, and a decision by the adjudicator concerned not to rehear the appeal will be final. Written notification of the decision on the application for a rehearing will be sent to the appellant and to the Authority, giving reasons for the decision where the application is refused.

82.   Where an appeal is to be reheard, the adjudicators who determined the appeal originally will not take part in the rehearing, and paragraphs 64 (onus on appellant), 65 (inspection of injury), and 72–78 (oral hearings) will apply.

Implementation and transitional provisions

83.   The provisions of this Scheme come into force on 1 April 1996. All applications for compensation received by the Criminal Injuries Compensation Board ('the Board') on or after that date will be passed to the Authority to be dealt with under this Scheme.

84.   Subject to paragraphs 85–87, applications for compensation received by the Board before 1 April 1996 will be dealt with according to the provisions of the non-statutory Scheme which came into operation on 1 February 1990 ('the old Scheme'), which includes the earlier Schemes mentioned therein insofar as they continue to have effect immediately before 1 April 1996 by virtue of the old Scheme or corresponding provisions in an earlier Scheme.

85.   The Board will cease to exist on such date ('the transfer date') as the Secretary of State may direct. Immediately before the transfer date, the Board will transfer to the Authority all its records of current and past applications.

86.   On and after the transfer date, applications required by paragraph 84 to be dealt with according to the provisions of the old Scheme will be so dealt with by the Authority, and:

(a)   any decision authorised under the old Scheme to be made by a Single Member of the Board may be made by a single legally qualified member of the Panel appointed for the purposes of this Scheme;

(b)   any decision authorised under the old Scheme to be made by at least two Members of the Board may be made by at least two legally qualified members of the Panel;

(c)   any decision authorised under the old Scheme to be made by the Chairman of the Board may be made by the Chairman of the Panel.

In this paragraph 'legally qualified' means qualified to practise as a solicitor in any part of Great Britain, or as a barrister in England and Wales, or as an advocate in Scotland.

87.   On and after the transfer date, any application to re-open a case under paragraph 13 of the old Scheme (or any corresponding provision in any of the earlier Schemes) must be addressed to the Authority, which will deal with it according to the provisions of the old Scheme, applying paragraphs 84 and 86 above as appropriate.

Notes to the Scheme
(see paragraph 8)

Note 1   Definition of Great Britain

(a)   For the purposes of paragraph 8 of this Scheme, an injury is sustained in Great Britain where it is sustained:

(i)   on a British aircraft, hovercraft or ship (see Note 2); or

(ii)   on, under or above an installation in a designated area within the meaning of section 1(7) of the Continental Shelf Act 1964 or any waters within 500 metres of such an installation; or

(iii)   in a lighthouse off the coast of Great Britain.

(b)   For the purposes of paragraph 8 of this Scheme, Great Britain includes that part of the Channel Tunnel designated part of Great Britain by the Channel Tunnel Act 1987. Within that part of the Tunnel or in the control zones within the meaning of the Channel Tunnel (International Arrangements) Order 1993 (SI No. 1813), this Scheme applies to:

(i)   anyone injured by a UK 'officer' (as defined by Article 1(d) of the Protocol made under the Channel Tunnel Treaty signed at Sangette on 25 November 1991) in the exercise of his duties, and

(ii)   any UK 'officer' injured in the exercise of his duties, but it does not apply to:

(iii)   anyone (except a UK 'officer' in the exercise of his duties) injured by a non-UK 'officer' in the exercise of his duties, and

(iv)   any non-UK 'officer' injured in the exercise of his duties, and such persons must pursue their remedy under the relevant national law.

Note 2   Definition of British craft

In Note 1 above:

(a)   'British aircraft' means a British controlled aircraft within the meaning of section 92 of the Civil Aviation Act 1982 (application of criminal law to aircraft), or one of Her Majesty's aircraft;

(b)   'British hovercraft' means a British controlled hovercraft within the meaning of that section (as applied in relation to hovercraft by virtue of provision made under the Hovercraft Act 1968), or one of Her Majesty's hovercraft; and

(c)   'British ship' means any vessel used in navigation which is owned wholly by persons of the following descriptions, namely:

(i)   British citizens, or

(ii)   bodies corporate incorporated under the law of some part of, and having their principal place of business in, the United Kingdom, or

(iii)   Scottish partnerships, or one of Her Majesty's ships.

The references in this Note to Her Majesty's aircraft, hovercraft or ships are references to aircraft, hovercraft or ships which belong to, or are exclusively used in the service of, Her Majesty in right of the government of the United Kingdom.

Note 3   Illustrative Multipliers
(see paragraph 32)

Years of Loss	Multiplier	Years of Loss	Multiplier
5	5	15	10.5
6	5.5	16	11
7	6	17	11.5
8	7	18	12
9	7.5	19	12.5
10	8	19	13
11	8.5	25	15
12	9	30	16
13	9.5	35	17
14	10	40	18

CRIMINAL INJURIES COMPENSATION SCHEME

Levels of compensation

Level 1	£1,000
Level 2	£1,250
Level 3	£1,500
Level 4	£1,750
Level 5	£2,000
Level 6	£2,500
Level 7	£3,000
Level 8	£3,500
Level 9	£4,000
Level 10	£5,000
Level 11	£6,000
Level 12	£7,500
Level 13	£10,000
Level 14	£12,500
Level 15	£15,000
Level 16	£17,500
Level 17	£20,000
Level 18	£25,000
Level 19	£30,000
Level 20	£40,000
Level 21	£50,000
Level 22	£75,000
Level 23	£100,000
Level 24	£175,000
Level 25	£250,000

TARIFF OF INJURIES

Description of Injury	Levels	Standard Amount £
Bodily functions: hemiplegia (paralysis of one side of the body)	21	50,000
Bodily functions: paraplegia (paralysis of the lower limbs)	24	175,000
Bodily functions: quadriplegia/tetraplegia (paralysis of all 4 limbs)	25	250,000
Brain damage: moderate impairment of social/intellectual functions	15	15,000
Brain damage: serious impairment of social/intellectual functions	20	40,000
Brain damage: permanent — extremely serious (no effective control of functions)	25	250,000
Burns: multiple first degree: covering at least 25% of body (For other burn injuries see under individual parts of the body)	19	30,000
Epilepsy: serious exacerbation of pre-existing condition	10	5,000
Epilepsy: fully controlled	12	7,500
Epilepsy: partially controlled	14	12,500
Epilepsy: uncontrolled	20	40,000
Fatal injury (one qualifying claimant)	13	10,000
Fatal injury (each qualifying claimant if more than one):	10	5,000
Head: burns: minor	3	1,500
Head: burns: moderate	9	4,000
Head: burns: severe	13	10,000
Head: ear: fractured mastoid	1	1,000
Head: ear: temporary partial deafness — lasting 6 to 13 weeks	1	1,000
Head: ear: temporry partial deafness — lasting more than 13 weeks	3	1,500
Head: ear: partial deafness (one ear) (remaining hearing socially useful)	8	3,500
Head: ear: partial deafness (both ears) (with hearing aid if necessary)	12	7,500
Head: ear: total deafness (one ear)	15	15,000
Head: ear: total deafness (both ears)	20	40,000
Head: ear: partial loss of ear(s)	9	4,000
Head: ear: loss of ear	13	10,000
Head: ear: loss of both ears	16	17,500
Head: ear: perforated ear drum	4	1,750
Head: ear: tinnitus (ringing noise in ears) — lasting 6 to 13 weeks	1	1,000
Head: ear: tinnitus — lasting more than 13 weeks	7	3,000
Head: ear: tinnitus — permanent (moderate)	12	7,500
Head: ear: tinnitus — permanent (very serious)	15	15,000
Head: eye: blow out fracture of orbit bone cavity containing eyeball	7	3,000
Head: eye: blurred or double vision — lasting 6 to 13 weeks	1	1,000
Head: eye: blurred or double vision — lasting more than 13 weeks	4	1,750
Head: eye: blurred or double vision — permanent	12	7,500
Head: eye: cataracts one eye (requiring operation)	7	3,000
Head: eye: cataracts both eyes (requiring operation)	12	7,500
Head: eye: cataracts one eye (permanent/inoperable)	12	7,500
Head: eye: cataracts both eyes (permanent/inoperable)	16	17,500
Head: eye: corneal abrasions	5	2,000
Head: eye: damage to iris resulting in hyphaema (bleeding in ocular chamber)	6	2,500
Head: eye: damage to irises resulting in hyphaema (bleeding in ocular chamber)	11	6,000

Head: eye: detached retina	10	5,000
Head: eye: detached retinas	14	12,500
Head: eye: degeneration of optic nerve	5	2,000
Head: eye: degeneration of optic nerves	10	5,000
Head: eye: dislocation of lens	10	5,000
Head: eye: dislocation of lenses	14	12,500
Head: eye: glaucoma	6	2,500
Head: eye: residual floaters	10	5,000
Head: eye: traumatic angle recession of eye	6	2,500
Head: eye: loss of one eye	18	25,000
Head: eye: loss of both eyes	23	100,000
Head: eye: loss of sight of one eye	17	20,000
Head: eye: loss of sight of both eyes	22	75,000
Head: eye: partial loss of vision — 6/9	12	7,500
Head: eye: partial loss of vision — 6/12	13	10,000
Head: eye: partial loss of vision — 6/24	14	12,500
Head: eye: partial loss of vision — 6/36	15	15,000
Head: eye: partial loss of vision — 6/60	16	17,500
Head: face: burns — minor	5	2,000
Head: face: burns — moderate	10	5,000
Head: face: burns — severe	18	25,000
Head: face: scarring: minor disfigurement	3	1,500
Head: face: scarring: significant disfigurement	8	3,500
Head: face: scarring: serious disfigurement	12	7,500
Head: facial: dislocated jaw	5	2,000
Head: facial: permanently clicking jaw	10	5,000
Head: facial: fractured malar and/or zygomatic — cheek bones	5	2,000
Head: facial: fractured mandible and/or maxilla — jaw bones	7	3,000
Head: facial: multiple fractures to face	13	10,000
Head: facial: temporary numbness/loss of feeling, lasting 6–13 weeks	1	1,000
Head: facial: temporary numbness/loss of feeling (lasting more than 13 weeks) — recovery expected	3	1,500
Head: facial: permanent numbness/loss of feeling	9	4,000
Head: nose: deviated nasal septum	1	1,000
Head: nose: deviated nasal septum requiring septoplastomy	5	2,000
Head: nose: undisplaced fracture of nasal bones	1	1,000
Head: nose: displaced fracture of nasal bones	3	1,500
Head: nose: displaced fracture of nasal bones requiring manipulation	5	2,000
Head: nose: displaced fracture of nasal bones requiring rhinoplasty	5	2,000
Head: nose: displaced fracture of nasal bones requiring turbinectomy	5	2,000
Head: nose: partial loss (at least 10%)	9	4,000
Head: nose: loss of smell and/or taste (partial)	10	5,000
Head: nose: loss of smell or taste	13	10,000
Head: nose: loss of smell and taste	15	15,000
Head: scarring: visible, minor disfigurement	3	1,500
Head: scarring: significant disfigurement	7	3,000
Head: scarring: serious disfigurement	10	5,000
Head: skull: balance impaired — permanent	12	7,500
Head: skull: concussion (lasting at least one week)	3	1,500

Head: skull: simple fracture (no operation)	6	2,500
Head: skull: depressed fracture (no operation)	9	4,000
Head: skull: depressed fracture (requiring operation)	11	6,000
Head: skull: subdural haematoma — treated conservatively	9	4,000
Head: skull: subdural haematoma — requiring evacuation	12	7,500
Head: skull: brain haemorrhage (full recovery)	9	4,000
Head: skull: brain haemorrhage (residual minor impairment of social/intellectual functions)	12	7,500
Head: skull: stroke (full recovery)	10	5,000
Head: teeth: fractured/chipped tooth/teeth requiring treatment	1	1,000
Head: teeth: chipped front teeth requiring crown	1	1,000
Head: teeth: fractured tooth/teeth requiring crown	1	1,000
Head: teeth: fractured tooth/teeth requiring apicectomy (surgery to gum to reach root — root resection)	5	2,000
Head: teeth: damage to tooth/teeth requiring root-canal treatment	1	1,000
Head: teeth: loss of crowns	2	1,250
Head: teeth: loss of one front tooth	3	1,500
Head: teeth: loss of two or three front teeth	5	2,000
Head: teeth: loss of four or more front teeth	7	3,000
Head: teeth: loss of one tooth other than front	1	1,000
Head: teeth: loss of two or more teeth other than front	3	1,500
Head: teeth: slackening of teeth requiring dental treatment	1	1,000
Head: tongue: impaired speech: slight	5	2,000
Head: tongue: impaired speech: moderate	10	5,000
Head: tongue: impaired speech: serious	13	10,000
Head: tongue: impaired speech: severe	16	17,500
Head: tongue: loss of speech: permanent	19	30,000
Head: tongue: loss of tongue	20	40,000
Lower limbs: burns — minor	3	1,500
Lower limbs: burns — moderate	9	4,000
Lower limbs: burns — severe	13	10,000
Lower limbs: fractured ankle (full recovery)	7	3,000
Lower limbs: fractured ankle (with continuing disability)	10	5,000
Lower limbs: fractured ankles (full recovery)	12	7,500
Lower limbs: fractured ankles (with continuing disability)	13	10,000
Lower limbs: fractured femur — thigh bone (full recovery)	7	3,000
Lower limbs: fractured femur (with continuing disability)	10	5,000
Lower limbs: fractured femur — both legs (full recovery)	12	7,500
Lower limbs: fractured femur — both legs (with continuing disability)	13	10,000
Lower limbs: fractured fibula — slender bone from knee to ankle (full recovery)	7	3,000
Lower limbs: fractured fibula (with continuing disability)	10	5,000
Lower limbs: fractured fibula — both legs (full recovery)	12	7,500
Lower limbs: fractured fibula — both legs (with continuing disability)	13	10,000
Lower limbs: fractured great toe	6	2,500
Lower limbs: fractured great toe — both feet	10	5,000
Lower limbs: fractured phalanges — toes	3	1,500
Lower limbs: fractured heel bone (full recovery)	6	2,500
Lower limbs: fractured heel bone (with continuing disability)	10	5,000
Lower limbs: fractured heel bone — both feet (full recovery)	10	5,000
Lower limbs: fractured heel bone — both feet (with continuing disability)	13	10,000
Lower limbs: fractured patella — knee cap (full recovery)	12	7,500
Lower limbs: fractured patella (with continuing disability)	13	10,000
Lower limbs: fractured patella — both legs (full recovery)	15	15,000

Lower limbs: fractured patella — both legs (with continuing disabiity)	17	20,000
Lower limbs: dislocated patella — both legs (full recovery)	5	2,000
Lower limbs: dislocated patella — both legs (with continuing disability)	16	17,500
Lower limbs: arthroscopy (investigative surgery/repair to knees) — no fracture	5	2,000
Lower limbs: fractured metatarsal bones (full recovery)	6	2,500
Lower limbs: fractured metatarsal bones (with continuing disability)	12	7,500
Lower limbs: fractured metatarsal bones — both feet (full recovery)	10	5,000
Lower limbs: fractured metatarsal bones — both feet (with continuing disability)	15	15,000
Lower limbs: fractured tarsal bones (full recovery)	6	2,500
Lower limbs: fractured tarsal bones (with continuing disability)	12	7,500
Lower limbs: fractured tarsal bones — both feet (full recovery)	10	5,000
Lower limbs: fractured tarsal bones — both feet (with continuing disability)	10	15,000
Lower limbs: fractured tibia — shin bone (full recovery)	7	3,000
Lower limbs: fractured tibia (with continuing disability)	10	5,000
Lower limbs: fractured tibia — both legs (full recovery)	12	7,500
Lower limbs: fractured tibia — both legs (with continuing disability)	13	10,000
Lower limbs: paralysis of leg	18	25,000
Lower limbs: loss of leg below knee	19	30,000
Lower limbs: loss of leg above knee	20	40,000
Lower limbs: loss of both legs	23	100,000
Lower limbs: minor damage to tendon(s)/ligament(s) (full recovery)	1	1,000
Lower limbs: minor damage to tendon(s)/ligament(s) (with continuing disability)	7	3,000
Lower limbs: moderate damage to tendon(s)/ligament(s) (full recovery)	5	2,000
Lower limbs: moderate damage to tendon(s)/ligament(s) (with continuing disability)	10	5,000
Lower limbs: severe damage to tendon(s)/ligament(s) (full recovery)	7	3,000
Lower limbs: severe damage to tendon(s)/ligament(s) (with continuing disability)	12	7,500
Lower limbs: scarring: minor disfigurement	2	1,250
Lower limbs: scarring: significant disfigurement	4	1,750
Lower limbs: scarring: serious disfigurement	10	5,000
Lower limbs: sprained ankle — disabling for at least 6–13 weeks	1	1,000
Lower limbs: sprained ankle — disabling for more than 13 weeks	6	2,500
Lower limbs: sprained ankle — both feet — disabling for at least 6–13 weeks	5	2,000
Lower limbs: sprained ankle — both feet — disabling for more than 13 weeks	8	3,500
Medically recognised illness/condition (not psychiatric or psychological) Significantly disabling disorder where the symptoms and disability persist for more than 6 weeks from the incident/date of onset		
lasting 6 to 13 weeks	1	1,000
lasting up to 28 weeks	9	4,000
lasting over 28 weeks — but not permanent	12	7,500
permanent disability	17	20,000
Minor injuries: multiple (see notes)	1	1,000
Neck: burns: minor	3	1,500
Neck: burns: moderate	9	4,000
Neck: burns: severe	13	10,000
Neck: scarring: minor disfigurement	3	1,500
Neck: scarring: significant disfigurement	7	3,000
Neck: scarring: serious disfigurement	9	4,000

Neck: strained neck — disabling for 6–13 weeks	1	1,000
Neck: strained neck — disabling for more than 13 weeks	4	1,750
Neck: strained neck — seriously disabling — but not permanent	10	5,000
Neck: strained neck — seriously disabling — permanent	13	10,000
Neck: whiplash injury: effects lasting 6–13 weeks	1	1,000
Neck: whiplash injury: effects lasting more than 13 weeks	4	1,750
Neck: whiplash injury: seriously disabling — but not permanent	10	5,000
Neck: whiplash injury: seriously disabling — permanent	13	10,000

Physical abuse of Children (where individual injuries do not otherwise qualify)

Minor abuse — isolated or intermittent assault(s) beyond ordinary chastisement resulting in bruising, weals, hair pulled from scalp etc	1	1,000
Serious abuse — intermittent physical assaults resulting in an accumulation of healed wounds, burns or scalds, but with no appreciable disfigurement	5	2,000
Severe abuse — pattern of systematic violence against the child resulting in minor disfigurement	7	3,000
Persistent pattern of severe abuse over a period exceeding 3 years	11	6,000

Sexual Abuse of Children (not otherwise covered by sexual assault)

Minor isolated incidents — non-penetrative indecent acts	1	1,000
Pattern of serious abuse — repetitive, frequent non-penetrative indecent acts	5	2,000
Pattern of severe abuse — repetitive, frequent indecent acts involving digital or other non-penile penetration and/or oral genital contact	7	3,000
Pattern of severe abuse over a period exceeding 3 years	11	6,000
Repeated non-consensual vaginal and/or anal intercourse over a period up to 3 years	13	10,000
Repeated non-consensual vaginal and/or anal intercourse over a period exceeding 3 years	16	17,500

Sexual Assault (single incident — victim any age)

Minor indecent assault — non-penetrative indecent physical act over clothing	1	1,000
Serious indecent assault — non-penetrative indecent act under clothing	5	2,000
Severe indecent assault — indecent act involving digital, or other non-penile penetration, and/or oral/genital contact	7	3,000
Non-consensual vaginal and/or anal intercourse	12	7,500
Non-consensual vaginal and/or anal intercourse by two or more attackers	13	10,000
Non-consensual vaginal and/or anal intercourse with other serious bodily injuries	16	17,500

Shock (see notes)

Disabling, but temporary mental anxiety, medically verified	1	1,000
Disabling mental disorder, confirmed by psychiatric diagnosis:		
lasting up to 28 weeks	6	2,500
lasting over 28 weeks to one year	9	4,000
lasting over one year but not permanent	12	7,500
Permanently disabling mental disorder confirmed by psychiatric prognosis	17	20,000

Torso: back: fracture of vertebra (full recovery)	6	2,500
Torso: back: fracture of vertebra (continuing disability)	10	5,000
Torso: back: fracture of more than one vertebra (full recovery)	9	4,000
Torso: back: fracture of more than one vertebra (continuing disability)	12	7,500
Torso: back: prolapsed invertebral disc(s) — seriously disabling — not permanent	10	5,000
Torso: back: prolapsed invertebral disc(s) — seriously disabling — permanent	12	7,500
Torso: back: ruptured invertebral disc(s) requiring surgical removal	13	10,000
Torso: back: strained back — disabling for 6–13 weeks	1	1,000
Torso: back: strained back — disabling for more than 13 weeks	6	2,500
Torso: back: strained back — seriously disabling — but not permanent	10	5,000
Torso: back: strained back — seriously disabling — permanent	12	7,500
Torso: burns: minor	3	1,500
Torso: burns: moderate	9	4,000
Torso: burns: severe	13	10,000
Torso: punctured lung	7	3,000
Torso: two punctured lungs	11	6,000
Torso: collapsed lung	8	3,500
Torso: two collapsed lungs	12	7,500
Torso: permanent and disabling damage to lungs from smoke inhalation	10	5,000
Torso: loss of spleen	9	4,000
Torso: damage to testes	4	1,750
Torso: dislocated hip (full recovery)	4	1,750
Torso: dislocated hip (with continuing disability)	12	7,500
Torso: fractured hip	12	7,500
Torso: dislocated shoulder (full recovery)	4	1,750
Torso: dislocated shoulder (with continuing disability)	10	5,000
Torso: fractured rib	1	1,000
Torso: fractured rib(s) (two or more)	3	1,500
Torso: fractured clavicle — collar bone	5	2,000
Torso: two fractured clavicles	10	5,000
Torso: fractured coccyx — tail bone	6	2,500
Torso: fractured pelvis	12	7,500
Torso: fractured scapula — shoulder blade	6	2,500
Torso: two fractured scapula	11	6,000
Torso: fractured sternum — breast bone	6	2,500
Torso: frozen shoulder	8	3,500
Torso: hernia	8	3,500
Torso: injury requiring laparotomy	8	3,500
Torso: injury to genitalia requiring medical treatment — no permanent damage	4	1,750
Torso: injury to genitalia requiring medical treatment — permanent damage	10	5,000
Torso: loss of fertility	21	50,000
Torso: loss of kidney	17	20,000
Torso: loss of testicle	10	5,000
Torso: scarring: minor disfigurement	2	1,250
Torso: scarring: significant disfigurement	6	2,500
Torso: scarring: serious disfigurement	10	5,000
Upper limbs: burns: minor	3	1,500
Upper limbs: burns: moderate	9	4,000
Upper limbs: severe	13	10,000

Upper limbs: dislocated/fractured elbow (with full recovery)	7	3,000
Upper limbs: dislocated/fractured elbow (with continuing disasbility)	12	7,500
Upper limbs: two dislocated/fractured elbows (with full recovery)	12	7,500
Upper limbs: two dislocated/fractured elbows (with continuing disability	13	10,000
Upper limbs: dislocated finger(s) or thumb — one hand (full recovery)	2	1,250
Upper limbs: dislocated finger(s) or thumb — one hand (with continuing disability)	6	2,500
Upper limbs: dislocated finger(s) or thumb(s) — both hands (with continuing disability)	12	7,500
Upper limbs: fractured finger(s) or thumb — one hand (full recovery)	3	1,500
Upper limbs: fractured finger(s) or thumb — one hand (with continuing disability)	8	3,500
Upper limbs: fractured finger(s) or thumb(s) — both hands (full recovery)	9	4,000
Upper limbs: fractured finger(s) or thumb(s) — both hands (with continuing disability)	12	7,500
Upper limbs: fractured hand (full recovery)	5	2,000
Upper limbs: fractured hand (with continuing disability)	10	5,000
Upper limbs: two fractured hands (full recovery)	8	3,500
Upper limbs: two fractured hands (with continuing disability)	12	7,500
Upper limbs: fractured humerus — upper arm bone (full recovery)	7	3,000
Upper limbs: fractured humerus (with continuing disability)	10	5,000
Upper limbs: fractured humerus — both arms (full recovery)	12	7,500
Upper limbs: fractured humerus — both arms (with continuing disability)	13	10,000
Upper limbs: fractured radius — smaller forearm bone (full recovery)	7	3,000
Upper limbs: fractured radius (with continuing disability)	10	5,000
Upper limbs: fractured radius — both arms (full recovery)	12	7,500
Upper limbs: fractured radius — both arms (with continuing disability)	13	10,000
Upper limbs: fractured ulna — inner forearm bone (full recovery)	7	3,000
Upper limbs: fractured ulna (with continuing disability)	10	5,000
Upper limbs: fractured ulna — both arms (full recovery)	12	7,500
Upper limbs: fractured ulna — both arms (with continuing disability)	13	10,000
Upper limbs: fractured wrist — including scaphoid fracture (full recovery)	7	3,000
Upper limbs: fractured wrist — including scaphoid fracture (with continuing disability)	11	6,000
Upper limbs: two fractured wrists — including scaphoid fracture (full recovery)	11	6,000
Upper limbs: two fractured wrists — including scaphoid fracture (with continuing disability)	13	10,000
Upper limbs: fractured wrist — colles type (full recovery)	9	4,000
Upper limbs: fractured wrist — colles type (with continuing disability)	12	7,500
Upper limbs: two fractured wrists — colles type (full recovery)	12	7,500
Upper limbs: two fractured wrists — colles type (with continuing disability)	13	10,000
Upper limbs: partial loss of finger (other than thumb/index) (one joint)	6	2,500
Upper limbs: partial loss of thumb or index finger (one joint)	9	4,000
Upper limbs: loss of one finger other than index	10	5,000
Upper limbs: loss of index finger	12	7,500
Upper limbs: loss of two or more fingers	13	10,000
Upper limbs: loss of thumb	15	15,000
Upper limbs: loss of hand	20	40,000
Upper limbs: loss of both hands	23	100,000
Upper limbs: loss of arm	20	40,000
Upper limbs: loss of both arms	23	100,000
Upper limbs: paralysis of arm	19	30,000
Upper limbs: paralysis of both arms	22	75,000
Upper limbs: permanently & seriously impaired grip — one arm	12	7,500
Upper limbs: permanently & seriously impaired grip — both arms	15	15,000
Upper limbs: scarring: minor disfigurement	2	1,250

Upper limbs: scarring: significant disfigurement	6	2,500
Upper limbs: scarring: serious disfigurement	9	4,000
Upper limbs: minor damage to tendon(s)/ligament(s) (full recovery)	1	1,000
Upper limbs: minor damage to tendon(s)/ligament(s) (with continuing disability)	7	3,000
Upper limbs: moderate damage to tendon(s)/ligament(s) (full recovery)	5	2,000
Upper limbs: moderate damage to tendon(s)/ligament(s) (with continuing disability)	10	5,000
Upper limbs: severely damaged tendon(s)/ligament(s) (full recovery)	7	3,000
Upper limbs: severely damaged tendon(s)/ligament(s) (with permanent disability)	12	7,500
Upper limbs: sprained wrist — disabling for 6–13 weeks	1	1,000
Upper limbs: sprained wrist — disabling for more than 13 weeks	3	1,500
Upper limbs: two sprained wrists — disabling for 6–13 weeks	5	2,000
Upper limbs: two sprained wrists — disabling for more than 13 weeks	7	3,000

Notes to the Tariff

1. Minor multiple injuries will only qualify for compensation where the applicant has sustained at least three separate injuries of the type illustrated below, at least one of which must still have had significant residual effects six weeks after the incident. The injuries must also have necessitated at least two visits to or by a medical practitioner within that six-week period. Examples of qualifying injuries are:

    (a)   grazing, cuts, lacerations (no permanent scarring)

    (b)   severe and widespread brusing

    (c)   severe soft tissue injury (no permanent disability)

    (d)   black eye(s)

    (e)   bloody nose

    (f)   hair pulled from scalp

    (g)   loss of fingernail

2. Shock or 'nervous shock' may be taken to include conditions attributed to post-traumatic stress disorder, depression and similar generic terms covering:

    (a)   such psychological symptoms as anxiety, tension, insomnia, irritability, loss of confidence, agoraphobia and pre-occupation with thoughts of guilt or self-harm; and

    (b)   related physical symptoms such as alopecia, asthma, eczema, enuresis and psoriasis. Disability in this context will include impaired work (or school) performance, significant adverse effects on social relationships and sexual dysfunction.

Appendix Four The New Scheme's Guide to Applicants for Loss of Earnings and Special Expenses

INTRODUCTION

1. The Scheme provides that in addition to a standard (tariff) amount for your injury, payment may also be made for your loss of earnings or earning capacity, and/or special expenses, *provided that you have been incapacitated for more than a full 28 weeks.*

2. This Guide explains the circumstances in which you may qualify for these additional payments and tells you how we calculate them. It is not a substitute for the provisions of the Scheme itself, under which your claim will be assessed according to your particular circumstances, but is simply aimed at enabling you to understand how these provisions work and to make a claim with as little trouble as possible. You may, of course, wish to seek professional or other advice. We do not require you to do so but if you choose to get such advice, you are reminded that the Scheme does not allow us to pay your costs.

3. If you are a police officer, firefighter, nurse or someone similarly in a structured career, you may have available the services of a trade union or staff association with arrangements to provide you with professional advice on the calculation of your claim and to present us with the details. If that is so, or you are otherwise represented, we will correspond with those acting on your behalf unless you tell us not to. In other cases, we will correspond directly with you to explain our assessment of your claim.

4. Where references are made in this Guide to paragraphs of the Scheme, the paragraph numbers are given in bold type.

ELIGIBILITY

5. The main eligibility rules for applications under the Scheme as a whole are in **Paragraphs 6** to **16** and explained in the Guide to the Criminal Injuries Compensation Scheme.

6.   There are additional rules and provisions applicable to claims for loss of earnings and special expenses which this section explains.

Loss of Earnings (Paragraph 30)

7.   The main rules are that:
the injury must have been the direct cause of your loss of earnings, or your loss of capacity to earn your living;
and
your loss must have lasted longer than 28 full weeks.
The period of 28 weeks will usually run from the date of the injury or if, for example, you returned to work the next day but later had to be admitted to hospital for lengthy treatment and convalescence as a result of the injury, the period would run from the date of your admission.

8.   *No compensation for loss of earnings is payable for the first 28 weeks.* The calculation of your loss of earnings therefore starts at week 29 from the date on which the loss began and runs to the date on which you returned to work, or for such period as is considered by us to be reasonable on the information we have about your claim.

9.   If you were not in work at the time of the injury but had an offer of employment which the injury prevented you from taking up, we will take any evidence you can provide about this into account.

Special Expenses (Paragraph 35)

10.   The main eligibility rule for a claim for special expenses is that the expenses must be a direct result of any injury which has caused you to lose earnings or earning capacity, or to be similarly incapacitated, *for longer than 28 weeks.*

11.   If you are not normally employed (for example retired, in full-time education or looking for work) we will assess from the medical information the extent to which you were incapacitated (i.e., prevented from going about the ordinary business of life) and whether the period of incapacity was, or is likely to be, longer than 28 weeks.

12.   Provided that you are incapacitated for a full 28 weeks, special expenses incurred by you from the date of the injury (provided the minimum qualifying period as above is met) can be taken into account in our assessment of the amount payable.

CALCULATION OF LOSS OF EARNINGS

13.   The calculation is based on a comparison of your earnings or other income before and after the injury. If there is a loss to you as a *direct result of the injury,* we take that figure and deduct from it any financial benefits you have received which also result from the injury.

14. **Paragraphs 30–34 (compensation for loss of earnings) and 45–49 (effect on awards of other payments)** are the detailed provisions. Before explaining these, the next paragraph gives examples of the factors which we take into account in our assessment.

15. We must be sure that your loss of earnings results directly from the criminal injury and not wholly or in part from other factors, for example:

— health problems before the injury;
— a previous injury (caused perhaps by sport, or an accident at work);
— the insecurity of your type of employment; or
— if you are self-employed, trading and cash-flow problems unconnected with the injury.

We need to be satisfied also that the loss could not reasonably be offset, at least in part, by other earnings, for example by your finding another job within your physical/intellectual capacity, if you lost your job because of the injury.

CALCULATION UP TO DATE OF ASSESSMENT (PAST LOSS)

16. **Paragraph 31** deals with claims where the loss of earnings has ended before, or continues to the date on which your claim is assessed. The calculation in most cases should be quite simple because it is based on what you can prove has actually happened to your earnings or other income, and our confirmation of any financial benefits you have received, as a result of the injury. The financial benefits have to be taken into account because you are not entitled to be compensated for the same amount of loss from more than one source of public money.

17. The following calculation is an example of how this is done:

Case Summary — 1

The applicant was assaulted, suffering a fractured femur in both legs. His regular net weekly pay (i.e., after deduction of income tax and national insurance contributions) was £400 at the time of the injury. He was unable to return to his job for 12 months, during which period he received social security benefits (assumed for this example to be £100 per week). In the meantime, his assailant had been convicted and ordered to pay him £500 under a court compensation order, of which £200 had been paid when his claim was assessed.

Calculation of Award	£	*Notes*
A Standard amount under Tariff of Injuries	7,500	**Paragraph 25 level 12**
Past loss of earnings week 29–52, 24 weeks at £400 per week	9,600	**Paragraph 31**
less Social security benefits (e.g., short-term incapacity benefit/income support) at £100 per week	2,400	**Paragraph 45(a)**
B Net loss	7,200	
Total award (A + B)	14,700	
less Court compensation paid	200	**Paragraph 48(c)(iii)**
Award payable	14,500	

CALCULATION OF LOSS CONTINUING FROM DATE OF ASSESSMENT (FUTURE LOSS)

18.   The calculation of what loss of earnings you can reasonably be expected to suffer in future as a result of the injury may be more complicated. It often involves some assessment, at the time when the loss as in the example above is calculated, about whether it will continue, for how long and at what rate. Because ordinary life is subject to so many uncertainties, no one can say for sure what your future earnings would have been had you not been injured. The calculation of future loss may therefore be based on an estimate of what your future earnings might have been without the injury and what you can still earn.

The multiplicand

19.   The first step in the calculation is to work out the annual rate of loss, otherwise known as the *multiplicand*, **(Paragraph 32)**. That is done from the figures given in the example above, with adjustments to take account of any changes to the annual rate of loss which are likely to arise in the future. You may, for example, have had a valid expectation of promotion which would have increased your earnings, or, if you have had to leave your former employment because of the injury, you may be capable of obtaining other employment which would reduce your loss. Or where the injury caused your early/medical retirement under an occupational pension scheme, we assess your claim on the basis of your pension and any benefits or earnings to the point of normal occupational retirement and for periods beyond. We therefore need to obtain as much information as we can from you, your employer(s) and the Benefits Agency where appropriate.

20.   It follows that there may be different multiplicands applicable to different future periods of loss. In all cases, an assessment of how long the period or periods will be, in terms of years, is made.

The multiplier

21.   The multiplier is the number by which the multiplicand is to be multiplied in order to convert your future annual losses into a single capital lump sum payable now.

22.   Because this lump sum is intended to be the *present value* of losses which will be incurred in future, account has to be taken of the interest which you could receive from investing it. The table in **Note 3** to the Scheme (reproduced below) illustrates that, for example, a loss continuing for 10 years from the present could attract a multiplier of 8. This is because for an annual loss of, say, £10,000 starting now, a capital sum of £80,000 suitably invested could produce, from payment of interest and gradual withdrawal of capital, an annual income of £10,000 for the full 10 years.

Illustrative Multipliers

Years of loss	Multiplier	Years of Loss	Multiplier
5	5	15	10.5
6	5.5	16	11
7	6	17	11.5
8	7	18	12
9	7.5	19	12.5
10	8	20	13
11	8.5	25	15
12	9	30	16
13	9.5	35	17
14	10	40	18

23.   **Paragraph 32** also says that, in choosing a multiplier, we may refer to Actuarial Tables for use in Personal Injury and Fatal Accident Cases published by the Government Actuary's Department and take account of any factors and contingencies which we think are relevant.

24.   The Actuarial Tables, which can be purchased from HMSO, provide a range of multipliers according to age, the different life expectancy of men and women, their different retirement ages, and when the loss starts (either from the present or at some future point). We use them where appropriate to refine our selection of the multiplier.

25.   Neither **Note 3** to the Scheme, not the Actuarial Tables, however, take account of the risks or chances in normal life (contingencies) or special factors which may be present in individual cases (other than mortality). As a general rule, when considering loss of earnings, we will reduce the multiplier by 10% to take account of ordinary risks such as illness, redundancy, temporary unemployment or accident.

Where we consider it appropriate, a further reduction will be made for particular factors such as a likelihood that the applicant would not always have been in full employment right up to normal retirement.

26.   The following is an example of a future loss assessment in a case where the applicant, although having to change his job as a result of the injury, remains capable of earning, albeit at a lower income level than before the injury.

Case summary — 2

The example follows on from the previous one and assumes that the broken femurs have resulted in a continuing disability, which prevents the applicant, now aged 40, from returning to the job he had before the injury. He is nevertheless re-employed on other work by his company where his net pay is now £300 instead of £400 per week. His future net earnings loss is therefore assessed at £100 per week, or £5,200 per year. His company pension would also be £1,000 less on retirement at age 65. There is a general risk of redundancy in his field of work.

	Calculation of Award	£	*Notes*
A	Standard amount under Tariff of Injuries	10,000	**level 13**
B	Past loss of earnings (as in case summary 1)	7,200	**Paragraphs 31 and 45(a)**
	Future loss of earnings from age 40 to 65:		**Paragraph 32**
	Net annual loss or *multiplicand*: £5,200; Period of loss: 25 years; *Multiplier*: 15 less 10% for ordinary contingencies and 10% for insecurity of his type of employment apart from		
C	the injury: 12 × £5,200	62,400	
	Loss of pension from age 65: Net annual loss or *multiplicand*: £1,000; *Multiplier* (from Actuarial Tables) to take account of payment now for a loss to be incurred in 25 years		
D	time: 2 × £1,000	2,000	
	Total award (A + B + C + D)	81,600	
	less Court compensation paid	200	**Paragraph 48(c)(iii)**
	Award payable	81,400	

27.   **Paragraph 34** applies a ceiling to the net loss of earnings which we can take into account. The figure is one and a half times the gross average industrial earnings *at the time when your claim is assessed*. The current figure (at February 1996) is some £28,500 a year, so net ('take-home') pay which is above that amount cannot be considered.

CALCULATION OF SPECIAL EXPENSES

27.   **Paragraph 35** enables us to consider claims for practical, medical and care costs, provided you have been incapacitated for longer than 28 weeks as a direct result of your injury. *These costs are payable from the date of the injury.* Social security benefits in respect of any of these costs will be deducted, as will payments from personal insurance in claims made under **Paragraph 35(c)** and **(d)**.

28.   **Paragraph 35(a)** covers damage to property or equipment belonging to you on which you relied as a physical aid. This is intended to enable us to make payments for items such as spectacles and dentures. We will ask you for the relevant receipts.

29.   **Paragraph 35(b)** covers expenses such as national health prescriptions, dental and optical charges and costs of travel to and from hospital for treatment. These must have been met by you. Help may be availble for these costs from the Benefits Agency. You can obtain information from your local office or from the Benefits Agency, Health Benefits Division, Sandyford House, Newcastle, NE2 1DB.

30.   **Paragraph 35(c)** enables us to consider the cost of private treatment. Both the treatment itself and the cost of it must be considered reasonable in the circumstances of your case. It may be that the particular kind of treatment you require is not routinely available under the NHS in your area — some types of cosmetic surgery or special dental work for example — but it will be for you to show that private treatment is a reasonable option.

31.   **Paragraph 35(d)** covers special equipment, adaptations to your home, and/or the costs of caring for you either at your home or, for example, in a nursing home. Claims under this paragraph will usually come from those who are most seriously injured. If you are in that situation, the following notes may be helpful.

— *Special equipment* covers aids to mobility whether at home or outside, including specially adapted vehicles, wheelchairs, walking aids, and kitchen implements designed to help those with weakened grip. We will ask you for receipts or an estimate of costs as applicable.

— *Adaptations to accommodation* can include both internal and external works to improve mobility and access. We will ask you for plans and estimates.

— *Care* costs are assessed on the basis of what is reasonably necessary in your case. We will consider your circumstances carefully, taking account of the services which may be provided to you free of charge from other sources, such as the NHS or local authority. If you are being looked after at home by a relative or friend we will consider what the costs are to the carer in question and the level of care provided.

32.   Where there will be recurring annual, or periodic special expenses (for example in the replacement of equipment), we will calculate a multiplicand and select a multiplier (see **Paragraphs 19–23** of this Guide) to produce a lump sum payable against your future expenses. Because these may be more predictable than loss of earnings, the multiplier indicated by **Note 3** to the Scheme and refined as appropriate by reference to the Actuarial Tables (Paragraph 24 of this Guide) is more likely to stand without much, if any, adjustment.

MAXIMUM AMOUNT PAYABLE AND METHOD OF PAYMENT

33.   The total maximum amount payable in respect of the claim as a whole (covering standard (tariff) amount, loss of earnings, and/or special expenses) is £500,000 **(Paragraph 23)**.

34.   Awards under the Scheme are normally paid as a single lump sum **(Paragraph 51**, which also covers interim payments), but **Paragraph 52** enables us, on the instructions of the applicant or his representative, to pay an award, or part of it, in the form of an annuity, which can provide a secure, tax-free income. Any expenses incurred in such instructions will be met from the award.

REOPENING, REVIEW AND APPEAL

35.   The Guide to the Criminal Injuries Compensation Scheme briefly explains the provisions for reopening of cases **(Paragraph 56)**, review of decisions made by the Authority, **(Paragraphs 58–60)** and for appeals against reviewed decisions to the Criminal Injuries Compensation Appeals Panel **(Paragraphs 61–82)**. Your attention is simply drawn here to those rights to seek redress if you consider that our assessment is wrong.

Appendix Five   The New Scheme's Guide to Applicants for Compensation in Fatal Cases

INTRODUCTION

1.   Where a victim has died as a result of a criminal injury, compensation may be payable if you are a qualifying claimant under the provisions of the Scheme. Supplementary compensation may also be payable if the victim has died following, but not as a result of a criminal injury. The reasonable cost of funeral expenses may also be reimbursed to anyone who has paid them, even if he or she would otherwise be ineligible under the Scheme.

2.   This Guide explains the circumstances in which you may qualify for compensation and tells you how it is calculated. It is not a substitute for the provisions of the Scheme itself, under which your claim will be assessed according to your particular circumstances, but is simply aimed at enabling you to understand how these provisions work and to make a claim with as little trouble as possible. You may, of course, wish to seek professional or other advice. We do not require you to do so but if you choose to get such advice, you are reminded that the Scheme does not allow us to pay your costs.

3.   You do not need to obtain the services of a solicitor or trade union to represent you in connection with your application, but if you choose to be represented you must tell us whether we should correspond directly with your representative or with you.

4.   Where references are made in this Guide to paragraphs of the Scheme, the paragraph numbers are given in bold type.

ELIGIBILITY

5.   Consideration of applications for compensation in respect of fatal cases is subject to the main eligibility requirements of the Scheme and apply to the applicant and the deceased (**Paragraphs 13 and 14**).

WHO CAN APPLY

6.   You can apply for compensation if you are a dependant or relative (as shown in the next paragraph) of someone who died as a result of a criminal injury, or who was criminally injured but died from some other cause.

7.   A dependant or relative will be known, for the purposes of the Scheme, as a qualifying claimant, who at the time of the deceased's death was:—

(a)   *the spouse* of the deceased, who was formally married to and living with the deceased as husband and wife in the same household immediately before the date of death; or

(b)   *a person* who, though not formally married to the deceased, lived with the deceased as husband and wife in the same household immediately before the date of death and had been so living for at least two years before that date; or

(c)   *the spouse* of the deceased who, though not living with the deceased immediately before the date of death, was at that time financially supported by him/her; *Note: a spouse living apart from and not financially dependent on the deceased is not a qualifying claimant.*

(d)   *a former spouse* of the deceased, who was financially supported by him/her immediately before the date of death; *Note: a former spouse does not qualify for the standard amount of compensation under **Paragraph 39** of the Scheme.*

(e)   *a parent* of the deceased, whether or not the natural child, provided that he/she was accepted by the deceased as a child of his/her family or was dependent on him/her. *Note: The definition of a 'child' is not restricted to a person below the age of 18.*

Any of the above may also apply where the victim has died from the injuries, even if an award has been made to the victim while still alive.

COMPENSATION FOR DEATH AS A RESULT OF A CRIMINAL INJURY

8.   If you are a qualifying claimant and the deceased died as a result of the criminal injury, we will assess your eligibility for compensation in the form of a Fatal Award. A Fatal Award can comprise one or more of the compensation payments listed below:

*Standard Amount of Compensation (**Paragraph 39** of the Scheme).*

*Dependency (**Paragraph 40** of the Scheme).*

*Loss of Parental Services for a child under 18 years of age (**Paragraph 42** of the Scheme).*

STANDARD AMOUNT

9.   It is of course impossible to say that any amount of money can make up for the death of a close relative. The standard amount set by the Tariff is intended to give some recognition to the grief and distress caused by a death resulting from a criminal injury.

10.   Where there is only one qualifying claimant the standard amount of compensation will be Level 13 of the Tariff. Where there is more than one qualifying claimant the standard amount of compensation for each claimant will be Level 10 of the Tariff. The Scheme does not provide for the standard amount of compensation to be paid to a former spouse of the deceased. **(Paragraph 39.)**

DEPENDENCY

11.   If you are a qualifying claimant who was financially dependent on the deceased, you may be eligible to apply for additional compensation for that dependency. The period of loss will begin from the date of the deceased's death. Financial dependency will not be applicable however, if the deceased's only normal income was from social security benefits. Cases where, for example, the deceased relied temporarily on social security benefits but had an offer of employment which he or she was expecting to take up, would however be considered on the basis of the information supplied. **(Paragraph 40.)**

12.   To calculate the compensation for loss of financial support we first assess the total net annual loss to the qualifying claimant which we call the 'multiplicand'. A multiplier is then applied. It is calculated by taking the number of years the qualifying claimant would have been dependent on the deceased (where the claimant is the widow/widower, this period would usually run to the date on which the deceased would have retired) and applying the figure indicated by the *illustrative* table in **Note 3** to the Scheme. This is further explained in **Paragraphs 14** to 17 below.

LOSS OF PARENTAL SERVICES

13.   A qualifying claimant under 18 years of age may be eligible, in addition to any sum apportioned under Paragraph 14, for compensation for loss of a parental services at an annual rate of Level 5 to the Tariff. Compensation may also be payable to meet other resultant losses, e.g., any additional costs of childcare or loss of earnings suffered by an adult in looking after the child. An appropriate multiplier, applied to the period until the child reaches the age of 18, will be used.

Note:— Unlike assessments under the Fatal Accidents Act, the Scheme recognises the services contributed by both mothers and fathers to the upbringing of children. Children who claim personally and who were receiving parental services from the deceased parent receive a Level 5 loss of services award whether it was the mother or the father who was the victim.

THE MULTIPLICAND

14.   When the claim for financial dependency is made by an adult who was living with the deceased, we start the calculation to determine the dependency by taking the total amount of the deceased's annual earnings and deducting a percentage for the

cost of the deceased's personal expenses. Where the deceased had a spouse (which includes someone with whom the deceased was living, as explained in Paragraph 7) and there were no children 33 per cent will normally be deducted. Where there was a spouse and children 25 per cent will normally be deducted. Where the spouse was also earning, his/her net earnings will also be taken into account. Part of the total sum assessed may be apportioned to the children.

15.   We will also take account of any changes to the annual rate of loss which may have arisen, e.g., the promotion prospects of the deceased.

16.   In assessing the dependency we must also deduct any social security benefits, and any insurance payments, pensions or other entitlements resulting from the death and which have not accrued solely as a result of payments by the deceased or a dependant, because you are not entitled to be compensated for the same loss from more than one source.

17.   There may be different multiplicands for different periods or types of loss or benefits received.

THE MULTIPLIER

18.   The multiplier is the number by which the multiplicand will be multiplied to determine the amount payable as a capital lump sum representing the present value of the dependency over the years ahead. It may also be used to calculate the value of benefits to be received which are to be deducted in the calculation of dependency. The multiplier will be selected by reference to **Note 3** of the Scheme and to the Actuarial Tables for use in Personal Injury and Fatal Accident cases as published by the Government Actuary's Department. We may take account of any factors and contingencies which we think are relevant.

19.   The Actuarial Tables, which you can purchase from HMSO, provide a range of multipliers according to age, the different life expectancy of men and women and their different retirement ages and when the loss starts (either from the present or at some future point). We use them, where appropriate, to refine our selection of the multiplier.

20.   Neither **Note 3** to the Scheme nor the Actuarial Tables, however, take account of the risks or chances in normal life (contingencies) or special factors which may be present in individual cases (other than mortality). As a general rule, we will reduce the multiplier by 10 per cent to take account of ordinary risks. Where we consider it appropriate, a further reduction will be made for particular factors such as a likelihood that the deceased would not always have been in full employment up to the normal retirement age.

FUNERAL EXPENSES

21.   Where the victim dies as a result of a criminal injury, an application will be considered for reimbursement of reasonable funeral expenses from the person incurring those expenses, even where that person is otherwise ineligible to claim

under the Scheme (**Paragraph 37**). In calculating the expenses to be reimbursed we will take account of the religious and cultural background of the victim and his/her family.

EXAMPLE

22.   The example at the end of the guide shows how the approach to calculation and assessment in a fatal application described in paragraphs 9 to 21 above can work in practice.

AWARD TO VICTIM BEFORE DEATH

23.   Applications for compensation in fatal cases can be made even if an award has previously been made to the victim for that injury, before his/her death. Applications will be subject to the conditions in **Paragraphs 56–7** of the Scheme (reopening of cases). Any compensation (except funeral expenses and the standard amount of compensation) payable to qualifying claimants will be reduced by the amount paid to the victim.

DEATH FOLLOWING, BUT NOT AS A RESULT OF, A CRIMINAL INJURY

24.   A qualifying claimant who was financially dependent on a victim may be eligible for supplementary compensation in respect of the victim's loss of earnings (except for the first 28 weeks) and any special expenses incurred if the victim died, but the death was not as a result of the criminal injury. Supplementary compensation is not payable if the victim [had (sic)] not been awarded compensation for such loss of earnings or special expenses prior to death.

MAXIMUM AWARD AND LIMIT ON RATE OF LOSS

25.   **Paragraphs 23, 43 and 44** of the Scheme impose an overall limit of £500,000 payable in respect of fatal injury, irrespective of the number of claimants.

25.   **Paragraph 34** of the Scheme applies a limit on the net loss of earnings which we can take into account when assessing applications under **Paragraphs 40, 41, 43** and **44** of the Scheme. The figure is one and a half times the gross average industrial earnings of the deceased and qualifying claimant(s) at the time when an application is assessed. The current figure (at February 1996) is £28,500 a year, so net ('take-home') pay which is above that amount cannot be considered.

METHOD OF PAYMENT

26.   Awards under the Scheme are normally paid as a single lump sum (**Paragraph 51**), but **Paragraph 52** enables us, on the instructions of the applicant or his representative, to pay an award, or part of it, in the form of an annuity, which

can provide a secure, tax-free income. Any expenses incurred in such instructions will be met from the award.

REOPENING, REVIEW AND APPEAL

27.   The Guide to the Criminal Injuries Compensation Scheme briefly explains the provisions for re-opening of cases (**Paragraph 56**), review of decisions made by the Authority (**Paragraphs 58–60**) and for appeals against reviewed decisions to the Criminal Injuries Compensation Appeals Panel (**Paragraphs 61–82**). Your attention is simply drawn here to those rights to seek redress if you consider that our assessment is wrong.

EXAMPLE OF FATAL INJURY CALCULATION

Husband and Wife, Both Working, Two Young Children

The husband was aged 32 when he died as a result of a criminal injury. He had been in full time employment for the past 10 years and was earning £240 net per week before his death. His employers certified that he had been due for promotion shortly, taking his net earnings to £265 per week. His wife, 30, was earning £96 net per week. There are two children, aged five and three.

	£	*Scheme references*
Dependency		
Joint weekly income (£265 + £96) is £361. Dependency is 75 per cent of that figure (£271) less the wife's income (£96) = £175 per week or £9,100 per year. The period of loss (to deceased's retirement at age 65) is 33 years, for which the indicative multiplier is 17, reduced to 15 to take account of contingencies. 15 × £9,100 =	136,500	**Note 3**
Less		
Widow's benefit (lump sum)	1,000	**Paragraph 45**
Widowed mother's allowance £3,060 per year to age 45 when the younger child becomes 18; multiplier 10 =	30,600	
Widow's children's allowance:		
1 aged 3, £575 per year to age 18, multiplier 10	5,750	**Note 3**
1 aged 5, £512 per year to age 18, multiplier 9	4,610	

Widow's pension from age 45, £920 per year, multiplier 5 (remainder of dependency multiplier of 15)	4,600	
Employer's pensions		
Employer pays widow £1,500, and children £400 each per year (until aged 18). These sums are taxable so only half is deductible.		**Paragraph 47**
Widow £750 per year × 15	11,250	**Note 3**
younger child £200 × 10	2,000	
older child £200 x 9	1,800	
Widow also received a taxable gratuity of £2,000, of which half is deductible	1,000	**Paragraph 47**
Total to be deducted	62,610	
Dependency total	73,890	
Dependency award to widow (see below for children's awards)	55,890	
Fatal injury payment	5,000	**Paragraph 39**
	60,890	

Children's awards

Younger child, loss of parental services £2,000 × £0	20,000	**Paragraph 42**
Fatal injury payment	5,000	
Dependency apportionment	10,000	
Older child, loss of parental services £2,000 × 9	18,000	
Fatal injury payment	5,000	
Dependency apportionment	8,000	
	66,000	

Funeral expenses

Cost paid by widow	950	**Paragraph 37**

Summary

Total award (including funeral expenses) to widow	61,840	
Total award to younger child	35,000	
Total award to older child	31,000	
	127,840	

Index

Abandoned application 38–9
Accountability
  complaints procedure 28
  internal 28
  judicial review 13, 26–8, 59, 145–6
  New scheme 24–5, 28
  Old Scheme 24, 26–8
  ombudsman 24, 25, 257–8
  parliamentary 24–5, 258–9
Adjournment of hearings 73–4
Adjudicators 20, 21, 68–9, 71
Administration of awards 50–1
Animals, causing injury 83
Appeals
  adjournments 73–4
  adjudicators 68–9, 71
  burden of proof 64, 67
  categories 63–4
  concerning awards 65–6, 279–80
  concerning time limits 64, 279
  confidentiality 72–3
  decisions 70
  evidence 63, 69
  extension of time 63
  failure to attend 75
  fatal injuries 306
  fresh determination 66–7
  frivolous or vexatious 71
  hearing summary 67–8
  New Scheme 63–75
  oral hearings 65–75, 280–1
  privacy 72–3
  procedure 63, 67–71
  reducing amount of award 71
  rehearings 74–5, 281–2

Appeals — continued
  reopening of cases 64
  review compared 61
  review decisions 278–9
  witnesses 68, 69
  written notice 67
Applicants see Eligible persons
Application
  abandoned 38–9
  co-operation with authorities in 156
  costs 51
  decision to apply 36–7
  determination see Determination of
      application
  false 38–9
  fraudulent 38–9
  initial determination 39–42
  procedure 37
  proportion of successful applicants
      42–3
  reference number 38
  time limits 141–3
    discretion to waive 143–6
  verification 37–8
Application rates 30–7
  decision to apply 36–7
  ignorance of rights 34–6
  number of crimes of violence 31–4
  report to police precondition 33
Arson 86, 98
Assessment of compensation
  common law basis 186–9
  fatal accident actions 186, 189
  fatal injuries 272–4
    bereavement award 135, 219–20

Assessment of compensation — *continued*
   cause of death
      New Scheme   218–19
      Old Scheme   216–18
   children of the family   223
   cohabitees   222
   death not result of criminal injury
      305
   deductions   221–2
   example of calculation   306–7
   funeral expenses   223, 304–5
   general damages   219–20
   loss of dependency   218–19, 303
   loss of parental services
      221, 223–5, 303
   loss of support   220–3
   maximum award   305
   payment method   305–6
   pre-death award   305
   qualifying claimants   218–19
   special damages   220–3
   standard amount   219–20, 302–3
  levels   284
  maximum amounts   300, 305
  mitigation of loss   189
  multiplicand   188, 209–10, 224, 296,
     303–4
  multipliers   188, 197, 209–10, 224–5,
     297–8
   fatal injuries   304
   illustrative   284, 297
  New Scheme *see* tariff scheme
  Old Scheme   186–9
  personal injuries
   adaptations to accommodation   214
   bands   199
   care   214–16
     carer's loss of earnings   215
     future   188
     long term   211, 214–15
   common law damages   192–5
   expenses of application   216
   general damages   192–202
     Board's guidelines
       levels   194
       tariffs compared   200
   loss or damage to property   212
   loss of dependency   191
   medical expenses   211, 212–14
   multiple injuries   202–3
   New Scheme, tariff   197–202, 285–02
   Old Scheme   192–7

Assessment of compensation — *continued*
   rape and aftermath   195–7, 204
   review of tariff *see* tariff scheme
   Secretary of State powers   199
   special damages   204–16
   special equipment   214
   special expenses   211–16, 272,
     299–300
   unprovided for injuries   203–4
   see also Loss of earnings and earning
     capacity
  personal injury actions   186, 189
  remarriage prospects   222, 234
  Scottish law   188–9
  size of award   189–90
  tariff scheme   187, 190–2, 197–202,
    285–92
   annual review   199–200
   Board's guidelines compared   200
   insufficiency   201–2
   Secretary of State powers   199
   total maximum   191–2
   unlawful   190
Association of Personal Injury
    Lawyers   19
Awards
  administration   50–1
  appeals   65–6, 279–80
  assessment *see* Assessment of
    compensation
  entitlement   43–5
  interim   45
  management   50–1
  notification of outcome   42–3, 44
  payment   49–50
   fatal injuries   305–6
  personal representatives   44–5
  personal to applicant   44
  proportion of successful applicants
    42–3
  'qualifying award'   50
  reconsideration of decisions   47–9
  reduction by adjudicators   71
  reopening   45–7
  size   189–90
  structured settlements   50–1
  tariff scheme *see* Tariff scheme
  time of vesting   43–4

Bereavement award   135, 219–20
British Crime Survey   32, 33
Burden of proof, appeals   64, 67

Bystanders 29
law enforcement 100–1

Care 214–16
carer's loss of earnings 215
future 188
long term 211, 214–15
Channel Tunnel 78, 283
Character of applicant *see* Undeserving
applicants
Character of victim, investigation 37
Children
abuse within family 130–1, 132
dangerous games 169–70
interest of child 131–2
juvenile convictions 177
local authorities 129–30
management of awards 50–1
personal injuries 129–32
persons with parental rights 129, 132
sex abuse 144–5
social services directors 130
victims 129–32, 144–5, 169–70
waiving time limits 144–5
Cohabitees, domestic violence 137–8
Common law damages, compensation
based on 17
Compensable persons *see* Eligible persons
Compensation
assessment *see* Assessment of
compensation
award *see* Awards
Compensation orders 11
deduction from award 239–41
Complaints procedures 28
Confidentiality 72–3
Consent, mistaken belief 90
Co-operation with authorities 151–6
application 156
bringing offender to justice 155–6
Old Scheme 151–2, 153
reporting incident 33, 151
'appropriate authority' 154
circumstances of injury 152–5
earliest opportunity 153–4
Costs
of application 51
expenses 51
Council on Tribunals 25
Crimes of violence 79–90
acts and omissions 83
animals 83

Crimes of violence — *continued*
consent 90
defining 79–82
external elements 82–8
fault elements 88–90
intention 85–6
numbers 31–4
pre-birth 88–9
property crimes 3, 84–5
rail track suicides 80–1
reasonable use of force 89–90
recklessness 85–6, 88
suicides on rail track 90–2
victimising events *see* Victimising events
see also individual crimes eg Arson; Sex
offences
Criminal injuries 76–9
establishment 120–7
causation 125–7
proof of victimising event 120–5
jurisdiction 77–9
aircraft 77, 283
Channel Tunnel 78, 283
European Convention countries 78–9
land borders 77, 283
Scotland 79
territorial waters 77–8
minor injuries 149–50
proof of victimising event 120–5
traffic accidents *see* Traffic accidents
victimising events *see* Victimising events
Criminal Injuries Compensation Act (1995),
text 251–60
Criminal Injuries Compensation Appeals
Panel 20, 21–2
Criminal Injuries Compensation
Authority x, 20–2
Criminal Injuries Compensation Board
ix, 1
hearing reference by 54
Criminal Injuries Compensation Scheme
ix
creation 1–29
new scheme *see* New Scheme
old scheme *see* Old Scheme
tariff scheme introduction 1–2
unlawfulness of tariff scheme 2
see also individual aspects
Criminal record 170–81
aggregation of points 177–8
discretion of Board 170–1
going straight 176

Criminal record — *continued*
juveniles 177
New Scheme 173–81
Old Scheme 170–3
penalty points 173–81
rehabilitation 162, 176–7, 178–9
unconnected with injury
158–9, 171–2
see also Undeserving applicants

Damages *see* General damages; Special
damages
Decisions
reconsideration *see* Reconsideration of
decisions
review *see* Reviews
Deductions 226–41, 274–5
compensation awards 227
compensation from offender 239–41
deductible benefits and payments 227
establishment of payments received
231–2
exempt payments 227
fatal injury compensation 221–2
financial minimum and 147
impact on award 228
insurance payments 208, 209, 226, 227
occupational arrangements 237–9
personal and non-employer insurance
235–7
loss of earnings and earning capacity
compensation 208, 209
non-deductible payments 228
children born of rape compensation
231
funeral expenses compensation
230–1
pension payments 208, 209, 221–2,
226, 227
fatal injuries 221–2
occupational arrangements 237–9
personal and non-employer insurance
235–7
previous compensation payments
241
social security benefits 208, 209, 221–2,
226, 227, 232–5
fatal injuries 221–2
impact of provisions 234–5
income tax payments 233–4
remarriage prospects 234
scope 232–3

Delay
determination of application delays
40, 42
interim awards and 45
in reporting incident 153–4
Dependants
eligibility for award *see* Eligibility
fatal injury claims 133, 134–5, 136
loss of dependency 19, 191, 218–19,
303
undeserving 161
Deterioration in condition of victim 15
interim awards 45–6, 47
Determination of application 276
delays 40, 42
delegation to administrative staff 40–1
initial 39–42
New Scheme 42
Old Scheme 39–42, 247–9
Disease 105
Domestic violence 137–9
award benefiting assailant 138, 139
cohabitees 137–8

Eligibility 140–85
co-operation with authorities 151–6
application 156
bringing offender to justice 155–6
Old Scheme 151–2, 153
reporting incident 33, 151
'appropriate authority' 154
circumstances of injury 152–5
earliest opportunity 153–4
'deserving characteristics' 159
fatal injuries 300
financial minimum
deductions 147
implementation 149–50
increase in threshold 150–1
minor injuries 149
multiple minor injuries 149–50
New Scheme provision 147–9
Old Scheme provision 146–7
policy 146
reduction of claim for character of
applicant 148
threshold 32
good character relevance 160–1
loss of earnings 293–4
special expenses 293–4
time limits 141–3
discretion to waive 143–6

Eligibility — *continued*
  ignorance of Scheme 145
  judicial review of decision 145–6
  to apply for compensation 266–7
  to receive compensation 267–8
  undeserving applicants *see* Undeserving
    applicants
Eligible persons 128–39
  character *see* Undeserving applicants
  child victims
    abuse within family 130–1, 132
    interest of child 131–2
    local authorities 129–30
    personal injuries 129–32
    persons with parental rights 129, 132
    sex abuse 144–5
    social services directors 130
    waiving time limits 144–5
  conditions *see* Eligibility
  criminal records *see* Criminal record;
    Undeserving applicants
  domestic violence 137–9
    award benefiting assailant 138, 139
    cohabitees 137–8
    'same roof' rule 139
  fatal injuries 302
    criminal injury cause 135–6
    dependants 133, 134–5, 136
    discretion to award 136
    ex gratia payments 133
    non-survival of compensation 133
    pre-birth 132
    qualifying claimants 133–5
    spouse 133, 134
    supplementary compensation 136
  personal injuries
    adult victims 128–9
    child victims 129–32
  potentially uncompensable persons,
    domestic violence 137–9
  undeserving *see* Undeserving applicants
Emergency services 98–100
European Convention on the Compensation
  of Victims of Violent Crimes
  (1990) 19
  deduction of awards from 241
  jurisdiction 78–9
Evidence, appeals 63
Ex gratia payments, from employers
  239
Expenses *see individual types eg* Funeral
  expenses; Medical expenses

False application 38–9
Fatal injuries
  applicants 302
    criminal injury cause 135–6
    dependants 133, 134–5, 136
    discretion to award 136
    ex gratia payments 133
    non-survival of compensation
      133
    pre-birth 132
    qualifying claimants 133–5
    spouse 133, 134
    supplementary compensation 136
  assessment of compensation 272–4
    bereavement award 135, 219–20
    cause of death
      New Scheme 218–19
      Old Scheme 216–18
    children of the family 223
    cohabitees 222
    death not result of criminal injury
      305
    deductions 221–2
    funeral expenses 223, 304–5
    general damages 219–20
    loss of dependency 218–19, 303
    loss of parental services 221, 223–5,
      303
    loss of support 220–3
    maximum award 305
    payment method 305–6
    pre-death award 305
    qualifying claimants 218–19
    special damages 220–3
    standard amount 219–20, 302–3
  reopening, review and appeal
    306
Financial minimum
  deductions 147
  implementation 149–50
  increase in threshold 150–1
  minor injuries 149
  multiple minor injuries 149–50
  New Scheme provision 147–9
  Old Scheme provision 146–7
  policy 146
  reduction of claim for character of
    applicant 148
  threshold 32
Firefighters 98, 99
Fraudulent application 38–9
Funding 16

Funeral expenses   43, 147, 161,
    304–5
  assessment   223
  deduction exception   230–1
Future care   188

General damages
  fatal injuries   219–20
  personal injuries   192–202
Guide to Applicants for Compensation in
    Fatal Cases   220–1
  eligibility   300
  text   301–7
Guide to Applicants for Loss of Earnings
    and Special Expenses   192, 210
  eligibility   293–4
  text   293–30
Guide to the Criminal Injuries
    Compensation Scheme   29

Hearing
  of appeals   65–75, 280–1
  New Scheme   65–75
    adjournments   73–4
    adjudicators   68–9, 71
    burden of proof   67
    confidentiality   72–3
    decisions   70
    evidence rules   69
    failure to attend   75
    fresh determination   66–7
    hearing summary   67–8
    privacy   72–3
    procedure   67–71
    reducing amount of award   71
    rehearings   74–5
    witnesses   68, 69
    written notice   67
  Old Scheme
    grounds   54–5, 56–7
    reconsideration   55, 59–60
    reference by Board   54
    refusal   58–9
    request   44, 52–4
    review   55–60
    right to   54

Immoral conduct   169
Incapacitated applicant, management of
    awards   50–1
Income tax, taking account of
    payments   233–4

Injury
  severity   32, 33
  see also Criminal injuries; Fatal injuries;
      Mental injury; Personal injuries
Insurance payments
  deductions from award   208, 209, 226,
      227
    occupational arrangements   237–9
    personal and non-employer
        insurance   235–7
Intention (of violent crime)   85–6
Interim awards   45
  permanent   45
Interpretation
  New Scheme   29
  Old Scheme   28–9
Intoxication, undeserving applicants
    168–9, 172–3

Judicial review   26–8, 59
  Old Scheme   13
  time limits   145–6
Jurisdiction   77–9
  aircraft   77, 283
  Channel Tunnel   78, 283
  European Convention countries   78–9
  land borders   77, 283
  Scotland   79
  territorial waters   77–8
Justification
  for Criminal Injuries Compensation
      Scheme   9–13
    common law damages   10
    compensation orders   11
    industrial injury compensation   9
    new tariff scheme   2–4
  for state compensation   4–9
    distribution of losses   7–8
    negligence law   4–6
    social welfare   7
  state compensation for victims of
      crime   4–9
Juvenile convictions   177

Law enforcement, victimising events
    92–101
  accidental injuries   96–7, 100
  'apprehension'   93, 94
  'attempted apprehension'   94
  'attempted prevention of offence'   97
  bystanders   100–1
  emergency services   98–100

Law enforcement, victimising events
— *continued*
exceptional risk qualification   96–101
firefighters   98, 99
'offender'   93, 95
paramedics   98
'prevention of offence'   93, 95–6, 97
reasonable use of force   89–90
'suspected offender'   95
traffic accidents   99–100
Long term care   211, 214–15
Loss of dependency   19, 191, 218–19
amount   303
Loss of earning capacity *see* Loss of
earnings and earning capacity
Loss of earnings and earning capacity
188, 191, 270–2
28 week rule   205–6, 207
calculation   294–9
future loss   296–9
past loss   295–6
carer's loss   215
ceiling on   211
compensation for personal injuries
204–11
deductions   208, 209
eligibility   294
injury direct cause   207
pension rights   208
qualification for benefit   205–6
qualifying period   205–7
tariff scheme   191
Loss of parental services   221, 223–5, 303
Loss of pension rights   208
Loss of support   220–3

Management of awards   50–1
Material change in condition   45–6, 47
Medical expenses   211, 212–14
Mental disability, waiving time limits
143–4
Mental injury   105–6
applicant as primary victim   109–12
applicant as secondary victim   112–18
causal link   113
event proximity   115–18
immediate aftermath   115–18
close involvement   116–17
non-consenting sex offence victims
118–19
presence at event   115
relational proximity   114

Mental injury — *continued*
time proximity   117–18
trespass on railway   119
meaning   106–7
phone calls   111–12
post traumatic stress   107–8
see also shock
psychiatric damage or illness   106
rescuers   109–10
sex offences   118–19
shock   106, 107, 150
sole injury   108–19
stalking   111–12
triggered by physical injury   107–8
Minimum threshold *see* Financial minimum
Minor injuries   149
multiple   149–50
Minors *see* Children
Mitigation of loss   189
Motor Insurers' Bureau   102–3
Multiple minor injuries   149–50
Multiplicand   188, 209–10, 224, 296,
303–4
Multipliers   188, 197, 209–10, 224–5,
297–8
fatal injuries   304
illustrative   284, 297

Negligence
compensation by law of   4–6
proximity   5
event   115–18
relational   114
time   117–18
public policy rejection   6
New Scheme
accountability
complaints procedure   28
parliamentary   24–5
adjudicators   20, 21
appeals
burden of proof   64, 67
categories   63–4
concerning awards   65–6
concerning time limits   64
evidence   63
extension of time   63
frivolous or vexatious   71
procedure   63
reopening of cases   64
review compared   61
see also oral hearings

New Scheme — *continued*
Appeals Panel   20, 21–2
assessment of compensation *see* Tariff
scheme
Authority   20–2
award *see* Awards
criminal convictions   173–81
determination of application   42
European Convention   19
financial minimum   147–9
funding   16
implementation   22–3
interpretation   29
justifications   2–4
loss of dependency   19
oral hearings   65–75
adjournments   73–4
adjudicators   68–9, 71
burden of proof   67
confidentiality   72–3
decisions   70
evidence rules   69
failure to attend   75
fresh determination   66–7
hearing summary   67–8
privacy   72–3
procedure   67–71
reducing amount of award
71
rehearings   74–5
witnesses   68, 69
written notice   67
reconsideration of decisions
48–9
review   60–75
appeals compared   61
of decisions   61–3
grounds   62
procedure   62–3
scheme manager   20
standard of proof   23–4
tariffs   17–18
text   261–92
transitional arrangements
22–3
undeserving applicants   160–1
unlawfulness   20
White Paper   16–20
see also individual aspects and Tariff
scheme
Notification of award   42–3, 44
hearing request   44

Old Scheme
accountability
complaints procedure   28
judicial   26–8
parliamentary   24
amendment   15–16
assessment of compensation   186–9
award *see* Awards
client satisfaction   53
constituted by Act of Crown   13–14
co-operation with authorities   151–2,
153
criminal convictions   170–3
determination of applications
39–42, 247–9
financial minimum   146–7
hearing
grounds   54–5, 56–7
reconsideration   55, 59–60
refusal   58–9
request   44, 52–4
review   55–60
right to   54
implementation   249–50
interpretation   28–9
judicial review   13
legal status   13–15
need for statutory scheme   16
reconsideration   47–8, 55, 59–60
review   55–60
text   242–50
time limits   15
undeserving applicants   159–60
see also individual aspects
Ombudsman   24, 25, 257–8

Paramedics   98
Parliamentary Commissioner for
Administration   24, 25, 257–8
Parliamentary control   24–5, 258–9
Payment of awards   49–50, 305–6
Penal Practice in a Changing Society
(White Paper)   10–11
Pension payments
deductions from award   208, 209,
221–2, 226, 227
fatal injuries   221–2
occupational arrangements   237–9
personal and non-employer
insurance   235–7
Pension rights, loss of   208
Permanent interim awards   45

Personal injuries
  applicants
    adult victims 128–9
    child victims 129–32
  assessment of compensation 186, 189
    adaptations to accommodation 214
    bands 199
    care 214–16
      carer's loss of earnings 215
    common law damages 192–5
    future care 188
    general damages 192–204, 285–92
      Board's guidelines
        levels 194
        tariffs compared 200
    long term care 211, 214–15
    loss or damage to property 212
    loss of dependency 191
    medical expenses 211, 212–14
    multiple injuries 202–3
    New Scheme, tariff 197–202,
      285–92
    Old Scheme 192–7
    rape and aftermath 195–7, 204
    review of tariff *see* tariff scheme
    Secretary of State powers 199
    special damages 204–16
    special equipment 214
    special expenses 211–16, 272,
      299–300
    unprovided for injuries 203–4
    see also Loss of earnings and earning
      capacity
  compensable persons
    adult victims 128–9
    child victims 129–32
  definition 104–19
  disease 105
  mental *see* Mental injury
  physical injury 104–5
Personal representatives 44–5
Persons due compensation *see* Eligible
  persons
Phone calls, mental injury caused by
  111–12
Police
  information given on rights 35
  law enforcement *see* Law enforcement,
    victimising events
  see also Co-operation with authorities
Post traumatic stress 107–8
  see also Shock

Pre-birth injuries
  fatal 132
  violence 88–9
Pregnancy, resulting from rape
  196–7, 204, 231
Privacy, oral hearings 72–3
Proof
  burden 64, 67
  standard 23–4
Property crimes 3, 84–5

Railways, suicides on rail tracks
  80–1, 90–2, 119
Rape
  aftermath 204
  compensation 195–7, 204
  pregnancy resulting from 196–7, 204,
    231
Recklessness 85–6, 88
Reconsideration of decisions 47–9, 276
  initiative to reconsider 48–9
  New Scheme 48–9
  Old Scheme 47–8, 55, 59–60
Rehabilitation 162, 176–7, 178–9
Rehearings 74–5, 281–2
Remarriage prospects 222, 234
Reopening of cases 277
  appeals concerning 279
  award 45–7
  fatal injuries 306
  time limit 46
Reporting incident 33, 151
  'appropriate authority' 154
  circumstances of injury 152–5
  earliest opportunity 153–4
Rescuers, mental injury 109–10
Reviews
  appeals compared 61
  of decisions 61–3, 277–8
    appeals against 278–9
    grounds 62
    procedure 62–3
  fatal injuries 306
  New Scheme 60–75
  Old Scheme 55–60

Scheme manager 20
Severity of injury 32, 33
Sex offences 32, 86–8
  children 144–5
  mental injury 118–19
  rape and aftermath 195–7, 204, 231

Shock   106, 107–8, 150
Social security benefit deduction
        208, 209, 221–2, 226, 227, 232–5
    fatal injuries   221–2
    impact of provisions   234–5
    income tax payments   233–4
    remarriage prospects   234
    scope   232–3
Special damages
    fatal injuries   220–3
    personal injuries   204–16
Spouse, fatal injury claims   133, 134
Stalking   111–12
Standard of proof   23–4
Store detectives, use of force   89–90
Structured settlements   50–1
Suicides
    on rail track   80–1, 90–2, 119
        mental injury   119

Tariff scheme   17–18
    assessment of compensation
        190–2, 197–202, 285–92
        annual review   199–200
        Board's guidelines compared
            200
        Secretary of State powers   199
        total maximum   191–2
        unlawful   190
    Board's guide compared   200
    introduction   1–2
    New Scheme justifications   2–4
    Secretary of State powers   199
    unlawfulness   2, 20
Time limits   141–3
    appeals concerning   279
    discretion to waive   143–6
    eligibility   141–3
        discretion to waive   143–6
        ignorance of Scheme   145
        judicial review of decision   145–6
    ignorance of Scheme   145
    judicial review of decision   145–6
    Old Scheme   15
    reopening award   46
Traffic accidents   101–3
    deliberate attempt to injure
        101–2
    justification for exclusion   102
    Motor Insurers' Bureau   102–3
    police officers   99–100
    untraced drivers agreement   102–3

Trespass on railway
    mental injury   119
    suicides on track   80–1, 90–2, 119

Undeserving applicants
    'clean hands'   157
    common law compared *see* tort compared
    conduct before, during or after incident
        162, 165–70
    criminal record   170–81
        aggregation of points   177–8
        discretion of Board   170–1
        going straight   176
        juveniles   177
        New Scheme   173–81
        Old Scheme   170–3
        penalty points   173–81
        rehabilitation   162, 176–7, 178–9
        unconnected with injury
            158–9, 171–2
    dangerous games   169–70
    dependant not deceased   161
    evidence available to claims officer
        184–5
    'fair fights'   166–8
    immoral conduct   169
    intoxication   168–9, 172–3
    New Scheme   160–1
    Old Scheme   159–60
    policy   156–9
    reduction of claim below minimum   148
    tort compared   161–4
        contributory negligence   162, 163–4
        ex turpi non oritur actio
            161, 162, 163
        novus actus interveniens   161
        volenti non fit injuria   161, 163
    unlawful conduct   182–4
    voluntary fights   166–8
Unlawful conduct   182–4

Vesting of award   43–4
Victim Support   19, 199
    information given on rights   35
Victimising events   79–90
    crimes of violence   79–90
        acts and omissions   83
        animals   83
        consent   90
        external elements   82–8
        fault elements   88–90
        intention   85–6

Victimising events — *continued*
 pre-birth 88–9
 property crimes 3, 84–5
 reasonable use of force 89–90
 recklessness 85–6, 88
 suicides on rail track 90–2
law enforcement 92–101
 accidental injuries 96–7, 100
 'apprehension' 93, 94
 'attempted apprehension' 94
 'attempted prevention of offence' 97
 bystanders 100–1
 emergency services 98–100
 exceptional risk qualification 96–101
 firefighters 98, 99
 'offender' 93, 95
 paramedics 98
 'prevention of offence' 93, 95–6
  attempted 97
 reasonable use of force 89–90
 'suspected offender' 95
 traffic accidents 99–100
proof of 120–5
trespass on railway 90–2
 intention to derail 92
 suicides on track 80–1, 90–2, 119

Victims
 character investigation 37
 common law damages 10
 deterioration in condition
  15, 45–6, 47
 justification for Criminal Injuries
  Compensation Scheme
  9–13
  common law damages 10
  compensation orders 11
  industrial injury compensation
   9
 justification for state compensation
  4–9
  distribution of losses 7–8
  negligence law 4–6
  social welfare 7
 politisation 10
 preferment of victims of crime over
  victims of accidents 2–3
 property crimes 3, 84–5
 see also Children; Eligible persons
Victim's Charter 9, 35
Violent crime *see* Crimes of violence

Witnesses, oral hearings 68, 69